D1236316

The World Trade System

The World Trade System

Trends and Challenges

Jagdish N. Bhagwati, Pravin Krishna, and
Arvind Panagariya, editors

The MIT Press
Cambridge, Massachusetts
London, England

This book was set in Sabon LT by Toppan Best-set Premedia Limited. Printed and bound in the United States of America.

Library of Congress Cataloging-in-Publication Data

Names: Bhagwati, Jagdish N., 1934– editor. | Krishna, Pravin, editor. | Panagariya, Arvind, editor.
Title: The world trade system : trends and challenges / edited by Jagdish N. Bhagwati, Pravin Krishna, and Arvind Panagariya.
Description: Cambridge, MA : MIT Press, 2016. | Includes bibliographical references and index.
Identifiers: LCCN 2016016599 | ISBN 9780262035231 (hardcover : alk. paper)
Subjects: LCSH: International trade. | International economic relations.
Classification: LCC HF1379 .W676 2016 | DDC 382/.9--dc23 LC record available at https://lccn.loc.gov/2016016599

10 9 8 7 6 5 4 3 2 1

Contents

Preface

This volume, edited by Professors Jagdish Bhagwati and Arvind Panagariya of the School of International and Public Affairs (SIPA) at Columbia University and Professor Pravin Krishna of the School of Advanced International Studies (SAIS) at Johns Hopkins University, is the product of a deep collaboration between the two institutions and represents a state-of-the-art analysis of the important trends in the world trading system today. It should prove to be an important contribution to the ongoing debate in the United States about the international trading system, the merits of mega-regional initiatives such as the Trans-Pacific Partnership (TPP) Agreement and the Trans-Atlantic Trade and Investment Partnership (TTIP), and the future role of the World Trade Organization (WTO).

The contributors to this volume include some of the world's leading trade economists and lawyers. The essays focus on a cluster of the most pressing issues facing the global trading system today, some widely discussed and others understudied and deserving of more scrutiny. The negotiation of multilateral rules and the Doha "development round" negotiations that started in 2001 have experienced a virtual demise, and international trade agreements are increasingly controversial, both within countries and in relations between them. This volume clarifies where progress has been achieved at the multilateral level, the emergence and spillover consequences of regional trade agreements and their effect on the multilateral system both economically and politically, and the nature and consequences for both developed and developing economies. Analytical and empirical, these illuminating essays advance our understanding of the evolving nature of the international trading system and should be read by anyone with an interest in understanding what is at stake.

Merit E. Janow
Dean and Professor of Practice, International Economic Law & International Affairs
School of International and Public Affairs (SIPA), Columbia University

Vali Nasr
Dean
School of Advanced International Studies (SAIS), Johns Hopkins University

Acknowledgments

The landscape of the international trade system has undergone substantial change in recent decades. While many multilateral successes were achieved under the GATT, the failure of the WTO member countries to successfully close the Doha Round of trade negotiations has now engendered a mood of pessimism regarding the future of the multilateral system. Countries have turned to preferential (and thus discriminatory, albeit GATT-legal) trade agreements and many new deals are now under negotiation, including the "mega-regional" agreements—the Trans-Pacific Partnership (TPP) between the United States and Pacific Rim countries and the Transatlantic Trade and Investment Partnership (TTIP) between the United States and the European Union. At the same time, developing countries having expanded their participation in international trade, challenging the international system to accommodate their interests and aspirations. Finally, worsening global economic conditions and a populist focus on the alleged links between the inequality of incomes within countries and globalization have generated a protectionist backlash. This has been, for instance, a dominant theme in the ongoing presidential campaign in the United States.

In an effort to assess these important trends, the School of International and Public Affairs (SIPA) at Columbia University and the School of Advanced International Studies (SAIS) at Johns Hopkins University organized two back-to-back conferences in the fall of 2014 titled "Challenges Facing the World Trade System," with panels and research presentations at both locations involving complementary contributions by leading scholars and policy makers. This volume gathers together the papers from these conferences, which provide theoretical and empirically based discussions of recent trends in world trade as well as institutional and regional perspectives. In addition to the authors of the various chapters, we are grateful to the paper discussants Chad Brown, Anu

Bradford, Lucian Cernat, Alan Deardorff, Caroline Freund, Amit Khandelwal, Michael Levi, Matthias Matthijs, and Heiwai Tang and to participants in panel discussions, Swedish Trade Minister Ewa Bjorling, Koichi Hamada, Merit Janow, Anne Krueger, Hugh Patrick, Indian Ambassador Manjeev Puri, James Riedel, and Jan Svejnar for their many insightful contributions.

We also recognize, with gratitude, the co-sponsorship of this event by Dean Merit Janow at Columbia SIPA and by Dean Vali Nasr at the School of Advanced International Studies (SAIS) at Johns Hopkins University and by Professor Jan Svejnar at the Center on Global Economic Governance at Columbia SIPA. We are grateful as well to May Yang and Michael Falco at Columbia and to Kelley Kornell at Johns Hopkins, who worked tirelessly to ensure the success of the two conferences and to Jane MacDonald and Kathleen Caruso at the MIT Press, whose editorial support at the MIT Press has been crucial in developing this volume and expediting it through the publication process.

1

The World Trade System Today

Jagdish N. Bhagwati, Pravin Krishna, and Arvind Panagariya

When the Uruguay Round was successfully closed in 1994, and the General Agreement on Tariffs and Trade (GATT) metamorphosed into the World Trade Organization (WTO), the despondency that had characterized the protracted multilateral trade negotiations (MTN) was replaced by euphoria. The GATT had been an "agreement" on tariff reduction with an improvised set of rules governing goods trade rather than the International Trade Organization (ITO) that many had sought as the third pillar of the international economic superstructure following World War II. While the International Monetary Fund and the World Bank, the other two pillars of this superstructure, had emerged with sparkling colors out of the Bretton Woods conference, the ITO did not do so well. The Havana Charter creating the ITO was signed in March 1948 but it was never ratified by the United States Congress and was, thus, stillborn. On January 1, 1995, the WTO finally emerged as that missing institution.

A key function of the WTO is the implementation of existing agreements among member countries. When the WTO replaced GATT, it greatly expanded the scope of multilateral discipline. It expanded sectoral coverage by bringing textiles, agriculture, and services into the fold of multilateral rules.[1] It created a uniform intellectual property rights (IPRs) regime. And it replaced the relatively weak dispute settlement mechanism of the GATT with a system that made dispute resolution virtually binding on member governments.

However, casting a shadow over the future of the WTO are the failure of its member countries to comprehensively close the Doha Round of trade negotiations initiated in 2001 for an extended period and the simultaneous breaking out of bilateral and plurilateral preferential trade agreements (PTAs) as the preferred option of major powers such as the United States and the European Union (EU).

The Bali meetings of the WTO in December 2013 achieved some preliminary but important successes in improving trade facilitation, in reducing trade barriers against imports from the least developed countries (LDCs) and in shielding, on an interim basis, food security programs in developing countries. While these developments offer hope for broader multilateral liberalization success in the future, the situation, nevertheless, is a challenging one and calls for a critical assessment of the prospects for the world trade system. To this end, we analyze here the major trends in international trade in recent years, as well as the opportunities they present and the challenges they pose to the world trade system.

We begin in section 1.1 by noting that there is much to celebrate about the progress made under the WTO in achieving a liberal trading system. We discuss the trends in world trade protection and trade flows and discuss the important role played by the WTO in supporting further liberalization of trade, in the implementation of existing agreements and the settling of disputes between member countries through its dispute settlement mechanism (DSM).

We discuss next, in section 1.2, the enhanced participation of the developing countries in the WTO and in world trade. Overall, low- and middle-income countries in the "South" more than doubled their share of global trade in the last two decades. In parallel, South–South trade flows have expanded substantially over the same time period: the share of exports from Southern countries going to other countries in the South has nearly doubled. There has also been a growing appreciation among the developing countries of the need to safeguard their trade interests and they have accomplished it through more effective participation in the WTO. All in all, developing countries now represent a much greater share of the multilateral trade system and, importantly, constitute a new set of interests for the system to engage and accommodate.

Despite the successes of the multilateral process in expanding trade, it is readily evident that both developed and developing countries have systematically moved in the direction of WTO-legal preferential trade arrangements in recent years. Indeed, both developing and developed countries have negotiated multilaterally with their gaze at least partially oriented toward opportunities for preferential trade agreements. Developed countries have also found it more attractive to either sign agreements with each other or negotiate bilaterally with individual or small groups of developing countries than to substantially engage the multilateral process. Indeed, these countries have used the threat of proceeding on the bilateral track to bend the multilateral process in their preferred direction. As then United States Trade Representative (USTR) Susan Schwab pointedly noted in June 2006, "Everyone knows that if there is no Doha Agreement, we are perfectly capable of moving ahead on the bilateral track."

While bilateral initiatives have resulted, in most cases, in only limited expansion of intra-PTA trade, thus suggesting the continued importance of multilateral initiatives, the momentum toward bilateral agreements has accelerated over time. Indeed, the Obama administration has been pursuing both a "Transatlantic Trade and Investment Partnership" (TTIP) with the European Union and a "Trans-Pacific Partnership" (TPP) with countries in the Asia Pacific region, while possibly diminishing U.S. investment in rescuing the Doha Round. Developing countries have found bilateral agreements to be increasingly appealing as well, especially because South–South agreements may be entered into via the "Enabling Clause" of the GATT, whose requirements are far less stringent than the restrictions imposed by Article XXIV on North–North and North–South Agreements. We discuss preferential trade agreements in section 1.3 and argue there that this is an unhealthy trend which greatly risks undermining the multilateral trading system.

In section 1.4, we turn to the current state of negotiations, focusing on the Doha Round, the TPP, and the TIPP. While some progress was made in the Doha negotiations at the latest 2013 ministerial meeting in Bali, the status remains very far from the agenda of the original declaration that launched the round. As regards TPP, we take a skeptical view of its provisions on intellectual property protection that seek to raise standards, not just above those in the WTO Agreement on Trade-Related Aspects of Intellectual Property (TRIPS) but also above those in previous United States bilateral agreements. Given these provisions and the labor standards clauses, it is unlikely that two of the largest countries in Asia, China and India, will join this agreement. As such, if the TPP is successfully signed—by no means a done deal—it will only lead to fragmentation of the trading system. We also argue that the prospects for a successful negotiation of the TTIP are quite poor. In section 1.5, we discuss how the proliferation of preferential agreements may have adverse consequences on the essential functions of the WTO such as rule making and dispute settlement. We conclude the chapter in section 1.6.

1.1 Multilateral Trade Liberalization: A Success

The multilateral trading system has had great success in the last two decades. World trade in goods and services is much freer today than it was in the pre-WTO world. Tariff barriers and nontariff barriers have been significantly reduced with tariff protection against industrial products at a historically low level in almost all countries.[2]

Specifically, developed countries have bound virtually all their tariffs, while developing countries have bound a substantial proportion of their tariff lines. Further, applied tariffs have dropped to their lowest levels in recent history. In developed countries, simple average tariffs uniformly stand below 5 percent. Tariff reductions in developing countries have been equally impressive. India, which was a highly protected country, now has applied tariffs averaging around 10 percent, while the corresponding figure in China stands even lower at 8.7 percent. Even Latin America, where tariffs are higher, averages below 15 percent.

Furthermore, the proportion of tariff lines—specifically, the share of Harmonized System (HS) six-digit subheadings—with applied tariff rates exceeding 15 percent is also generally low (see *World Tariff Profiles 2011*, published by the WTO). In the developed countries, the proportion is uniformly below 3 percent, with Canada being the major exception. Remarkably, this proportion in India stands at 6.7 percent and is significantly below the 11.6 percent level in China.

Trade outcomes have mirrored this liberalization, with goods as well as services trade expanding at an accelerated pace. The simple average of annual growth rates of world merchandise exports rose in nominal terms from 5.6 percent during 1981–1994 to 8.9 percent during 1995–2010.[3] Trade has grown faster than GDP (which grew globally at an annual average of 2.2 percent annually during both periods). Further, merchandise exports have shown remarkable growth in the three major regions of the world: Europe, North America, and Asia. In Europe, they have more than doubled and in Asia, they have almost tripled during the last decade. Growth in North America has been slower but still impressive with exports rising from $1225 billion in 2000 to $1965 billion in 2010. Remarkably, though exports are much smaller in magnitude, export growth in the remaining three regions—Africa, the Middle East, and the Commonwealth of Independent States—has been as impressive as in Asia. In each case, merchandise exports have more than tripled during the decade.

Growth in the exports of commercial services has been similarly spectacular. In North America, they have almost doubled; in Europe, they have more than doubled; and in Asia, they have more than tripled between 2000 and 2010, suggesting significant WTO success in facilitating trade.[4]

A key function of the WTO is to implement the existing agreements among member countries. When the WTO replaced GATT on January 1, 1995, it replaced the relatively weak dispute settlement system of the GATT with a binding system backed by the right to retaliate on the part of the damaged party in case of noncompliance by the offending party. Davey (2012) discusses in detail the functioning of WTO dispute settlement and concludes that, despite some shortcomings, it has lived up to expectation. First, after an initial surge, the number of cases brought for consultations has been cut to half of their level in the 1990s and the number of cases has been reasonably steady during the 2000s—suggesting that a steady state may have been reached. Second, only relatively few cases have experienced delays (the two massive subsidy cases involving Airbus and Boeing being the major exceptions). Third, rulings in almost all cases have been implemented, even if with some delay. Finally, developing countries in general and smaller countries in particular have been able to access the system and use it effectively to protect their trading rights.

It is also noteworthy that despite the major financial crisis, which created prolonged and high levels of unemployment in the major industrial economies that continue till today, trade disruption has been minimal. This is in contrast to the Great Depression when similar dislocations led to a virtual trade war between Europe and the United States that led to the enactment of the infamous Smoot–Hawley tariffs in the latter. On the whole, trade has recovered relatively quickly in the aftermath of the crisis.

1.2 Developing Countries Embrace Liberalization and the WTO

The last two decades have also seen a serious shift in the attitudes and policies of developing countries toward international trade. In the 1950s and 1960s, development thinking was dominated by the view that developing countries needed to foster industrialization and that this required protection of manufacturing against competition from well-established foreign suppliers. Reliance on exports was seen as a nonstarter because it was thought that the demand for developing country exports, which consisted of largely primary products, exhibited low elasticity with respect to both price and income. Low price elasticity meant that any efforts by the developing countries to expand exports would be frustrated by such large endogenous decline in the terms of trade that expanded exports would end up fetching reduced revenues. And the low income elasticity meant that over time, as incomes rose in the industrial countries, their demand would shift in favor of manufactures and services and away from developing country exports with the result that the developing countries would experience an exogenous secular decline in their terms of trade.

This line of thinking inevitably led the developing countries to seek "special and differential" (S&D) treatment in framing the rules of international trade under the auspices of GATT. Under S&D, developing countries enjoyed automatic extension of any tariff reductions undertaken by developed countries, without having to reciprocate with matching trade concessions. Two outcomes followed. First, since tariff reductions "bought" them nothing at the GATT, many developing countries chose egregiously high levels of protection for many decades, with disastrous economic outcomes. Second, developed countries, in turn, negotiated multilateral tariff reductions only on products of interest to themselves (ignoring, for instance, textiles and agriculture until recently).

By the late 1980s, however, three factors led to a change in the ethos in the developing countries in favor of trade liberalization. First, the outstanding economic performance of the few developing countries such as South Korea and Taiwan, which switched to liberal trade regimes early on, demonstrated that liberal trade was beneficial. Second, the failure of their own wholesale protection to produce industrialization and growth reinforced this view. And finally, the aggressive push toward liberal trade by the World Bank and IMF under loan conditionality, though initially resented, has also contributed to the shift in domestic attitudes toward reform.

The outcomes have been impressive. Spurred by trade liberalization and other market-friendly reforms, China and India both experienced double-digit growth in their exports averaging around 15 percent annually between 1990 and 2010. Middle-income economies like Brazil, Turkey, South Korea, Indonesia, and Thailand grew their exports at nearly 10 percent annually. Overall, low- and middle-income countries more than doubled their share of global trade, from roughly 20 percent in 1990 to over 40 percent in 2010. In parallel, with the increased importance of the South in overall world trade, South–South trade flows have also increased substantially.[5] Specifically, the share of exports from low-income countries going to low- and middle-income markets has nearly doubled from around 22 percent to over 40 percent of the total and the share of exports from middle-income countries to low- and middle-income markets has increased from around 30 percent to nearly 50 percent. Furthermore, overall trade shares of those countries have risen much faster than the growth in their output.

While special and differential treatment for developing countries continues at the WTO, developing countries today participate much more effectively in the activities of the WTO. This is observed on three principal dimensions.

First, developing country membership has increased considerably over time. More than thirty countries have joined the system after the WTO was formed and more than twenty countries are currently negotiating accession. A number of interrelated factors have contributed to this development. Developing countries have become major exporters of manufactures and have thus favored an outward orientation. The establishment of the WTO has resulted in a number of changes requiring additional participation by developing countries. The WTO covers a variety of new areas, such as services, standards, and intellectual property rights, and it has been engaging in a number of ongoing negotiations in the liberalization of different sectors that require member countries' continuous involvement.

Second, the extent of the engagement of developing countries in multilateral negotiation, principally, the Doha Round, has been far more substantial than it was in the past. To begin with, the Doha Round, billed the Doha "development round," has focused significant attention on agriculture, a sector of key importance to developing countries, thus automatically increasing developing countries' interest in the proceedings. The emergence of the G-20 grouping prior to the 2003 WTO ministerial meeting and its success in getting the developed countries to drop three of the four "Singapore issues" from the Doha negotiating agenda offers one example of their involvement in the negotiating process. Their continued involvement at the Hong Kong ministerial meeting in 2005 and then again in the 2008 negotiations in Geneva that produced a deadlock between developed and developing countries offers another example of the intensity and relevance of their engagement.

Third, developing countries have also come to use the dispute settlement body (DSB) to assert and defend their trading rights. Hoekman (2012), who makes this point cogently, points out that while developing countries were defendants in only 8 percent of the cases under the GATT, under the WTO they have been defendants in 35 percent of the cases. Developing countries have also emerged as complainants, accounting for one-third of all cases brought to DSB during 1995–2011. Even more interestingly, as many as 44 percent of the developing country cases have been against other developing countries. In a highly visible case, India challenged the EU's Generalized System of Preferences (GSP) plus program in 2003 with adverse implications for the neighboring Pakistan who benefited from the program. In another similar case, Brazil challenged the EU export subsidy on sugar that had benefited the African, Caribbean, and Pacific (ACP) countries through guaranteed access to the highly protected EU market.

Finally, we note that although nearly all developing countries have moved away from antitrade policies of the 1950s and 1960s, there are vast differences among them in their trade interests and in their approaches toward trade policy. At one extreme, we have the LDCs that still insist on, and enjoy, overwhelming one-way trade preferences without offering reciprocal liberalization. They have tariff-free access to the internal EU market under the "everything but arms" (EBA) initiative. Developing countries in Sub-Saharan Africa, the vast majority of them also LDCs, enjoy significant one-way preferences in the U.S. market under the Africa Growth and Opportunity Act (AGOA). At the other extreme, larger developing countries such as China, Brazil, India, and Indonesia have become vocal demanders of concessions in the negotiations. Developing countries including Brazil, Argentina, Indonesia, and Colombia played an important role in bringing agriculture into the negotiations even under the Uruguay Round.

This emergence of developing countries as significant players in the world trade system and the heterogeneity of interests among them has had its own impact on the multilateral process, as we will discuss in greater detail in section V.

1.3 Proliferating PTAs Derail Multilateralism

A cornerstone of the World Trade Organization is the principle of nondiscrimination: member countries may not discriminate against goods entering their borders based upon the country of origin. However, in an important exception to its own central prescription, the WTO, through Article XXIV of GATT and Article V of the General Agreement on Trade in Services, does permit countries to enter into PTAs in the form of free trade areas (FTAs) and customs unions (CUs) with one another. Additional derogation of the principle of nondiscrimination is included in the Enabling Clause, which allows one-way tariff preferences to be granted by developed to developing countries and permits preferential trade agreements among developing countries that are not subject to the disciplines imposed by the GATT Article XXIV.

Such preferential agreements are now in vogue, with hundreds of them having been negotiated during the last two decades and with every member country belonging to several of them. Nevertheless, ever since PTAs began gathering momentum, it has been argued that they were an unfortunate development and pose a threat to multilateral liberalization.[6] The proponents of bilateral agreements have argued that PTAs would complement rather than supplant multilateral liberalization and that bilateral approaches may yield faster liberalization than what can be achieved through multilateral negotiation. They also defend a "WTO Plus" approach to trade liberalization.

The actual record on trade liberalization undertaken through bilateral negotiations suggests a different picture, however, and the analysis provided by the recent *World Trade Report 2011* (WTO 2011) is instructive in this regard. *World Trade Report 2011* indicates that there has been a significant increase in the value of trade taking place between PTA members. In 1990, trade between PTA partners (excluding intra-EU trade) made up around 18 percent of world trade and this figure rose to 35 percent by 2008. When the intra-EU trade is included, intra-PTA trade is placed at 28 percent in 1990 and 50 percent in 2008. In dollar terms, the value of intra-PTA trade, excluding intra-EU trade, rose from $537 billion in 1990 to $4 trillion by 2008 and from $966 billion to nearly $8 trillion once the intra-EU trade is included.

Looked at this way, a large share of world trade is now taking place between PTA members. However, as *World Trade Report 2011* points out, these statistics vastly overstate the role of preferential trade liberalization. This is because much of the trade between PTA members is in goods on which they impose MFN tariffs of zero in the first place. And goods that are subject to high MFN tariffs are also often subject to exemptions from liberalization under PTAs, so that the volume of trade that benefits from preferences is, on average, quite low.

Specifically, *World Trade Report 2011* calculations indicate that despite the recent explosion in PTAs, only about 16 percent of world trade takes place on a preferential basis when we exclude intra-EU trade and 30 percent when we include it. Furthermore, less than 2 percent of trade (4 percent when the intra-EU trade is included) takes place in goods that receive a tariff preference that is greater than 10 percent. For instance, well over 50 percent of Korean imports enter with zero MFN tariffs applied to them. Korea offers preferences on about 10 percent of its imports, but a preference margin greater than 10 percent on virtually none of its imports. Similarly, in India, goods entering under preference are about 5 percent of overall imports with over 50 percent of imports entering under zero MFN tariffs and virtually no imports receiving a preference of greater than 10 percent. A similar picture emerges on the exporting side. One of the countries that have actively negotiated PTAs is Chile and 95 percent of Chilean exports go to countries with which it has PTAs. However, only 27 percent of Chilean exports are eligible for preferential treatment and only 3 percent of its exports benefit from preference margins greater than 10 percent. For most PTAs, the majority of their trade takes place under zero MFN tariffs. It is only a small fraction of trade that enters on a preferential basis, especially outside of the EU and NAFTA.[7]

Of note it is also now clear that PTAs have become a stumbling block to multilateral liberalization. Export interests, especially in the developed countries, have learned that they get better deals through PTAs since they gain an upper hand over nonmembers within the union. Therefore, they prefer a bilateral rather than a multilateral route to liberalization. This is also often true of firms with multinational investments. For instance, it is argued that the multilateral process in the United States has also suffered because large U.S. firms have increasingly turned multinational, with investments in multiple foreign countries, thus cutting their incentive to seek through the U.S. Trade Representative (USTR) liberalization in those countries that would open them up to competition in these foreign markets from firms in the rest of the world. Symmetrically, their own credibility with the USTR has suffered since the USTR does not see them as necessarily pushing purely U.S. interests. This has worked to weaken a major lobby within the United States that favored multilateral liberalization. At the same time, this has been less of an impediment to preferential liberalization, as this only extends to firms in the home country and, further, specific sectors may be chosen for liberalization and some others excluded.

That PTAs may impede multilateral liberalization is even truer in the context of developed country lobbies pushing nontrade agenda items consisting of intellectual property rights and labor standards. Large developing countries such as India, China, and Brazil are strictly opposed to further proliferation of nontrade issues in the WTO. That naturally diverts the lobbies to PTAs where they face much weaker developing country partners and have relatively free play. The United States in particular is playing the game almost entirely as Bhagwati (1994) had predicted: a hegemonic power is likely to gain a greater payoff by bargaining *sequentially* with a group of nonhegemonic powers rather than *simultaneously*.

Avoiding multilateral negotiations also allows countries to maintain distortions in agriculture. As an example, absent their consideration in multilateral negotiations, the United States cotton subsidies can continue indefinitely. Buyers of cotton such as Bangladesh use cotton in apparel that they export and profit from the lower prices that subsidies imply. At the same time, other cotton exporters such as the small West African countries and India cannot challenge the subsidies in the WTO.

Finally, we should discuss here the link between forums for trade negotiation and the evolving phenomena of production fragmentation and trade. Production fragmentation refers to a context in which various components of a good are produced in multiple countries and possibly traverse national borders many times before being assembled into a final form that is sold to the consumer.[8] It is now argued that the fragmentation of global production provides a new basis for countries to achieve preferential integration regionally and at a "deeper" level. (See, for instance, Baldwin 2014.) While this argument is gaining currency in some quarters, it would seem that production fragmentation should provide greater incentives instead for broader multilateral liberalization.[9] After all, the most efficient producers of any given intermediate good need not lie within the jurisdictional boundaries of any specific preferential agreement and the identity and location of the efficient producers of intermediates may be expected to vary faster than any country's ability to sign new preferential agreements. Furthermore, with increased fragmentation, the identification of the origin of goods, so that preferences may be suitably granted, is itself a major challenge. As a practical matter, if PTAs were designed to support fragmented production networks, we might expect to see greater geographic concentration of trade over time as many production networks are regional in nature. As the WTR 2011 notes, however, the share of intra-regional trade in Europe has remained roughly constant at around 73 percent between 1990 and 2009. While Asia's intra-regional trade seems to have risen from 42 to 52 percent during the same period, North America's intra-regional trade shares rose from 41 percent in 1990 to 56 percent in 2000 and fell back to 48 percent in

2009.[10] Thus, it cannot be argued that preferential agreements have been designed to support or benefit from fragmented production networks. Finally, the multiple crossings of borders by a single good before it takes its final form only makes the WTO more relevant—since, in this case, knocking down tariffs multilaterally, or otherwise facilitating trade (as negotiated recently at the multilateral level in Bali), has even greater value.

1.4 Whither Trade Negotiations: Doha, TPP, and TIPP

Any consideration of the global trading system is incomplete without a discussion of ongoing negotiations concerning major trade agreements. Three such negotiations are of particular importance in view of their coverage in terms of countries or the volume of trade or both. These include the multilateral Doha Round and the two major preferential initiatives by the United States, the TPP, and the TTIP.

The Doha Round

The multilateral Doha Round of trade negotiations, also called the Doha Development Agenda, because of its putative focus on the improvement of the trading prospects for developing countries, was launched in 2001. The Doha ministerial declaration gave this round its mandate to negotiate liberalization on agriculture, services, and intellectual property rights. To date, despite several attempts to advance the negotiations, this round has not been successfully closed, although a preliminary agreement on less contentious issues such as trade facilitation and removal of trade barriers against exports from the least developed countries was at last achieved at the latest December 2013 WTO ministerial meetings in Bali. Until this admittedly minor breakthrough, many observers had concluded that the round had reached an impasse, with some going so far as to suggest that it should now be officially killed.

A key question is why the Doha negotiations have stalled. Several explanations may be advanced, which, taken together, account for the situation as it currently stands. Because the Doha discussions have lasted well over a decade, with the changing domestic and global economic environment and changing negotiating details, individual countries' positions have varied over time. Below, we discuss the key reasons for the impasse.

First, having been labeled the "development round," the expectations of the developing countries for the Doha Round were at least partly based on the idea that the previous round of negotiations (the Uruguay Round) had effectively damaged them and the new round would be about treating those injuries. This impression was greatly reinforced by repeated subsequent assertions by the heads of international institutions, press, NGOs, and many influential academics to the effect that (1) agricultural protection is largely a developed country problem; (2) subsidies and protection in developed countries hurt the poorest developing countries the most; (3) it is wrong to ask poor countries to liberalize when rich countries heavily protect their own markets; and (4) rich countries' agricultural subsidies and protection reflect their double standards and hypocrisy. The effect of these assertions was to harden considerably the stance of the developing countries and to give them the false hope that they deserved one-way concessions from the developed countries, especially in agriculture.

Second, on agricultural policies, while the initial goal of many food-exporting developing countries was the reduction of developed country production and export subsidies (so that the price of their exports—food—would rise), the 2007–2008 food price crisis, when shortages of particular commodities led to sharp increases in food prices, led them to reevaluate this position. Indeed many developing countries are now more interested in keeping food prices in check than in eliminating developed country subsidies. Equally, some countries have been fearful of the contrary outcome whereby imports might push agricultural prices too far down. For instance, in 2008, there was insoluble disagreement between India and China on the one hand and the United States on the other over the special safeguard mechanism (SSM), a measure ostensibly designed to protect poor farmers by allowing countries to impose a special tariff on certain agricultural goods in the event of an import surge. Thus, countries have shown a degree of ambivalence toward rationalization of the agricultural policy and perhaps see this as less of a priority than they did in the past.

Further, even without agreement at Doha, agricultural export subsidies have nearly disappeared and actionable domestic agricultural subsidies have come down considerably in both the European Union and United States. As of February 2011, export subsidies in the EU continued to be available for cereals, beef and veal, poultry meat, pig meat, eggs, sugar, and some processed goods but they had not been used on cereals since July 2006 or on sugar since October 2008.

As a result of reforms of the Common Agricultural Policy, support for beef, olive oil, and fruits and vegetables, as measured by the current total AMS (aggregate measure of support), has either declined sharply or ceased altogether. Support for cereals, dairy, and sugar remains more significant but the overall support has seen considerable decline. In 2000–2001 and 2007–2008, Amber Box subsidies (which are recommended to be reduced) in the EU had dropped to 12.4 billion euros. Similarly, in the United States, the total support in 2007 fell to $84.65 billion, of which $76.2 billion was under the Green Box (permitted subsidies). The AMS was down to $6.3 billion.

Finally, as we have previously discussed, the heft of emerging economies has increased dramatically in recent years. A much greater fraction of the addition to world GDP came from developing countries in the last decade than it did in the preceding decade. So rich countries are much more concerned about access to emerging markets than they were when the goals for the Doha Round were first set. Indeed, the United States sees the Doha talks as an important opportunity to get fast-growing emerging economies to reduce their duties on imports of manufactures, which have been reduced in previous rounds but remain higher than those in developed countries.

Interestingly, markets in industrial goods and services in the developing countries have also undergone significant liberalization in the 2000s. This is particularly true of two major countries: China and India. As a part of the conditions for its 2001 entry into the WTO, China undertook major obligations to liberalize. It not only undertook this liberalization de facto but also bound it at the WTO giving it international legal force. India continued to bring its tariffs down and to open services sectors to direct foreign investment until at least 2007–2008 as a part of its national liberalization. As a result, outside of agriculture, which remains highly protected, India has a very open trade regime with the trade in goods and services as a proportion of the GDP rising to above 50 percent. These developments perhaps have left some of the major developing country players more or less satisfied in terms of market access but without the appetite for further opening of their own markets that would be necessary to bring the Doha Round to a conclusion.

We note that at the recent (December 2013) meetings of the WTO in Bali, some partial successes were indeed achieved. These included broad multilateral agreement on improving trade facilitation and agreement for the reduction of lowering barriers to exports from LDCs. Importantly, in the more contentious area of agricultural liberalization, an interim agreement was reached on the shielding of public stockholding programs for food security in developing countries, so that they would not be challenged legally even if a country's agreed limits for trade-distorting domestic support were breached. This may open the door to more ambitious agreements in the agricultural sphere and thus revives optimism that a multilateral agreement can be achieved in the future.

The Trans-Pacific Partnership (TPP)

The TPP is a trade agreement currently under negotiation among twelve countries: Australia, Brunei, Chile, Canada, Japan, Malaysia, Mexico, New Zealand, Peru, Singapore, the United States, and Vietnam. The TPP is sometimes seen as a competing proposal to the Regional Comprehensive Economic Partnership (RCEP), the agreement championed by China and now being discussed by ASEAN's ten member states—along with Australia, China, Japan, India, South Korea, and New Zealand. From the perspective of the United States, which has led the TPP negotiations, the agreement promises to provide a link to the dynamic economies of the Asia-Pacific and insures against its exclusion from the RCEP.

While the agreement covers many standard items such as the liberalization of trade in goods and services, several of its provisions have been criticized for being excessively restrictive. For instance, the provisions relating to intellectual property protection—the enforcements of patent and copyrights—provide restraints well beyond even those in previous bilateral trade agreements negotiated by the United States let alone the WTO TRIPS Agreement. In particular, concerns have been expressed that the TPP focuses on protecting intellectual property to the detriment of efforts to provide access to affordable medicine in the developing world, thus going against the foreign policy goals of the Obama administration.

In addition, there have been strong domestic pressures within the United States seeking the inclusion of a "labor chapter" that, for instance, insures that workers in any TPP country have the ability to unionize and engage in collective wage bargaining.

The TTP is widely discussed and considered as a prelude to far broader economic integration, encompassing much of the Asia-Pacific. Proponents argue that it could establish an "open regionalism" framework for other countries to sign on, without being subject to the exhausting negotiations required for bilateral agreements. Specifically, countries could simply elect to join the TPP, via what has been described as a "docking" arrangement. It has been suggested that the TPP could be the *last* trade agreement the United States negotiates and that from now on, other countries could simply elect to join the Trans-Pacific Partnership. Whether such a "docking" arrangement will indeed be built into the TPP is unclear. Further, as Bhagwati (2014) had noted, if accepting the TPPs demands on nontrade issues, such as intellectual property protection and labor standards, remains the precondition for joining TPP, it may just be that the result is a fragmentation of Asia into "TPP, China and India."

Transatlantic Trade and Investment Partnership (TTIP)

The TTIP is a trade agreement that is being negotiated at present between the European Union and the United States. Announced with an ambitious timetable for completion (end of 2014), it is already clear that the agreement is highly unlikely to be achieved due to the current economic circumstances as well as the longstanding differences between the United States and the EU on a number of issues that would be key to successful negotiation of a joint trade agreement.

It is clear that economic circumstances in a number of EU countries remain dire. The Eurozone has not yet recovered from the banking and financial crisis of recent years. Unemployment stands at around 12 percent overall and is significantly higher in the hardest-hit countries such as Greece (where the unemployment rate stands at nearly 30 percent with youth unemployment numbers being higher still at nearly 65 percent). Under these circumstances, it seems most unlikely that an ambitious trade program with potentially major distributional consequences will find support among the twenty-eight different EU states.

Moreover, while tariff barriers between the United States and the EU are already quite low, the negotiations are likely to be plagued by differences between the two on a number of economic and regulatory matters. Decades-long differences of perspective and priorities exist in areas such as agricultural subsidies and protection, health and safety, cultural diversity and protection, competition policy, services regulation, genetically modified (GM) foods, and environmental regulations. It is extremely unlikely that the persistent differences in viewpoints, supported by popular sentiment, entrenched interest groups and domestic regulators, will be ironed out despite the priority evidently given to the proposed agreement by the top political leadership. Indeed, powerful political actors on both sides have already taken tough negotiating positions, insisting on their favored regulatory templates, such as on GM foods and environmental standards, while insisting that any attempts to pursue an agreement with more limited goals would be doomed to failure.

1.5 Rule Making and Dispute Settlement: Bilateral versus Multilateral Settings

Doha Round negotiations cover a variety of issues and sectors such as agriculture, services, investment and intellectual property, which are now being comprehensively negotiated within the realm of the WTO. In addition to market access discussions, much needs to be done in all of these and other areas in terms of rule making. For instance, rules governing trade in services require negotiation over a number of complex issues in areas such as competition policy, domestic regulation, and government procurement.

While rule making in the past has largely been done during multilateral negotiation rounds, it is unclear how this will evolve in the future. As Bhagwati (2013) has noted, the question before the system is whether the weakening of the multilateral trade process and the popularity of bilateral processes might damage the rule-making function of the WTO and result in bilateral-agreement-specific rules that exist in an uncomfortable disharmony and possible legal indeterminacy with rules made in the context of negotiations in other bilateral agreements.

The problem is an especially acute one for developing countries.The regulatory intensity of services trade and the complexity of the consultative processes at both the domestic and international level and the informational deficit on institutional best practices and commercial interests of individual countries have implied a level of cautiousness and defensiveness in their approach to rule making in the multilateral forums. While progress on these matters has been admittedly slow at the multilateral level, the current drive for bilateral agreements raises the worrisome possibility that the developing country markets will be harvested individually by dominant trading partners who set the rules to reflect their own interests.

A similar issue arises in the context of the dispute settlement mechanism. DSM would also weaken if the WTO is viewed as weakened or merely optional and disputes are resolved in other bilateral and regional forums instead. Many of the preferential agreements that have been negotiated since the WTO came into existence cover areas that are already the subject of obligations under WTO agreements (for instance on intellectual property, services, government procurement, and technical barriers to trade). These PTAs typically contain details on dispute settlement that establishes committees and procedures for handling disputes between the parties to the agreement and this is potentially problematic, as these procedures and committees need not coincide with those at the WTO. For instance, as Drahos (2005) has noted, one of the distinctive features of the PTAs that the United States has signed is that the dispute settlement chapters contain "choice of forum" provisions that give the complaining state their choice of forum in those cases where "the state complained against has breached an obligation under more than one trade agreement and both states are parties to the relevant trade agreements." The ability of a dominant state to choose its legal "battleground" has potentially important implications for weaker states. This is especially true if the stronger state were to choose a setting other than that of WTO DSB to settle the case. As Drahos concludes, "weaker states are probably making themselves worse off by agreeing to such provisions."

Finally, we note that failure of the Doha Round will effectively lead the Dispute Settlement Body (DSB) itself to write the rules rather than to just interpret them. When the legislature (WTO Ministers) fail to clarify the rules and the cases come to the DSB, judgments are delivered under ambiguity of the extant rules. Once these judgments are given, however, new rules are effectively created through precedence—even if the "precedent effect" at the WTO is regarded as somewhat more fluid than is often the case in domestic judicial systems. Thus, it remains essential that multilateral negotiations succeed in the rule making.[11]

1.6 Concluding Remarks

In this chapter we have offered an overview of trends in the global trading system. We began by noting that the world trade system remains open and world trade has seen healthy growth since the inception of the WTO. Remarkably, the Lehman Brothers bankruptcy crisis in 2008 did not do any lasting damage to the institution and global trade recovered remarkably rapidly after a brief setback. This being said, there remains a threat to the WTO as long as the Doha Round is not closed satisfactorily. Despite the recent success in Bali and the innovations that have been suggested to move the negotiations forward, such as "mini-ministerial" meetings, failure to achieve the main goals of the Doha Round remains a distinct possibility. This would leave PTAs as the only game in town, which would undermine not only the trade liberalization function of the WTO, but also its rule-making role. In this context, the United States' near-singular focus on the two major PTAs—TPP and TIPP—recently is worrisome. If these arrangements become reality, they would greatly diminish the interest of the United States in the

WTO, a fact that would relegate the institution to a secondary role. As it stands, the prospects for a successful negotiation of the TTIP look dim and the successful closure of even the TPP faces numerous uphill tasks. We shall see.

Notes

1. While the textile sector was significantly liberalized in the Uruguay Round, both agriculture and services remain subject to enormous distortions and thus offer the potential for significant economic gains, if suitably liberalized—a fact that appears to have been overlooked by the recent commentators expressing the concern that multilateral liberalization has little to offer, as much of the liberalization has already been undertaken in preceding multilateral negotiation rounds.

2. For details on trade liberalization going beyond what we report in this chapter, see Panagariya 2013.

3. These rates have been calculated using the annual growth rates, appendix table A1 in *International Trade Statistics 2011*, published by the WTO.

4. However, we need to recognize that trade liberalization occurs in other ways as well, including through unilateral trade reform—resulting, for instance, from the recognition that trade barriers inflict damage on oneself or from conditionality being imposed by donor institutions such as the IMF and the World Bank. We should also note the study of Rose (2004), which critically evaluated the role of the WTO and found no significant effect of GATT/WTO membership on trade. However, neither his contention concerning the inefficacy of the GATT/WTO process, nor the arguments of his critics (for instance, Subramanian and Wei [2007]) have been based on meaningful counterfactuals (i.e., a world in which the GATT/WTO simply did not exist).

5. Further details on these patterns of South–South trade can be found in Krishna and Matthias 2014.

6. The earliest systematic critique of the PTAs was provided by Bhagwati (1993). Subsequent contributions in this spirit include Bhagwati and Panagariya 1996; Panagariya 1996, 1999; and Krishna 2013. Panagariya 2000 provides an accessible survey of the theory of preferential trading.

7. Ironically, it is conceivable that the difficulty with complying with the rules of origin (ROO) within preferential agreements is large enough, especially for small and medium-sized enterprises, to explain, at least partially, the low take up of PTA preferences by firms. See *World Trade Report 2011* for a detailed discussion.

8. The fragmentation of trade and its increased relevance over time has been well documented in the economics literature For instance, Varian (2007) points out that the popular iPod music player is made out of well over four hundred parts that originate in a number of different countries and are finally assembled in China.

9. Indeed, at a more basic level, the various theoretical aspects of production networks, such as trade in intermediates, foreign investment, and multinational production and so on are old issues in the literature and do not interfere with the basic welfare propositions concerning the dominance of multilateral free trade over other policy alternatives.

10. The principal factor driving the rise in intra-regional trade in Asia is the liberalization and faster growth in the countries within this region. This fact also explains in large part the decline in the intra-regional trade in North America during the 2000s despite the North American Free Trade Agreement (NAFTA), which has worked to divert trade toward regional partners.

11. As an example, experts are sharply divided on whether the current WTO rules allow a carbon tax on imports. Under these circumstances, if a country such as the United States were to introduce a carbon tax on imports and it were challenged in the WTO, the DSB would have to take a view on the matter even though the existing rules do not provide clear guidance one or the other way.

References

Baldwin, Richard. 2014. "Multilateralizing 21st Century Regionalism." Paper presented at OECD Global Forum on Trade, Paris, November 4.

Bhagwati, Jagdish. 1993. "Regionalism and Multilateralism: An Overview." In *New Dimensions in Regional Integration*, ed. Jaime de Melo and A. Panagiriya, 22–51. Cambridge, UK: Cambridge University Press.

Bhagwati, Jagdish. 1994. "Threats to the World Trading System: Income Distribution and the Selfish Hegemon." *Journal of International Affairs*, Spring.

Bhagwati, Jagdish. 2013. "Dawn of a New System." *Finance & Development* 50 (4).

Bhagwati, Jagdish, and Arvind Panagariya. 1996. "Preferential Trading Areas and Multilateralism: Strangers, Friends or Foes?" In *The Economics of Preferential Trading*, ed. J. Bhagwati and A. Panagariya, 1–78. Washington, DC: AEI Press.

Davey, William. 2012. "The Future of the WTO: What Is Next for the WTO?" Paper presented at Stanford University Conference on the Future of the WTO, Stanford Center for International Development, April 26–27.

Drahos, Peter. 2005. "The Bilateral Web of Trade Dispute Settlement." Paper presented at the Conference on WTO Dispute Settlement and Developing Countries, Centre for World Affairs and the Global Economy, University of Wisconsin-Madison, May.

Hoekman, B. 2012. "WTO Reform: A Synthesis and Assessment." In *The Oxford Handbook on the World Trade Organization*, ed. A. Narlikar, M. Daunton, and R. M. Stern, 743–775. Oxford: Oxford University Press.

Krishna, Pravin. 2013. "Preferential Trade Agreements and the World Trade System: A Multilateralist View." In *Globalization in an Age of Crisis:*

Multilateral Economic Cooperation in the Twenty-First Century, ed. Robert C. Feenstra and Alan M. Taylor, 131–164. Chicago: University of Chicago Press.

Krishna, Pravin, and Matthias Matthijs. 2014. "Trading Up or Trading Down: Emerging Markets' Changing Interests in the World Trade System." *SAISPHERE 2013–2014: Emerging Markets on the World Stage* (School of Advanced International Studies, Johns Hopkins University), 28–31. http://www.sais-jhu.edu/sites/default/files/resource-article/files/SAISPHERE%202013-2014.pdf, accessed June 8, 2016.

Panagariya, Arvind. 1996. "The Free Trade Area of the Americas: Good for Latin America?" *World Economy* 19 (5) (September): 485–515.

Panagariya, Arvind. 1999. "The Regionalism Debate: An Overview." *World Economy* 22 (4) (June): 287–331.

Panagariya, Arvind. 2000. "Preferential Trade Liberalization: The Traditional Theory and New Developments." *Journal of Economic Literature* 38 (June): 477–511.

Panagariya, Arvind. 2013. "Challenges to the Multilateral Trading System and Possible Responses." *Economics: Open-Access, Open-Assessment E-Journal* 7 (2013-10) (March 15): 1–25. http://dx.doi.org/10.5018/economics-ejournal.ja.2013-10.

Rose, Andrew. 2004. "Do We Really Know That the WTO Increases Trade?" *American Economic Review* 94 (1): 98–114.

Subramanian, Arvind, and Shang-Jin Wei. 2007. "The WTO Promotes Trade, Strongly but Unevenly." *Journal of International Economics, Elsevier* 72 (1): 151–175.

Varian, Hal. 2007. "An iPod Has Global Value, Ask the (Many) Countries That Make It." *New York Times*, June 28.

World Trade Organization. 2011. *World Trade Report 2011—The WTO and Preferential Trade Agreements: From Co-existence to Coherence*. Geneva: WTO. https://www.wto.org/english/res_e/booksp_e/anrep_e/world_trade_report11_e.pdf.

I

Issues in Trade Policy

2

Border Tax Equalization

Steve Charnovitz

The topic of "border tax equalization"[1] does not match any treaty terms in the World Trade Organization (WTO) Agreement (Goode 2007, 61). Rather, the phrase "border tax equalization" is used synonymously with a border tax adjustment, which is a public policy that seeks to use fiscal measures for trade purposes. As Professor Shinya Murase explains, "The whole idea of border-tax-adjustment is, ostensibly, to ensure an equality of competitiveness in each country's market" (Murase 2011, 102). A border tax adjustment is a process by which imports are subjected to and exports exempted from internal taxation (Rosendahl 1970, 88n11) in order to match (for imports) or counteract (for exports) the effects of a domestic fiscal policy on trade. The economic rationale for a border tax adjustment was recognized by economists at least as far back as the early nineteenth century when David Ricardo argued that when a domestic tax raised the price of corn, "a duty should be imposed on its importation" (Ricardo 1822, 15).[2]

This chapter explores several facets of border tax equalization as one of the challenges facing the world trading system. In particular, the chapter will address the following two questions: First, in section 2.1, under what circumstances does the law of the World Trade Organization (WTO) permit border tax equalization?[3] Second, in section 2.2, what are the implications of those disciplines for current multilateral challenges such as climate change? Relatedly, should the WTO law on border tax equalization, including the General Agreement on Tariffs and Trade (GATT), be revised in order to better achieve the goals of the trading system and other multilateral goals?

2.1 Overview of the WTO Law on Border Tax Equalization

Governments are known to apply a variety of policy measures at the border and to imported products within the domestic market. Such measures include, inter alia, tariffs, duties, taxes, charges, regulations, and subsidies. Although perhaps of diminishing significance, the most important border measure is the common tariff. In WTO law, such a tariff is known as an "ordinary customs duty" (OCD). Besides OCDs, governments utilize many other border measures that go by names such as a transitional surcharge, foreign exchange fee, and exceptional duties. Such fees, charges, and duties fall within the GATT nomenclature of "other duties and charges" (ODC). Another type of border measure is the antidumping duty or countervailing duty applied to imported products. When taxes or charges apply (equally or unequally) to both domestic and imported products, such measures are often referred to as "internal taxes" or "internal charges." Such taxes or charges can be imposed on imports or exempted from exports. The economic instrument of an internal regulation is often substitutable with a tax. Such *internal regulations* can be applied solely to imports (for example, a sanitary regulation) or to both imports and domestic production in a symmetric fashion. Although this is not typically done, a *subsidy* applied to domestic production could also be applied to a like imported product. Much more common is the subsidy applied to the exportation of a good, known in the WTO as an (prohibited) export subsidy. The rebating of taxes upon exportation can also be an export subsidy depending on the type and amount of tax rebated. Of course, some tax rebates at time of exportation are not considered export subsidies if they are WTO-allowable border adjustments.

The rationale for the use of such governmental instruments can reflect either domestic or foreign policy interests, or both. The instruments of ODC, OCD, antidumping and countervailing duties, internal taxes and charges, internal regulations, subsidies, and tax rebates are employed by governments principally to achieve a domestic policy purpose (but could also have secondary foreign policy purposes). By contrast, other instruments, including quantitative restrictions, import bans, and export bans, are commonly used not only for domestic policy purposes, but also for international policy purposes. Such quantitative restrictions and import/export bans lie outside of the scope of this chapter.

ODCs, OCDs, trade remedies, taxes, charges, regulations, and subsidies have a variety of motivations including raising revenues, shielding domestic producers from competition, protecting consumers, leveling the playing field, and avoiding double taxation. All of these purposes can be legitimate under WTO law in certain circumstances as noted in the following examples: Purely protective OCDs are permitted in GATT provided that they exact at levels below or equal to any tariff binding and are imposed on a most-favored-nation basis (or consistently with a preferential trade agreement).[4] Consumer regulations applying to domestic products can generally be applied to imported products provided that the like imported product is not being treated less favorably and the regulation is not more trade restrictive than necessary to fulfill a legitimate objective.[5] A tax on imports intended to raise revenues is permitted provided that the imported product is not being treated less favorably than the like domestic product. The remission at the border of accrued indirect taxes on exported products is permitted.[6] Certain direct taxes related to exports can be remitted in order to avoid the double taxation of foreign source income.[7]

Although the WTO Agreement does not detail legitimate objectives of measures that are legally allowed, within WTO policy discourse several of the preceding measures are justified for the purpose of leveling the playing field with a competing economy. For example, antidumping duties imposed on imports are calibrated to equilibrate to the "full margin of dumping or less" of the foreign production.[8] The highest permitted countervailing duty is equalized to the amount of the foreign subsidy found to exist, "calculated in terms of subsidization per unit of the subsidized and exported product."[9] Although the WTO Agreement on Subsidies and Countervailing Measures (SCM) prohibits employing a subsidy as a "specific action against a subsidy of another Member," governments do regularly take into account the domestic subsidies offered by their trading partners in determining whether to provide parallel domestic subsidies.

Like the other measures, taxes and charges can be imposed or remitted for all of the same reasons noted earlier. An excise tax on a domestically made product is imposed on the like imported product to level the playing field and perhaps to raise revenue. A value-added tax imposed on domestic products is remitted on export to level the playing field and avoid double taxation despite the reduction in revenue for the government.

As noted, the policy rationale in favor of the border tax adjustment can be traced back to the British political economist David Ricardo. After pointing out that a tax on income does not subject the domestic economy to any disadvantage in foreign commerce, Ricardo explained:

> A tax, however, which falls exclusively on the producers of a particular commodity tends to raise the price of that commodity. ... If no protecting duty is imposed on the importation of a similar commodity from other countries,

> injustice is done to the producer at home. ... It is for the interest of the public that he should not be driven from a trade which, under a system of free competition, he would have chosen, and to which he would adhere if every other commodity were taxed equally with that which he produces. ... The growers of corn are subject to some of these peculiar taxes, such as tithes, a portion of the poors' rate, and perhaps one or two other taxes, all of which tend to raise the price of corn, and other raw produce, equal to these peculiar burdens. In the degree then in which these taxes raise the price of corn, a duty should be imposed on its importation. ... By means of this duty and this drawback, the trade would be placed on the same footing as if it had never been taxed, and we should be quite sure that capital would neither be injuriously for the interests of the country, attracted towards, nor repelled from it. (Ricardo 1822, 13–15)

In other words, in order to avoid injustice to home producers and to promote the interest of the public, when a domestic commodity is taxed, an equivalent duty should be imposed on the importation of a similar commodity from other countries. Ricardo promoted such an adjustment for domestic taxes that burden producers of a commodity and that raise the price of the commodity. He illustrated his principle by pointing to "peculiar taxes, such as tithes, a portion of the poors' rate, and perhaps one or two other taxes."

The GATT has always provided policy space for such Ricardian duties. Although GATT Article II:1(b) second sentence prohibits the imposition of ODCs,[10] GATT Article II:2(a) carves out from that discipline "a charge equivalent to an internal tax" in respect of the like domestic product. Specifically, Article II:2(a)[11] provides the following: "Nothing in this Article shall prevent any contracting party from imposing at any time on the importation of any product: (*a*) a charge equivalent to an internal tax imposed consistently with the provisions of paragraph 2 of Article III* in respect of the like domestic product or in respect of an article from which the imported product has been manufactured or produced in whole or in part." In other words, as Frieder Roessler explains, this provision clarifies that governments have a right to burden imports with the collection of the charges specified in Article II:2(a) (Roessler 2010, 267).[12] Furthermore, Roessler observes that the purpose of the border adjustment is "To equalize conditions of competition" (268).

The logic of the GATT-permitted border adjustment is trade neutrality (Leontiades 1966, 173–174). The motivating idea is that while indirect taxes are shifted into the price of the product, direct taxes are shifted back to producers taxes (174). Thus, in allowing adjustments for indirect taxes on products, the GATT was thought to be trade neutral for exports by stripping out the taxes imposed at the origin. Similarly, by enabling tax adjustments to imported products, the GATT was thought to be trade neutral for imports by allowing the imposition of a charge to reflect whatever internal product tax exists. Of course, whether this framework for border adjustments achieves neutrality depends on the accuracy of the assumption that indirect taxes are fully shifted forward and direct taxes are fully shifted back. Yet as trade experts recognized by the 1950s,[13] this economic assumption was unwarranted, and therefore the allowable and disallowable border adjustments would not necessarily achieve trade equality. Moreover, as Jagdish Bhagwati and Petros Mavroidis observe, "it is far from easy to distinguish between direct and indirect taxes" (Bhagwati and Mavroidis 2007, 305).

Another legal issue is whether a regulation can be border adjusted via a fiscal charge on the import. For example, can a domestic regulatory cap and trade system be decomposed into a cap-and-trade equivalent charge to be applied to imported products? Traditionally, commentators have denied that such cross-adjustment was a possibility pursuant to GATT Article II:2(a). For example, Professor Rick Kirgis explained in his seminal article on trade and environment that "if legal regulation is used in place of the production tax, it almost certainly could not be supplemented by cost-equilibrating import charges on bound items without running afoul of [GATT] article II" (Kirgis 1972, 900). Paola Conconi and Jan Wouters wrote in 2010 that "the exception under Article II:2(a) seems to require that there exist a domestic *charge* (e.g. not product standard) that is counterbalanced by a border charge" (Conconi and Wouters 2010, 258; emphasis in original). Most WTO law commentators (including me) would continue to deny the possibility of cross-regulation/tax adjustment, but a comprehensive analysis would have to take into account public policy defenses under GATT Article XX. Moreover, as Don Regan has noted, whether a measure for border adjustment purposes is a tax or a regulation may not be clear (Regan 2009, 122), an ambiguity reflected in the U.S. Obamacare debate.

GATT and WTO caselaw is sparse regarding the interpretation of border adjustment rules. The GATT Article II provision came into play in the GATT *Superfund* case, where Canada and the European Economic Community (EEC) challenged a U.S. tax on certain imported substances.[14] Under this U.S. tax, "the amount of tax on any of the imported substances equals in principle the amount of the tax which would have been imposed under the Superfund Act on the chemicals used as materials in the manufacture or production of the imported substance if the taxable chemicals had been sold in the United States for use in the manufacture or production of the imported substance."[15] In defending itself against a claim of a GATT violation, the United States pointed to GATT Article II:2(a) and argued that the Superfund Act "imposed the same fiscal burden on imported and like domestic substances."[16] The panel agreed with the United States that its excise tax adjustment was consistent with GATT Articles II:2(a) and III.[17]

Superfund was a highly precedential case in explicating the contours of the GATT Article II:2(a) exemption to border tax adjustments for environmental purposes. The EEC argued that the U.S. tax was not "eligible for border tax adjustment" because "It was a tax on pollution ...," not a sales or excise tax imposed for general revenue purposes.[18] In addition, the EEC and Canada argued that the pollution created in the production of the imported substances did not occur in the United States, and "it was therefore inappropriate to tax these substances upon entry in the United States."[19] In addition, the EEC argued that "it was incorrect to assume that the border tax adjustments were necessary to avoid giving foreign producers an unfair advantage."[20] Rather, the EEC suggested that the foreign competitors of the United States "could be assumed to have paid for the pollution caused by the production of the chemicals and substances either directly—by paying a tax for the removal of pollution—or indirectly—by meeting regulatory requirements designed to prevent pollution."[21] Based on that theoretical construct, the EEC then argued that the U.S. border tax adjustments gave U.S. producers an unfair advantage because a chemical exported from the EEC to the United States "would have to bear the costs of environmental protection twice: once in the exporting country in accordance with the Polluter-Pays Principle and upon importation into the United States under the Superfund Act."[22] The EEC further argued that it was inappropriate for the United States to exempt export sales of the involved chemical from the excise tax "because the pollution caused by the production of those chemicals occurred in the United States whether the chemicals were sold in the domestic market or abroad."[23]

The panel rejected the entire line of reasoning put forward by Canada and the EEC. Notably, the panel did not view the contested measure as a tax on pollution, but rather a tax on a product. According to the panel, the purpose of a tax is irrelevant: "Whether a sales tax is levied on a product for general revenue purposes or to encourage the rational use of environmental resources, is therefore not relevant for the determination of the eligibility of a tax for border tax adjustment."[24] The panel went on to explain that although the GATT's rule on tax adjustment set maxima limits for adjustment, governments were free to impose a lower tax or no tax at all on like imported products.[25] In addition, the panel did not buy the EEC's argument that the putative double taxation occurring from the burden of the environmental tax being imposed both in the exporting country and in the importing country needed to be taken into account in making a border adjustment. In other words, the panel affirmed the view of the United States that GATT's border adjustment rules were inward looking and formalistic.

The *Superfund* case played an important role in 1987 in teeing up several difficult issues that were discussed extensively in the trade and environment debate of the 1990s and that continue to complicate the trading system today. These issues include (1) what kind of taxes or charges are eligible for border adjustment; (2) when rebates on environmental or energy taxes are a prohibited export subsidy; (3) how a defendant government shows that a border tax equalization qualifies for the carveout in GATT Article II:2(a); (4) whether environmental purposes are still irrelevant under GATT Articles II:2(a) and III:2; and (5) how recourse to Article XX (General Exceptions) by the defendant would make a difference in cases challenging policy-motivated border tax adjustments.

Only one dispute has occurred during the WTO era under GATT Article II:2(a), the case of *India—Additional Import Duties and Extra-Additional Duties on Imports from the United States*. In this dispute, the complainant United States challenged certain additional and extra-additional duties levied on imports into India that were designed to "counterbalance" domestic sales taxes, value-added taxes, and various other local taxes. Ultimately, neither the panel nor the Appellate Body found any violations. But the Appellate Body in dicta suggested that many of the Indian border charges challenged did not meet the conditions of GATT Article II:2(a).

In doing so, the Appellate Body offered some important interpretations of the relevant GATT rules, and in particular of the availability of GATT Article II:2(a) to justify an ODC with respect to its alleged "corresponding" domestic "counterparts":[26]

- ODCs cover only duties and charges (on imports) that are not OCDs.[27]
- Article II:2(a) "exempts" a charge from the coverage of Article II:1(b) only when the Article II:2(a) conditions are met.[28]

- Whether a measures is a "charge" under Article II:2(a) or an "internal tax or other internal charge" under the Ad Note to GATT Article III "has to be decided in the light of the characteristics of the measure and the circumstances of the case."[29]
- An ODC is not necessarily of a nature that it discriminates against imports.[30]
- The term "equivalent" in Article II:2(a) needs to be interpreted "harmoniously" with the requirement of consistency with Article III:2.[31]
- The requirement for consistency with Article III:2 applies both to an internal tax as well as a charge.[32]
- The requirement for equivalence between a charge and an internal tax requires a comparative assessment that is both qualitative and quantitative in nature; such an assessment needs to include elements of effect, amount, and value, and a look at the "relative function" of the charge and the tax.[33]
- Consistency with Article III:2 is a necessary condition to qualification under Article II:2(a).[34]
- A plaintiff in making a prima facie claim under Article II:1(b) may be required not only to present arguments regarding that provision, but also to present arguments that the challenged measure is *not* justified under Article II:2(a).[35]

Although these holdings suggest many avenues for finding charges and taxes to be equivalent, no follow-on jurisprudence has discussed the many implications of this decision. So this case and the GATT-era *Superfund* case continue to remain the only significant jurisprudence on border adjustments under Article II:2(a).

The WTO law on border adjustments is also informed by the talismanic 1970 *Report of the Working Party on Border Tax Adjustments* (GATT 1970), which has been cited by five Appellate Body reports. The Working Party begins its report by defining "border tax adjustments"—based on a definition elaborated upon in the Organization for Economic Co-operation and Development (OECD)—as measures that "enable exported products to be relieved of some or all of the tax charged in the exporting country in respect of similar domestic products sold to consumers on the home market and which enable imported products sold to consumers to be charged with some or all of the tax charged in the importing country in respect of similar domestic products" (GATT 1970, para. 4). In addition, the Working Party made several points that undergird the current doctrine on border adjustments. First, the GATT provisions on border tax adjustment "set maxima limits for adjustment (compensation)" (para. 11).[36] Second, taxes "directly levied on products were eligible for tax adjustment," such as excise duties, sales taxes, and value-added taxes (para. 14). Third, "certain taxes[37] that were not directly levied on products were not eligible for tax adjustment," such as payroll taxes (14).[38] Fourth, no GATT consensus existed as to the eligibility for adjustment of "taxes occultes" (hidden taxes), which are certain consumption taxes on capital equipment, and taxes on advertising, energy, machinery, and transport (para. 15(a)). Fifth, no consensus existed on other taxes, such as property taxes, which "are not generally considered eligible for tax adjustment" (para. 15(b)). Sixth, the Working Party made the useful suggestion that the term "border tax adjustments" be replaced with "tax adjustments applied to goods entering into international trade" (para. 5). Seventh, the Working Party provided excursus on the term "like product" (para. 18) and this is the part of the report that has been regularly alluded to in the WTO jurisprudence. Of course, the WTO caselaw on "like product" has continued to evolve and is more nuanced today than suggested by a rereading of the 1970 Working Party report. In addition, the Working Party made a statement that continues to be cited but that clearly is no longer good law, even if it was good law at the time.[39] That is, the Working Party asserted that "GATT provisions on tax adjustment applied the principle of destination[40] identically to imports and exports" (para. 10).

With regard to exports, the rules are in the original GATT and the SCM Agreement. The GATT clarified that the exemption of an exported product from duties or taxes "borne by the like product when destined for domestic consumption" shall not be deemed to be a subsidy."[41] In 1960, the GATT Working Party on Subsidies enacted an interpretation of "subsidy" that included the remission on exported goods of "direct taxes or social welfare charges on industrial or commercial enterprises" (GATT 1960). This interpretation was brought forward into the SCM Agreement which prohibits adjustments for direct taxes and social welfare charges and permits adjustments for indirect taxes so long as the adjustment is not in excess of the domestic tax.[42] Direct taxes are defined to be taxes on wages, profits, interest, rent, and all other forms of income including the ownership of real property. Indirect taxes, however, are defined more inclusively to include sales and excise taxes, but also "border taxes and all taxes other than direct taxes and import charges."[43] Since direct taxes are defined by example, and the examples do not include taxes occultes, one could argue that taxes occultes are treated by the SCM Agreement as indirect taxes rather than formalistically as direct taxes. The inclusion of "border taxes" as an indirect tax is puzzling, but one probably should not assume that any tax applied at the border is an indirect tax.

This ambiguity about the meaning of "indirect taxes" leaves open the possibility that export rebates are possible for energy or environmental taxes. For example, a carbon or energy tax could be an indirect tax "levied in respect of the production" of a product.[44] Indeed, on the one hand, one scholar has recently opined that rebates of energy and carbon taxes are justified under the SCM Agreement (Coppens 2014, 518). On the other hand, a carbon tax could be a "social welfare" charge for which an export rebate has been prohibited since 1960.

Although the *Report of the Working Party on Border Tax Adjustments* applies just as much (or more) to exports as it does to imports, the report is less relevant today for exports because export law has been clarified by the SCM Agreement, which seems to permit adjustments beyond those validated in the report. For example, the SCM Agreement allows the rebate of prior-stage cumulative indirect taxes levied on "inputs" that are consumed in the production of the exported product.[45] "Inputs consumed in the production process are defined as "inputs physically incorporated, energy, fuels and oil used in the production process."[46] After this 1994 provision had been finalized by negotiators and publicly released, praise for the new text in some quarters provoked negotiators to reexamine the treaty and to assert that it was not intended to apply the destination principle to energy-intensive exports (Hufbauer 1996, 49–50). So far, this provision has not been interpreted in WTO dispute settlement but based on WTO jurisprudence, a textual interpretation would be favored over one premised on tenth-inning negotiating history.

By defining inputs to include energy and oil used in the production process, the SCM Agreement would seem to allow export rebates of taxes on inputs such as energy. Thus, the SCM Agreement does not follow a physical incorporation principle in distinguishing between a permissible export rebate and an export subsidy. By contrast, the 1979 GATT Subsidies Code had limited export remission to indirect taxes on goods that were "physically incorporated" into the exported product" (GATT 1979, Annex item (h)). That rule reflected U.S. countervailing duty policy at the time, which distinguished between tax rebates that were not subsidies and those that were subsidies, such as rebates of tax occultes, which were subject to U.S. countervailing duties (Hufbauer and Shelton-Erb 1984, 56–57).

Putting all this together, one can restate the WTO law on border tax equalization. Three basic principles can be noted. First, imports and exports are not treated symmetrically. Second, with regard to imports, a government may impose a border charge on an imported product when such charge is equivalent to (and not in excess of) an internal tax on a like domestic product. Under GATT Article II:2(a), a government may also impose a border charge on an imported product when such charge is equivalent to an internal tax in respect of an article "from which"[47] the imported product has been manufactured or produced in whole or in part.[48] Moreover, because Article II:2(a) incorporates Article III:2, a charge imposed on an import cannot be in excess of a tax or charge applied directly or indirectly to a like domestic product. Third, with regard to exports, a government may remit (or relieve) from an exported product an indirect tax, but may not remit in excess of those taxes levied in respect of the production or distribution of like products when sold for domestic consumption. In addition, internal payroll or social security tax cannot be rebated on exports.

This restatement of WTO law on border equalization is summarized in table 1.1.

Having restated the positive law, this chapter should also underline the lacunae in the law. In my view, three fundamental issues remain unresolved: First, would a tax occultes be border adjustable on imports or exports, particularly when such a tax—for example, a pollution tax or an energy tax (Charnovitz 2003, 148)—is crafted as a tax on a product? The *Superfund* case teaches that certain environmental taxes can be border adjustable on imports, but its holding does not extend to taxes on producers rather than taxes on products.

Second, are property taxes adjustable? Footnote 58 of the SCM Agreement precludes adjustment on exports of property taxes.[49] But how about imports? In introducing the concept of a border adjustment and explaining why it was sound economic policy, Ricardo gave examples of tithes and the poors' rate, which in English law were fiscal, or in-kind measures imposed on property production and income. (The poors' rate was a tax used to assist the poor.) Ricardo viewed such taxes as burdening producers and raising commodity prices. Of course, GATT law need not match Ricardo's categories, but a rereading of his works raises the question of whether the "peculiar taxes" that Ricardo discussed are necessarily taxes

Table 1.1
When do WTO rules prohibit border equalization of social and environmental taxes?

	Measure	WTO law status
On imports		
	Application of charge equivalent to a domestic tax on like products	Permitted by GATT Art. II:2(a)
	Application of a charge equivalent to a domestic tax on inputs physically incorporated in the imported product	Permitted by GATT Art. II:2(a)
	Application of a charge equivalent to a domestic tax on inputs used in making the imported product	Arguably prohibited by GATT Art. III:2 and II:2(a), but status unclear
	Application of a charge equivalent to the economic effect of a domestic regulation on like products	Prohibited by Article II:2(a)
On exports		
	Exemption of a tax or charge borne by the domestic product	Permitted by SCM Agreement and GATT, ad art. XVI
	Exemption of a tax on inputs physically incorporated in the exported product	Permitted by SCM Annex I item (h)
	Exemption of a tax on inputs used in making the exported product	Arguably permitted by SCM Annex II, but status unclear

of the type for which border adjustments are precluded on imports. Recall again that the GATT Working Party left the question of property taxes unsettled.[50]

Third, how narrowly does the accordion of product likeness contract in comparing an imported and a domestic product, each of which has different environmental or social externalities? In other words, is a widget made with clean energy a *like* product to a widget made with carbon energy? A recent development in WTO caselaw, discussion of which follows, makes the answer appear to be no.

A border tax adjustment on imports that violates GATT Articles I, II, or III could be defended by the General Exceptions in GATT Article XX that can exculpate measures that would otherwise violate the GATT. Even though Article XX could save a border tax equalization, most of the legal debate revolves around justifying such adjustments under baseline GATT rules. After all, if the Article XX exception ultimately is needed, then there would be no particular benefit in using a border adjustment over some other instrument.

Although a restatement of Article XX doctrine and caselaw is beyond the scope of this chapter, four key points can be noted: First, traditionally border tax adjustments were used to achieve trade and competitiveness purposes. That motivation is clearly insufficient for an Article XX justification. As noted in the World Economic Forum, "measures taken to ensure continued competitiveness in the marketplace are not environmental measures eligible for the GATT defence" (World Economic Forum 2010, 11).[51] Second, a climate border adjustment may reflect mixed motives of both trade and environment. Although a tax measure instituted to make a domestic regime politically feasible would be viewed by a WTO panel as falling outside of allowable environmental purposes, using a border measure on imports to incentivize foreign behavior could be a valid Article XX defense.[52] Back in 1972, Frederic L. Kirgis expressed skepticism that Article XX(b) could be used to justify a border charge for health purposes, stating that the "bond between the charge and the health measure is too tenuous" (Kirgis 1972, 901). Over forty years later, there is GATT caselaw wherein the Article XX(b) justification has been accepted, but none of those cases involved something as tenuous as applying a tax to address a production externality in another country. Third, a border adjustment on exports that violates the SCM rules by being a prohibited subsidy cannot be saved by GATT Article XX (Shadikhodjaev 2015, 499–500). Moreover, even aside from the problem of SCM as higher law than the GATT, the terms of Article XX could not shield a remission of a tax on export because there would not be any environmental reason to do so. Fourth, to qualify under Article XX, a measure must pass scrutiny under the chapeau of Article XX which requires "that such measures are not applied in a manner which would constitute a means of arbitrary or unjustifiable discrimination between countries where the same conditions prevail, or a disguised restriction on international trade." This provision has been interpreted to require transparency, due process, and flexibilities for individual exporting countries (Voigt 2009, 228–231). In my view, these requirements preclude imposing on imports a charge calculated on the basis of the carbon content in domestic production (as opposed to the production in the country of export).[53]

2.2 Using Border Adjustments for Climate Challenges

The interface of climate and international trade was recognized from the beginning of the climate regime. The UN Framework Convention on Climate Change (UNFCCC) states the general principle that "Measures taken to combat climate change, including unilateral ones, should not constitute a means of arbitrary or unjustifiable discrimination or a disguised restriction on international trade" (Art. 3.5). Neither the UNFCCC nor any subsidiary acts discuss border tax equalization.

Over the past fifteen years, considerable attention has been devoted to the idea of imposing and adjusting carbon taxes at the border. For example, one recent study defines a "carbon-motivated border tax adjustment" (CBTA) as "a tax on the emissions of products imported by any region or country to compensate for different carbon policies (and especially carbon taxes) on products from different origins that compete in the same market."[54]

Can a domestic carbon tax be imposed at the border to imports? This simple question should be easy for a WTO lawyer to answer, but unfortunately, the answer is not clear. To elaborate the question, suppose a government imposed a domestic tax on carbon emissions entailed in the upstream production of a widget. Or suppose that a government imposed a domestic tax based on the sources of energy used in making the widget. Would it be legal for the government to impose a border charge on imported like widgets?

If such a carbon charge is to be GATT-legal, it would have to have an extraterritorial character. In other words, the importing country government would have to calculate the charge to be equal to the tax that would have been imposed on the widget had its law applied to the production.[55] The *U.S.—Gasoline* case, the WTO's first environmental case, certainly teaches us that an effort to use a shortcut, such as imposing on the import the average domestic tax, would be viewed as a violation of national treatment. Note that the calculation of the border carbon charge based on facts occurring in a foreign country is no different than what occurs in antidumping law.

Whether such a carbon charge on imports would meet GATT's border adjustment rules depends on the status of the taxes involved. As noted earlier, the legal status of so-called taxes occultes is not settled in GATT law and therefore a tax on either energy consumed or pollution emitted might or might not qualify for a border adjustment. One of the leading WTO law experts, Frieder Roessler, has written that GATT Articles II and III "do not permit Members to offset the competitive impact of internal taxes borne by producers (such as energy taxes raising the costs of transportation) and regulations affecting exclusively production (such as emission regulations increasing the cost of production)" (Roessler 2010, 271). In support of that position, one could note the failure of Germany's efforts at the GATT in 1954–1955 to clarify that under Article III, the border adjustment could reflect internal taxers at various stages of production including "the power consumed for the production" of the finished products" (GATT 1995, 144–145).

Roessler's position may be a majority view, but other analysts disagree. For example, I believe that a true carbon tax matched to the carbon footprint of a product could be adjusted at the border (Hufbauer, Charnovitz, and Kim 2009, 67–69). Roessler seems to want to distinguish between taxes on products and taxes on producers, but products veritably do not pay taxes. The payer of taxes is the taxpayer. So, for example, a so-called indirect sales tax on the sale of a product is paid by the seller or the buyer. Thus, while GATT doctrine holds that sales taxes are border adjustable, there is no obvious way to distinguish the adjustability of different kinds of indirect taxes. For example, if an excise tax on a vendor for the "privilege" of selling[56] is adjustable, why not an excise tax on a manufacturer for the privilege of polluting?

When the GATT Working Party discussed taxes occultes in 1970, the Working Party indicated that the scarcity of complaints indicated a relative lack of importance justifying its decision to conduct no further examination (GATT 1970, para. 15). Today the issue has grown in importance and should such taxes be border adjusted, there would be a lot of trade complaints. At the same time, the ranks of carbon border adjustment defenders have been growing. For example, a study from 2011 suggests that applying domestic energy and pollution taxes to imports would be "indirect" product taxes with a nexus between the tax and the product based on the goal of "creating a level playing field between like products in the country of destination" (Kaufmann and Weber 2011, 520). A more recent study finds that "BTA [border tax adjustment] can serve as a device to ensure a level playing field between countries with high and such with lax or no environmental policies" (Weber 2015, 4).

Being able to impose a border charge on an import based on its production process raises the issue of PPMs, an acronym for processes and production methods. The legal question is whether a WTO court would ever treat two otherwise "like" products as *not* like based on the PPMs used in producing the product. That matters because if the imported high-carbon-footprint widget is a like product to the domestic low-carbon-footprint widget, then imposing the border charge on the imported widget would be a violation of national treatment (GATT Article III:2).

For many decades, trade law doctrine has denied that PPMs could lead to product unlikeness, but the caselaw has evolved on how to consider the factor of "consumers tastes and habits" identified in the *Report of the Working Party on Border Tax Adjustments* (GATT 1970) as one of the relevant factors in determining product likeness. Indeed, two leading WTO law commentators, Jagdish Bhagwati and Petros Mavroidis, contend that "a consumer (in the eyes of the Appellate Body) who is aware of the environmental (and eventually health) hazard that global warming might represent, will treat the two goods (*Kyoto Protocol*-compatible, *Kyoto Protocol*-incompatible) as unlike goods" (Bhagwati and Mavroidis 2007, 308; original footnotes omitted).

Although it did not consider product likeness, the recent decision of the Appellate Body in *Canada—Renewable Energy/FITs* shows an important evolution of the caselaw. In that dispute, the central issue was whether the Ontario renewable energy subvention was a subsidy as defined in the SCM Agreement (Cosbey and Mavroidis 2014, 23). A contested question was whether the feed-in-tariff provided a "benefit" to the recipient and for that, the Appellate Body held that the relevant market for analysis was not the wholesale electricity market, but rather electricity produced from certain renewable energy.[57] The Appellate Body did not specifically state that electricity made from renewable energy was not a like product to electricity made from carbon energy, but based on past jurisprudence, if two products do not compete in the same market, then not only are they not "like" under GATT Article III:2 first sentence, but they are also not "directly competitive" under GATT Article III:2 second sentence. The legal significance is that when two products are not like, then treating the imported product less favorably cannot be a violation of national treatment. This holding has important implications for the PPM question.

The MFN Problem for Carbon Adjustments

The application of border adjustments to imports also raises issues under the most-favored nation disciplines in GATT Article I.[58] Consider an easier and then a harder question. The easier question is whether the border adjustment on a widget from Country A can be higher than on a widget from Country B if the production process in A is more carbon intensive than in B. In my view, the answer has to be yes, assuming that a border adjustment linked to carbon intensity is permissible in the first place. In *Superfund*, the amount of the tax on the imported substance could have differed from country to country depending on the product composition. But if two countries had an identical production process, then the tax for those two countries ought to be the same.

The harder question is whether the border tax adjustment can treat exporting countries differently not based on the production process used for a shipment of products, but rather on the laws of the exporting country. To put this more concretely, if Country A already imposes a carbon tax on a good and does not remit the tax on export, can importing Country E refrain from taxing the imported product so as to avoid double taxation or double burdening? Such double burdening would arguably make the imported product uncompetitive. Or in other words, if Country E refrains from border taxing the import from green Country A but Country E does impose the border tax on environmentally indifferent Country B, would Country B be able to complain to the WTO that there is illegal discrimination?

This problématique arose early in the GATT in the *Belgian Family Allowances* case in 1952.[59] To complement the domestic tax revenue it was using to pay for family allowances, Belgium had imposed a parallel domestic tax on imported goods purchased by public bodies.[60] Yet in an exercise of comity, Belgian had exempted from taxation imports from countries whose system of family allowances met requirements similar to Belgium's system. (Belgium was not using its provision to encourage other countries to adopt a similar social policy, but rather was presumably seeking to avoid double taxation.) Norway and Denmark had been denied the exemption and brought a case to the GATT seeking to show that they were as qualified for the exemption as France and other countries, and alleging discrimination. The complainants won the case but on much broader grounds because the panel ruled that the entire system of policy-linked exemptions violated GATT Article I:1.

Belgian Family Allowances established an important precedent in the trading system that remains good law today although one should note that Article XX would be available as a defense for a policy motivated system of exemptions if that policy is covered within Article XX. In addition, one should note that WTO jurisprudence has left open the issue of whether certain origin-neutral distinctions (e.g., based on corporate characteristics) could be consistent with GATT Article I. The most recent Appellate Body holding came in the 2014 *EC–Seal Products* case where the appellators stated that "Article I:1 permits regulatory distinctions to be drawn between like imported products, provided that such distinctions do not result in a detrimental impact on the competitive opportunities for like imported products from any Member."[61]

The issue of whether to exempt the imported product from a border adjustment for policy reasons was at the forefront of the 1970 *Superfund* case and has reappeared in discussions of trade and the environment since then. As noted earlier, the EEC argued that the United States should have assumed that foreign producers had already paid a tax on pollution and therefore its exports should have been exempt from the border adjustment so that its producers would not have to bear the costs of environmental protection twice.[62] The panel rejected this line of reasoning, holding that the United States was entitled to a tax adjustment to match its tax on like domestic products.

The two GATT panel holdings—*Superfund* and *Belgian Family Allowances*—combine to create a policy conflict. On the one hand, the adjustment on imports is allowed to equilibrate competition. Yet on the other hand, applying the adjustment to imports from certain countries could disequilibrate competition because the exported product would already be bearing the burden of the tax at home. But GATT Article I and *Belgian Family Allowances* rule out distinguishing imports based on their origin.

One traditional answer to this conundrum going back to early OECD studies is that if all countries remitted such a domestic tax on exports, then in principle there would be no double taxation. But the problem is that relevant government instruments are broader than just taxes on products. Taxes on processes and producers may not be rebatable on exports under the SCM Agreement and the cost of regulations cannot be remitted to exporters. Furthermore, a government for environmental (or even budget) reasons may not want to remit taxes on exports. Thus, GATT Article I will constrain the ability of a government to tailor its border adjustments to conditions in other countries.

Legality of Proposed U.S. Border Carbon Equalization

Several governments considering climate legislation have floated proposals to utilize border adjustments to address so-called carbon leakage or to avoid competitiveness impact. Such proposals have been a particularly salient feature in the U.S. legislative process (Durán Medina and Polanco Lazo 2011, 31). For example, consider the Healthy Climate and Family Security Act of 2014 (H.R. 5271), introduced by Congressman Chris Van Hollen and colleagues in July 2014. This bill caps carbon emissions, auctions carbon pollution permits, and returns these auction receipts to American residents. In addition, the Van Hollen bill includes a chapter on "Border Adjustments" that would impose a "carbon equivalency fee" on imports of carbon-intensive goods. The amount of the carbon equivalency fee would be set equal to the cost that domestic producers of a comparable carbon-intensive good incur as a result of (1) prices paid in the acquisition of carbon permits by covered entities; and (2) carbon equivalency fees paid by importers of carbon-intensive goods used in the production of the comparable carbon-intensive good. The bill also provides for a payment to exporters of carbon-intensive goods produced in the United States. The amount of the payment would be equal to the cost that domestic producers of the carbon-intensive good incur as a result of (1) prices paid in the acquisition of carbon permits by covered entities; and (2) carbon equivalency fees paid by importers of carbon-intensive goods used in the production of the comparable carbon-intensive good. The bill also contains a sunset provision for the import and export provisions that states that these programs shall cease to have effect at such time as and to the extent that (1) an international agreement requiring countries that emit greenhouse gases and produce carbon-intensive goods for export markets to adopt equivalent measures comes into effect; or (2) the country of export has implemented equivalent measures. The bill defines an "equivalent measure" as a tax, or other regulatory requirement that imposes a cost, on manufacturers of carbon-intensive goods located outside the United States, by reason of greenhouse gas emissions in the production of such goods by such manufacturers, approximately equal to the cost imposed by this legislation on manufacturers of comparable carbon-intensive goods located in the United States. The bill does not discuss its relationship to WTO law, and no statement by Van Hollen has come to my attention analyzing the WTO implications of this bill. Moreover, unlike some other U.S. legislation over the years,[63] the bill does not contain a provision for suspending a challenged measure should it be found to be a trade law violation.

In August 2014, the *Washington Post* praised the Van Hollen bill in its editorial "An Answer to Global Warming" (Washington Post 2014, A16.) The editorial opines that the border charge "will be hard to pull off efficiently. Officials will have to calculate the carbon footprint of various goods from various points of origin, and other countries will accuse the United States of protectionism. Yet any carbon pricing plan will have to include some trade adjustment. Otherwise U.S. industry will be disadvantaged." The *Post* editorial omits any discussion of the WTO law problems with the scheme they praise.

The question of whether the Van Hollen bill would be consistent with WTO border adjustment rules is straightforward. It would not. The carbon equivalency fee would not qualify under GATT Article II:2(a) because there would be no equivalent internal tax or charge to mirror. Rather, there would be a domestic regulation that would require producers to purchase carbon permits. The payment to exporters would be a prohibited export subsidy because there is no domestic indirect tax to be rebated at the border. The exemption for imports of particular goods from countries with taxes or regulations that impose a cost on local manufacturers approximately equal to the cost imposed by U.S. law would violate GATT Article I and would not fit within Article XX, which contains no exception to assure that foreign regulatory costs are as high as U.S. regulatory costs. Furthermore, the Article XX chapeau would rule out a program that shifts cost to foreign countries based solely on costs to domestic producers. Even if it were true that for domestic U.S. political reasons any carbon plan will have to include some trade adjustment, as the *Post* avers, that domestic political constraint would not buttress the case for WTO legality before a WTO panel.

Besides the vulnerability to WTO litigation, a government that put in place a unilateral border adjustment for climate policy would also be subject to tit-for-tat retaliation (Houser et al. 2008, 42; Bhagwati 2009, 176). That is because any country could enact an idiosyncratic Van Hollen type measure to protect local competitors from the real or imagined harms imposed by domestic environmental laws. I say imagined harms because as OECD Secretary-General José Àngel Gurría has noted, "fears about the potential impact of leakage and loss of competiveness are exaggerated" (Gurría 2009). Moreover, as Robyn Eckersley has noted, "border measures could potentially poison the international climate negotiations by angering major developing countries, such as India and China, against which such measures are primarily directed" (Eckersley 2010, 379). So the simplistic, jingoistic answer to global warming trumpeted by the *Washington Post* is hardly an answer to complex environmental and trade questions.

What Can Be Done?

The last section of this chapter reflects on whether WTO law needs to be changed to accommodate climate measures. Is there anything wrong with current law? One answer could be that current WTO law is adequate because governments should not attempt to shift the costs of their domestic policies onto their trading partners. But that is not a satisfactory answer given the justification for at least some adjustments in Ricardian economics and the longtime accommodation in trade rules for border equivalency measures. The fact that climate change is a global challenge also makes it hard to rule out in principle all unilateral measures seeking to induce multilateral solutions. While it may be true that if all governments agreed to identical climate measures there might not be need for border measures, that condition of consensual climate policymaking does not exist.

Another problem with current WTO law is that it is ambiguous. Although a stupidly designed legislative proposal such as the Van Hollen bill is clearly WTO-legal, whether a well-designed border carbon adjustment would be legal or not is debatable. In my view, WTO law should not be inscrutable. Governments contemplating climate policy should know in advance whether the tool of a border adjustment is available. To that end, one could imagine legislative refinements to GATT Article II:2(a) and to SCM Annex I. Over four decades ago, a leading scholar of border tax adjustments called for clarification of their application particularly to the tax occultes (Rosendahl 1970, 140).

Two types of reforms can be considered: One is to rationalize border tax adjustments overall. The other is to seek a special law for climate-related adjustments.

On border equalization generally the most radical proposal came thirty years ago in a landmark study by Gary Clyde Hufbauer and Joanna Shelton Erb. They recommended that in order to "restore fiscal sovereignty" to GATT parties, "the international community should embrace the full destination principle as a *permissible* (not *mandatory*) method of border tax adjustment, for both direct and indirect taxes" (Hufbauer and Erb 1984, 55).[64] In other words, a country that wants to shelter its industries from the consequences of high taxation could provide destination-principle border adjustments, and a country that did not wish to shelter its production could refrain from them. How such a flexible tax adjustment scheme might have worked out in practice would be an interesting gaming exercise.

With regard to climate, the Peterson Institute study (Hufbauer, Charnovitz, and Kim 2009, 105–106) called for the negotiation of an international Trade and Climate Code that would include permission for the imposition of carbon equivalent taxes at the border based on domestic climate-related taxes. This proposal also called for a credit for imports from countries that imposed equivalent carbon taxes on their production and exports. Not much progress toward such a code has occurred since 2009, but a group of academics has prepared a very helpful guidance document for border adjustments.[65]

Looking ahead, one step forward might be for multilateral stakeholders in the trade and climate regimes to devise a template carbon-adjustment scheme that could be copied by governments into their domestic climate legislation and considered by climate negotiators for inclusion within climate law norms. International trade norms would be important to consider in this exercise but equally important are international environmental norms. As I have pointed out in a previous study, the unilateral application of carbon charges to imports may be inconsistent with environmental law (Charnovitz 2010, 411). Furthermore, as one leading climate analyst has concluded, "a border adjustment on carbon-intensive manufactured goods from countries that have not taken comparably effective action to address climate change, as commonly proposed today, would do little to reduce overall leakage and have little environmental benefit" (Bordoff 2009, 52). Thus, the best path ahead may be to avoid trade conflicts through the imposition of unilateral carbon border adjustments and instead strive to improve multilateral cooperation on climate policy including free trade in environmental goods and services.

Notes

Thanks to Jagdish Bhagwati and Michael Levi for their helpful comments.

1. Note that the terms "border equalization tax" (on exports) and "import equalization taxes" (on imports) were used in Feller's landmark article on border adjustments in international trade Feller 1969, 51–52). The terms "equalization charge" and "equalization tax" were also used in Dam's classic treatise on GATT in his chapter on border tax adjustments (Dam 1970, 212).

2. At the time that Ricardo wrote his treatise, border tax adjustments on exports were already in existence (e.g., the U.S. Whiskey Act of 1791 §14, 15, 51, 1 Stat. 199).

3. This article addresses only general WTO law, not the individual laws of accession applying to WTO members, such as China, that joined the WTO pursuant to sui generis rules. In addition, this article only addresses trade in goods, not trade in services.

4. The WTO Appellate Body has quoted approvingly the statement of the Turkey–Textiles panel that "A basic principle in the GATT system is that tariffs are the preferred and acceptable form of protection." Appellate Body Report, *India—Additional Import Duties*, adopted November 17, 2008, para. 159 footnote 316 (citing Panel Report, *Turkey–Textiles*, para. 9.63).

5. GATT Art. III:4, Agreement on Technical Barriers to Trade (TBT Agreement), Arts. 2.1, 2.2.

6. Agreement on Subsidies and Countervailing Measures (SCM Agreement), Art. 1.1(a)(1)(ii) and footnote 1, and Annex I, items (g), (h).

7. SCM Agreement, Annex I, para. (e), footnote 59, para. 2.

8. Antidumping Agreement, Art. 9.1.

9. SCM Agreement, Art. 19.4.

10. GATT Article II:1(b) states: "Such products shall also be exempt from all other duties or charges of any kind imposed on or in connection with the importation in excess of those imposed on the date of this Agreement or those directly and mandatorily required to be imposed thereafter by legislation in force in the importing territory on that date." This means that no new ODCs can be imposed (on at least bound items) following a government's entry into the GATT or the WTO. See WTO Understanding on the Interpretation of Article II:1(b) of the General Agreement on Tariffs and Trade 1994. Former GATT legal adviser Frieder Roessler goes further in saying, "The second sentence obliges Members to reduce the number and diversity of import duties or charges by prohibiting, in principle, all duties and charges on bound items other than ordinary customs charges" (Roessler 2010, 266, 269 table 1.1). Yet as Roessler also notes, there is suggestion in the caselaw that an ODC validly recorded in the GATT Schedule of Concessions would be permitted (ibid., 267).

11. The original proposal for what became Article II:2(a) came from a U.S. proposal that was based on U.S. bilateral trade agreements with Canada, The Netherlands, and Switzerland Rosendahl 1970, 144–145).

12. The remainder of Article II:2 clarifies that governments have a right to burden imports with antidumping and countervailing duties and with import fees commensurate with the costs of services rendered.

13. Stewart, Salonen, and McDonough 2007, 37.

14. GATT Panel Report, *United States—Taxes on Petroleum and Certain Imported Substances*, adopted June 17, 1987. Another issue in the case was a U.S. tax on petroleum. This dispute is known as the *Superfund* case.

15. Ibid., para. 2.5.

16. Ibid., para. 3.2.5.

17. Ibid., paras. 5.2.7, 5.2.8, 5.2.10.

18. Ibid., para. 3.2.7.
19. Ibid.
20. Ibid., para. 3.2.8.
21. Ibid.
22. Ibid.
23. Ibid., para. 3.2.7.
24. Ibid., para. 5.2.4.
25. Ibid., para. 5.2.5.
26. Appellate Body Report, *India—Additional Import Duties*, paras. 208, 211.
27. Ibid., para. 151.
28. Ibid., para. 153.
29. Ibid., para. 153, footnote 304.
30. Ibid., para. 158.
31. Ibid., para. 170.
32. Ibid.
33. Ibid., paras. 170–175.
34. Ibid., para. 181.
35. Ibid., para. 190.
36. This point was picked up in the *Superfund* case and remains a good interpretation today.
37. Note that the Report does not say that all taxes not levied on products are not eligible for border adjustment.
38. This remains good law and was broadened and enacted with respect to exports in the SCM Agreement (SCM Agreement, Annex I, para. E).
39. Gary Hufbauer argues that it was never good law (Hufbauer 1996, 56). However, even if it was good law until 1994, such symmetry was overturned by the adoption of the SCM Agreement, which trumps the GATT in the event of an inconsistency. The SCM Agreement provides distinctive rules for border adjustments for exports that do not apply to imports. Thus, the SCM Agreement may permit or prohibit adjustments for exports that would not be permitted or prohibited by the GATT.
40. The destination principle means taxing a good should be taxed where it is consumed as contrasted with the origin principle of taxing a good where it is produced.
41. GATT Ad Note GATT Art. XVI (added in 1957).
42. See SCM Agreement, Annex I, items (e), (g).
43. SCM Agreement, Annex I, footnote 58.
44. See SCM Agreement, Annex I, item (g). World Trade Organization and UN Environment Programme 2009, 105.

45. SCM Agreement, Annex I, item (h) and Annex II.

46. Ibid., Annex II, footnote 61.

47. There has been considerable scholarly debate on whether the term "from which" necessitates physical incorporation of inputs or whether one might say more broadly, for example, that coal produces energy from which a widget is manufactured. According to one commentator, "The words 'from which' suggest that any input from which the imported product is manufactured should be eligible for adjustment regardless of physical incorporation, including energy and catalysts, which are consumed in the production process and are not found in the final product" (Maruyama 2011, 691). Other scholars have pointed to the French version of Article II:2(a), which seems to imply that only taxes on items incorporated in the imported product can be collected at the border (Holzer 2014, 100, footnote 337). Another stream of scholarship points out that charges on byproducts of the production process, such as carbon emissions, may not be eligible for a border adjustment. See Veel 2009, 774; Low, Marceau, and Reinaud 2012, 492, 497.

48. To wit, "Offsetting domestic taxation by imposing similar taxes on imports at the border is considered lawful under Article II" (Cottier, Nartova, and Shingal 2014, 1019).

49. SCM Agreement, Annex I, para. (e), footnote 58.

50. See GATT 1970, para. 15(b). Four years before the GATT Working Party report, one border adjustment scholar pondered whether property taxes could be indirect taxes (Leontiades 1966, 174).

51. See also O'Brien 2009, 1095, 1109.

52. Whether Article XX could be used to prevent so-called carbon leakage presents a slightly different question. To wit, Country A has an export sector in widgets that may relocate abroad to polluter haven B if A imposes higher environmental regulation. Here the problem A faces is that B is a polluter haven. Certainly, A may need to take some action to green B's policies, but incentivizing A's widget sector to remain addresses only a minuscule part of the B problem. Perhaps the best solution for A short term would be to subsidize its widget sector for adaptation costs to higher environmental regulation. Such a subsidy was specifically permitted in SCM Article 8 but the WTO allowed that right of subsidy to expire in 2000 (Luengo 2007, 158).

53. It is interesting to note that recently, two distinguished trade policy scholars endorsed a border adjustment based on the carbon content in domestic production (Mattoo and Subramanian 2013).

54. Rocchi et al. 2015, 7.

55. In other words, the charge would be outwardly looking in the sense that it would be based on facts occurring in a foreign country. But the charge would be inwardly looking in applying the internal rules for the charge to the foreign facts available.

56. See D.C. Code Ann. §§ 47–2002 to 47–2004.

57. Canada—Certain Measures Affecting the Renewable Energy Generation Sector/Canada—Measures Relating to the Feed-In Tariff Program, WT/DS412, WT/DS426, adopted May 24, 2013, paras. 5.177–5.178.

58. GATT Article I:1 states:

With respect to customs duties and charges of any kind imposed on or in connection with importation or exportation or imposed on the international transfer of payments for imports or exports, and with respect to the method of levying such duties and charges, and with respect to all rules and formalities in connection with importation and exportation, and with respect to all matters referred to in paragraphs 2 and 4 of Article III, any advantage, favour, privilege or immunity granted by any contracting party to any product originating in or destined for any other country shall be accorded immediately and unconditionally to the like product originating in or destined for the territories of all other contracting parties.

59. *Belgian Family Allowances*, BISD 1S/59, adopted November 7, 1952.

60. Belgium's tax was an internal tax reviewed solely under Article III; Belgium did not raise a defense under Article II:2(a).

61. *EC–Seal Products*, WT/DS400,401/AB/R, adopted June 18, 2014, paras. 5.88, 5.95.

62. GATT Panel Report, *United States—Taxes on Petroleum and Certain Imported Substances*, para. 3.2.8.

63. For example, 22 USCA §1978(a).

64. Compare Leontiades 1966, 180, suggesting that direct and indirect taxes "should be abandoned as useful concepts for applying border price adjustments."

65. Cosbey et al. 2012.

References

Bhagwati, Jagdish, and Petros C. Mavroidis. 2007. "Is Action against US Exports for Failure to Sign Kyoto Protocol WTO-Legal?" *World Trade Review* 6:299–310.

Bhagwati, Jadish. 2009. "Reflections on Climate Change and Trade." In *Climate Change, Trade and Competitiveness: Is a Collision Inevitable?*, ed. Lael Brainard and Isaac Sorkin, 171–176. Washington, DC: Brookings Institution Press.

Bordoff, Jason E. 2009. "International Trade Law and the Economics of Climate Policy: Evaluating the Legality and Effectiveness of Proposals to Address Competitiveness and Leakage Concerns." In *Climate Change, Trade and Competitiveness: Is a Collision Inevitable?*, ed. Lael Brainard and Isaac Sorkin, 35–59. Washington, DC: Brookings Institution Press.

Brainard, Lael, and Isaac Sorkin, eds. 2009. *Climate Change, Trade and Competitiveness: Is a Collision Inevitable?* Washington, DC: Brookings Institution Press.

Charnovitz, Steve 2003. "Trade and Climate: Potential Conflicts and Synergies." In *Beyond Kyoto. Advancing the International Effort Against Climate Change*, ed. J. Aldy et al., 141–170. Washington, DC: Pew Center on Global Climate Change.

Charnovitz, Steve. 2010. "Reviewing Carbon Charges and Free Allowances Under Environmental Law and Principles." *ILSA Journal of International and Comparative Law* 16 (2): 398–412.

Conconi, Paola, and Jan Wouters. 2010. "Appellate Body Report, India—Additional and Extra-Additional Duties on Imports from the United States (WT/DS360/AB/R, adopted on 17 November 2008)." *World Trade Review* 9:239–263.

Coppens, Dominic. 2014. *WTO Disciplines on Subsidies and Countervailing Measures: Balancing Policy Space and Legal Constraints*. Cambridge, UK: Cambridge University Press.

Cosbey, Aaron, Susanne Droege, Carolyn Fischer, Julia Reinaud, John Stephenson, Lutz Weischer, and Peter Wooders. 2012. *A Guide for the Concerned: Guidance on the Elaboration and Implementation of Border Carbon Adjustment*. Entwined Policy Report 03, November.

Cosbey, Aaron, and Petros C. Mavroidis. 2014. "A Turquoise Mess: Green Subsidies, Blue Industrial Policy and Renewable Energy: The Case for Redrafting the Subsidies Agreement of the WTO." *Journal of International Economic Law* 17:11–47.

Cottier, Thomas, Olga Nartova, and Anirudh Shingal. 2014. "The Potential of Tariff Policy for Climate Change Mitigation: Legal and Economic Analysis." *Journal of World Trade* 48:1007–1038.

Dam, Kenneth W. 1970. *The GATT: Law and International Economic Organization*. Chicago: University of Chicago Press.

Durán Medina, Valentina, and Rodrigo Polanco Lazo. 2011. "A Legal View on Border Tax Adjustments and Climate Change: A Latin American Perspective." *Sustainable Development Law & Policy* 11 (3): 29–34, 43–45.

Eckersley, Robyn. 2010. "The Politics of Carbon Leakage and the Fairness of Border Measures." *Ethics & International Affairs* 24:367–393.

Feller, Peter Buck. 1969. "Mutiny Against the Bounty: An Examination of Subsidies, Border Tax Adjustments, and the Resurgence of Countervailing Duty Law." *Law and Policy in International Business* 1:17–76.

GATT. 1960. *Provisions of Article XVI:4*, report adopted November 19, 1960. GATT BISD 9S/185.

GATT. 1970. *Report by the Working Party on Border Tax Adjustments*. BISD 18S/97, adopted Dec. 2, 1970.

GATT. 1979. *Agreement on the Interpretation and Application of Articles VI, XVI, and XXIII of the General Agreement on Tariffs and Trade*.

GATT. 1995. *Analytical Index*. http://www.wto.org/english/res_e/booksp_e/gatt_ai_e/gatt_ai_e.htm (accessed June 1, 2016).

Goode, Walter. 2007. *Dictionary of Trade Policy Terms*. 5th ed. Geneva: WTO.

Gurría, José Àngel. 2009. "Carbon Has No Place in Global Trade Rules." *Financial Times*, November 5.

Holzer, Kateryna. 2014. *Carbon-Related Border Adjustment and WTO Law*. Cheltenham, UK: Edward Elgar.

Houser, Trevor, Rob Bradley, Britt Childs, Jacob Werksman, and Robert Heilmayr. 2008. *Leveling the Carbon Playing Field*. Washington, DC: Peterson Institute for International Economics.

Hufbauer, Gary Clyde, assisted by Carol Gabyzon. 1996. *Fundamental Tax Reform and Border Tax Adjustments*. Washington, DC: Institute for International Economics.

Hufbauer, Gary Clyde, Steve Charnovitz, and Jisun Kim. 2010. *Global Warming and the World Trading System*. Washington, DC: Peterson Institute for International Economics.

Hufbauer, Gary Clyde, and Joanna Shelton-Erb. 1984. *Subsidies in International Trade*. Washington, DC: Institute for International Economics.

Kaufmann, Christine, and Rolf H. Weber. 2011. "Carbon-related Border Tax Adjustment: Mitigating Climate Change or Restricting International Trade?" *World Trade Review* 10:497–525.

Kirgis Frederic L., Jr. 1972. "Effective Pollution Control in Industrialized Countries: International Economic Disincentives, Policy Responses, and the GATT." *Michigan Law Review* 70:859–918.

Leontiades, Milton. 1966. "The Logic of Border Taxes." *National Tax Journal* 19 (2): 173–183.

Low, Patrick, Gabrielle Marceau, and Julia Reinaud. 2012. "The Interface between the Trade and Climate Change Regimes: Scoping the Issues." *Journal of World Trade* 46:485–544.

Luengo Hernandez de Madrid, Gustavo E. 2007. *Regulation of Subsidies and States Aids in WTO and EC Law*. AH Alphen aan den Rijn: Kluwer Law International.

Maruyama, Warren H. 2011. "Climate Change and the WTO: Cap and Trade versus Carbon Tax?" *Journal of World Trade* 45:679–726.

Mattoo, Aaditya. and Arvind Subramanian 2013. "Four Changes to Trade Rules to Facilitate Climate Change Action." CGD Policy Paper 021.

Murase, Shinya. 2011. *International Law: An Integrative Perspective on Transboundary Issues*. Tokyo: Sophia University Press.

O'Brien, Julia. 2009. "The Equity of Levelling the Playing Field in the Climate Change Context." *Journal of World Trade* 43:1093–1114.

Regan, Donald H. 2009. "How to Think about PPMs (and Climate Change)." In *International Trade Regulation and the Mitigation of Climate Change*, ed. Thomas Cottier, Olga Nartova and Sadeq Z. Bigdeli, 97–123. Cambridge, UK: Cambridge University Press.

Ricardo, David. 1822. *On Protection to Agriculture*. 3rd ed. London: J. Murray.

Rocchi, Paola, Iñaki Arto, Jordi Roca, and Mónica Serrano. 2015. "Carbon-Motivated Border Tax Adjustment: A Proposal for the EU." Universitat de Barcelona Economics Working Papers E15/327, July 2015.

Roessler, Frieder. 2010. "India: Additional and Extra-Additional Duties on Imports from the United States." *World Trade Review* 9:265–272.

Rosendahl, Roger W. 1970. "Border Tax Adjustments: Problems and Proposals." *Law and Policy in International Business* 2:85–146.

Shadikhodjaev, Sherzod. 2015. "Renewable Energy and Environmental Support: Time to 'Green' the SCM Agreement?" *World Trade Review* 14 (3): 479–506.

Stewart, Terence P, Eric P. Salonen and Patrick J. McDonough 2007. "More Than 50 Years of Trade Rule Discrimination on Taxation: How Trade with China Is Affected." The Trade Lawyers Advisory Group, http://www.uscc.gov/Research/more-50-years-trade-rule-discrimination-taxation-how-trade-china-affected (accessed June 1, 2016).

Veel, Paul-Erik. 2009. "Carbon Tariffs and the WTO: An Evaluation of Feasible Policies." *Journal of International Economic Law* 12:749–800.

Voigt, Christina. 2009. *Sustainable Development as a Principle of International Law. Resolving Conflicts between Climate Measures and WTO Law*. Leiden: Martinus Nijhoff Publishers.

Washington Post. 2014. "An Answer to Global Warming: Congress Doesn't Have to Make It Complicated." *Washington Post*, August 28, A16.

Weber, Rolf H. 2015. "Border Tax Adjustment—Legal Perspective." *Climactic Change* 13 (3): 407–417.

World Economic Forum. 2010. *From Collision to Vision: Climate Change and World Trade*. Ad Hoc Working Group on Trade and Climate Change, November.

World Trade Organization and UN Environment Programme 2009. *Trade and Climate Change*.

3

Trade, Poverty, and Inequality

Devashish Mitra

Bhagwati (2004) has elegantly and clearly described "the scientific analysis of the effect of trade on poverty" as being "centered on a two-step argument: that trade enhances growth, and that growth reduces poverty." While trade has long been recognized as "an engine of growth," that there are gains from trade is a much older proposition. The gains from trade proposition, simply stated, is that trade leads to an increase in the per capita real income of a country. Obviously, during the period of transition to that higher per capita income, growth will increase. Moreover, that trade raises the per capita real income of a country is strongly supported by recent econometric evidence that controls for the possibility of reverse causation (Frankel and Romer 1999; Irwin and Tervio 2002). In fact, as far back as the 1960s and 1970s, several individual country studies undertaken by the OECD (directed by Ian Little and Maurice Scott) and by the National Bureau of Economic Research (NBER) (directed by Jagdish Bhagwati and Anne Krueger) clearly showed that import substitution policies had not worked. These studies were all showing an unambiguous support for an outward orientation in trade policy.

In addition, as pointed out by Bhagwati (2004) and Bhagwati and Panagariya (2013), the need for growth for the purpose of poverty reduction has also long been recognized. For example, Jawaharlal Nehru, India's first prime minister was aware of this need based on nothing more than basic arithmetic. When per capita incomes are as low as what one saw in low-income countries around the middle of the last century, perfect equality in the economy's income distribution puts everyone below the poverty line. As a result, growth is necessary for poverty reduction. But is it also sufficient? While poverty-enhancing or poverty-neutral growth is a theoretical possibility if there is a sharp and offsetting worsening of the income distribution accompanying economic growth, most of the recent empirical work shows that the poor gain when the economy grows and, in fact, the incomes of the poor grow no slower than the overall economy (Ravallion and Datt 1999; Ravallion 2001; Dollar and Kraay 2002). Thus, given the preceding, it is not surprising to find that most recent studies on trade and poverty find that trade is good for the poor and that it pulls them out of poverty.

Like any policy change, trade liberalization will create both winners and losers. If the people on the lower end (and in the middle range) of the income distribution are the losers (or they don't gain proportionally as much as the rich) we get a worsening of the income distribution, in other words, a rise in income inequality. This can happen even when the incidence of poverty declines. Even though poverty has declined during the last two to three decades in major parts of the developing world, income inequality has increased in large parts of it, including China and India. However, whether trade has had a major role to play in this increase in inequality or not is debatable.

Piketty's recent book entitled *Capital in the Twenty-First Century* has brought the issue of rising inequality into focus. Piketty (2014) invokes Harvard philosopher John Rawls's "difference principle" to argue that we should care about rising inequality. According to this principle, inequality is compatible with justice only if it improves the lives of the least well off. It is important here to note that Piketty's focus is mainly on the developed world (where the kind of extreme poverty we see in low-income countries is nonexistent), in many parts of which during recent decades the poorest citizens have not really seen a perceptible improvement in their living standards in the presence of rapid rises in the incomes of the rich. In contrast, trade reforms in developing countries, even though inequality-increasing, within the last couple of decades have been accompanied by a halving of world poverty. Since these reforms have made those in extreme poverty better off, they are compatible with the Rawlsian idea of justice. Sunstein (2014) points out that the demanding difference principle is rejected by many people in philosophical circles, in which context he suggests an alternative principle that allows for more inequality: "Ensure that average income in a society is as high as possible while also making adequate provisions for those at the bottom." Sunstein argues that surveys conducted in various countries show support for such an alternative principle and a rejection of the difference principle, without much enthusiasm for a ceiling on the incomes of the rich. Trade reforms in developing countries seem to pass the alternative principle test with flying colors, since they have resulted in large growth accelerations along with poverty reductions, even though they may have increased inequality.

Bhagwati (2004) argues that whether increased inequality matters or not depends on the context and the society in question. For example, it depends on whether the rich spend their surplus incomes ostentatiously or for social upliftment, in other words, whether on "self- indulgence" or "doing social good." He argues, "If a thousand people become millionaires, the inequality is less than if Bill Gates gets to make a billion all by himself. But the thousand millionaires, with only a million each, will likely buy expensive vacations, BMWs, houses in the Hamptons and toys at FAO Schwartz. In contrast, Gates will not be able to spend his billion even if he were to buy a European castle a day and the unconscionable wealth would likely propel him, as in fact it has, to spend the bulk of his money on social good." Based on his difference principle, I think John Rawls would prefer not to replace Bill Gates with a thousand millionaires.

Also, how we view inequality should depend on the degree of social mobility. According to Bhagwati (2004), "Another way in which inequality becomes acceptable is if those who are at the bottom of the scale feel that they can also make it: inequality is accepted because it excites not envy but aspirations and hope."

Bernstein (2013) has discussed some of the recent theoretical arguments in favor of the proposition that inequality is bad for economic growth. First, higher inequality can lead to higher inequality of education, which in turn leads to a less productive workforce, an argument made by Joseph Stiglitz in some of his writings. Second, higher inequality increases the incentives for the rich to lobby to protect that inequality at the expense of growth, for example, "high-income tax cuts instead of investments in infrastructure and R&D." Third, higher inequality can lower consumer spending and therefore aggregate demand, as the rich have a lower marginal propensity to consume than the poor. Finally, "inequality can lead to credit bubbles and financial crises." This can happen since, with the incomes at the top growing and those at the bottom stagnating, we can get an increase in the demand for cheap credit. The middle class and lower income groups need to borrow, while the rich have surplus money to lend together with their power to influence and push policy in favor of "looser financial rules." However, Bernstein has also argued that there isn't yet clear empirical evidence supporting these stories. While I believe there is enough evidence supporting the view that, other things remaining equal, higher inequality leads to greater political and economic instability, in the case of trade reforms one can argue that the poverty reduction it brings about is an offsetting force (an instability reducing force).

An important point often raised in various discussions of Piketty's recent work is that inequality leads to the capture of the policymaking process by the rich. However, in developing countries, trade liberalization is exactly the kind of policy reform the rich capitalists of those countries would not like to see happen as it reduces the return to their factor of production—capital (scarce factor in developing countries)—and destroys the monopoly power of the firms they own.

3.1 Theoretical Linkages

Having introduced the topic, we discuss the various channels through which trade can affect poverty and inequality and their theoretical underpinnings. International trade leads to increases in average real incomes through two main channels: efficiency gains from specialization and exchange; and the availability of larger varieties of final and intermediate goods. While the greater variety of final goods directly improves welfare (or real income), the greater variety of intermediate inputs increases productivity (and, in turn, real income) through greater division of labor and better input–output matching.

Even though the theoretical literature on trade and endogenous growth does not provide clear predictions on the overall relation between trade and growth (as different models lead to different predictions), it does identify quite a few growth-accelerating channels. For example, trade can spur innovation by enhancing industrial learning since it facilitates international exchange of technical information; can improve the efficiency of global research since it eliminates the duplication of research efforts in different countries; and can, through procompetitive effects, increase the incentives for domestic producers to innovate. By holding the distribution of incomes around the average fixed income (or moving the same distribution by the amount of the increase in average income), increases in the average income should reduce poverty, as fewer people will remain below the poverty line. Or if everyone experiences the same rate of income growth, it is obvious that poverty should decline. These effects on poverty through aggregate income growth, however, depend on the extent to which trade creates winners and losers and who these winners and losers are.

We know from standard trade theory that, under plausible conditions, the winners from trade liberalization are the relatively abundant factors of production in a country and the losers are the scarce factors. Unskilled labor, being an abundant factor in developing countries, is expected to benefit from trade liberalization in such countries. As a result, we should expect to see trade reforms lead to poverty reduction in such countries. There are a number of things that can get in the way of this prediction. The first is the lack of mobility of factors, including labor, from one sector to another (or from one region to another). The reasons are twofold. First, the overall gains from specialization as well as those to the abundant factor take place through the reallocation of factors from one sector to another. Second, in the absence of intersectoral labor mobility, workers who are not able to get out of shrinking sectors will see a decline in their incomes or will be thrown into a state of unemployment.

There are some other arguments that have been discussed in the literature against the poverty-reducing impact of trade. First, capital goods, which require skilled labor as a complementary input, become better available and cheaper through trade. In other words, a reduction in the tariff on the imports of capital goods will lead to an increase in the demand for skilled relative to unskilled labor (Goldberg and Pavcnik 2007a). Along similar lines, as argued by Davis and Mishra (2007), when a tariff on a noncompeting import is reduced, we will see a departure from the standard Stolper–Samuelson predictions. On the one hand, if these imported products are inputs into sectors that use skilled relative to unskilled workers more intensively, then reducing tariffs on them will raise skilled wages and lower unskilled wages, thereby increasing poverty and inequality. On the other hand, if this noncompeting import is consumed by all final consumers, then reducing the tariff on it increases everyone's real income, leading to poverty reduction.

Trade, especially in capital goods, facilitates the offshoring of parts of the production process that are the least skill intensive in developed countries and yet end up being the most skill intensive within developing countries (Feenstra and Hanson 1996, 1997). This raises the relative demand for skilled labor in both the developing and the developed world, thereby leading to an increase in wage inequality everywhere. However, it is possible that although the relative wages of the unskilled workers goes down, their actual real wages actually do not go down (Feenstra and Hanson 1999), in which case poverty should not go up.

Next, trade results in firms upgrading their quality in response to greater import competition or to sell in the export market. Production of higher quality products is more skill intensive (Verhoogen 2008). In addition, the more productive firms as well as those selling higher quality products will expand their market share in response to trade. All these changes will increase the relative demand for skilled labor and reduce the relative demand for unskilled labor. These are all factors that increase wage inequality. However, there could be a productivity-enhancing effect here, which might lead to an increase in the wages of both the skilled and the unskilled.

To summarize, trade can in theory affect poverty and inequality through a large number of channels. There is the standard Stolper-Samuelson effect that benefits the abundant factor and hurts the scarce factor. Through this channel trade is expected to reduce poverty and inequality in developing countries that are abundant in less-skilled labor. However, several factors can potentially interfere with the Stolper-Samuelson effect. These primarily include the various types of labor-market frictions, such as lack of mobility across sectors or unemployment. In addition, trade in intermediate and capital goods complementary to skilled labor might overturn the standard Stolper-Samuelson results. Besides, there are predictions from quality-based models of firm heterogeneity that show how trade can increase wage inequality.

3.2 A Tale of Two Large Developing Countries

Having discussed a number of theoretical linkages, we need to check their empirical validity. I start that process here by looking at two large developing countries, China and India. With high rates of poverty until the 1980s (together accounting until that decade for more than half of world's extreme poverty), China and India are two countries that have experienced huge reductions in poverty over the last three decades. Both also have had dramatic trade reforms. Figures 3.1–3.6 show us the changes in poverty, inequality, trade, and trade protection over the last two to three decades in these two countries.[1] Trade reforms started slowly in China in the late 1970s. According to the World Development Indicators (WDI), trade as a proportion of GDP in China was roughly 18 percent in 1984, while Naughton (2007) reports this ratio to be 10 percent in 1978. By 2005 it was around 70 percent. By 2008 it fell to 62 percent and the world financial crisis led to a big fall in the trade-to-GDP ratio, to around 49 percent in 2009. Overall average tariff rates fell from roughly 32 percent in 1992 to about 4 percent in 2009 according to the WDI data. During the period 1984–2009, the WDI data show

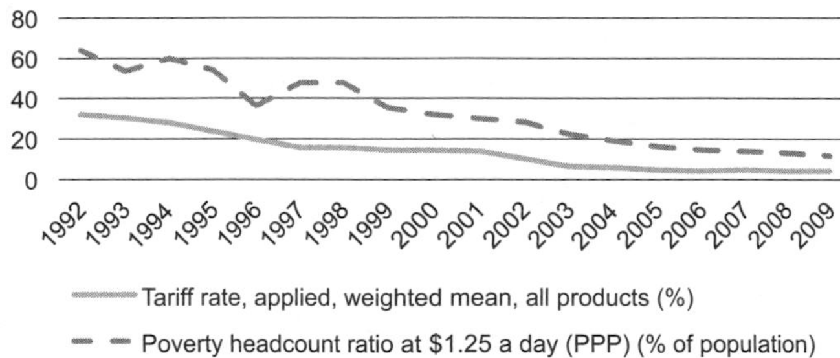

Figure 3.1
China's import protection and poverty (1992–2009).

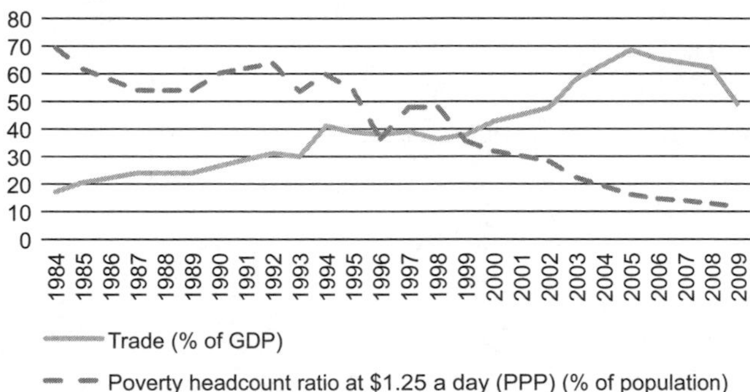

Figure 3.2
China's trade and poverty (1984–2009).

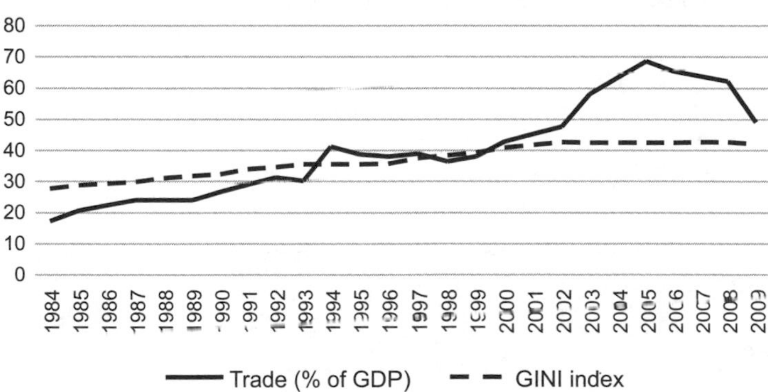

Figure 3.3
China's trade and inequality (1984–2009).

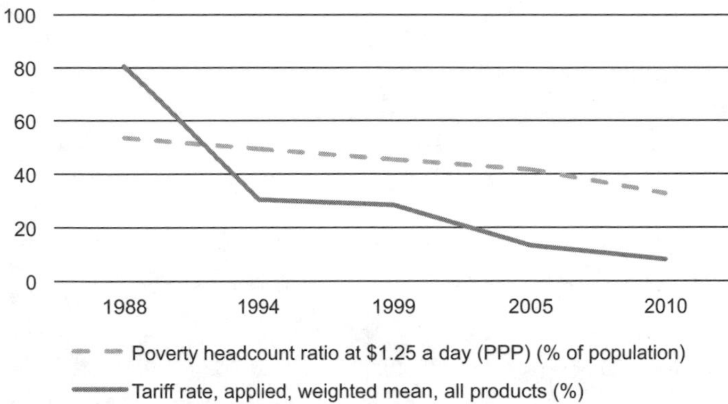

Figure 3.4
India's import protection and poverty (1988–2010).

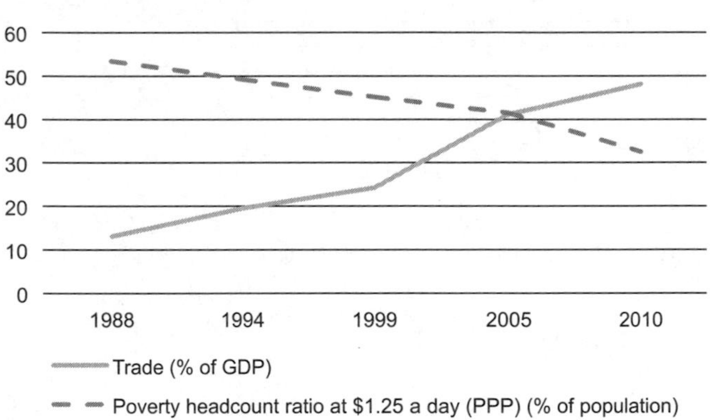

Figure 3.5
India's trade and poverty (1988–2010).

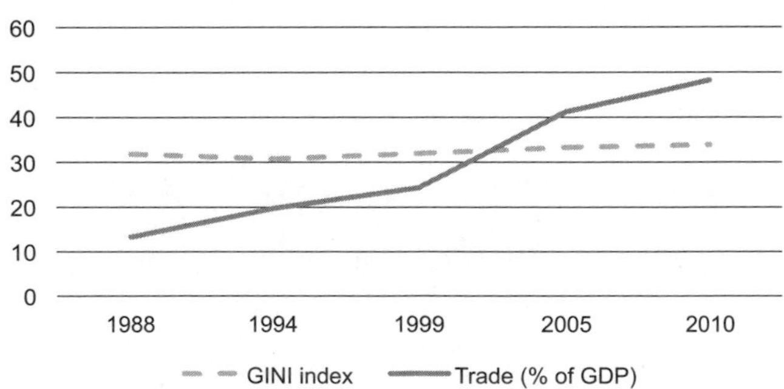

Figure 3.6
India's trade and inequality (1988–2010).

that the percentage of population below the $1.25-a-day poverty line (a measure of extreme poverty) fell from 69 percent to 12 percent. During this period, barring the years 1989 and 1990, the annual growth rate of GDP in China has been in the range of roughly 8–15 percent. These high growth rates have translated into huge reductions in poverty. Rough calculations show that about 700 million people have been lifted out of poverty in China. Inequality, on the other hand, has been growing in China.

The WDI Gini index for China has grown from roughly 28 in 1984 to roughly 42 in 2009. In this period, according to the WDI, the income share of the bottom 10 percent of the population has dropped from 3.7 percent to 1.7, while that of the top 10 percent has increased from 22 percent to 30 percent. In other words, the ratio of the incomes of the top 10 percent to the bottom 10 percent has gone up from 6 to 18. However, despite this increase in inequality China has experienced a huge reduction in poverty due to the high GDP growth it has sustained over the last three decades. In other words, in the case of poverty reduction the direct effect of the high GDP growth has much more than offset the accompanying effect on poverty reduction of increasing inequality. It is not clear what would have happened to the growth rate in China if resources were directly used to keep the increase in inequality in check. If this could have been done without reducing growth, then it is obvious that poverty reduction would have been even greater. However, if government revenues had been switched toward redistributive purposes from infrastructure, the effect of the consequent reduction in growth could have possibly (more than) offset the effect of the reduction in inequality on poverty. Thus poverty could have risen in that case.

Naughton (2007) argues that "the most important single factor in Chinese inequality is the urban-rural gap" and that "ultimately market reforms contributed to inequality because they contributed to urban economic growth." He goes on to invoke the Kuznets' hypothesis that inequality rises first during the process of economic development and then starts falling. He believes that China is still in the upward rising part of the Kuznets curve, the amplification of which has been caused by three factors: limited spillovers due to China's size and geographic diversity, the concentration of the effects of foreign trade and investment in coastal cities, and the reinforcement of the rural–urban divide through its socialist institutions. In other words, the increase in inequality might have been magnified by the interaction of foreign trade and investment with its long history of socialist institutions.

While an argument can be made that high inequality can lead to political instability and as a result to lower growth, we are not sure whether inequality had reached such high levels in China. While China's inequality might be among the highest within Asia it is nowhere close to what we see in Latin America. Compared to China's Gini coefficient of 42, Brazil's and Mexico's are much higher at 59 and 55 respectively. Certainly, inequality in China so far does not seem to be high enough to make it economically and politically unstable. As mentioned earlier, despite this increasing inequality China has grown very rapidly and has managed to drastically reduce its incidence of poverty.

We next turn to India. During the period 1988–2010, India's trade-to-GDP ratio increased from roughly 13 percent to 48 percent. The average tariff rate during this period went down from 80 percent to 10 percent, and the $1.25-a-day poverty rate went down from 53 percent to 32 percent. The most rapid decline in poverty was during the five-year period 2005–2010 from 41.6 percent to 32.7 percent. This was also a period of rapid growth in the range of 8–10 percent (barring the year 2008), considered by many experts to be a lagged response to the trade reforms of the 1990s and early 2000s. Inequality in India during this period was fairly stable. It increased only a little from about 32 to 34. The share of the top 10 percent in national income increased from roughly 27 percent to 29 percent, while the share of the bottom 10 percent decreased from 3.91 percent to 3.75 percent. In other words, the ratio of the incomes of the top 10 percent to the bottom 10 percent has gone up by only slightly above 10 percent from 6.9 to 7.7.

Thus, the increase in inequality in India was been relatively modest, especially in comparison with what we see in China. Yet, the rate of poverty reduction while substantial was much smaller than in China, which also had a higher growth rate overall sustained over a much longer period of time. Thus, while both countries have performed well after their trade reforms in terms of growth and poverty reduction, the country with the greater rise in inequality, namely China, did better in those two areas.

We next move to some cross-country regression analysis, the results from which we will use to revisit the Chinese and Indian cases.

3.3 Cross-Country Evidence

Here I provide some cross-country evidence on how poverty and inequality are related to trade and trade protection using a panel of developing countries for the period 1981–2013. Aisbett, Harrison, and Zwane

(2008) performed a similar cross-country study. I use here an updated poverty series from the World Bank's WDI. Compared to Aisbett, Harrison, and Zwane, not only the data that I use are for more recent years, but also the new poverty headcount ratio based on the $1.25-a-day poverty line is much improved due to a major overhaul of the World Bank's poverty numbers based on better funding of and significant improvements in the *International Comparisons Project* as well as the availability of many more countrywide household surveys (see Chen and Ravallion 2010).

The regression results are provided in table 3.1. Following Aisbett, Harrison, and Zwane, my variables listed on the right-hand side, namely trade as a percentage of GDP and import tariff, are lagged by three years. While Aisbett, Harrison, and Zwane also ran instrumental variables (IVs) regressions with three-period lagged tariff (or trade-GDP ratio) to instrument current tariff (or trade-GDP ratio) as a right-hand side variable, I only present reduced form regressions with the three-year lagged tariff and alternatively the three-year lagged trade as the right-hand side variables. I present pooled ordinary least squares (OLS) regressions, country fixed-effects regressions, and country and year fixed-effects regressions. As seen from the first panel of table 3.1, there is fairly strong evidence of a negative relationship between poverty and trade and a positive relationship between poverty and tariffs. While the pooled OLS and country fixed-effects results are significant at the 1 percent level, the results become insignificant when both country and year fixed effects are thrown in at the same time. This is not surprising given that the timing and the magnitude of trade reforms by various developing countries have been quite close to each other. The Uruguay Round of the GATT led to tariff declines in many countries at the same time. In addition, unilateral trade liberalization took place roughly at the same time in many developing countries in the 1980s and 1990s. As a result, throwing in both country and year effects simultaneously in our regressions will not leave any variation in the tariffs or trade to identify the effects we are interested in.

In order to get a sense of the magnitudes of the effects, we focus on the regressions with the country fixed effects. Here we are hoping that the country fixed effects are able to capture the differences in institutions and time-invariant characteristics across countries. We see here that a percentage point increase in trade leads to a poverty decline of 0.149 percentage points. During the period 1984–2005, trade as a percentage of GDP went up in China by 52 percentage points (from 17 to 69

Table 3.1
Cross-country evidence on poverty and inequality vs. trade and protection (1981–2013)

Dependent variable: POVERTY

$Trade_{t-3}$			$Tariffs_{t-3}$		
Pooled OLS	Country FE	Country and Year FE	Pooled OLS	Country FE	Country and Year FE
-0.263***	-0.149***	0.005	0.879***	0.401***	0.005
(0.037)	(0.053)	(0.035)	(0.241)	(0.095)	(0.178)
350 (67)	350 (67)	350 (67)	129 (45)	129 (45)	129 (45)

Dependent variable: GINI coefficient

$Trade_{t-3}$			$Tariffs_{t-3}$		
Pooled OLS	Country FE	Country and Year FE	Pooled OLS	Country FE	Country and Year FE
0.024	0.007	0.020	-0.215***	-0.048**	-0.105***
(0.016)	(0.016)	(0.017)	(0.048)	(0.024)	(0.026)
352 (71)	352 (71)	352 (71)	127 (46)	127 (46)	127 (46)

***, **, * indicate statistical significance at 1%, 5%, and 10% respectively. Numbers in parentheses in the penultimate row of each panel are robust standard errors. The last row in each panel shows the number of observations (countries).

percent).[2] Based on the regression coefficient in the country fixed-effects regression, this would represent a poverty reduction of 7.8 percentage points, which represents more than a seventh of the actual poverty decline of 53 percentage points (from 69 percent to 16 percent) in China that we see in this period. India's trade as a percentage of its GDP went up by 35 percentage points from 13 percent to 48 percent in the period 1988–2010. Based on the regression coefficient of the third column of the first panel of table 3.1, this should lead to a 5.25 percentage point reduction in poverty, which is a fourth of the actual decline in poverty of 21 percentage points (from 53 percent to 31 percent) during this period.

Moving to tariffs, we see from column 5 of the first panel of table 3.1 that a percentage point decline in tariff leads to a 0.4 percentage point decline in poverty. It is important to note that a percentage point decline in the average tariff can be brought about in many ways. One way could be a uniform decline by a percentage point each in the tariff rate on each importable good at constant import shares. Considering this, our regression coefficient is not large enough in magnitude to cause any concerns about possible overestimation. We see that China's tariff fell from 32 percent to 5 percent in the period 1992–2005 and to almost 4 percent by 2009. This is a decline in tariff of almost 27–28 percentage points, which represents a poverty reduction of roughly 11 percentage points, which is a fifth of the actual decline in poverty of about 53–57 percentage points that took place in China. Moving to India, during the period 1988–2010, the tariff rate went down by 72 percentage points from 80 percent to 8 percent. The regression estimate in column 5 of the first panel of 3.1 predicts a 29 percentage point decline in poverty, which strangely is greater than the 21 percentage point decline in poverty that we see in India. Thus the poverty reduction in China has been much more than what is predicted by our regression based on the trade liberalization that has taken place, while in India it has been less than predicted. There are two interpretations possible. One is that while there have been poverty-reducing factors in addition to trade liberalization operating in China, in India there may have been some offsetting factors. An alternative explanation is that China has been much more efficient than the average developing country in getting poverty reductions out of their trade reforms, while India has been less efficient that the average developing country in obtaining such gains from trade reforms for its poor. More specifically, this could mean differences in complementary policies and institutions.

Moving next to the inequality regressions in the second panel of table 3.1, we see that while trade as a percentage of GDP has a statistically insignificant effect on inequality across all three specifications, tariff reductions do lead to increases in inequality in a statistically significant way. Using column 5 of this panel, we see that a percentage point reduction in the average tariff leads to a 0.048 point increase in the Gini coefficient (measured on a scale of 0–100). In the case of India where the tariff rate has gone down by 72 percentage points, this predicts an inequality increase of about 3.5 points. India's Gini coefficient during this period went up by only 2 points from 32 to 34 during this period. Other redistributive policies may have been responsible for this smaller increase. In China's case, the 28 percentage point decline in tariff during the period 1992–2009, based on the regression coefficient in column 5 of the second panel, translates into a prediction of a very small (1.3 point) increase in the Gini coefficient. The actual increase in inequality was 7 points (from 35 to 42). Thus only a fifth of the blame for the rise in inequality can be put on trade liberalization. In both China and India, trade reforms have been associated with an increase in inequality but this inequality increase has been relatively small in India. As seen later, the work by Krishna and Sethupathy (2012) shows that with better measures of inequality this result does not hold for Indian states. They find no effect of trade liberalization on inequality.

Thus on the one hand, the cross-country regressions using $1.25 a day as the poverty line show the strong possibility of a poverty-reducing effect of trade reforms. I call this a "possibility" since having both time and country effects at the same time makes the tariff and the trade variables insignificant. On the other hand, the regressions with the inequality as the right-hand side variable (including the one with both country and year effects) show an inequality-increasing effect of trade. However, these effects are small in magnitude.

I next turn to the existing literature on the evidence regarding the effects of trade on poverty. This is a large literature, as a result of which not all important contributions can be covered here.[3]

3.4 Trade and Poverty: Review of Existing Evidence

Indirect Evidence

It has been argued by Bhagwati (2004) that trade, by fostering growth, leads to higher incomes and in turn a reduction in poverty. Also, Winters, McCulloch, and McKay (2004) in their survey piece on the evidence regarding trade liberalization and poverty write: "In the long run, economic growth is the key to the alleviation of absolute poverty." Bhagwati and Panagariya (2013) call this strategy of reducing poverty through promoting growth a "pull-up" strategy as opposed to a "trickle down" effect of growth. Therefore, we first review the literature on the effects of trade barriers on growth and income, which have been studied empirically since the early 1990s. This is followed by a review of the literature on the effect of growth on poverty.

Various cross-country macro studies, using different measures of openness, have showed positive effects of trade on growth (see, for instance, Dollar 1992, Sachs and Warner 1995, and Edwards 1998). However, these papers have been strongly criticized by Rodriguez and Rodrik (2001) for the problems with their openness and protection measures, their econometric techniques, and the difficulty in establishing the direction of causality. While the measure of openness used by Sachs and Warner (1995), as argued by Rodriguez and Rodrik (2001), captures many aspects of the macroeconomic environment in addition to trade policy, Baldwin (2003) has defended that approach on the grounds that the other policy reforms captured in the measure accompany most trade reforms. Therefore, the use of such a measure tells us the value of the entire package of trade and accompanying reforms. Wacziarg and Welch (2003) have updated the Sachs-Warner dataset and have again shown the positive growth effects of such reforms.

Papers since the late 1990s have focused on the effects of trade on income levels rather than growth rates. Frankel and Romer (1999) using gravity- and geography-based predicted trade flows as instruments find positive effects of trade on income levels that are greater than the estimates produced by ordinary least squares. Irwin and Tervio (2002) demonstrate the robustness of these results, with the same approach applied to cross-country data from various periods in the twentieth century.

Rodrik, Subramanian, and Trebbi (2002) have looked at the simultaneous effects of institutions, geography, and trade on per capita income levels. Using a measure of property rights and the rule of law to capture institutions and the trade-GDP ratio to capture openness in trade, and appropriately instrumenting them, they find that "the quality of institutions trumps everything else." However, trade and institutions have positive effects on each other, so trade does have indirect effects on income in Rodrik, Subramanian, and Trebbi's empirical analysis.

In this context, it is also important to look at some of the micro-level studies on the impact of trade on productivity growth, since it is productivity growth at the micro level that is one of the two main proximate drivers (the other being structural change in the economy) of overall per capita income growth. Extending Solow's approach modified by Hall (1988) and Domowitz, Hubbard, and Peterson (1988) to include imperfect competition and nonconstant returns to scale, Harrison (1994) finds a strong correlation between trade reforms and firm-level productivity growth in Cote d'Ivoire. Using a similar approach and allowing the returns to scale to be flexible and to change over time, Krishna and Mitra (1998) find some evidence of an increase in the growth rate of firm productivity after the dramatic 1991 trade reforms in India. An increase in productivity due to trade liberalization in the Indian case has also been confirmed, using a more updated dataset and more modern techniques in production function estimation to take care of endogeneity and measurement error problems as well as selection issues, by Topalova and Khandelwal (2011). They find that both a procompetitive effect of the liberalization of tariffs on final good imports as well as cheaper and better inputs arising from a reduction in the tariffs on input imports have been responsible for this increase in firm-level productivity, with the latter making a bigger contribution than the former. In the trade literature, the use of this class of econometric techniques for productivity estimation was pioneered by Pavcnik (2002) who, using plant-level panel data on Chilean manufacturers, found "evidence of *within* plant productivity improvements that can be attributed to a liberalized trade for the plants in the import-competing sector." In addition, she found aggregate productivity improvements due to the reallocation of resources and output from less to more efficient producers. Similar results were found in the case of Colombian plants by Fernandes (2007) after she addressed certain remaining technical shortcomings at that time in the literature. In this context, it is important to mention a paper by Kim (2000) who examined Korean industry-level data for the period 1966–1988 and found that trade liberalization led to both greater productivity and scale efficiency, with the reforms in quantitative restrictions contributing more than reductions in tariffs.

Recently, Atkin, Khandelwal, and Osman (2014) have used a randomized control trial where a few rug manufacturing firms in Egypt are randomly selected to receive export orders. They find that there is learning by exporting: in controlling for product specifications, exporting firms experience an increase in product quality and productivity relative to the control firms. These improvements also translate into an improvement in profits.

Having looked at the impact of trade on incomes, productivity, and growth, we next turn to the impact of growth on poverty. Dollar and Kraay (2002) in a cross-country study of ninety-two countries over the last four decades find that the growth rates of average incomes of people in the bottom quintile are no different from the growth rates of overall per capita incomes, with the former growth always associated with the latter. Also, policies that promote overall growth promote growth in the incomes of the poor. These policies include trade openness, macroeconomic stability, moderate government size, financial development, and strong property rights and the rule of law. In another paper, Dollar and Kraay (2004) use data from the post-1980 "globalizing developing economies" to argue that per capita income growth arising from expansion in trade in those countries led to a sharp fall in absolute poverty over the next two decades.

Similarly, Ravallion (2001) finds that an increase in the per capita income by 1 percent can reduce the proportion of people below the $1-a-day poverty line by about 2.5 percent on average. This varies across countries, depending how close the poor are to the poverty line. Research by Ravallion and Datt (1999) on the determinants of poverty reduction across India's major states between 1960 and 1994 also shows empirically the importance of initial conditions, such as literacy and health. That is why they find that a 1 percent increase in nonagricultural state domestic product leads to a 1.2 percent decline in poverty rates in the states of Kerala and West Bengal versus only a 0.3 percent decline in Bihar.

Thus there is strong evidence that trade has increased incomes. The evidence survives controlling or correcting for two-way causation. In addition, most of the evidence suggests that growth in average incomes is accompanied by growth in the incomes of the poor and, therefore, a reduction in the poverty rate. We next look at some of the direct evidence on the impact of trade on poverty

Direct Reduced-Form Evidence on Trade and Poverty

There are by now a few intra-country studies examining directly the empirical relationship between trade and poverty in a reduced-form way (i.e., regressing poverty measures on trade protection). Three of these studies are for India. This is not surprising since between a quarter and a third of the world's poor live there. Also, the institutional diversity and differing exposure to trade across the various Indian states, regions, and districts provide the kind of variations applied econometricians love to exploit. The three studies on trade and poverty noted earlier are Topalova (2007), Hasan, Mitra, and Ural (2007), and Cain, Hasan, and Mitra (2012).

Topalova examined the impact of trade liberalization on district-level poverty in India. Her main findings were that while rural districts with a greater concentration of "industries more exposed to trade liberalization experienced a slower progress in poverty reduction," there was "no statistically significant relationship between trade exposure and poverty in urban India" (but with point estimates still in the same direction as in rural poverty). In fact, she goes on to claim, based on her regressions, that greater trade exposure could have resulted in a significant "setback" in poverty reduction.

The results from the Hasan-Mitra-Ural study are quite different from Topolova's. They, in fact, find that states facing greater exposure to foreign competition by way of employment composition tend to have lower rural, urban, and overall poverty rates (and poverty gaps) and have experienced greater poverty reduction due to trade liberalization, with these effects being more pronounced in states with more flexible labor markets. Their results hold at varying strengths and significance for overall, urban, and rural poverty, and are robust to using the National Sample Survey Organization (NSSO) regions in place of states.

It is quite possible for the conclusions from a district-level study to be different from those from a state-level (or a region-level) study, since the results seen at the latter level could be driven by compositional changes of the population living in the various districts.[4] In other words, people within a state could be moving from poorer to richer districts. This is possible since the evidence shows there is lack of mobility between states but there is no evidence on the lack of inter-district mobility within states. However, it is also important to note that there are some additional methodological differences between the two studies with regard to the treatment of the nontradable sectors in the calculation of the state-level protection measure, the inclusion of the 1993–1994 round (the round being included in the Hasan-Mitra-Ural study but not in Topolova's study) and the variety of protection and poverty rate measures in the two studies (with a greater variety included in Hasan, Mitra, and Ural).

Cain, Hasan, and Mitra (2012) update the Hasan-Mitra-Ural study to include a new round of NSSO survey. In addition, Cain, Hasan, and Mitra also allow the gains in poverty reduction from trade liberalization to vary by road connectivity and financial development. The basic flavor of the results from the Cain-Hasan-Mitra study is summarized in figure 3.7 where we see there is a tight positive correlation between the change in poverty in a state between 1987 and 2004 and the change in the state's weighted tariff. Table 3.2 shows us a positive correlation between the various measures of the reduction in poverty and the reduction in protection (from Cain, Hasan, and Mitra). The regressions from Cain-Hasan-Mitra (not presented in this chapter) show that that a 38 percent reduction in poverty during 1987–2004 can be attributed to the change in the exposure to foreign trade. Since their regressions use time and state/region controls, the negative sign of the coefficient of the state-level protection variable indicates that trade liberalization (and the greater exposure of the labor force to foreign competition) actually speeded up poverty

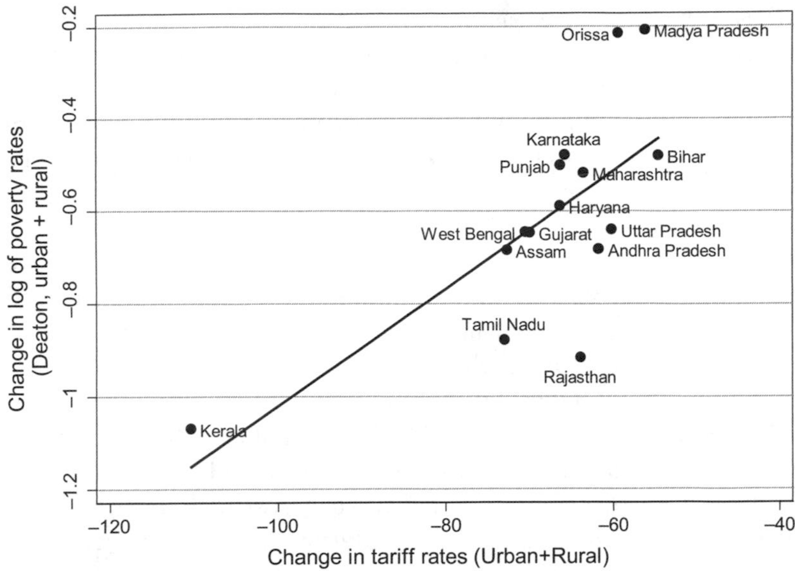

Figure 3.7
Change in poverty vs. change in protection in Indian states.
Source: Based on data from Cain, Hasan, and Mitra 2012.

Table 3.2
Pairwise correlations: Reductions in poverty and lagged protection in Indian states, 1987 and 2004

	Reductions in poverty		
	Deaton	Expert group	Reductions in tariffs
Reductions in expert group poverty	0.8494		
Reductions in tariffs	0.6216	0.6465	
Reductions in nontariff barriers	0.7536	0.7687	0.7357

Source: Cain, Hasan, and Mitra 2012.

reduction. They find an urban poverty-reducing effect of tariff reforms, the extent of which has been larger in states with flexible labor regulations, higher road density, and more advanced banking and financial systems. In the case of rural poverty, the basic impact of trade on poverty goes in the same direction but does not vary by labor-market flexibility, road density, and financial development.

The study by Mukim and Panagariya (2012) responds to and rebuts the main criticism of these types of studies that while poverty may have fallen in the aggregate after trade reforms, the socially disadvantaged classes have become poorer. Mukim and Panagariya study the evolution of poverty separately within the scheduled castes (SC), the scheduled tribes (ST), and the nonscheduled (NS) castes. Looking at the five thick NSSO rounds for the period 1983–2005, they find that the poverty rate continuously fell for each of these three groups, and this was true in each of the ten largest states of India. They also find some evidence for the favorable impact of openness and growth on poverty reduction for each of these groups, and no evidence whatsoever for any adverse impact.

We next move to reduced-form studies for other countries. Goldberg and Pavcnik (2007b) look at the impact of trade liberalization on poverty in Colombia. They find that there are certain labor market variables such as the unemployment rate and informal-sector employment rate that positively correlate with poverty. They then investigate whether trade affects any of these labor market conditions and find it does not. Unable to identify the various channels, they go on to look at the direct effect of trade on urban poverty in Colombia. They find that while the poverty of workers in a sector is unrelated to tariffs, it is positively related to the volume of imports of competing products from the rest of the world. Exports, on the other hand, do not have a significant role to play in this.

Goh and Javorcik (2007) study the impact of Poland's trade liberalization on wages and indirectly on poverty for the period 1994–2001. They find that trade liberalization increased wages in all industries, controlling for individual worker characteristics, geographical variables, and industry and time effects. However, tariff cuts were the deepest in more unskilled labor industries, leading to greater increases in their wages. These indicate a possible labor productivity increase in response to foreign competition. Given the high rate of poverty among the unskilled workers in Poland, an increase in their wages was expected to result in a decline in the poverty rate.

Hanson (2007) studies Mexico in the 1990s where he compares high-exposure states with states with low exposure to globalization, as measured by the share of foreign direct investment, imports, or export assembly in state GDP. He finds that poverty incidence declined in the high-exposure states relative to the low-exposure states (poverty increased in the former from 21 percent to 22 percent, while in the latter it went up from 32 to 40 percent).

Finally, there are a couple of cross-country studies. Hasan, Quibria, and Kim (2003) argue, using cross-country evidence, that "policies and institutions that support economic freedom are critical for poverty reduction." Economic freedom indicators used by these authors include those pertaining to government size, price stability, freedom to trade with foreigners, absence of overregulation of markets, and civil liberties as reflected in property rights, rule of law, and so on.

Aisbett, Harrison, and Zwane (2008), using cross-country data on developing countries with $1-a-day poverty as the dependent variable, do not find any effect of trade or tariffs on poverty once country effects are introduced. However, they find evidence separately for the income-increasing effect of trade and for the poverty-reducing effect of growth. It is then surprising that the direct effect of trade on poverty vanishes, which means only the growth that is independent of trade (not due to trade openness) reduces poverty, for which it is very hard to find any intuition.

The reduced form regressions give us the bottom line on whether trade increases or decreases, or does not affect poverty. They cannot identify or account for all the different channels through which trade affects poverty. For this we can get some help from the new literature on empirical general equilibrium welfare analysis.

Empirical General Equilibrium Welfare Analysis

There is a growing literature on the evaluation of the impact of trade reforms on income distribution and poverty. It is important to note here the word "empirical" as opposed to "computable" in computable general equilibrium (CGE) analysis. This approach captures empirically the various general-equilibrium channels through which trade affects the real welfare of individuals at all of the different points on the income distribution, as a result of which it is possible to determine fairly comprehensively the impact of trade on poverty and inequality.

The pioneering paper in this literature is by Porto (2006). It is a direct application of the calculation of compensating variation from price changes based on household-level data. Porto incorporates the relationship between tariff changes and price changes of tradables into this calculation of compensating variation. Further, he estimates the endogenous impact of tariffs on tradables on prices of nontradables. Thus, he is able to estimate the parts of price changes for both tradables and nontradables that can be attributed to the entire tariff change vector. In turn, he plugs them into the formula derived by Angus Deaton for the calculation of compensating variation. These price changes attributable to tariff changes interact with individual budget shares to determine the compensating variation. In addition, Porto adds the welfare change that takes place due to wage changes attributable to tariff changes, for which he estimates the elasticity of wage with respect to tariff for three different classes of skills (skilled, semi-skilled, and unskilled).

Porto uses this approach to look at the impact of Mercosur (a trade bloc, in the form of a customs union, of Latin American countries) on real income changes at each point on the income distribution. While this would normally be quite different from an analysis of unilateral trade reforms, in Porto's analysis it is not very different as he ignores the trade diversion effects and focuses only on the trade creation effect in the determination of his domestic price changes as well as of the consumption of varieties coming from within the region and from outside. Substitution possibilities between these two classes of product varieties are ignored. Overall, Porto finds that there are statistically significant gains for the poor and middle-income households, and that the welfare effects are negative but insignificant for the rich (upper tail of the distribution). On the whole, he finds a reduction in wage inequality and the incidence of poverty. While it is well known that in Argentina poverty and inequality increased in the 1990s, these results from Porto's study tell us that in the absence of the trade creating effects of Mercosur the adverse impact on poverty and income inequality would have been even greater. Also, important to note is that the focus is only on wage income and other factor incomes are ignored, which is a weakness of this paper by Porto.

Ural Marchand (2012) extends the Porto methodology to allow for incomplete price transmission of tariff changes across the various states of India and across rural and urban areas. In addition, she allows for wage effects to differ across skill categories and age cohorts to create a "quasi panel" using a dataset of repeated cross sections, which is not a panel (since all the same households are not surveyed as one moves from one NSSO round to another). In addition, she takes the evidence on the lack of labor mobility across sectors seriously and, as a result, allows wages at the same skill level to vary across sectors. Therefore, the industry-specific wage for a given skill level responds to changes in tariffs for that industry. Like Porto, she abstracts from changes in capital and land incomes in response to tariff changes (due to the lack of availability of relevant data), but in addition she also assumes that nontradable prices do not respond to trade reforms. In other words, we could think of this (as well as Porto's) exercise an evaluation of the impact of trade on the distribution of real labor incomes and poverty. Overall, Ural Marchand finds a pro-poor effect of trade reforms both in rural and urban areas with the effect being larger in the states where the transmission of tariff changes is high and in urban areas. Separately the consumption effect (the change in the cost of consuming a given basket) and the wage effect of trade reforms turn out to be pro-poor. An implication of these results is that trade reforms contributed to the reduction in poverty, and, in fact, the gains to the people significantly below the poverty line were greater than to those who were just below it (and were able to cross that line).

Two other applications of this approach need mention here. The first one by Porto (2006) is the application to the impact of agricultural liberalization in the developed world on poverty in Argentina. He finds that as a result of such liberalization Argentinian poverty would decline by about 1.5 percentage points. Seshan (2014) modifies the approach to take into account household production in Vietnamese agriculture and examines the impact of trade liberalization during the period 1993–1998, which consisted mainly of relaxing export restrictions on agricultural products and import restrictions, including those on chemicals and fertilizers. He finds a reduction in inequality as well as poverty. While this trade liberalization can explain a third of the decline in overall poverty during this period, it can explain about half of the decline in rural poverty.

The fact that expenditure shares of different goods vary across individual incomes is also taken seriously in a recent path-breaking paper by Fajgelbaum and Khandelwal (2014), where they estimate from a non-homothetic gravity equation the elasticity of imports with respect to trade costs as well as the income elasticity of import demand product by product. Using their model estimation, they are able to calculate the elasticity of expenditure shares with respect to both prices and income. They are then able to calculate the "unequal" impact of trade on the welfare of individuals within each economy who differ in their income levels. Their "multi-sector model implies a strong pro-poor bias of trade in every country" (Fajgelbaum and Khandelwal 2014).

3.5 Trade and Inequality: Existing Evidence

From poverty we move to inequality. As we will see, there are many important aspects of inequality. But it is wage inequality that has been studied in depth in the trade literature. There has also been some recent work on labor shares and some work on overall income inequality. I start with the impact of trade on wage inequality.

Trade and Wage Inequality

Goldberg and Pavcnik (2007a) is a comprehensive survey of research on the impact of globalization on all aspects of inequality, including wage inequality. Therefore, to minimize duplication of effort, I will discuss only the main papers in the pre-2007 literature and some important contributions from 2007 onward.

Using state-level, two-digit data for Mexico for the period 1975–1988 Feenstra and Hanson (1996, 1997) found that wage inequality went up as a result of trade, specifically input trade. They attributed this to the shifting of the least skill-intensive production activities of the United States across the border to Mexico where the same activities were more skill intensive than any other existing production activity. This resulted in an increase in the relative demand for skilled labor in both the United States and Mexico, resulting in rising inequality in both countries. Feliciano (2001) also found that trade reforms in Mexico between 1986 and 1990 had led to a rise in wage inequality. However, she found that while the import license coverage ratios were positively related to wage inequality, tariffs did not have a statistically significant effect.

Attanasio, Goldberg, and Pavcnik (2004) and Goldberg and Pavcnik (2005) find an increase in wage inequality arising from the "drastic trade liberalization" episodes of the 1980s and 1990s in Colombia. They find that tariff cuts reduced wages at the sector level and that the initially most protected sectors were the most unskilled labor intensive as well as the ones paying the lowest wages. One of the goals of the tariff liberalization was uniformity in tariffs, which meant that these were also the sectors with the biggest tariff cuts. As a result, these sectors had the largest wage declines and because they were unskilled labor intensive, overall unskilled workers' wages declined proportionally more than those of skilled workers. Also, the labor market was rigid, which meant that workers in declining sectors could not easily move to expanding sectors. As a result, many of them moved from the formal to the informal sector (that pays lower wages) within the same industry. Also, these sectors were now facing more competition from the rest of the world as a result of the trade liberalization and they responded by upgrading their technology, which was a more skill-intensive one. For all these reasons, trade liberalization increased wage inequality in Colombia.[5] However, it is important note that the impact of trade reforms on wage inequality was small in magnitude.

Pavcnik et al. (2004) study the impact of the 1988–1994 trade reforms in Brazil on the structure of wages across manufacturing industries in Brazil. They found that industry affiliation was an important determinant of the wage but also that changes in these industry wage premiums were not related to changes in trade policy. Thus trade did not seem to affect wage inequality in Brazil. According to Pavcnik et al., the contrasting results of Colombia and Brazil highlight the role of country characteristics in determining the impact of trade on wage inequality. On the one hand, I can think of the extent of labor mobility across sectors and regions differing between the two countries. On the other hand, the existence of industry wage premiums is not consistent with labor mobility across sectors.

Kumar and Mishra (2008) have looked at the impact of tariff reductions on wage premiums in India and have found that tariff reductions result in increases in industry wage premiums. Note that since skill variables such as education and experience are controlled for, these are not the premiums for additional skills. However, as Kumar and Mishra argue, "since different industries employ different proportions of skilled workers, changes in wage premiums translate into changes in the relative incomes of skilled and unskilled workers." They in fact find that tariff reductions have been larger in the more unskilled labor-intensive industries, where the increases in the "industry wage premiums" have also been bigger. As a result, they infer a reduction in wage inequality in India. This is consistent with the Stolper–Samuelson effect, or it is simply that the increase in productivity gets passed on as an increase in the industry wage premium, both being greater in the labor-intensive industries where tariff reductions have been bigger.

In the context of wage inequality as well, it is important to return to the literature that uses the general equilibrium welfare approach, which we already discussed in detail in the context of poverty. One of the weaknesses of that literature is that it ignores the impact of trade on nonlabor factor incomes, but does a fairly comprehensive job on labor incomes based on skill level and, in one of the papers, on age cohorts as well. It also takes into account differences in consumption bundles depending on household income level, which lead to different effects of a given change in the price vector on different households. Thus, Porto (2006) and Ural Marchand (2012) effectively are able to do a very good job in looking at the impact of trade on the inequality of real labor incomes. In fact, while the authors explicitly have not calculated Gini coefficients, the pro-poor impact—due to which the proportional increase in real labor income is higher in the left tail than in the right tail of the income distribution—is suggestive of an improvement in the distribution of real labor incomes. As mentioned earlier, this is done by factoring in the differences in the structure of consumption across income levels.

Recent work by Helpman and colleagues (Helpman et al. 2014) looks at Brazilian employer-employee data for the 1990s. They document that most of the wage inequality occurs within industries and occupations, driven mainly by between- rather than within-firm inequality, with these patterns being robust to controlling for worker characteristics. The authors estimate a model of firm heterogeneity in productivity, export-market entry costs, and worker screening costs to match the preceding observations about the data. The prediction of the model estimated using Brazilian data is an inverted-U-shaped relationship between the variance of the logarithm of worker wages (which is a measure of wage inequality) and the logarithm of market access. As trade costs go down from a prohibitive level, initially only a few firms are able to jump their fixed costs of exporting and to earn higher profits. These are the firms that were making relatively higher profits to begin with. Now their larger market beyond their home country increases their profits further, which they share with their own workers. As a result, inequality goes up. With further declines in trade costs, many more firms start exporting, as a result of which wage inequality declines. For the period analyzed, the trade costs for Brazil had not gone down far enough to result in inequality reduction, predicted by their estimated model.

Krishna, Poole, and Senses (2014) use the same dataset to analyze the impact of trade on wage inequality from a different angle. In investigating the impact of trade on wages, they introduce firm-worker-match fixed effects, which they can do with employer-employee matched data. In other words, they believe that, based on characteristics unobservable to the econometrician, a worker "fits" a particular firm better than other firms, as a result of which one could think of there being additional productivity from that match. Once this is controlled for, Krishna, Poole, and Senses find that exporters do not actually pay a higher wage than others. They also find that trade results in better matches and, as a result, higher productivity in exporting firms for which workers are paid a higher wage. Thus if there is higher wage inequality it corresponds closely to the greater productivity heterogeneity among workers.

Trade and Overall Income Inequality

Goldberg and Pavcnik (2007a) have looked at trends in overall income inequality and in trade flows and protection for a number of countries that liberalized their trade regimes in the 1970s, 1980s, and 1990s. In Mexico, they observe that during the liberalization phase inequality first increased and then declined. In Brazil and Colombia there have been non-monotonic changes in inequality (first declined, then increased, and after that fairly stable), while Argentina and Chile has shown a steady increase during the liberalization phase. These trends do not show us a clear pattern. However, as mentioned earlier, even a clear pattern would not definitively tell us anything about causation. One could expect intra-country studies to be more useful in this regard.

In an intra-country study on India, Krishna and Sethupathy (2012) compute Theil's inequality index from Indian household survey data for each of the four NSSO "thick" survey rounds during the period 1988–2005. The attractive property of this inequality index is that if the entire population can be divided into groups then the overall inequality is the sum of within-group and between-group inequality. Krishna and Sethupathy find that the inequality between states or between rural and urban areas is much smaller than that within these aggregates, the latter accounting for more than 70 percent of the overall inequality in India. Overall inequality fell from the year 1988 to 1994, rose in the period 1994–2000 and subsequently fell again. These trends are robust to using alternative measures of inequality such as the Gini coefficient or the variance of the logarithm of expenditures.

In addition to finding a non-monotonic movement in inequality in the post reform period, Krishna and Sethupathy fail to find any correlation between state-level inequality and state-level employment-weighted measures of tariff and nontariff barriers. Thus there seems to be no association between trade and overall inequality.

Trade and Labor Shares

In most of the work on trade and inequality the focus has been on the inequality of labor incomes. However, overall inequality can grow due to a reduction of the share of labor income since the rich derive a lot of their income from assets like capital or land, which are very unequally distributed. ILO (2011) shows a declining labor share of national income since the early 1990s in many countries, with this decline more rapid in developing countries. The trend in the labor share of corporate value added has been no different (Karabarbounis and Neiman 2013). Atkinson (2009) argues that this declining labor share can possibly explain the rising inequality in recent years. Since this decline in the labor's share as well as the rise in income inequality in many parts of the world have coincided with an increase in world trade, it is important for the trade and inequality literature to go beyond looking at the rising skilled-unskilled wage gap.

Ahsan and Mitra (2014) fill this gap in the literature by empirically examining the impact of India's 1991 trade reforms on labor's share of firm revenue among a sample of Indian firms. They find that the share of wages in total revenue increased rapidly between the initial point and the end point of their sample period among smaller firms in the sample, while the share of wages in total revenue declined among the larger firms. It is important to note that this finding also holds with respect to changes in the share of wages in value added. It is important to note that the smaller firms are more labor intensive than the larger firms. Ahsan and Mitra run a regression that has the share of labor compensation in total firm revenue on the left-hand side and on the right-hand side they have a one-year lagged tariff, the interaction of this tariff with their labor intensity measure (or alternatively with their firm size indicators), firm and year fixed effects, and numerous controls.[6] Their results indicate that trade liberalization raised labor's share of revenue for firms that are, based on translog production function estimates, sufficiently labor intensive (about 34.6 percent of the firms in their sample). When they use firm size indicators as their proxy for labor intensity, they find that trade liberalization led to an increase in the share of wages in total revenue for small firms (whose sales in any given year are below the 33rd percentile of the sample's sales distribution. For such firms, the elasticity of wage share with respect to tariff, evaluated at the mean, is -0.05. The results also suggest that trade liberalization led to a decrease in the share of wages for large firms. These are firms whose sales in any given year are above the 67th percentile. In this case, the elasticity, evaluated at the mean, is 0.09. These results are consistent with the predictions of a model they developed that incorporates firm-labor union bargaining in the presence of imperfect competition in the product market.

Using China's Annual Survey of Industrial Production data, Kamal, Lovely, and Mitra (2014) estimate the effect of Chinese tariff cuts during the period 1998–2007 on manufacturing firms' labor shares relative to economy-wide trends. Regressions estimated with this large panel of firms provide evidence of a positive and statistically significant effect of output and input tariff cuts on labor shares of output. Alternatively, reductions in effective rates of protection increase labor shares of value added. This is true despite the fact that both tariffs and labor shares were falling during this period. In other words, the fall in labor shares could have been more rapid in the absence of these tariff cuts. It is interesting to note that the effects of trade liberalization on labor shares increase in strength with proximity to ports and are also dependent on ownership type (domestic private, foreign, and state-owned).

Thus this literature on trade reforms and labor shares does not show a negative impact of the former on the latter. While in India, in the case of smaller, labor-intensive firms trade reforms have raised labor shares, in China the positive impact of trade reforms on labor shares in firms seems to hold on average across all firms. Thus, it is quite possible that income inequality would have gone up even more had there not been trade reforms of the magnitude these countries had experienced in the last two decades.

3.6 Concluding Remarks

In this chapter I have reviewed the literature on the impact of trade on poverty and inequality. Before going to the evidence, I have surveyed the various theories from which we can derive predictions regarding the impact of trade on poverty and inequality. The evidence on the whole that trade reduces poverty is quite strong. There is some evidence of a possible poverty-reducing effect of trade reforms in the cross-country regressions I have run and presented in this chapter. In addition, a vast majority of the intra-country studies, including both of the direct reduced form type as well as those relying on empirical general-equilibrium welfare analysis, strongly support the poverty-reducing impact of trade reforms. Also, there is strong empirical evidence that trade increases incomes and that growth reduces poverty, which together support the view that trade reduces poverty.

The evidence on the impact of trade on inequality is quite mixed in several respects. First, the impact on inequality is different for wage inequality and overall income inequality. Even in the case of wage inequality, once we bring in the heterogeneity in consumption bundles across income classes and how their costs change as a result of reforms, the results change from an inequality-increasing effect of trade reforms to an inequality-reducing effect of trade. Furthermore, when we focus on within-country variation in income inequality it can be non-monotonic with respect to both time and trade openness. This is true of overall income inequality trends reviewed by Goldberg and Pavcnik (2007a) and the trends for Indian states studied by Krishna and Sethupathy (2012). It is also true of the predictions generated about the inequality of labor incomes by the model estimated using Brazilian data in Helpman et al. (2014). However, cross-country regressions do show some evidence of an inequality-increasing effect of trade liberalization. Also, for India as a whole and for China inequality post reforms has exhibited an overall increasing trend. Nevertheless, it seems that trade has had a relatively small role to play in this rise in inequality. In fact, labor shares in output at the firm level in India and China do not seem to be declining with respect to trade liberalization across all types of firms. On average, this share is increasing for relatively small, labor-intensive firms in India. It is also increasing on average for Chinese firms with respect to tariff cuts. Since a falling wage share is associated with rising inequality, as shown by Atkinson (2009), the positive empirical relationship between labor shares and tariff cuts shows us one way in which trade might have been relatively inequality reducing rather than enhancing (compared to the counterfactual).

We need to be aware here that the impact of trade on poverty and inequality depends on domestic institutions and complementary domestic policies. Bhagwati (2004) emphasizes the importance of "appropriate policies" for trade reforms to yield maximum benefits. In particular, he discusses diversifying away from specializing in products that might experience steeply falling world prices over time while still specializing according to one's factor abundance-based comparative advantage. Bhagwati also discusses suitable agricultural policies, policies promoting financial development, provision of property rights (giving people title to assets they can borrow against for production purposes), infrastructure development such as building roads (to facilitate the transmission of price changes from tariff reforms to remote parts of the country), and so on. Cain, Hasan, and Mitra (2012) actually find evidence that better road density (more extensive road infrastructure), labor regulations making for more flexible labor markets, and greater financial development enhance the beneficial impact of trade reforms on urban poverty. While this means that increased road density more completely translates price changes at the border into local price changes, financial development leads the banking system to respond to changes in producers' credit needs as they face greater competition through trade liberalization as well as their need to increase production scale or invest in more modern techniques. Similarly, Krishna, Mitra, and Sundaram (2010) show how trade liberalization is relatively less effective in reducing poverty in India's lagging states (those further away than average from the closest port). They also find that it is the price transmission from tariff changes that is relatively more imperfect in such states, which in turn weakens the poverty-reducing effect of trade reforms. Thus building more ports and roads should reduce uneven regional development and promote more effective poverty reduction in response to trade reforms.

Notes

1. Missing WDI data for a few intermediate years have been interpolated based on the observations available for the closest years to make the graphs in these figures appear continuous. These interpolations have no impact on the qualitative inferences from these graphs.

2. Actually, it had gone up to 69 percent by 2005 but continuously went down over the next four years to 49 percent in 2009. Given that this might be related to the slowdown in the world economy, we do our calculations for the period up to 2005.

3. For an excellent, comprehensive survey of the evidence on the globalization-poverty linkage, see Harrison 2007.

4. The NSSO sampling methodology is not constructed with the aim of making the sample within a district random. In addition, it is extremely difficult, if not impossible, to keep controlling for frequent changes in district boundaries. See Hasan, Mitra, and Ural 2007 for details.

5. It is important to note that these results are obtained upon controlling for time-invariant unobservable industry characteristics along with observable worker and industry characteristics. These results survive instrumenting tariffs with initial tariffs interacted with macro variables.

6. They address concerns about the endogeneity of tariffs, if any, by adopting a variant of the instrumental variable (IV) strategy used by Goldberg and Pavcnik (2005). Also, to rule out alternative channels working through other firm characteristics correlated with firm size or labor intensity, they tried controlling for tariff interactions with R&D expenditure, export status, import status, etc.

References

Ahsan, Reshad N., and Devashish Mitra. 2014. "Trade Liberalization and Labor's Slice of the Pie: Evidence from Indian Firms." *Journal of Development Economics* 108:1–16.

Aisbett, Emma, Ann Harrison, and Alix Zwane. 2008. "Globalization and Poverty: What Is the Evidence?" In *Trade, Globalization and Poverty*, ed. E. Dinopoulos, P. Krishna, A. Panagariya, and K. Wong, 33–61. London: Routledge.

Atkin, David, Amit K. Khandelwal, and Adam Osman. 2014. "Exporting and Firm Performance: Evidence from a Randomized Trial." Mimeo., Columbia Business School, Columbia University.

Atkinson, Anthony. 2009. "Factor Shares: The Principal Problem of Political Economy?" *Oxford Review of Economic Policy* 25 (1): 3–16.

Attanasio, Orazio, Nina Pavcnik, and Pinelopi K. Goldberg. 2004. "Trade Reforms and Income Inequality in Colombia." *Journal of Development Economics* 74:331–366.

Baldwin, Robert. 2003. "Openness and Growth: What Is the Empirical Relationship?" NBER Working Paper No. 9578, National Bureau of Economic Research, Cambridge, MA.

Bernstein, Jared. 2013. "The Impact of Inequality on Growth." Mimeo, Center for American Progress, Washington, DC.

Bhagwati, Jagdish. 2004. *In Defense of Globalization*. New York: Oxford University Press.

Bhagwati, Jagdish, and Arvind Panagariya. 2013. *Why Growth Matters: How Economic Growth in India Reduced Poverty and the Lesson for Other Developing Countries*. New York: Public Affairs.

Cain, Jewelwayne, Rana Hasan, and Devashish Mitra. 2012. "Trade Liberalization and Poverty Reduction: New Evidence from Indian States." In *India's Reforms: How They Produced Inclusive Growth*, ed. J. Bhagwati and A. Panagariya, 91–185. New York: Oxford University Press.

Chen, Shaohua, and Martin Ravallion. 2010. "The Developing World Is Poorer Than We Thought, but No Less Successful in the Fight Against Poverty." *Quarterly Journal of Economics* 125 (4): 1577–1625.

Davis, Donald R., and Prachi Mishra. 2007. "Stolper-Samuelson Is Dead: And Other Crimes of Both Theory and Data." In *Globalization and Poverty*, ed. Ann Harrison, 87–108. Chicago: University of Chicago Press.

Dollar, David. 1992. "Outward-Oriented Developing Economies Really Do Grow More Rapidly: Evidence from 95 LDCs, 1976–1985." *Economic Development and Cultural Change* 40 (3): 523–544.

Dollar, David, and Art Kraay. 2002. "Growth Is Good for the Poor." *Journal of Economic Growth* 7 (3): 195–225.

Dollar, David, and Art Kraay. 2004. "Trade, Growth, and Poverty." *Economic Journal* 114 (493): F22–F49.

Domowitz, Ian, R. Glenn Hubbard, and Bruce C. Peterson. 1988. "Market Structure and Cyclical Fluctuations in U.S. Manufacturing." *Review of Economics and Statistics* 70:55–66.

Edwards, Sebastian. 1998. "Openness, Productivity and Growth: What Do We Really Know." *Economic Journal* 108 (447): 383–398.

Fajgelbaum, Pablo, and Amit K. Khandelwal. 2014. "Measuring the Unequal Gains from Trade." Mimeo., Columbia Business School, Columbia University, New York.

Feenstra, Robert C., and Gordon H. Hanson. 1996. "Foreign Investment, Outsourcing and Relative Wages. In *Political Economy of Trade Policy: Essays in Honor of Jagdish Bhagwati*, ed. R. C. Feenstra et al., 89–127. Cambridge, MA: MIT Press.

Feenstra, Robert C., and Gordon H. Hanson. 1997. "Foreign Direct Investment and Relative Wages: Evidence from Mexico's Maquiladoras." *Journal of International Economics* 42:371–393.

Feenstra, Robert C., and Gordon H. Hanson. 1999. "The Impact of Outsourcing and High-Technology Capital on Wages: Estimates for the US, 1979–90." *Quarterly Journal of Economics* 114 (3): 907–940.

Feliciano, Zadia. 2001. "Workers and Trade Liberalization: The Impact of Trade Reforms in Mexico on Wages and Employment." *Industrial & Labor Relations Review* 55 (1): 95–115.

Fernandes, Ana M. 2007. "Trade Policy, Trade Volumes and Plant-Level Productivity in Colombian Manufacturing Industries." *Journal of International Economics* 71 (1): 52–71.

Frankel, Jeffrey, and David Romer. 1999. "Does Trade Cause Growth?" *American Economic Review* 89 (3): 379–399.

Goh, Chor-Ching, and Beata S. Javorcik. 2007. "Trade Protection and Industry Wage Structure in Poland." In *Globalization and Poverty*, ed. A. E. Harrison, 337–372. Chicago: University of Chicago Press.

Goldberg, P., and N. Pavcnik. 2005. "Trade Protection and Wages: Evidence from the Colombian Trade Reforms." *Journal of International Economics* 66 (1): 75–105.

Goldberg, Pinelopi K. and Nina Pavcnik. 2007a. "Distributional Effects of Globalization in Developing Countries." *Journal of Economic Literature* 45 (1): 39–82.

Goldberg, Pinelopi K., and Nina Pavcnik. 2007b. "The Effects of the Colombian Trade Liberalization on Urban Poverty." In *Globalization and Poverty*, ed. A. E. Harrison, 241–289. Chicago: University of Chicago Press.

Hall, Robert E. 1988. "The Relation between Price and Marginal Cost in U.S. Industry." *Journal of Political Economy* 96 (5): 921–947.

Hanson, Gordon H. 2007. "Globalization, Labor Incomes and Poverty in Mexico." In *Globalization and Poverty*, ed. A. E. Harrison, 241–289, 417–476. Chicago: University of Chicago Press.

Harrison, Ann E. 1994. "Productivity, Imperfect Competition and Trade Reform: Theory and Evidence." *Journal of International Economics* 36 (1–2): 53–73.

Harrison, Ann E. 2007. "Globalization and Poverty: An Introduction." In *Globalization and Poverty*, ed. A. E. Harrison, 1–30. Chicago: University of Chicago Press.

Hasan, Rana, Devashish Mitra, and Beyza P. Ural. 2007. "Trade Liberalization, Labor Market Institutions, and Poverty Reduction: Evidence from Indian States." India Policy Forum, 2006-07, New Delhi, India.

Hasan, Rana. M. G. Quibria, and Y. Kim. 2003. "Poverty and Economic Freedom: Evidence from Cross-Country Data." East-West Center Working Paper, The East-West Center, University of Hawaii-Manoa, Honolulu, Hawaii.

Helpman, Elhanan, Oleg Itskhoki, Marc Andreas Muendler, and Stephen Redding. 2014. "Trade and Inequality: From Theory to Estimation." Mimeo., Harvard University, Cambridge, MA.

International Labour Organization (ILO). 2011. *World of Work Report 2011: Making Markets Work for Jobs*. Geneva: International Labour Office.

Irwin, D., and J. M. Tervio. 2002. "Does Trade Raise Income? Evidence from the Twentieth Century." *Journal of International Economics* 58:1–18.

Kamal, Fariha, Mary E. Lovely, and Devashish Mitra. 2014. "Trade Liberalization and Labor Shares in China." Mimeo., Syracuse University, Syracuse, NY.

Karabarbounis, L., and B. Neiman. 2013. "The Global Decline of the Labor Share." NBER Working Paper No. 19136, National Bureau of Economic Research, Cambridge, MA.

Kim, Euysung. 2000. "Trade Liberalization and Productivity Growth in Korean Manufacturing Industries: Price Protection, Market Power, and Scale Efficiency." *Journal of Development Economics* 62:55–83.

Krishna, Pravin, and Devashish Mitra. 1998. "Trade Liberalization, Market Discipline and Productivity Growth: New Evidence from India." *Journal of Development Economics* 56 (2): 447–462.

Krishna, Pravin, Jennifer P. Poole, and Mine Zeynep Senses. 2014. "Wage Effects of Trade Reform with Endogenous Worker Mobility." *Journal of International Economics* 93:239–252.

Krishna, Pravin, and Guru Sethupathy. 2012. "Trade and Income Inequality in India." In *India's Reforms: How They Produced Inclusive Growth*, ed. J. Bhagwati and A. Panagariya, 247–278. New York: Oxford University Press.

Krishna, Pravin, Devashish Mitra, and Asha Sundaram. 2010. "Do Lagging Regions Benefit from Trade?" In *The Poor Half Billion in South Asia: What Is Holding Back Lagging Regions?*, ed. E. Ghani, 137–177. Oxford: Oxford University Press.

Kumar, Utsav, and Prachi Mishra. 2008. "Trade Liberalization and Wage Inequality: Evidence from India." *Review of Development Economics* 12 (2): 291–311.

Mukim, Megha, and Arvind Panagariya. 2012. "Growth, Openness and the Socially Disadvantaged." In *India's Reforms: How They Produced Inclusive*

Growth, ed. J. Bhagwati and A. Panagariya, 186–246. New York: Oxford University Press.

Naughton, Barry J. 2007. *The Chinese Economy: Transitions and Growth*. Cambridge, MA: MIT Press.

Pavcnik, Nina. 2002. "Trade Liberalization, Exit, and Productivity Improvements: Evidence from Chilean Plants." *Review of Economic Studies* 69:245–276.

Pavcnik, Nina, Andreas Blom, Pinelopi K. Goldberg, and Norbert Schady. 2004. "Trade Policy and Industry Wage Structure: Evidence from Brazil." *World Bank Economic Review* 18 (3): 319–344.

Pavcnik, Nina, Andreas Blom, Pinelopi K. Goldberg, and Norbert Schady. 2004. "Trade Policy and Industry Wage Structure: Evidence from Brazil." *World Bank Economic Review* 18 (3): 319–344.

Piketty, Thomas. 2014. *Capital in the Twenty-First Century*. Cambridge, MA: Harvard University Press.

Porto, Guido G. 2006. "Using Survey Data to Assess the Distributional Effects of Trade Policy." *Journal of International Economics* 70 (1): 140–160.

Ravallion, M. 2001. "Growth, Inequality, and Poverty: Looking Beyond Averages." *World Development* 29 (11): 1803–1815.

Ravallion, M., and G. Datt. 1999. "How Important to India's Poor Is the Sectoral Composition of Economic Growth?" *World Bank Economic Review* 1 (10): 1–25.

Rodriguez, Franciso, and Dani Rodrik. 2001. "Trade Policy and Economics Growth: A Skeptic's Guide to the Cross-National Evidence." In *Macroeconomics Annual 2000*, ed. B. Bernanke and K. S. Rogoff, 261–338. Cambridge, MA: MIT Press.

Rodrik, Dani, Arvind Subramanian, and Francesco Trebbi. 2002. "Institutions Rule: The Primacy of Institutions over Geography and Integration in Economic Development." NBER Working Paper No. 9305, National Bureau of Economic Research, Cambridge, MA.

Sachs, Jeffrey D., and Andrew Warner. 1995. "Economic Reform and the Process of Global Integration." *Brookings Papers on Economic Activity* 26 (10): 1–118.

Seshan, Ganesh. 2014. "The Impact of Trade Liberalization on Household Welfare in a Developing Country with Imperfect Labor Markets." *Journal of Development Studies* 50 (2): 226–243.

Sunstein, Cass. 2014. "Why Worry About Inequality?" *Bloomberg View*, May 13. http://www.bloombergview.com/articles/2014-05-13/why-worry-about-inequality (accessed September 10, 2014).

Topalova, Petia. 2007. "Trade Liberalization, Poverty and Inequality: Evidence from Indian Districts." In *Globalization and Poverty*, ed. A. E. Harrison, 291–335. Chicago: University of Chicago Press.

Topalova, Petia, and Amit Khandelwal. 2011. "Trade Liberalization and Firm Productivity: The Case of India." *Review of Economics and Statistics* 93 (3): 995–1009.

Ural Marchand, Beyza. 2012. "Tariff Pass-Through and the Distributional Effects of Trade Liberalization." *Journal of Development Economics* 99 (2): 265–281.

Verhoogen, Eric. 2008. "Trade, Quality Upgrading and Wage Inequality in the Mexican Manufacturing Sector." *Quarterly Journal of Economics* 123 (2): 489–530.

Wacziarg, Romain, and Kevin H. Welch. 2003. "Trade Liberalization and Growth: New Evidence." NBER Working Paper No. 10152, National Bureau of Economic Research, Cambridge, MA.

Winters, Alan L., Neil McCulloch, and Andrew McKay. 2004. "Trade Liberalization and Poverty: The Evidence So Far." *Journal of Economic Literature* 42 (March): 72–115.

4

Dial PTAs for Peace: The Influence of Preferential Trade Agreements on Litigation between Trading Partners

Petros C. Mavroidis and André Sapir

The WTO dispute settlement mechanism (DSM) has been widely described as "the crown jewel of the WTO system." Recently, however, doubts have been expressed about the solidity of the jewel's value due to the proliferation of preferential trade agreements (PTAs), and the threat they represent. The fear is that as WTO members turn away from multilateral to bilateral or regional trade agreements they will also turn away from the WTO to bilateral or regional mechanisms for the settlement of trade disputes. This fear has further intensified with the launch of mega PTAs, such as the Transatlantic Trade and Investment Partnership (TTIP) currently negotiated between the United States and the European Union, respectively the first and second most active participants in WTO disputes during the first two decades of the WTO.

The purpose of this chapter is to provide a framework to assess the impact of PTAs on WTO disputes and ultimately on the WTO dispute settlement mechanism itself. This will be done using evidence from existing and currently negotiated EU and U.S. PTAs.

Our starting point is a twofold observation pertaining to the behavior of the EU. The first one is that the EU is the world's biggest participant in PTAs: in 2014, the EU had PTAs with fifty-eight trading partners accounting for one-third of its external trade and was involved in trade negotiations with other trading partners that would bring this amount to two-thirds. The second observation is that the EU often litigates before the WTO but almost never with PTA partners. After the United States, the EU is the most active participant to WTO disputes. During the period 1995–2014, it was involved in 183 disputes (out of a total of 486 WTO disputes): 93 times as complainant, 90 as respondent. Yet, only seven of these disputes were with (three) PTA partners.

The chapter provides answers to two sets of questions. The first set concerns whether the EU is special. In particular, we ask whether the

United States—the most active participant in WTO disputes with 223 disputes during the period 1995–2014—behaves toward its PTA partners differently from or similarly to the EU. The second set of questions pertains to the consequences of TTIP for WTO dispute settlement: Would bilateral EU-U.S. disputes before the WTO (accounting for 51 of the 486 WTO disputes during the period 1995–2014) stop? Would the EU and the United States (together accounting for 345 of the total WTO disputes) stop litigating at the WTO? Would the WTO's DSM become irrelevant?

To this effect, we have put together data of all the WTO disputes between, on one hand, the EU and the United States, and, on the other, their PTA partners, both before and after PTAs were signed and/or entered into force.[1]

The EU and the United States are party to some PTA agreements (such as NAFTA) that predate the creation of the WTO in 1995, and have entered into several new agreements afterward. For pre-WTO PTAs, we focus on PTA partners with whom the EU or the United States has engaged in WTO disputes. For post-WTO PTAs, we concentrate on PTA partners with whom the EU or the United States had WTO disputes before the signature of the PTA agreement. Consequently, we do not include in our data information about all PTAs signed by the two transatlantic partners, but only those involving partners with whom the EU or the United States had at least one WTO dispute after (for pre-WTO PTAs) or before (for post-WTO PTAs) the signature of the PTA.

We do not purport to suggest that we will come up with some sort of causal link between PTA-partnership and litigation behavior. It is doubtful that such a conclusion can be reached, not to mention that it is doubtful that economic analysis has much to say about causation in general. We simply want to see whether litigation behavior is *correlated* with the occurrence of the signature of a PTA (or the launch of negotiation).

The rest of the chapter is organized as follows: Section 4.1 includes the data. In section 4.2 we discuss the data and explain why in our view it supports the observation that the signature of a PTA signals the reduction of litigation between PTA partners before the WTO (and elsewhere). Section 4.3 offers, instead of conclusions, an evaluation of the impact that the prospect of reduced litigation between the EU and the United States might have for the WTO.

4.1 The Data

We reproduce the data used for this chapter in tables 4.1–4.8.

Tables 4.1 and 4.2 present the PTAs that we examine in this chapter. Recall that we focus on a subset of all EU and U.S. PTAs, namely, those where the EU or the United States had at least one WTO dispute after (for pre-WTO PTAs) or before (for post-WTO PTAs) the signature of the PTA.

Tables 4.3–4.6 represent the litigation that the EU and the United States have had with their PTA partners since the entry into force of the WTO (January 1, 1995). It is by comparing the date that a request for consultations was submitted before the DSB (Dispute Settlement Body at the WTO) to the date of PTA signature (or launch of negotiations) that we come up with the number indicating that we observe fewer disputes post-signature of a PTA.

Table 4.1
EU trade agreements covered

Name	Date of signature of PTA	Coverage	Dispute settlement	Binding
Pre-WTO PTAs				
EU-Norway	May 14, 1973	Goods	No	n.a.
Post-WTO PTAs				
EU-Mexico	December 8, 1997	Goods, Services	Yes	Yes
EU-Chile	November 18, 2002	Goods, Services	Yes	Yes
EU-Korea	October 6, 2010	Goods, Services	Yes	Yes
EU-Colombia/Peru	June 26, 2012	Goods, Services	Yes	Yes
EU-Central America [Costa Rica, El Salvador, Guatemala, Honduras, Nicaragua, Panama]	June 29, 2012	Goods, Services	Yes	Yes

Table 4.2
U.S. trade agreements covered

Name	Date of signature of PTA	Coverage	Dispute settlement	Binding
Pre-WTO PTAs				
NAFTA	January 29, 1993 (goods) March 1, 1995 (services)	Goods, Services	Yes	Yes
Post-WTO PTAs				
U.S.-Chile	December 16, 2003	Goods, Services	Yes	Yes
U.S.-Central America [Costa Rica, El Salvador, Guatemala, Honduras, Nicaragua] and Dominican Republic	August 5, 2004	Goods, Services	Yes	Yes
U.S.-Australia	December 22, 2004	Goods, Services	Yes	Yes
U.S.- Korea	March 15, 2012	Goods, Services	Yes	Yes
U.S.-Colombia	May 8, 2012	Goods, Services	Yes	Yes

Table 4.3
EU as complainant against PTA partners

Respondent	Date of signature of PTA	Case number	Date of request	DS stage reached	Subject matter
Chile	18/11/2002	DS87	6/4/1997	AB	GATT
		DS110	12/15/1997	AB	GATT
		DS193	4/19/2000	C	GATT
Korea	10/6/2010	DS40	5/5/1996	MAS	GATT
		DS75	4/2/1997	AB	GATT
		DS98	8/12/1997	AB	GATT SG
		DS273	10/21/2002	P	SCM
Mexico	12/8/1997	DS53	8/27/1996	C	GATT
		DS314	2/12/2004	C	AG SCM
		DS341	3/31/2006	P	AG GATT SCM

Table 4.4
EU as respondent against PTA partners

Complainant	Date of signature of PTA	Case number	Date of request	DS stage reached	Subject matter
Chile	18/11/2002	DS14	7/24/1996	P MAS	GATT TBT
		DS326	2/8/2005	C	GATT SG
Colombia	6/26/2012	DS361	7/21/2008	C	GATT
Guatemala	6/29/2012	DS16	9/28/1995	C	GATS GATT ILA
		DS27	2/5/1996	AB MAS	AG GATS GATT ILA TRIMS
		DS158	1/20/1999	C	ILA
Honduras	6/29/2012	DS16	9/28/1995	C	GATS GATT ILA
		DS27	2/5/1996	AB MAS	AG GATS GATT ILA TRIMS
		DS158	1/20/1999	C	ILA
Korea	10/6/2010	DS299	7/25/2003	P	GATT SCM
		DS301	9/3/2003	P	GATT SCM
		DS307	2/13/2004	C	GATT SCM
Mexico	12/8/1997	DS16	9/28/1995	C	GATS GATT ILA
		DS27	2/5/1996	AB MAS	AG GATS GATT ILA TRIMS
		DS158	1/20/1999	C	ILA
Norway	7/1/1973	DS328	3/1/2005	C	GATT SG
		DS337	3/17/2006	P	AD GATT
		DS401	11/5/2009	AB	AG GATT TBT
Peru	6/26/2012	DS231	3/20/2001	AB MAS	GATT TBT

Table 4.5
United States as complainant against PTA partners

Respondent	Date of signature of PTA	Case number	Date of request	DS stage reached	Subject matter
Australia	12/22/2004	DS21	11/20/1995	C MAS	GATT SPS
		DS57	10/7/1996	C	SCM
		DS106	6/11/1998	C	SCM
		DS126	7/24/2000	P MAS	SCM
Canada	1/29/1993	DS31	3/11/1996	AB	GATT
		DS103	10/8/1997	AB MAS	AG GATT SCM ILA
		DS170	5/6/1999	AB	TRIPS
		DS276	12/17/2002	AB	GATT TRIMS
		DS338	3/17/2006	C	AD SCM GATT
Chile	12/16/2003	DS109	12/11/1997	C	GATT
Korea	3/15/2012	DS3	4/4/1995	C	AG GATT SPS TBT
		DS5	7/20/1995	C MAS	AG GATT SPS TBT
		DS41	5/24/1996	C	AG GATT SPS TBT
		DS84	5/23/1997	AB	GATT
		DS161	2/1/1999	AB	AG GATT ILA
		DS163	3/16/2004	P	GATT
Mexico	1/29/1993	DS101	9/4/1997	C	AD
		DS132	5/8/1998	AB	AD
		DS203	7/10/2000	C	AG AD SPS TBT GATT
		DS204	8/17/2000	P	GATS
		DS295	6/16/2003	AB	AD SCM GATT
		DS308	3/16/2004	AB	GATT

Table 4.6
United States as respondent against PTA partners

Complainant	Date of signature of PTA	Case number	Date of request	DS stage reached	Subject matter
Australia	12/22/2004	DS178	7/23/1999	AB	GATT SG
		DS217	12/21/2000	AB	AD GATT SCM
Canada	1/29/1993	DS144	9/25/1998	C	AG GATT SPS TBT
		DS167	3/19/1999	C	AG SCM
		DS180	9/6/1999	C	AG GATT
		DS194	5/19/2000	P	SCM
		DS221	1/17/2001	P	AD GATT SCM
		DS234	5/21/2001	AB	AD SCM GATT
		DS236	8/21/2001	P MAS	GATT SCM
		DS247	3/6/2002	C MAS	AD
		DS257	5/3/2002	AB MAS	GATT SCM
		DS264	9/13/2002	AB MAS	AD GATT
		DS277	12/20/2002	AB MAS	AD SCM GATT
		DS310	4/8/2004	C	AD SCM GATT
		DS311	4/14/2004	C MAS	SCM GATT
		DS357	1/8/2007	C	AG SCM GATT
		DS384	12/1/2008	AB	GATT ROO SPS TBT
Chile	12/16/2003	DS109	12/11/1997	C	GATT
Colombia	5/15/2012	DS78	4/28/1997	C	GATT SG

Table 4.6 (continued)

Complainant	Date of signature of PTA	Case number	Date of request	DS stage reached	Subject matter
Costa Rica	8/5/2004	DS24	12/22/1995	P	T&C
Korea	3/15/2012	DS89	7/10/1997	C	AD GATT
		DS99	8/14/1997	P	AD GATT
		DS179	7/30/1999	P	AD GATT
		DS202	6/13/2000	AB	GATT SG
		DS217	12/21/2000	AB	AD GATT SCM
		DS251	3/20/2002	AB	GATT SG
		DS296	6/30/2003	AB	GATT SCM
		DS402	11/24/2009	P	AD GATT
		DS420	1/31/2011	C	AD GATT
		DS464	8/29/2013	C	AD GATT SCM
Mexico	1/29/1993	DS49	1/1/1996	C	AD
		DS234	5/21/2001	AB	AD SCM GATT
		DS280	2/21/2003	C	SCM
		DS281	1/31/2003	C MAS	AD GATT
		DS282	3/18/2003	AB	AD GATT
		DS325	1/5/2005	C	AS GATT
		DS344	5/26/2006	AB	AD GATT
		DS381	10/24/2008	AB	GATT TBT
		DS386	12/17/2008	AB	GATT ROO SPS TBT

Two caveats are in order here. First, we include all disputes that were formally launched (e.g., the DSB was notified of a request for consultations) before the WTO. We do not care if disputes are of a certain magnitude (for instance in terms of trade flows) or not.[2] Second, we do not ask questions regarding the "optimal" number of disputes that the EU and the United States should have had because of their size.[3] We take the number of disputes as given.

Finally, tables 4.7 and 4.8 show the PTAs, which are being negotiated by the EU and the United States at the moment of writing.

Table 4.7
EU trade negotiations launched

Name	Date of launch	Coverage	EU partners
EU-India	March 2007	Goods, Services	India
EU-Singapore	October 2010	Goods, Services	Singapore
EU-Japan	April 2013	Goods, Services	Japan
TTIP (Trans-Atlantic Trade and Investment Partnership)	July 2013, first round of negotiations	Goods, Services	U.S.
EU-Canada	October 2013	Goods, Services	Canada

Table 4.8
U.S. trade negotiations launched

Name	Date of launch	Coverage	U.S. partners
TPP (Trans-Pacific Partnership)	November 2009 (U.S. announces participation) November 2011 inaugural conference	Goods, Services	Australia, Brunei, Canada, Chile, Japan, Malaysia, New Zealand, Peru, Singapore, Vietnam
TTIP (Trans-Atlantic Trade and Investment Partnership)	July 2013, first round of negotiations	Goods, Services	EU

Pre-WTO PTAs

At the time of creation of the WTO, the EU had already signed PTAs with numerous partners. In the next twenty years, the EU did not bring a single case before to the WTO against all but one of these partners: it brought three cases against Norway (see tables 4.3 and 4.4).

The situation with the United States is exactly the opposite. When the WTO was created, the United States was party to only two PTAs (U.S.-Israel, and NAFTA), but it has litigated many times before the WTO with its two NAFTA partners during the period 1995–2014: Twenty times with Canada (five as complainant, fifteen as respondent); and fifteen with Mexico (six as complainant, nine as defendant). Tables 4.5 and 4.6 reflect this point.

Post-WTO PTAs

The EU greatly increased its participation in PTAs after the creation of the WTO but has had few WTO disputes with its new PTA partners since the PTA agreements were signed. With partners of the five new EU PTAs (listed in table 4.1) with whom the EU litigated at least once before the WTO either before or after signature of the PTAs, the EU was involved in twenty disputes: sixteen before signature of the PTAs (eight times as complainant and eight as respondent), but only four after (two times as complainant and two as respondent).[4] Tables 4.3 and 4.4 reflect this point.

The situation with the United States is fairly similar. With partners of the five new U.S. PTAs (listed in table 4.2) with whom the United States had litigated at least once before the WTO either before or after signature of the PTAs, the United States was involved in twenty-five disputes: twenty-four before signature of the PTAs (eleven times as complainant and thirteen as respondent), but only once after (as respondent),[5] as our tables 4.5 and 4.6 indicate.

PTAs under Negotiation

The EU is currently negotiating PTAs with Canada, India, Japan, Singapore, and the United States. See table 4.7.

The EU and the United States have not initiated a WTO complaint against each other since July 2013, when the TTIP negotiation was launched. Previously, they had litigated fifty-one times before the WTO: the EU acted as complainant against the United States thirty-two times and as respondent nineteen times.[6]

The EU litigated before the WTO fifteen times with Canada before the launch of bilateral negotiations (six times as complainant and nine as defendant, and none after the launch). It litigated fourteen times with India before the launch of bilateral negotiations (nine times as complainants and five as defendant), and also litigated three times afterward (one time as complainant and two times as respondent). It litigated seven times with Japan before the start of their bilateral negotiations (six times as complainant and once as respondent), but not after the launch of negotiations. The EU has never litigated with Singapore.

The United States is currently negotiating two PTAs: the TPP (Trans-Pacific Partnership) with Australia, Brunei, Canada, Chile, Japan, Malaysia, New Zealand, Peru, Singapore, andVietnam; and the TTIP with the EU, as per our table 4.8.

Regarding the TPP partners, we limit our observations to Brunei, Japan, Malaysia, New Zealand, Peru, Singapore, and Vietnam since the United States has already concluded PTAs with the other TPP partners.

The United States litigated fourteen times with Japan before the launch of the TPP negotiations (six times as complainant and fourteen as defendant), and none after the launch. It litigated once with Malaysia, the United States acting as defendant, before the launch of the negotiations and none ever since. It acted as defendant twice against New Zealand before the launch of negotiations and none after that. And, finally, it litigated twice with Vietnam, always as defendant, once before and once after the launch of the TPP negotiations. The United States never litigated with Brunei, Peru, and Singapore.

4.2 Interpreting the Data

In Principle, Few(er) Disputes

The numbers in and of themselves tell a story here.

The pattern of the EU and the United States is the same as far as post-WTO PTAs are concerned. The EU has never litigated with Colombia, Guatemala, Honduras, and Peru and only once with Chile and Korea and twice with Mexico after the signature of PTAs with any of them. The number of litigations with these countries fell from sixteen prior to the PTAs to four afterward (see tables 4.3, 4.4, 4.10, and 4.11). Similarly, the United States never litigated with Australia, Chile, Colombia, and Costa Rica, and only once with Korea after the signature of PTAs with any of them. The number of litigations with these countries went down from twenty-four prior to the PTAs to one afterward (see tables 4.5, 4.6, 4.10, and 4.11).

But where the main contrast lies between the EU and the United States is with respect to PTAs that predate the creation of the WTO. Although the EU was party to many more PTAs than the United States at the time, it has litigated only three times before the WTO with an "old" PTA partner, each time with Norway. In comparison, the United States has litigated thirty-five times before the WTO with its two NAFTA partners (twenty times with Canada and fifteen times with Mexico).

Our tentative conclusion at this point is therefore that the EU and the United States behave similarly with their PTA partners: the two rarely, if at all, litigate with their partners before the WTO either as complainant or as defendant. Thus the EU does not appear to be special. However, it seems that NAFTA is different, an issue that we will examine further.

Even Fewer, If We Discount for Old Battles

It is reasonable to hypothesize that ongoing WTO disputes between future PTA partners are one of the subjects addressed during negotiations leading to the signature of a PTA. We define as "old" disputes those WTO (or even GATT) disputes litigated before the signing of a PTA, and "new" WTO disputes as those initiated after the signature of the PTA. We then discount such old disputes from our counting when measuring the litigation behavior of PTA partners. Our hypothesis (tested in section 3.5) is that there are even fewer WTO disputes between the EU or the United States and their PTA partners, if we discount for disputes that predate the signature of the PTAs. The intuition is that new issues are resolved in ways other than submitting a formal dispute before a WTO Panel.

Even Fewer Disputes after the Launch of Negotiations

The United States has litigated before the WTO only once with Vietnam since the launch of TPP negotiations, and never with the EU since the launch of the TTIP negotiations. The same holds for the EU, which has not litigated with Canada, Japan, or the United States since the launch of their PTA negotiations. The timespan, however, for all these cases is quite short and does not allow for strong conclusions. Interestingly the EU has litigated three times only with India since the launch of their bilateral negotiations. These negotiations have lasted longer than other PTA negotiations, casting doubt on the successful conclusion of the whole endeavor.

Fewer Disputes in General: No Forum Diversion

We also check disputes raised before the bilateral or regional PTA forum to see whether forum diversion has occurred. In this case, the EU and the United States would be "doves" before the WTO, because they behave like "hawks" in the bilateral or regional forum. Our data does not support this hypothesis. The EU and the United States become "doves" across the board after signing PTAs.

According to Chase et al. (2013), dispute settlement mechanisms in PTAs fall in three categories: political/diplomatic, quasi-judicial, and judicial. Political or diplomatic mechanisms are those that have no dispute settlement provisions at all, that provide exclusively for negotiated settlement among the parties, or that provide for referral of a dispute to a third-party adjudicator but with the PTA members having a right to veto such referral. By contrast, both quasi-judicial and judicial systems involve decisions by an adjudicating body, but only the latter implies the existence of a permanent adjudicating body such as the WTO's DSB.

As table 4.12 indicates, two-thirds of the PTAs notified to the WTO until 2012 belonged to the quasi-judicial category. Table 4.13 indicates that today all the PTAs involving the United States are quasi-judicial. The situation is slightly different for PTAs involving the EU. Here the majority is also quasi-judicial, but PTAs with some European partners have political/diplomatic dispute settlement mechanisms.

Turning to the PTAs examined in this chapter, we observe that all but one contain a quasi-judicial dispute settlement mechanism. Moreover these mechanisms are binding. What do we mean by "binding," and why is it important for the purposes of our work?

We define "binding" dispute settlement regimes as those that allow for countermeasures by parties facing uncooperative behavior (nonimplementation of adverse rulings).[7] If no dispute settlement exists, or if it exists but it has no teeth (it is not "binding"), then we should contemplate the following: either the EU and the United States have become "doves," and they litigate neither before the PTA forum (where it is impossible to litigate at all), nor before the WTO; or they act as "hawks" before the WTO. The outlier is the EU-Norway PTA signed on July 1, 1973, which contains no dispute settlement regime at all. We suggest it should not be treated as an outlier, however, since Norway can of course access the EFTA (European Free Trade Association) Court, which is a binding regime that handles, inter alia, disputes between EEA (European Economic Area) members, which include both Norway and the EU.

As stated earlier, our data supports the view that the EU and the United States become doves after the signature of an FTA. Ideally, we would like to have a binomial—say 0 is "dove" and 1 is "hawk." Unsurprisingly, this is wishful thinking that has no support in empirics. The emerging picture though, largely supports the conclusion that both the EU and the United States behave more like doves toward their PTA partners. This conclusion is even more robust when we adopt the old/new dispute dichotomy explained earlier. We are not suggesting that the EU and the United States become doves because of the signing of the FTA. We are simply stating that they become doves after this event.

Is NAFTA an Outlier?

The United States has been involved in thirty-five WTO disputes with its two NAFTA partners but only in one WTO dispute with a PTA partner other than NAFTA (Korea) after the PTA signature. Why such difference?

The facts, first: the United States has litigated before the WTO fifteen times with Mexico since January 1, 1995, six of which acting as complainant (DS 101, 132, 203, 204, 295, 308), and nine times as defendant (DS 49, 234, 280, 281, 282, 325, 344, 381, 386).

When we apply our distinction between old and new disputes to NAFTA, this is what we obtain.

DS 101, 132, 308 refer to the old sugar disputes between Mexico and the United States. Huerta-Goldman (2009) reports unsuccessful attempts to resolve these disputes during the NAFTA negotiations. DS 280, 282, 325, 344 refer to steel disputes that had been raised before the advent of the WTO, and which were then discussed during the NAFTA negotiations, however, without the NAFTA partners managing to resolve their differences. DS 281 also refers to an old cement dispute. Mexico had submitted a GATT dispute on this issue, which had gone unresolved before the creation of the WTO. DS 381 is an offshoot of the notorious GATT dispute between the two NAFTA partners regarding the marketing of tuna products in the United States market. DS 386 is about the treatment of cattle, another issue that had been negotiated without success during the NAFTA negotiations.

As a result, there are only five disputes (DS 49, 203, 204, 234, 295) between Mexico and the United States that qualify as genuinely WTO disputes ("new" disputes, as per our terminology), and not as continuations of GATT disputes that remained unresolved during the NAFTA negotiations. Note also that no new dispute between Mexico and the

United States is reported since 2008. Of the five new disputes between the United States and Mexico, three are so-called "Chapter 20" cases (DS 49, 203, 204), which could not have been raised before a NAFTA Panel because the adjudication of disputes under this chapter of the NAFTA agreement is in reality impossible, due to the deadlock between partners regarding the selection of panelists.[8] The end result is that United States and Mexico have litigated five new disputes since the advent of the WTO (which almost coincides with the advent of NAFTA), and have not litigated at all for almost seven years now.

The United States and Canada have litigated against each other before the WTO twenty times: the United States acted as complainant five times (DS 31, 103, 170, 276, 338), and as defendant fifteen times (DS 144, 167, 180, 194, 221, 234, 236, 247, 257, 264, 277, 310, 311, 357, 384).

Applying again the old/new dispute distinction, this is what we obtain.

The softwood lumber disputes are longstanding battles between Canada and the United States due to the so-called "stumpage programs" adopted by Canada that the United States always considered constituted a subsidy. They date from the GATT era and were finally amicably resolved in 2008 after numerous WTO disputes (DS 236, 257, 247, 264, 277, 311).

Cattle, dairy products, and grain have been extensively litigated both in the Canada-U.S. FTA as well as NAFTA without the two partners managing to resolve the issue. This led to a number of WTO disputes (DS 103, 144, 167, 276, 310, 338, 357, 384).

The cultural exception in the bilateral agreement between Canada and the United States, as well as in NAFTA, was insufficient to resolve the dispute on split-run periodicals and led to one WTO dispute (DS 31).

The sugar syrup (high fructose) dispute (DS 180) arose because NAFTA was poorly drafted with respect to access to sugar markets, and was resolved after 2008 with the removal of export restrictions.

This leaves only four Canada-U.S. WTO disputes that qualify as new disputes, namely DS 170, 194, 221, 234, and no dispute at all since 2008. As was the case of the Mexico U.S. dispute, therefore, adopting the old/new dispute criterion mitigates the image of NAFTA as an outlier when compared to other PTAs.

Had Canada and the United States litigated more often before NAFTA? Is there, in other words, forum diversion?

Of the four new cases between the United States and Canada, only DS 234 concerned contingent protection, and could have been litigated either before the WTO or before a NAFTA Panel. The other three cases are Chapter 20 NAFTA disputes. The amount of litigation before the WTO therefore equals the total amount of litigation between Canada and the United States. Three disputes in twenty years between two intensely integrated partners is a very low number by any reasonable benchmark. Litigation before NAFTA is confined to contingent protection cases.

The situation in the EU is both different and similar to the U.S. situation. What is different is that although all EU PTAs examined here (including EU-Norway when considering the possibility of using the EFTA Court) contain quasi-judicial, binding dispute settlement mechanisms, they have never been used. It seems that disputes between the EU and its PTA partners are either resolved politically or give rise to (scarce) litigation before the WTO. What is similar between the EU and the United States is that many of the WTO disputes between the EU and its PTA partners are, like those between the United States and its two NAFTA partners, old GATT disputes. This is the case for most of the disputes that took place before the signature of the PTAs, in particular the three banana disputes with Guatemala, Honduras, and Mexico (DS 16, 27, 158), which all date back to the GATT era.

Taking Stock

Our tentative conclusion has been reinforced by our examination of disputes before the PTA-forum and our distinction between old and new disputes. The EU and the United States rarely, if at all, litigate with their PTA partners before the WTO or the PTA forum either as complainant or as defendant. Neither the EU nor NAFTA is special in this respect.

Although a full analysis is beyond the scope of this chapter, it is nonetheless tempting to speculate about the reasons why there appears to be a (negative) correlation between PTA partnership and formal trade litigation. One reason may be that countries choose to sign PTAs, or to launch PTA negotiations, with trade partners with whom they have few trade disputes. While this factor may be at play in some cases, there are also plenty of other cases pointing to the opposite logic, including the TTIP negotiations. A second reason may be that PTA partners find it politically costly to litigate in open or semi-open multilateral (i.e., WTO) or regional and bilateral (i.e., PTA) forums and prefer to resolve their disputes through nontransparent political mechanisms even though quasi-judicial mechanisms are available. The final reason may simply be that PTAs create a framework to solve most past disputes between the partners and to anticipate many future disputes. The content of modern PTAs to some extent underscores this intuitive finding. One of the main conclusions of our work in Horn, Mavroidis, and Sapir 2010 was that the overwhelming majority of PTAs concern "regulatory" issues. Especially, the PTAs signed by the EU establish a forum of "permanent" and "steady" cooperation on a host of issues that directly or indirectly affect trade. It is to be expected that with increased transparency regarding the preparation and shaping of national policies, understanding about their rationale increases, and behavior is not predicated on the presence of some adverse trade effects. Transparency can work as a substitute for litigation, and increased transparency across PTA partners is a plausible contributing factor explaining why the amount of litigation across PTA partners has steadily decreased.

Our main finding is in line with the results of a recent econometric study by Li and Qiu (2014), which investigates the effects of the formation of PTAs on trade disputes. Using a dataset covering 110 countries and 1,130 trade disputes from 1995 to 2007 and controlling for economic size, economic growth, and trade shares, the study finds that a PTA between two countries reduces the occurrences of trade disputes between them.

4.3 Are Fewer Disputes Good News for the WTO?

Of the nearly five hundred disputes that have been brought to the WTO during the past twenty years, more than 70 percent involve the EU or the United States, usually against third parties but also sometimes against each other.

As table 4.9 indicates, the number of WTO disputes has steadily declined over the past twenty years. From an average of thirty-seven per year during the first five years, it declined to twenty-seven during the next five years and has averaged sixteen during the last ten years. Part of the reason for this decline has to do with the fact that the WTO inherited a stock of disputes that had been left unresolved during the GATT era, which the WTO's dispute settlement mechanism was able to resolve decisively during its first decade of operation. But the other reason is that, independently of the previous reason, the EU and the United States have sharply reduced their litigation activity, which dropped by more 50 percent between 1995 and 2004 and 2005–2014.

This chapter suggests that one factor behind the decreased litigation activity in the WTO has been the increasing number of PTAs among

Table 4.9
WTO disputes initiated per period: Number of disputes (#) and share of all WTO disputes (%), 1995–2014

Period	All WTO disputes (#)	Disputes with the EU and the U.S. as complainants			Disputes with the EU and the U.S. as respondents			EU-U.S. bilateral disputes	
		EU (#)	U.S. (#)	EU + U.S. (%)	EU (#)	U.S. (#)	EU + U.S. (%)	(#)	(%)
1995–1999	187	47	56	55.1	38	40	41.7	37	19.8
2000–2004	137	20	20	29.2	23	47	51.1	18	13.1
2005–2009	78	13	13	33.3	16	20	46.2	5	6.4
2010–2014	84	13	14	32.1	13	13	31.0	1	1.2
1995–2014	486	93	103	40.3	90	120	43.2	61*	12.7

*Including nine complaints by the United States against individual EU members in 1995–1999 and one in 2000.

WTO members. Indeed the chapter documents that, at least as far as the EU and the United States are concerned, the signature (or even perhaps the start of negotiation) of PTAs is associated with a sharp reduction in litigation activity between PTA members. It is to be expected, therefore, that the successful conclusion of the TPP and TTIP negotiations as well as the EU-India and EU-Japan negotiations would further reduce the number of WTO disputes, at least those involving the EU or the United States or both.

While a reduction in trade litigation should in principle be welcomed, there are also reasons for caution about the fact that PTAs seem to be associated with a reduction in WTO litigation. To the extent that the WTO's dispute settlement mechanism is characterized by fairness and transparency, its relative demise could be a loss for weaker parties within and outside the PTAs.

Table 4.10
Number of WTO disputes initiated each year by the EU and the United States against PTA partners, 1995–2014

	Pre- and post-WTO EU PTAs					Pre- and post-WTO U.S. PTAs				
	Pre-WTO PTAs	Post-WTO PTAs*				Pre-WTO PTAs	Post-WTO PTAs*			
	Norway	All 3	Chile	Korea	Mexico	NAFTA	All 3	Australia	Chile	Korea
1995	0	0/0	0	0	0	0	3/0	1	0	2
1996	0	2/0	0	1	1	1	2/0	1	0	1
1997	0	4/0	2	2	0	2	3/0	1	1	1
1998	0	0/0	0	0	0	1	1/0	1	0	0
1999	0	0/0	0	0	0	1	2/0	0	0	2
2000	0	1/0	1	0	0	2	0/0	0	0	0
2001	0	0/0	0	0	0	0	0/0	0	0	0
2002	0	1/0	0	1	0	1	0/0	0	0	0
2003	0	0/0	0	0	0	1	0/0	0	0	0
2004	0	0/1	0	0	1	1	0/0	0	0	0
2005	0	0/0	0	0	0	0	0/0	0	0	0
2006	0	0/1	0	0	1	1	0/0	0	0	0

Table 4.10 (continued)

	Pre- and post-WTO EU PTAs					Pre- and post-WTO U.S. PTAs				
	Pre-WTO PTAs	Post-WTO PTAs*				Pre-WTO PTAs	Post-WTO PTAs*			
	Norway	All 3	Chile	Korea	Mexico	NAFTA	All 3	Australia	Chile	Korea
2007	0	0/0	0	0	0	0	0/0	0	0	0
2008	0	0/0	0	0	0	0	0/0	0	0	0
2009	0	0/0	0	0	0	0	0/0	0	0	0
2010	0	0/0	0	0	0	0	0/0	0	0	0
2011	0	0/0	0	0	0	0	0/0	0	0	0
2012	0	0/0	0	0	0	0	0/0	0	0	0
2013	0	0/0	0	0	0	0	0/0	0	0	0
2014	0	0/0	0	0	0	0	0/0	0	0	0
1995–2014	0	8/2	3/0	4/0	1/2	11	11/0	4/0	1/0	6/0

*Number of disputes before the PTA/number of disputes after the PTA. A shaded cell indicates the year of entry into force of the PTA.

Table 4.11
Number of WTO disputes initiated each year against the EU and the United States by PTA partners, 1995–2014

	Pre- and post-WTO EU PTAs					Pre- and post-WTO U.S. PTAs				
	Pre-WTO PTAs	Post-WTO PTAs*				Pre-WTO PTAs	Post-WTO PTAs*			
	Norway	All 3	Chile	Korea	Mexico	NAFTA	All 3	Australia	Chile	Korea
1995	0	2/0	1	0	1	0	0/0	0	0	0
1996	0	1/0	0	0	1	1	0/0	0	0	0
1997	0	0/0	0	0	0	0	2/0	0	0	2
1998	0	0/0	0	0	0	1	1/0	0	1	0
1999	0	0/1	0	0	1	2	2/0	1	0	1
2000	0	0/0	0	0	0	1	3/0	1	1	1
2001	0	0/0	0	0	0	4	0/0	0	0	0
2002	0	0/0	0	0	0	4	1/0	0	0	1
2003	0	2/0	0	2	0	3	1/0	0	0	1
2004	0	1/0	0	1	0	2	0/0	0	0	0
2005	1	0/1	1	0	0	1	0/0	0	0	0
2006	1	0/0	0	0	0	1	0/0	0	0	0

Table 4.11 (continued)

	Pre- and post-WTO EU PTAs					Pre- and post-WTO U.S. PTAs				
	Pre-WTO PTAs	Post-WTO PTAs*				Pre-WTO PTAs	Post-WTO PTAs*			
	Norway	All 3	Chile	Korea	Mexico	NAFTA	All 3	Australia	Chile	Korea
2007	0	0/0	0	0	0	1	0/0	0	0	0
2008	0	0/0	0	0	0	3	0/0	0	0	0
2009	1	0/0	0	0	0	0	1/0	0	0	1
2010	0	0/0	0	0	0	0	0/0	0	0	0
2011	0	0/0	0	0	0	0	1/0	0	0	1
2012	0	0/0	0	0	0	0	0/0	0	0	0
2013	0	0/0	0	0	0	0	0/1	0	0	1
2014	0	0/0	0	0	0	0	0/0	0	0	0
1995–2014	3	6/2	1/1	3/0	2/1	24	11/1	2/0	2/0	7/1

*Number of disputes before the PTA/number of disputes after the PTA. A shaded cell indicates the year of entry into force of the PTA.

Table 4.12
Frequency of dispute settlement mechanism (DSM) in WTO-notified PTAs, as of end of 2012

DSM model	Share of all PTAs (%)
Political	30
Quasi-judicial	65
Judicial	5
All	100

Source: Chase et al. 2013.

Table 4.13
Dispute settlement mechanism used in EU and United States pre- and post-WTO PTAs, as of 2014

	EU	US
Pre-WTO PTAs	Nearly all quasi-judicial Main political exceptions: EU-Iceland, EU-Norway, EU-Switzerland	All quasi-judicial
Post-WTO PTAs	Nearly all quasi-judicial Main political exceptions: EU-Albania, EU-FYROM	All quasi-judicial

For the weaker party to a PTA, like most partners of the EU and the United States, the absence of WTO (and also formal PTA) litigation might mean that disputes are resolved in the old political/diplomatic fashion, which naturally gives more power to the stronger party. Unfortunately this study has not been able to establish why the signature of PTAs with the EU or the United States might lead to a lowering of WTO litigation, or whether there are disputes between the parties and if so how they are resolved. Certainly the TTIP would be different from other PTAs in this respect since the two partners are of equal economic size. Whether this means that bilateral EU-U.S. disputes would continue to be adjudicated by the WTO or instead would go to their bilateral DSM forum is obviously difficult to say based on this study.

For third parties, that is, countries outside a PTA, the absence of WTO litigation between PTA members might mean less transparency and potentially harmful consequences, especially if PTA disputes are resolved in a political/diplomatic fashion. Whether such harmful consequences rise with the aggregate economic size of the PTA members, as one would expect, and therefore that TTIP would be especially damaging in this respect, is again difficult to say based on this study.

In conclusion we can safely assert that PTAs seem to be associated with greater peace among PTA members, though we cannot say whether the benefits of such peace is fairly distributed between members and whether nonmembers benefit as well or suffer. These open questions urgently need answers at a time when PTAs are giving rise to mega PTAs, such as the Transatlantic Trade and Investment Partnership.

Notes

We would like to thank Anu Bradford, Marco Bronckers, Tessa Bridgeman, Bill Davey, Alan Deardorff, David Gantz, Henrik Horn, Jorge Huerta-Goldman, Gabrielle Marceau, Julie Pain, and Rhian-Mary Wood Richards for helping in preparing this chapter. We are indebted to Jagdish Bhagwati, Pravin Krishna, and Arvind Panagariya for including us in their conference, "Challenges Facing the World Trade System," held on September 30, 2014, at Columbia University in NYC, where we first presented this chapter.

1. PTAs between the United States and its partners typically enter into force at the same time or shortly after their signature. By contrast the delay between the time of signature and entry into force of PTAs between the EU and its partners is often one year or more.

2. Bown and Reynolds (2015) provide data to this effect.

3. Horn, Mavroidis, and Nordstrom (2005) advance thoughts on this score.

4. The total number of disputes adds up to twenty rather than twenty-six because Guatemala, Honduras, and Mexico all acted as complainants in the same three (banana) disputes with the EU.

5. The total number of disputes adds up to twenty rather than twenty-six because Guatemala, Honduras, and Mexico all acted as complainants in the same three (banana) disputes with the EU.

6. In addition the United States acted as complainant ten times against individual EU members.

7. Compare the results in Koremenos 2007.

8. Private parties have standing and can act as plaintiffs before a NAFTA Panel in certain disputes, including in antidumping cases. There have indeed been antidumping disputes between Mexico and the United States before NAFTA Panels. However it would be wrong to count these disputes as evidence that

either NAFTA partner has acted as "hawk," since it is at least doubtful whether Mexico or the United States would have agreed to a request to this effect, had private operators been obliged to act only through an instrument of diplomatic protection (à la WTO, where members represent private parties' interests).

References

Bown, Chad P., and Kara M. Reynolds. 2015. "Trade Flows and Trade Disputes." *Review of International Organizations* 10 (2): 145–177.

Chase, Claude, Jo-Ann Crawford, Pamela Ugaz, and Alan Yanovich. 2013. "Mapping of Dispute Settlement Mechanisms in Regional Trade Agreements, Innovative or Variations of a Theme?" WTO Discussion Paper ERSD-2013-07. Geneva: WTO.

Horn, Henrik, Petros C. Mavroidis, and Hakan Nordstrom. 2005. "Is the Use of the WTO Dispute Settlement System Biased? " In *The WTO and International Trade Law/Dispute Settlement*, ed. Petros C. Mavroidis and Alan O. Sykes, 454–486. Cheltenham, UK: Edward Elgar.

Horn, Henrik, Petros C. Mavroidis, and André Sapir. 2010. "Beyond the WTO? An Anatomy of EU and US Preferential Trade Agreements." *World Economy* 33:1565–1588.

Huerta-Goldman, Jorge. 2009. *Mexico in the WTO and NAFTA, Litigating International Trade Disputes*. Amsterdam: Kluwer.

Koremenos, Barbara. 2007. "If Only Half of International Agreements Have Dispute Resolution Provisions, Which Half Needs Explaining?" *Journal of Legal Studies* 36:189–221.

Li, Tan and Larry D. Qiu. 2014. "Free Trade Agreements and Trade Disputes." Mimeo., University of Hong Kong, Hong Kong, China.

5

Antidumping Provisions in Preferential Trade Agreements

Thomas J. Prusa

This chapter examines the economic rationale for and the implications of including antidumping (AD) provisions in preferential trade agreements (PTAs). Using information culled from 217 PTAs we find that nearly three out of four PTAs include either additional AD rules or prohibit the use of AD against PTA members. The provisions have the potential to significantly impact trade both through their direct effect on current protection and also as a possible signal of future developments in WTO AD rules.

AD provisions have a mixed welfare impact. PTA rules might make it easier to restrain intra-PTA imports. Such provisions may benefit global welfare by mitigating trade diversion stemming from preferential tariffs. More often, however, PTAs rules either prohibit AD protection against members or make AD protection harder to apply. As a result, PTAs may further tilt the playing field toward members by shifting contingent protection toward nonmembers—protection diversion.

We examine AD usage patterns by NAFTA countries as a case study of PTA rules. We find evidence that NAFTA rules have discouraged the intra-North American use of AD and likely increased the incidence against non-NAFTA countries. We also discuss usage trends across a wider set of PTAs and again find evidence that PTA rules have altered the pattern of AD activity, likely lowering the incidence against members and shifting the restrictions to nonmembers. These results confirm the theoretical possibility that PTA provisions shift the burden of trade restraints to nonmembers.

Overall, the findings highlight the need to be vigilant about the impact of these provisions. On the one hand, provisions first implemented in PTAs might be a guide to what to expect in future WTO negotiations (i.e., "beta" testing). On the other hand, PTA trade remedy provisions may erode the market access that nonmembers thought they had secured in prior WTO rounds.

5.1 Introduction

The question of whether PTAs are good or bad for the global trading system has always been contentious. With more experience our understanding of the consequences of PTAs has evolved. The traditional worries about welfare impacts associated with trade creation and diversion has been augmented with a multitude of new and unanticipated concerns.[1] This is partly due to the fact that over the past half century most countries have reduced tariffs across the board on a nondiscriminatory basis. As a result the value of PTA preferences has steadily fallen. How much trade creation and diversion can one expect when preferential rates are essentially the same as the most favored nation rates?[2] For many PTAs, therefore, the main welfare consequences likely stem from nontariff provisions. Indeed, as PTAs have evolved they increasingly address many issues beyond tariffs—government procurement, investor protections, labor standards, environmental protection, trade remedies, and so on.

This chapter examines the potential effects of one particular nontariff provision—antidumping. AD duties are designed to sanction exporters who engage in "unfair" trading practices that cause or threaten to cause *material* injury to domestic producers. When these unfair trading practices take the form of selling products below their "normal" price domestic producers can seek antidumping protection.[3]

While countervailing duty and safeguards are also important trade remedies, in this chapter we limit our focus to AD for two primary reasons. First, AD is used far more frequently than either countervailing duty or safeguards. According to Bown (2015), between January 1995 and December 2013 WTO members initiated 4,519 AD investigations, 335 countervailing duty (CVD) investigations, and 279 safeguard actions.[4] Second, in earlier work (Prusa and Teh 2011) we found PTAs are more likely to alter AD provisions than either countervailing duty or global safeguard rules.[5] This is partly due to the fact that few PTAs have created common policies on subsidies and state aid. Without such rules and given the global nature of subsidy distortions, there appears to be little motivation for PTA to limit the application of countervailing duty against members.

An important component of this study was the development of a database of the AD provisions contained in PTAs. Currently the database contains detailed information on AD provisions in 217 PTAs. Some PTAs include no discussion of or language related to AD. Other PTAs prohibit the use of AD against PTA members. Most often, however, we find PTAs allow the use of AD against PTA members but add some extra rules.

The remainder of this chapter is organized as follows. Section 5.2 discusses some of the political and economic justifications for including AD provisions in PTAs. As specific provisions are discussed, it is important to consider the possible conflicting motivations countries have when negotiating agreements. On the one hand, if AD duties serve primarily as "pressure release valves" (Fischer and Prusa 2003), then PTAs should include provisions that make it easier for domestic industries to raise barriers; on the other hand, if PTAs open closed home markets, then one of the traditional justifications for AD is eliminated and, consequently, PTAs should make it harder to impose AD duties, or possibly even prohibit AD against PTA members.

Section 5.3 examines the database and discusses the provisions included in these PTAs. PTAs are divided into three groups: those with AD rules, those that prohibit the use of AD, and those without any AD rules. In section 5.4 we will take a closer look at the pattern of AD use by NAFTA countries and the important issue of protection diversion. In section 5.5 we discuss the issue of protection diversion across a broader set of PTAs.

5.2 Background Issues

The Political Economy of Why Trade Remedies Are Needed in PTAs

Why do PTAs include trade remedy provisions? The rationale for PTAs to include preferential tariff schedules and definitions of rules of origin seems clear; however, it is less obvious why most PTAs should devote significant language amending and qualifying the use of trade remedies.[6]

One explanation for the widespread presence of AD rules in PTAs is the political economy of protectionism (Tharakan 1995). The long-term process of tariff liberalization during the post–World War II era has successfully reduced tariff rates to very low levels worldwide. Import-competing sectors continue to have an incentive to secure protection through whatever means they can find. Because the agreements have eliminated the most direct route to protection (tariffs), industries turn to the next best alternative, contingent protection. Given that the PTAs lower tariffs, industries may desire alternative language for offsetting provisions.

A second related explanation argues that contingent protection acts as a pressure release valve without which liberalization would not be able to proceed (Jackson 1997). Because trade liberalization often imposes costs of adjustment on uncompetitive industries, something needs to be done to manage the political consequences of these costs.[7] Incorporating AD rules in PTAs may be thought of as anticipating the possibility of this pressure and providing a means to deflate it with a temporary reversal of liberalization.

Bown and Crowley (2013) provide empirical evidence for this role. While motivated by Bagwell and Staiger's (1990) terms of trade theory, their results are consistent with the safety valve argument. In particular, among their conclusions they find the likelihood of these new contingent tariffs is increasing in the size of import surges. In effect, protection increases to offset increased imports. Bown and Tovar's (2011) findings are also consistent with this pressure release perspective. Their findings suggest temporary trade barriers (of which AD is the most widely used) increase as tariffs decrease.

Empirically, we find that the AD rules in PTAs generally make protection more difficult to grant. A third explanation addresses why this might be. The inclusion of PTA provisions that restrict their use is consistent with the view that AD protection is necessitated because countries are insufficiently open to trade. For example, Mastel (1998) argues that dumping is driven by closed home markets. The elimination of barriers for intra-PTA trade reduces the ability of firms to dump as they no longer have a protected home market where they can earn supernormal profits.[8]

Possible Economic Consequences

Each of the three explanations suggests that PTAs may alter the demand for AD protection. On the one hand, import-competing sectors need to be given assurance that they can protect themselves from the unanticipated consequences of the regional liberalization program. Retaining AD in the PTA helps maintain political support for the agreement. On the other hand, regional liberalization might also eliminate unfair trade.

To the extent that PTA provisions make AD protection easier to obtain, they are similar to long transition periods, complicated rules of origin, and carve-outs for sensitive sectors in PTAs, all of which result in a slower process of liberalization for import-competing sectors. Instead of directly cushioning the effects of the PTA by drawing out the process of tariff elimination, AD duties achieve a different cushioning effect by specifying a set of conditions under which the regional liberalization may be temporarily suspended or partially reversed. Such rules may hurt PTA partners and moderate beneficial trade creation; they may be beneficial from a global perspective, however, if they serve to lessen trade diversion.

PTA provisions that make AD protection more difficult to grant have more subtle effects. Abolishing or restricting the use of AD on PTA partners' trade will most likely increase intra-bloc trade. The welfare effects, however, are uncertain. The ambiguity stems from the well-known insight that preferential trade arrangements have both trade creation and trade diversion effects (Viner 1950). Rules on AD protection can clearly create and divert trade (Bown and Crowley 2007).

The danger is that as intra-regional trade expands because of preferential tariffs, AD protection will become increasingly directed at the imports of nonmembers. Bhagwati (1993) and Bhagwati and Panagariya (1996) foresaw this danger, arguing that the elastic and selective nature of contingent protection increases the risk of trade diversion from PTAs. Bhagwati states:

> My belief that FTAs will lead to considerable trade diversion because of modern methods of protection, which are inherently selective and can be captured readily by protectionist purposes is one that may have been borne out in the European Community. It is well known that the European Community has used antidumping actions and VERs profusely to erect Fortress Europe against the Far East. Cannot much of this be a trade-diverting policy in response to the intensification of internal competition among member states of the European Community? (Bhagwati 1993, 37)

So apart from discrimination introduced by preferential tariffs, Bhagwati and Panagariya are concerned that the establishment of PTAs can lead to more discrimination against non-PTA countries through more frequent AD actions. They conjecture that there is a protection analogue to the standard "trade creation-trade diversion" impact of PTAs. PTA members are spared from AD actions but non PTA members face even greater AD scrutiny.

The Incidence of Antidumping Actions

Before discussing the role of trade remedies in PTAs, it is useful to review the incidence of trade remedy actions over the past decade (Bown 2011b). Over the 1995–2013 period the WTO was notified of 4,519 AD investigations (Bown 2015). There has been a significant change in the use of these remedies. The four major users (Australia, Canada, the EC/EU, and the United States) accounted for more than 90 percent of the AD initiations during the 1980s and were also the target in more than 75 percent of the investigations (Prusa 2001). By contrast, countries from all parts of the world are now active users and targets of AD protection (Prusa 2005). Since 1995 nearly 50 countries have initiated AD cases and more than 100 countries have been the subject of AD investigations.[9] In a sense, the broadened set of uses and targets of AD remedies is just another example of increased globalization.

AD duties can reinforce the trade diversion effects of a PTA: on average the imposition of AD duties reduces subject imports from the targeted country by about half (Prusa 2001). When faced with contingent protection measures, non-PTA members will be at an even greater disadvantage than that created by the preferential tariffs. This is exactly the danger Bhagwati (1993) and Bhagwati and Panagariya (1996) predicted.

5.3 Antidumping Provisions in PTAs

A summary of the 217 PTAs surveyed is given in table 5.1. The PTAs in our survey represent 83 percent of the 263 regional and preferential agreements "notified to" the WTO. As seen, the coverage is quite thorough, involving PTAs from all corners of the world: Europe, North America, the Caribbean, Latin America, Eastern Europe, Asia, and the Pacific, Africa, and the Middle East.

The AD provisions for each PTA were mapped into three distinct groups: (1) those that *disallow* AD among the members,(2) those with *no language* regarding AD, and (3) those with specific *rules* regarding AD.

In table 5.2 we tabulate the PTAs by the agreement type and how they were notified to the WTO. The sample is dominated by free trade agreements—86 percent of the PTAs in our sample are free trade areas; 7 percent are customs unions; and the remaining are preferential trade agreements (table 5.2). There is not a significant variation in the type of AD provision in the PTA by agreement type—in all cases about two-thirds of the PTAs either prohibit AD or have additional rules governing the imposition of AD.

Table 5.1
PTA and antidumping rules

PTA name	**Year of entry into force**	**AD rules**
Andean Community (CAN)	1988	Rules
Armenia—Kazakhstan	2001	No Rules
Armenia—Moldova	1995	No Rules
Armenia—Russian Federation	1993	No Rules
Armenia—Turkmenistan	1996	No Rules
Armenia—Ukraine	1996	No Rules
ASEAN—Australia—New Zealand	2010	No Rules
ASEAN—China	2005	Rules
ASEAN—India	2010	Rules
ASEAN—Japan	2008	No Rules
ASEAN—Korea, Republic of	2010	Rules
ASEAN Free Trade Area (AFTA)	1992	No Rules
Asia Pacific Trade Agreement (APTA)	1976	No Rules
Australia—Chile	2009	Rules
Australia—New Zealand (ANZCERTA)	1983	Prohibited
Australia—Papua New Guinea (PATCRA)	1977	Rules
Brunei Darussalam—Japan	2008	No Rules
Canada—Chile	1997	Prohibited
Canada—Colombia	2011	Rules
Canada—Costa Rica	2002	Rules
Canada—Israel	1997	No Rules
Canada—Peru	2009	Rules
Caribbean Community and Common Market (CARICOM)	1973	Rules
Central American Common Market (CACM)	1961	No Rules
Central European Free Trade Agreement (CEFTA)	2007	Rules
Chile—China	2006	Rules
Chile—Colombia	2009	Rules

Table 5.1 (continued)

PTA name	Year of entry into force	AD rules
Chile—Costa Rica (Chile—Central America)	2002	Rules
Chile—El Salvador (Chile—Central America)	2002	Rules
Chile—Honduras (Chile—Central America)	2008	Rules
Chile—India	2007	Rules
Chile—Japan	2007	No Rules
Chile—Mexico	1999	No Rules
China—Costa Rica	2011	Rules
China—Hong Kong, China	2003	Prohibited
China—Macao, China	2003	Prohibited
China—New Zealand	2008	Rules
China—Singapore	2009	Rules
Colombia—Mexico	1995	Rules
Common Economic Zone (CEZ)	2004	Rules
Common Market for Eastern and Southern Africa (COMESA)	1994	Rules
Commonwealth of Independent States (CIS)	1994	Rules
Costa Rica—Mexico	1995	Rules
Dominican Republic—Central America	2001	Rules
Dominican Republic—Central America—United States Free Trade Agreement (CAFTA-DR)	2006	Rules
East African Community (EAC)	2000	Rules
EC Treaty	1958	Prohibited
Economic & Monetary Community of Central Africa (CEMAC)	1999	No Rules
Economic Community of West African States (ECOWAS)	1993	Rules
Economic Cooperation Organization (ECO)	1992	Rules
EFTA—Albania	2010	Rules
EFTA—Canada	2009	Rules

Table 5.1 (continued)

PTA name	Year of entry into force	AD rules
EFTA—Chile	2004	Prohibited
EFTA—Colombia	2011	Rules
EFTA—Egypt	2007	Rules
EFTA—Former Yugoslav Republic of Macedonia	2002	Rules
EFTA—Israel	1993	Rules
EFTA—Jordan	2002	Rules
EFTA—Korea, Republic of	2006	Rules
EFTA—Lebanon	2007	Rules
EFTA—Mexico	2001	Rules
EFTA—Morocco	1999	Rules
EFTA—Palestinian Authority	1999	Rules
EFTA—Peru	2011	Rules
EFTA—SACU	2008	Rules
EFTA—Serbia	2010	Rules
EFTA—Singapore	2003	Prohibited
EFTA—Tunisia	2005	Rules
EFTA—Turkey	1992	Rules
Egypt—Turkey	2007	Rules
EU—Albania	2006	Rules
EU—Algeria	2005	Rules
EU—Andorra	1991	No Rules
EU—Bosnia and Herzegovina	2008	Rules
EU—Cameroon	2009	Rules
EU—CARIFORUM States EPA	2008	Rules
EU—Chile	2003	Rules
EU—Côte d'Ivoire	2009	Rules
EU—Eastern and Southern Africa States EPA	2009	Rules
EU—Egypt	2004	Rules

Table 5.1 (continued)

PTA name	Year of entry into force	AD rules
EU—Faroe Islands	1997	Rules
EU—Former Yugoslav Republic of Macedonia	2001	Rules
EU—Iceland	1973	Rules
EU—Israel	2000	Rules
EU—Jordan	2002	Rules
EU—Korea, Republic of	2011	Rules
EU—Lebanon	2003	Rules
EU—Mexico	2000	Rules
EU—Montenegro	2008	Rules
EU—Morocco	2000	Rules
EU—Norway	1973	Rules
EU—Overseas Countries and Territories (OCT)	1971	No Rules
EU—Palestinian Authority	1997	Rules
EU—Papua New Guinea / Fiji	2009	Rules
EU—San Marino	2002	No Rules
EU—Serbia	2010	Rules
EU—South Africa	2000	Rules
EU—Switzerland—Liechtenstein	1973	Rules
EU—Syria	1977	Rules
EU—Tunisia	1998	Rules
EU—Turkey	1996	Rules
Eurasian Economic Community (EAEC)	1997	Rules
European Economic Area (EEA)	1994	Prohibited
European Free Trade Association (EFTA)	1960	Prohibited
Faroe Islands—Norway	1993	Rules
Faroe Islands—Switzerland	1995	No Rules
Georgia—Armenia	1998	No Rules
Georgia—Azerbaijan	1996	No Rules

Table 5.1 (continued)

PTA name	**Year of entry into force**	**AD rules**
Georgia—Kazakhstan	1999	No Rules
Georgia—Russian Federation	1994	No Rules
Georgia—Turkmenistan	2000	No Rules
Georgia—Ukraine	1996	No Rules
Guatemala—the Separate Customs Territory of Taiwan, Penghu, Kinmen, and Matsu	2006	Rules
Gulf Cooperation Council (GCC)	2003	No Rules
Honduras—El Salvador and the Separate Customs Territory of Taiwan, Penghu, Kinmen, and Matsu	2008	Rules
Hong Kong, China—New Zealand	2011	Rules
Iceland—Faroe Islands	2006	Rules
India—Afghanistan	2003	Rules
India—Bhutan	2006	No Rules
India—Japan	2011	Rules
India—Malaysia	2011	Rules
India—Nepal	2009	No Rules
India—Singapore	2005	Rules
India—Sri Lanka	2001	Rules
Israel—Mexico	2000	Rules
Japan—Indonesia	2008	Rules
Japan—Malaysia	2006	No Rules
Japan—Mexico	2005	No Rules
Japan—Mexico	2005	No Rules
Japan—Peru	2012	Rules
Japan—Philippines	2008	Rules
Japan—Singapore	2002	Rules
Japan—Switzerland	2009	No Rules
Japan—Thailand	2007	No Rules
Japan—Viet Nam	2009	No Rules

Table 5.1 (continued)

PTA name	Year of entry into force	AD rules
Jordan—Singapore	2005	Rules
Korea, Republic of—Chile	2004	Rules
Korea, Republic of—India	2010	Rules
Korea, Republic of—Singapore	2006	Rules
Kyrgyz Republic—Armenia	1995	No Rules
Kyrgyz Republic—Kazakhstan	1995	No Rules
Kyrgyz Republic—Moldova	1996	No Rules
Kyrgyz Republic—Russian Federation	1993	No Rules
Kyrgyz Republic—Ukraine	1998	No Rules
Kyrgyz Republic—Uzbekistan	1998	No Rules
Lao People's Democratic Republic—Thailand	1991	No Rules
Latin American Integration Association (LAIA)	1981	Rules
Melanesian Spearhead Group (MSG)	1994	Rules
MERCOSUR—India	2009	Rules
Mexico—Central America	2012	Rules
Mexico—Uruguay	2004	Rules
New Zealand—Malaysia	2010	Rules
New Zealand—Singapore	2001	Rules
Nicaragua and the Separate Customs Territory of Taiwan, Penghu, Kinmen, and Matsu	2008	Rules
North American Free Trade Agreement (NAFTA)	1994	Rules
Pacific Island Countries Trade Agreement (PICTA)	2003	Rules
Pakistan—China	2007	Rules
Pakistan—Malaysia	2008	Rules
Pakistan—Sri Lanka	2005	Rules
Panama—Chile	2008	Rules
Panama—Costa Rica (Panama—Central America)	2008	Rules
Panama—El Salvador (Panama—Central America)	2003	Rules
Panama—Honduras (Panama—Central America)	2009	Rules

Table 5.1 (continued)

PTA name	Year of entry into force	AD rules
Panama—Singapore	2006	Rules
Panama and the Separate Customs Territory of Taiwan, Penghu, Kinmen, and Matsu	2004	Rules
Pan-Arab Free Trade Area (PAFTA)	1998	Rules
Peru—Chile	2009	Rules
Peru—China	2010	Rules
Peru—Korea, Republic of	2011	Rules
Peru—Mexico	2012	Rules
Peru—Singapore	2009	Rules
Protocol on Trade Negotiations (PTN)	1973	No Rules
Singapore—Australia	2003	Rules
South Asian Free Trade Agreement (SAFTA)	2006	No Rules
South Asian Preferential Trade Arrangement (SAPTA)	1995	Rules
South Pacific Regional Trade and Economic Cooperation Agreement (SPARTECA)	1981	Rules
Southern African Customs Union (SACU)	2004	Rules
Southern African Development Community (SADC)	2000	Rules
Southern Common Market (MERCOSUR)	1991	Rules
Thailand—Australia	2005	Rules
Thailand—New Zealand	2005	Rules
Trans-Pacific Strategic Economic Partnership	2006	Rules
Turkey—Albania	2008	Rules
Turkey—Bosnia and Herzegovina	2003	Rules
Turkey—Chile	2011	Rules
Turkey—Croatia	2003	Rules
Turkey—Former Yugoslav Republic of Macedonia	2000	Rules
Turkey—Georgia	2008	Rules
Turkey—Israel	1997	Rules

Table 5.1 (continued)

PTA name	**Year of entry into force**	**AD rules**
Turkey—Jordan	2011	Rules
Turkey—Montenegro	2010	Rules
Turkey—Morocco	2006	Rules
Turkey—Palestinian Authority	2005	Rules
Turkey—Serbia	2010	Rules
Turkey—Syria	2007	Rules
Turkey—Tunisia	2005	Rules
Ukraine—Azerbaijan	1996	No Rules
Ukraine—Belarus	2006	Rules
Ukraine—Former Yugoslav Republic of Macedonia	2001	Rules
Ukraine—Kazakhstan	1998	No Rules
Ukraine—Moldova	2005	Rules
Ukraine—Russian Federation	1994	No Rules
Ukraine—Tajikistan	2002	No Rules
Ukraine—Uzbekistan	1996	No Rules
Ukraine -Turkmenistan	1995	No Rules
US—Australia	2005	No Rules
US—Bahrain	2006	No Rules
US—Chile	2004	No Rules
US—Israel	1985	No Rules
US—Jordan	2001	No Rules
US—Morocco	2006	No Rules
US—Oman	2009	No Rules
US—Peru	2009	Rules
US—Singapore	2004	No Rules
West African Economic and Monetary Union (WAEMU)	2000	Rules

Table 5.2
AD provisions in PTAs

	Prohibited	Rules	No rules	Total
Agreement type				
Customs union	1	10	5	**16**
	(6%)	(63%)	(31%)	
FTA	7	131	49	**187**
	(4%)	(70%)	(26%)	
Partial scope agreement	0	9	4	**13**
	(0%)	(69%)	(31%)	
Other	1	0	0	**1**
	(100%)	(0%)	(0%)	
Total	**9**	**150**	**58**	**217**
	(4%)	(69%)	(27%)	
How notified				
Enabling clause	0	22	8	**30**
	(0%)	(73%)	(27%)	
GATT Article XXIV	8	126	49	**183**
	(4%)	(69%)	(27%)	
Other/Not notified	1	2	1	**4**
	(25%)	(50%)	(25%)	
Total	**9**	**150**	**58**	**217**
	(4%)	(69%)	(27%)	

About 84 percent of the PTAs in our sample were notified under Article XXIV of GATT and 14 percent were notified under the Enabling Clause.[10] With few exceptions all the PTAs were notified to the WTO.[11] Once again, we do not find a significant variation in the type of AD provision in the PTA by notification method.

In previous work (Prusa and Teh 2011) we discussed the ways that PTAs can alter AD rules. Broadly stated, there are four primary categories of rules. First, there are *rules that affect the likelihood of imposing AD duties*. Some PTAs require parties to make greater efforts to negotiate a solution prior to the formal investigation. Other PTAs altered key requirements such as the *de minimis* dumping margins. Under WTO rules, an AD investigation is to be terminated immediately if the dumping margin is found to be less than 2 percent of the export price or if the volume of dumped imports from a particular country is less than 3 percent of imports. PTA provisions that specify higher *de minimis* dumping margins or higher *de minimis* volumes than the WTO benchmarks will treat PTA partners more favorably. This is because even though exports from PTA and non-PTA sources may be found to have the same dumping margin, the investigation against the PTA member will terminate while the investigation against non-PTA sources will continue if the margin turns out to be higher than the WTO benchmark but less than or equal to that prescribed in the PTA.

Second, there are *rules that affect the size of the duty*. This is often referred to as a lesser duty rule. Multilateral rules encourage but do not mandate the application of an AD duty that is less than the dumping margin if a lesser duty would be adequate to remove the injury to the domestic industry. A lesser duty rule or mandate in a PTA can provide a significant advantage to members. In the event that an AD action is taken by a country against a group of suppliers, some of which happen to be PTA members and others not, then PTA partners will face a lower AD duty even though the AD investigation might have found the same dumping margin against all suppliers.

Third, there are *rules that shorten the duration of the duties*. Under multilateral rules, definitive AD duties are to be terminated within five years from its imposition. Thus, PTAs that impose a shorter termination period on regional partners will give an advantage to exporters from those countries. AD duties against exports from PTA partners will already have been phased out while exports from non-PTA partners can continue to be restrained by the duties.

Fourth, there are *rules that create a regional body to conduct investigations or review or remand final determinations.* This is a unique innovation in PTAs. The PTA literature suggests that a regional institution can have a significant role on the frequency of AD initiations and measures against PTA partners. The best-known example of such a regional institution occurs in Chapter 19 of NAFTA, which allows a binational panel review of the final AD determination made by the authority of another NAFTA partner.

5.4 The NAFTA Experience

The inclusion of the binational panel review of AD determination in the NAFTA agreement was controversial (Mankiw and Swagel 2005). There are differing views on the impact of this specific provision. On the one hand, using a time dummy to control for the pre-/post-PTA effect Jones (2000) finds that there was a statistically significant reduction in both U.S. AD filings against Canada and Canadian AD filings against the United States after NAFTA took effect. On the other hand, Blonigen (2005) incorporates information on actual panel activity and finds no evidence that binational reviews under Chapter 19 of NAFTA affected the frequency of U.S. filings or affirmative determinations against Canada and Mexico.[12] The fact that the United States has refused to include a similar provision in any subsequent PTAs suggests that U.S. policymakers feel that the bi-national panels have altered the pattern of protection. Gagné and Paulin (2013) succinctly summarize the view from Washington:

> Past cases of trade disputes with Canada, such as Pork, Swine, and Lumber III, have made Congress more and more suspicious towards the NAFTA panel review system. In Lumber IV, some senators, representing lumber producing constituencies, complained against the ruling of the injury panel. For these senators, this "runaway" or "rogue" panel prevented the US from offsetting the effect of Canadian unfair trade practices and, thus, violated the rights of American industries and workers to be protected against such practices. These concerns were voiced by Senator Chambliss: "*We cannot allow our domestic industries and their workers to become defenseless against unfairly traded imports due to flawed decisions by runaway panels.*" For Senator Craig, "*the rights of US lumber producers to remedy against unfairly traded imports from Canada have been improperly curtailed by a runaway NAFTA Chapter 19 dispute settlement panel.*" Senator Lincoln found it troubling that panelists are empowered to review trade remedy cases as to whether they are consistent with US law, especially when decisions actually overturn US law. Revealingly, Senator

Craig commented: "Simply put, here we go again having *an international body full of individuals who disregard US law, dictating the US courts how to interpret our own laws*." (emphasis added, 419)

To get a perspective on the impact of AD rules on NAFTA AD activity we collected information on all AD filings by Canada, Mexico, and the United States since January 1980. For each year we calculated the number of cases initiated by the NAFTA members against nonmember countries and against fellow NAFTA members.[13] The results are given in figure 5.1 and table 5.3.

We begin by plotting NAFTA AD filings pre- and post-NAFTA enactment (figure 5.1). The dotted line depicts the number of AD cases filed by Mexico, Canada, or the United States against non-NAFTA countries and the solid line is the number of AD cases filed by NAFTA members against a fellow NAFTA country. As seen, it is clear that in broad terms the two series are clearly related. This suggests that AD activity is driven first and foremost by industry trade trends and secondarily by country-level considerations. That being said, the relationship clearly is not as tight following NAFTA. During the early period (pre-1994) the correlation is 0.82 compared with the later period (post-1994) when the correlation is 0.56. Without controlling for other factors the figure is consistent with the view that the incidence of intra-NAFTA disputes fell after 1994: the NAFTA line clearly falls below the non-NAFTA line for almost the entire 1994–2013 period.

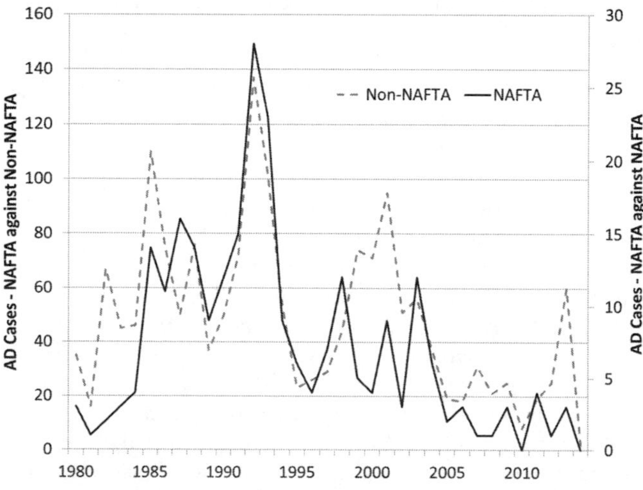

Figure 5.1
NAFTA antidumping cases.

Table 5.3
NAFTA antidumping cases, pre- and post-1994

1980–2013

	Canada	Mexico	USA	NAFTA	Non-NAFTA	Total
Canada	0	6	67	73	323	396
	(0%)	(2%)	(17%)	(18%)	(82%)	
Mexico	5	0	74	79	183	262
	(2%)	(0%)	(28%)	(30%)	(70%)	
USA	53	45	0	98	1198	1,296
	(4%)	(3%)	(0%)	(8%)	(92%)	
NAFTA total	58	51	141	250	1704	1,954
	(3%)	(3%)	(7%)	(13%)	(87%)	

Pre-NAFTA

	Canada	Mexico	USA	NAFTA	Non-NAFTA	Total
Canada	0	3	47	50	158	208
	(0%)	(1%)	(23%)	(24%)	(76%)	
Mexico	4	0	46	50	92	142
	(3%)	(0%)	(32%)	(35%)	(65%)	
USA	36	19	0	55	668	723
	(5%)	(3%)	(0%)	(8%)	(92%)	
NAFTA total	40	22	93	155	918	1,073
	(4%)	(2%)	(9%)	(14%)	(86%)	

Post-NAFTA

	Canada	Mexico	USA	NAFTA	Non-NAFTA	Total
Canada	0	3	20	23	165	188
	(0%)	(2%)	(11%)	(12%)	(88%)	
Mexico	1	0	28	29	91	120
	(1%)	(0%)	(23%)	(24%)	(76%)	
USA	17	26	0	43	530	573
	(3%)	(5%)	(0%)	(8%)	(92%)	
NAFTA total	18	29	48	95	786	881
	(2%)	(3%)	(5%)	(11%)	(89%)	

Table 5.3 presents a summary tabulation. The table is split into three parts: the upper panel reports all AD activity between January 1980 and December 2013, the middle panel reports AD activity for the pre-NAFTA period (between January 1980 and December 1993) and the bottom panel reports AD activity for the post-NAFTA period (between January 1994 and December 2013). Over the entire period, intra-NAFTA filings have accounted for just 13 percent of all NAFTA-sourced AD investigations. This is far less than NAFTA partners' share of overall trade. This preference to *not* file AD against fellow NAFTA partners is seen both in the pre- and post-NAFTA periods and echoes a finding in Blonigen 2005.

The key statistics for the purposes of this discussion is the incidence rate pre-NAFTA as compared with post-NAFTA. Pre-NAFTA intra-filings accounted for 14 percent of all AD filings. Post-NAFTA intra-filings accounted for 11 percent of all AD filings. This difference is statistically significant at the 1 percent level (binomial test). Again, without controlling for many other factors that could be influencing AD activity, the raw data does support the view that NAFTA has reduced intra-filings.

What is particularly fascinating is that the NAFTA review panel has been the source of considerable unhappiness in the United States (as already discussed). Growing U.S. resentment against international trade and international institutions is likely due to the fact U.S. commentators are reflecting on what they feel is the loss of U.S. autonomy in making its trade policy. The data suggests, however, that the commentators are missing the larger story: namely, that the NAFTA rules particularly seem to have altered Canadian and Mexican filing patterns targeting the United States. Consider the following. In both the pre- and post-NAFTA periods intra-NAFTA filings have accounted for 8 percent of U.S. AD filings. By this metric, Canada and Mexico have gained little as a result of the NAFTA provisions. Now, consider the filing behavior of Canada and Mexico. The data suggests the United States has gained disproportionately with respect to being targeted. Mexico's filing rate against the United States fell from 32 percent to 23 percent and Canada's filing rate against the United States fell from 23 percent to 11 percent. By contrast, Mexico's and Canada's filing rate against one another fell but by far less (certainly due in part to the low level of cases against one another throughout the period). Arguably, in terms of being subject to AD duties U.S. firms have been the big winner as a result of NAFTA.

While the overall data provides compelling evidence that there has been a change in filing incidence post-NAFTA, additional evidence can be found when we drill down and look at two large AD steel cases during the post-NAFTA period. In the 2001–2002 period the U.S. steel industry was struggling with a number of large steel producers declaring bankruptcy (e.g., National Steel, Bethlehem Steel, LTV Steel). During that time the U.S. steel industry was aggressively seeking protection, filing dozens of AD cases and also initiating the largest safeguard action in U.S. history.

Curiously, despite the industry's desperate attempts to reduce imports, Canadian and Mexican producers were conspicuously absent from most of the investigations. For instance, consider the 2000–2001 hot-rolled steel case and the 2001–2002 cold-rolled steel case. The hot-rolled case involved eleven major steel exporters: Argentina, China, India, Indonesia, Kazakhstan, Netherlands, Romania, South Africa, Taiwan, Thailand, and Ukraine. Moreover, this hot-rolled case followed on the heels of a just completed hot-rolled case involving three other steel exporters (Brazil, Japan, Russia). Taking the 1997–1998 and 2000–2001 cases together, fourteen of the seventeen largest hot-rolled suppliers to the United States were named. Noticeably absent were steel producers located in Mexico and Canada.[14] As shown in figure 5.2 the Mexican and Canadian steel producers exported large volumes at prices below those charged by other

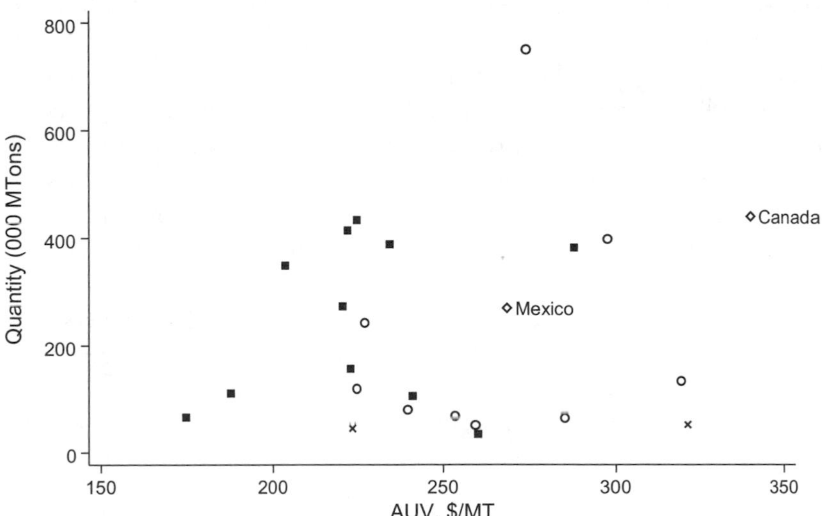

Figure 5.2
U.S. hot-rolled steel—antidumping case (2000–2001).
Source: USITC 2001.

countries named in the investigation. On the x-axis we graph the AUV ($/ton) charged by each country in the year before the case was initiated. On the y-axis we graph the quantity of exports sold to the United States (in the year prior to the filing). In the figure, the open circle marker represents the (price, volume) combination for non-named suppliers. The solid square markers denote the (price, volume) combination for named suppliers. The two X markers denote the (price, volume) for two of the countries (Brazil and Japan) named in the previous hot-rolled case and were already subject to an AD order.[15] As seen, while Canada charged high prices, its volume was larger than any other supplier to the U.S. market. Mexico, on the other hand, had a lower price than one named supplier (Netherlands) and a comparable price to another named supplier (Thailand). At least as damning, Mexico's volume was larger than six of the ten named suppliers. Given the U.S. Department of Commerce's discretion at computing margins, there is little doubt that Mexico would have been found to have dumped had it been included in the case.

The 2001–2002 U.S. cold-rolled steel case offers another clear example of the preferences that NAFTA seems to be providing NAFTA firms. This dispute involved a remarkable twenty countries: Argentina, Australia, Belgium, Brazil, China, France, Germany, India, Japan, Korea, Netherlands, New Zealand, Russia, South Africa, Spain, Sweden, Taiwan, Thailand, Turkey, and Venezuela. The case was the most expansive AD dispute in a decade. As shown in figure 5.3 Mexico and Canada stand out as true outliers—they were the fifth and sixth largest foreign suppliers to the United States. As in the previous figure, the open circle marker represents the (price, volume) combination for non-named suppliers. The solid square markers denote the (price, volume) combination for named suppliers. In terms of pricing, Mexico's prices were among the lowest third of all suppliers and Canada's prices were lower than five named countries. As with the hot-rolled case, the fact that both NAFTA partners were not-named suggests that NAFTA rules discourage U.S. producers from seeking to levy duties.

Interestingly, Bown (2013) finds a similar phenomenon we see happening with NAFTA and AD extends to application of the other major temporary trade barrier policy (safeguards). He examines steel safeguard protection by the United States and finds the altered pattern of protection (NAFTA preference) documented in the preceding discussion also happened with the U.S. application of the steel safeguard in 2001–2003 that exempted NAFTA countries.

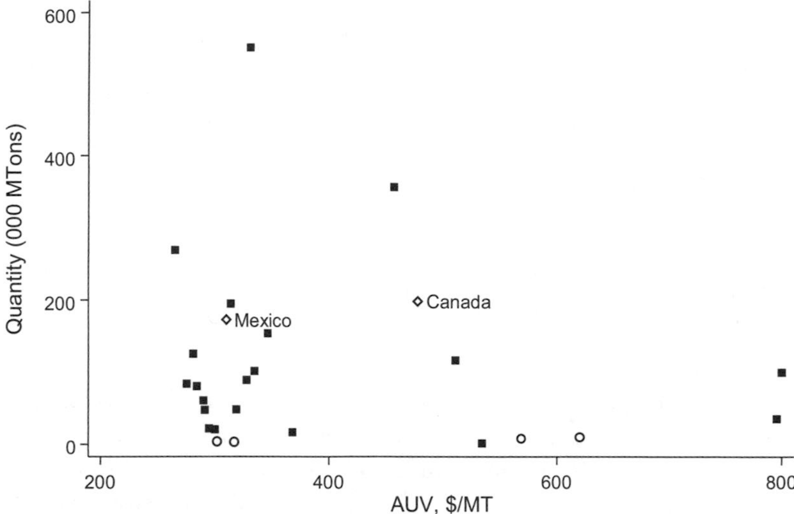

Figure 5.3
U.S. cold-rolled steel—antidumping and CVD case (2001–2002).
Source: USITC 2002.

Finally, by way of comparison we note that U.S. filings against partners in non-NAFA PTAs have also generally decreased post-enactment. In table 5.4 we present the average number of AD filings per year for four other PTAs (Australia-US, US-Chile, US-Israel, US-Singapore), none of which has an additional AD rules. While the level of AD activity has always been low, the data nevertheless shows that filings fell post-enactment for three of the four PTAs. This raises the specter that the effect attributed to AD provisions might indeed be related to PTA membership but not really driven by AD rules. For instance, the PTA might simply engender "good will" or political closeness. In Prusa and Teh 2010, we explore this issue at some length and find that on average, AD filing patterns do not change for PTAs without AD rules—and that the U.S. pattern is the outlier.

5.5 Trade and Protection Diversion

A concern with PTAs that prohibit or add additional rules to trade remedies is that the provisions do not guarantee that disputes will not occur. The rules may mean fewer cases will be filed against PTA members, but that tells us little about what may happen to *other* countries. The PTA

Table 5.4
U.S. AD cases against PTA partners (average per year), pre- and post-PTA enactment

	Australia-US	US-Chile	US-Israel	US-Singapore
Pre-PTA	0.28	0.33	0.20	0.38
Post-PTA	0.20	0.00	0.33	0.00
% change	-29%	-100%	67%	-100%

provisions might simply lead to fewer intra-PTA disputes but not change filings against non-PTA members. Or, it is possible that industries seeking to reduce overall import competition will file more cases against non-PTA countries. Bhagwati (1993) and Bhagwati and Panagariya (1996) argued that the elastic and selective nature of administered protection made "protection diversion" a particularly pernicious and unforeseen consequence of PTAs. Administered protection is elastic because it is arbitrary and the targets can be easily manipulated. So apart from discrimination introduced by preferential tariffs, PTAs can lead to more discrimination against nonmembers of the PTA through more frequent trade remedy actions against them: trade diversion begets protection diversion which begets more trade diversion.

AD is an ideal candidate for protection diversion. Given WTO rules, unfair trade is poorly measured; often all exporters to a market will be found guilty of dumping. Over the past decade it is increasingly rare for authorities to *not* determine unfair pricing exists.[16] Unfair trade may be practiced by suppliers within as well as outside the trade bloc. But given that PTA rules on AD make it more difficult (or for some agreements impossible) to apply AD against intra-bloc members, in these cases AD duties may get applied only against countries outside the bloc. AD duties are rarely less than 10 percent *ad valorem*, so it is quite possible the secondary trade diversion (caused by protection diversion) will surpass the primary trade diversion (caused by preferential tariff treatment).[17] Moreover, as Bhagwati has argued, the source of the industry's injury might be truly rooted in the PTA preferences but the PTA rules may result in the AD duties being imposed on non-PTA sources.

To get a sense of the extent of the changing incidence of AD protection we augmented the basic PTA database with information on worldwide AD activity dating back to 1980. The earlier years of data were gathered to allow for a better comparison of pre-PTA versus post-PTA filing patterns. All together, we have information on more than six thousand AD cases that were initiated by WTO countries that belong to at least one PTA.

For each importing country the annual number of AD disputes initiated by PTA members against PTA members (intra-PTA filings) is calculated. Given that PTAs are enacted in a variety of years, we abstract from calendar time and instead consider time as measured relative to the year the PTA was enacted. For each PTA, year zero is the year the PTA was enacted, year $t - 1$ is the year before, year $t - 2$ is two years before enactment, $t + 1$ is the year after, and so on. This view of time allows us to conveniently aggregate across PTAs.

In figure 5.4 the aggregate number of AD disputes relative to each PTA's inception is plotted.[18] This chart only looks at intra-PTA activity. The results are pretty compelling. During the years prior to the PTA enactment, intra-PTA AD activity is growing. The year the PTA is enacted ($t = 0$) the number of AD disputes drops sharply and remains much lower than the pre-PTA level. On average, during the ten years prior to the PTA there were 29.5 AD cases per year; by contrast, during the ten

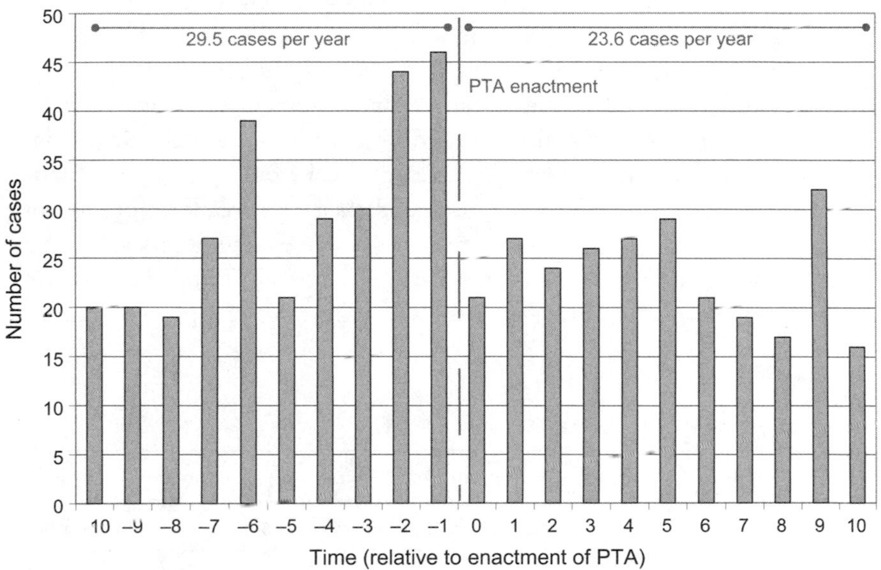

Figure 5.4
Intra-PTA AD filings.

years following the PTA there were just 23.6 cases per year—about a 20 percent reduction.

While the results are striking the analysis does not control for the possibility that AD activity in general—AD actions against both PTA and non-PTA members—may have fallen at a time coincidental with the enactment of the PTA. Said differently, the analysis is not able to distinguish the PTA effect from some other trend. For instance, given that the Uruguay Round was concluded in 1994 and given that a number of PTAs were enacted in the mid-1990s, it is possible that the observed decline in AD activity might be a result of AD provisions in the Uruguay Round rather than the PTA provisions.

To control for this possibility a "difference in difference" analysis is needed. The general idea of the approach is that to identify the effect of some sort of treatment by comparing the treatment group after treatment both to the treatment group before treatment and to some other control group. In our case, the "treatment" group is composed of countries that join a PTA and the "control" group is made up of countries not in a PTA. The comparison will therefore involve AD filings against PTA members and non-PTA countries both before and after each PTA is enacted.

The results are shown in table 5.5. The changing pattern of use is clearly seen. During the "pre-PTA" period 58 percent of the cases were filed against non-PTA countries and 42 percent were against PTA members. By contrast, during the "post-PTA" period, 90 percent of the cases were against non-PTA countries and only 10 percent were against PTA members. Using a binomial test, the difference in filing incidence is significant at the 1 percent level. So, during the "before" period the difference between PTA members and nonmembers is 16 percentage points but during the "after" period the difference is 80 percentage points yielding a "difference in difference" of 64 percentage points. The implied change on filing patterns is quite large—if pre-PTA filing rates (58 percent against

Table 5.5
AD activity by PTA status

	Target country	
	Non-PTA member	**PTA member**
Pre-PTA	58%	42%
Post-PTA	90%	10%

non-PTA, 42 percent against PTA) had continued during the post-PTA period the results imply that almost one-third of the AD cases filed during the post-PTA period were diverted from PTA members to non-PTA countries.

While these results are compelling they do not control for a variety of other factors that might be influencing the changing patterns. For instance, some PTAs also have additional investment rules that may encourage more intra-PTA FDI, which in turn might dampen the incentive to impose AD duties. Or, it could be that the main effect of PTAs is the political closeness not the AD rules—what one might call "kumbaya." If this were the case, there still would be protection diversion, but our sense of the cause of the diversion would be very different than if it is the rules that are the cause. Also, China has emerged as a major exporting country and this has led to a large number of AD cases against China. China, and not the growing number of PTAs, could be the basis for the changing patterns.

Prusa and Teh (2010) control for all of these factors using formal econometric techniques. In each case we find that the importance and significance of PTA rules remains. The findings clearly raise the specter of protection diversion and more subtle forms of trade diversion. Tariff preferences are small and might result in only modest amounts of trade diversion. This does not imply, however, that trade diversion is not a concern; rather, it appears that the larger source of discrimination might stem from other provisions in the PTA.

5.6 Concluding Comments

Overall, the findings highlight the need to be vigilant about the impact of AD provisions in PTAs. The trade remedy provisions vary greatly across PTAs and increase the overall complexity of the world trading environment. Trade remedy provisions in PTAs have a mixed welfare impact. This ambiguous finding partly reflects that trade creation and trade diversion are happening within the PTA. In some cases PTA rules appear to mostly promote trade creation and other times the rules seem to be simply trade diversion.

Some PTA rules make it easier to restrain intra-PTA imports. Such provisions may benefit global welfare by mitigating trade diversion stemming from preferential tariffs. More often, however, PTAs rules either prohibit AD protection against PTA members or make AD protection harder to apply against PTA members. This raises the very real possibility that PTAs induce protection diversion that in turn serves to produce more trade diversion.

There are other possible consequences of including AD provisions in PTAs. For instance, PTAs might serve as small-scale experiments that allow countries to better understand the practical effect of certain provisions. If parties find certain new rules attractive, those rules might be incorporated in future WTO negotiations. In this sense, PTAs might act as beta testing for the larger-scope WTO rounds. By giving members experience with new provisions, PTA rules could streamline future WTO negotiations.

On the other hand, the trade remedy provisions in PTAs may erode the market access that nonmembers thought they had secured in prior WTO rounds. The erosion is not limited to trade diversion stemming from preferential tariffs but also emerges from selective use of contingent protection rules. As a result PTAs may make it more difficult for non-PTA members to agree to future WTO liberalization because the requisite quid pro quo from PTA members may not be realized. The complicated pattern of inclusion of these provisions threatens the delicate give-and-take balancing of incentives that is at the crux of the GATT/WTO agreements.

Notes

1. World Bank 2005 contains an excellent discussion of the myriad of effects associated with the proliferation of PTAs.

2. There is growing evidence that a high percentage of PTA tariff preferences are never utilized. Amiti and Romalis (2007), Brenton and Ikezuki (2004), and Dean and Wainio (2009) discuss utilization for different countries, products, and time periods. Francois, Hoekman, and Manchin (2005) find a threshold preference margin of 4 percent below which preference margins are irrelevant likely due to high compliance costs such as paperwork and red tape.

3. The WTO agreement requires a link between trade volume change and the imposition of AD protection. An administrative body in the importing country generally determines the causal link.

4. Bown (2010, 2011b) offers an alternative product code metric for evaluating the incidence of protection. He finds that antidumping protection accounts for the vast majority of all the trade subject to any temporary trade barrier. That being said, Bown (2011b) finds at particular moments in time across a number of policy-implementing countries safeguard policies have affected a significant share of imports, especially when evaluated using the trade-weighting import coverage ratios.

5. Relative to antidumping, we found PTAs were almost twice as likely to have no countervailing duty rules and three times as likely to have no safeguard rules.

6. Bown, Karacaovali, and Tovar (2014) provide an excellent overview of many of the issues discussed in this section.

7. Fischer and Prusa (2003) argue that the risk of costly adjustment (or even exit) creates an insurance motive for AD.

8. This third explanation does not explain why PTAs simply do not prohibit the use of AD against PTA members. After all, from Mastel's (1998) perspective the elimination of intra-regional tariffs and other border barriers also means the raison d'être for AD is eliminated. We note that this third explanation is also consistent with the lack of CVD rules in PTAs. Specifically, because most PTAs have failed to strengthen anti-subsidy rules, the notion that there will be fewer subsidies, and in turn less need for CVD, is not supported.

9. The four traditional users now account for only about one-third of AD initiations.

10. These percentages are very comparable to those for all notified PTAs.

11. ASEAN-Korea, GCC, and Korea-India.

12. Both the Jones (2000) and Blonigen (2005) studies were done within a few years following the enactment of NAFTA and thus only had a few observations post-NAFTA.

13. Bown (2011a, 2011b) argues that a product-code basis is a more accurate measure of the extent of AD activity. In this chapter we opt for the simpler case metric.

14. The other large supplier that was not named was Korea. The explanation for Korea not being named was that the vast majority of Korea's hot-rolled imports were shipped to the United States as part of a joint venture with U.S. Steel. This joint venture later became a difficult issue during the U.S. safeguard action. As a way to placate its Korean partner, U.S. Steel cooperated with the USTR to get Korea the largest volume exemption to the safeguard order. Canada and Mexico were excluded from the safeguard protection.

15. The third country subject to the earlier case (Russia) had sufficiently small volume to not warrant including in the plot.

16. For example, Lindsey and Ikenson (2003) document that the U.S. Department of Commerce finds unfair pricing for more than 95 percent of all firms investigated. They also note that the Department of Commerce can go years between negative determinations.

17. Blonigen (2006) finds that the average U.S. dumping margin exceeds 60 percent.

18. Additional details are found in Prusa and Teh 2010.

References

Amiti, Mary and John Romalis. 2007. "Will the Doha Round Lead to Preference Erosion?" *IMF Staff Papers* 54 (2): 338–384.

Bagwell, Kyle, and Robert W. Staiger. 1990. "A Theory of Managed Trade." *American Economic Review* 80 (4): 779–795.

Bhagwati, Jagdish. 1993. "Regionalism and Multilateralism: An Overview." In *New Dimensions in Regional Integration*, ed. Jaime de Melo and Arvind Panagariya, 22–51. Cambridge, UK: Cambridge University Press.

Bhagwati, Jagdish, and Arvind Panagariya, eds. 1996. *The Economics of Preferential Trade Agreements*. Washington, DC: AEI Press.

Blonigen, Bruce A. 2005. "The Effects of NAFTA on Antidumping and Countervailing Duty Activity." *World Bank Economic Review* 19 (3): 407–423.

Blonigen, Bruce A. 2006. "Evolving Discretionary Practices of U.S. Antidumping Activity." *Canadian Journal of Economics. Revue Canadienne d'Economique* 39:874–900.

Bown, Chad P. 2010. "Assessing the G20 Use of Antidumping, Safeguards, and Countervailing Duties During the 2008–2009 Crisis." In *Unequal Compliance: The 6th GTA Report*, ed. Simon J. Evenett, 39–47. London: CEPR and VoxEU.org.

Bown, Chad P., ed. 2011a. *The Great Recession and Import Protection: The Role of Temporary Trade Barriers*. London: CEPR and the World Bank.

Bown, Chad P. 2011b. "Taking Stock of Antidumping, Safeguards and Countervailing Duties, 1990–2009. *World Economy* 34 (12): 1955–1998.

Bown, Chad P. 2013. "How Different Are Safeguards from Antidumping? Evidence from U.S. Trade Policies Toward Steel." *Review of Industrial Organization* 42 (4): 449–481.

Bown, Chad P. 2015. "Temporary Trade Barriers Database," World Bank, June. http://econ.worldbank.org/WBSITE/EXTERNAL/EXTDEC/EXTRESEARCH/EXTPROGRAMS/EXTTRADERESEARCH/0,,contentMDK:22561572~pagePK:64168182~piPK:64168060~theSitePK:544849,00.html (accessed April 26, 2016).

Bown, Chad P., and Meredith A. Crowley. 2007. "Trade Deflection and Trade Depression." *Journal of International Economics* 72 (1): 176–201.

Bown, Chad P., and Meredith A. Crowley. 2013. "Self-Enforcing Trade Agreements: Evidence from Time-Varying Trade Policy." *American Economic Review* 103 (2): 1071–1090.

Bown, Chad P., Baybars Karacaovali, and Patricia Tovar. 2014. "What Do We Know about Preferential Trade Agreements and Temporary Trade Barriers?" In *Trade Cooperation: The Purpose, Design and Effects of Preferential Trade Agreements*, ed. Andreas Dür and Manfred Elsig, 433–462. Cambridge, UK: Cambridge University Press.

Bown, Chad P., and Patricia Tovar. 2011. "Trade Liberalization, Antidumping, and Safeguards: Evidence from India's Tariff Reform." *Journal of Development Economics* 96 (1): 115–125.

Brenton, Paul, and Takako Ikezuki. 2004. "The Initial and Potential Impact of Preferential Access to the U.S. Market under the African Growth and Opportunity Act." Policy Research Working Paper Series 3262, World Bank, Geneva.

Dean, Judith M., and John Wainio. 2009. "Quantifying the Value of US Tariff Preferences." In *Trade Preference Erosion: Measurement and Response*, ed. B. Hoekman, W. Martin, and C. Braga, 29–64. New York: World Bank and Palgrave-MacMillan.

Fischer, Ronald, and Thomas J. Prusa. 2003. "WTO Exceptions as Insurance." *Review of International Economics* 11 (5): 745–757.

Francois, Joseph, Bernard Hoekman, and Miriam Manchin. 2005. "Preference Erosion and Antitrust in RTAs." *World Bank Economic Review* 29 (2): 197–216.

Gagné, Gilbert, and Michel Paulin. 2013. "The Softwood Lumber Dispute and US Allegations of Improper NAFTA Panel Review." *American Review of Canadian Studies* 43 (3): 413–423.

Jackson, John H. 1997. *The World Trading System: Law and Policy of International Economic Relations*. Cambridge, MA: MIT Press.

Jones, Kent. 2000. "Does NAFTA Chapter 19 Make a Difference? Dispute Settlement and the Incentive Structure of US/Canada Unfair Trade Petitions." *Contemporary Economic Policy* 18:145–158.

Lindsey, Brink, and Daniel J. Ikenson. 2003. *Antidumping Exposed: The Devilish Details of Unfair Trade Law*. Washington, DC: Cato Institute.

Mankiw, N. Gregory, and Phillip Swagel. 2005. "Antidumping: The Third Rail of Trade Policy." *Foreign Affairs* 84 (4): 107–119.

Mastel, Greg. 1998. *Antidumping Laws and the U.S. Economy*. Armonk, NY: ME Sharpe.

Prusa, Thomas J. 2001. "On the Spread and Impact of Antidumping." *Canadian Journal of Economics. Revue Canadienne d'Economique* 34 (3): 591–611.

Prusa, Thomas J. 2005. "Antidumping: A Growing Problem in International Trade." *World Economy* 28:683–700.

Prusa, Thomas J., and Robert Teh. 2010 "Protection Reduction and Diversion: PTAS and the Incidence of Antidumping Disputes." NBER Working Paper No. 16276.

Prusa, Thomas J., and Robert Teh. 2011. "Contingent Protection Rules in Regional Trade Agreements." In *Preferential Trade Agreements*, ed. Kyle W. Bagwell and Petros C. Mavroidis, 60–114. Cambridge, UK: Cambridge University Press.

Tharakan, P. K. M. 1995. "Political Economy and Contingent Protection." *Economic Journal* 105:1550–1564.

U.S. International Trade Commission. 2001. *Hot-Rolled Steel Products from China, India, Indonesia, Kazakhstan, The Netherlands, Romania, South Africa, Taiwan, Thailand, and Ukraine*. Investigations Nos. 701-TA-405-408 and 731-TA-899-904 and 731-TA-906-908 (Final). USITC Publication 3468, October.

U.S. International Trade Commission. 2002. *Certain Cold-Rolled Steel Products from Argentina, Australia, Belgium, Brazil, China, France, Germany, India, Japan, Korea, The Netherlands, New Zealand, Russia, South Africa, Spain, Sweden, Taiwan, Thailand, Turkey, and Venezuela*. Investigations Nos. 701-TA-422-425 and 731-TA-964-983. USITC Publication No. 3536, September, and Publication No. 3551, November.

Viner, Jacob. 1950. *The Theory of Customs Union Issue*. New York: Carnegie Endowment for International Peace.

World Bank. 2005. *Global Economic Prospects 2005: Trade, Regionalism, and Development*. Washington, DC: World Bank.

6

The Bali Trade Facilitation Agreement and Rulemaking in the WTO: Milestone, Mistake, or Mirage?

Bernard Hoekman

At the December 2013 ministerial meeting in Bali WTO members successfully concluded the first multilateral agreement since the launch of the Doha Round in 2001. The Agreement on Trade Facilitation (TFA) continues the trend that was initiated in the Uruguay Round for negotiated disciplines to center more on so-called positive integration—agreement to pursue specific practices as opposed to refraining from using certain policies (e.g., quotas, export subsidies) or commitments not to exceed a negotiated level of protection for a product (e.g., tariff bindings).

The TFA is noteworthy in a number of ways beyond being the first agreement on new rules to have been negotiated under WTO auspices in almost twenty years.

- It was part of a small package of decisions centering on matters of interest to developing country WTO members that was "harvested" from the broader set of issues on the table in the Doha Development Agenda (DDA) negotiations.
- While its disciplines apply to all WTO members, it embodies an extensive à la carte approach to determining the timing of implementation by developing countries of its various disciplines.
- It goes beyond trade policy disciplines, calling for joint action by donor countries and development agencies to assist developing countries to implement the agreement.
- It incorporates a mechanism to assess whether and why a developing country is not able to implement commitments before a dispute can be initiated.
- Despite having been agreed by consensus at the 9th WTO Ministerial Conference, it continues the pattern established during the Doha Round of not meeting deadlines set by ministers. The Bali ministerial

meeting called for a Protocol of Amendment incorporating the TFA into the WTO to be adopted by July 31, 2014. India blocked such adoption at the WTO General Council meeting held at the end of July 2014—not because it was opposed to the TFA but because it sought to use the leverage created by the need for the amendment to be adopted by consensus to pursue its demands in another area (agriculture). While the gambit failed and India eventually accepted the Protocol in December 2014, the episode illustrated the challenge of obtaining multilateral agreement and may further increase the incentives of countries to pursue preferential and plurilateral trade agreements.

The TFA reflects a major effort by WTO members to extend WTO rules in a way that addresses the concerns of developing nations regarding implementation costs and capacity constraints. It may be the shape of things to come for multilateral cooperation on trade policy matters. It may also constitute the end of efforts to conclude universal agreements under WTO auspices on regulatory policies. Very different views can be (and have been) expressed regarding the TFA by trade policy analysts. The narrative coming from the WTO Secretariat (e.g., Neufeld 2014; WTO 2015), international organizations, and many governments is that the TFA is a major milestone for the WTO because it addresses an area of policy that is of great importance for traders, for economic development and national welfare. It is also a milestone in demonstrating that WTO members are able to agree on new rules and disciplines that apply to *all* countries and that the organization is capable of fulfilling its legislative function in addition to its transparency and dispute settlement functions. It demonstrates an ability to be innovative in recognizing differences in implementation capacity across nations by calling on developing countries to determine when they will apply specific provisions of the agreement and by linking implementation of some disciplines to the delivery of assistance from developed nations.

But others, including observers who are otherwise strong supporters of national action on trade facilitation, worry that the TFA may have been a mistake for the WTO. They point to the fact that the TFA moves the WTO away from binding, enforceable commitments (as many of its provisions have elements of "best endeavors" language) and further moves the WTO Secretariat into the realm of development assistance, something in which it has little capacity or comparative advantage (Finger 2002; Winters 2007). Specific criticism has been expressed regarding the linkage that is established in the TFA between assistance from developed countries and the timing of implementation of commitments by developing countries, and the associated implication (and possible precedent) that governments must be "paid" for reforms that benefit their traders and consumers (Finger 2014). More generally, worries have been expressed that negotiating trade facilitation measures created perverse incentives to delay taking action to reduce national trade costs as a negotiating chip to obtain concessions in other areas of the DDA, with potentially significant opportunity costs (e.g., Finger 2008). Indeed, as will be discussed, many TFA provisions do not address a prisoner's dilemma situation where international cooperation generates payoffs that exceed what a country can obtain through unilateral action. As a result, the TFA may not be self-enforcing, raising the question of why this issue area should be dealt with in the WTO.

Others question the very premise that the TFA will generate important development benefits. They argue it will do little if anything to improve economic outcomes. There are different flavors of this "mirage" argument. One points to the fact that because implementation in many countries will only occur far in the future, the global gains will be much less than what has been projected in the policy research literature. Another points to "internal imbalances" in the provisions of the agreement that will distribute benefits in favor of high-income countries or large multinationals or both and worsen the balance of trade in developing countries (e.g., South Centre 2013). A related line of argument is that the case for trade facilitation is grossly overblown by proponents, that the net benefits for developing countries are very uncertain, and that the TFA may divert attention away from actions with a higher rate of return (e.g., Capaldo 2013). The specific matters addressed in the TFA may do little to reduce trade costs in a country or region because other factors—such as internal transport costs and corruption—account for the lion's share of total trade costs.

A basic motivation for large multilateral trade negotiating rounds that span many countries and subjects is that this allows issue linkages (Sebenius 1983). A large negotiating set allows countries to offset losses in one area against gains in another area. In the case of the DDA a broad package deal could not be constructed, leading to calls for smaller "self-balancing" deals that are Pareto-improving in the sense that they benefit many countries without making any nation worse off.[1] The TFA was negotiated in Bali as part of a small "development package" of ten ministerial decisions that mostly addressed matters of concern to developing countries (WTO 2013). These included an understanding on tariff-rate quota administration (for agricultural products); a call for WTO members to put in place preferential rules of origin for least developed countries (LDCs); a decision on operationalization of an LDC services waiver (calling for preferential treatment of LDC services exports); more extensive monitoring of duty-free, quota-free (DFQF) market access initiatives for LDCs; and the establishment of a "Monitoring Mechanism" to review the implementation of the many WTO provisions calling for special and differential treatment (SDT) of developing countries.

Another Bali decision concerned public stockholding programs for food security purposes. This called for revisiting the provisions of the WTO Agreement on Agriculture pertaining to domestic production support. It reflected concerns by India that its food stockholding program threatened to exceed the maximum permitted production subsidy under WTO rules (a cap of 10 percent of the value of domestic production), thus opening up the country to potential dispute settlement action.[2] A four-year "peace clause" was agreed in Bali for developing country public food stockholding programs, conditional on satisfying transparency-related reporting requirements, and ministers committed themselves to negotiating a permanent solution to this matter before the 2017 WTO Ministerial Conference. The decision by India to block adoption of the TFA protocol in July 2014 reflected India's view that WTO members had not given enough attention to discussing a permanent solution to the agricultural support question in the six-month period following the Bali conference.

This chapter discusses why trade facilitation was brought to the WTO and why and how the TFA can help improve upon what governments can (and should) do on their own. It also reflects on what the TFA negotiating experience may imply for future multilateral rule-making efforts in the WTO. Section 6.1 briefly discusses the genesis of the TFA talks and the economic rationale for negotiating on trade facilitation. Section 6.2 reviews some of the extant literature on the (potential) benefits and costs of trade facilitation and the state of knowledge available to negotiators and policymakers more generally regarding what to negotiate and focus on. Section 6.3 describes the main elements of TFA. Section 6.4 reflects on some of the factors that arose during the negotiations and that affected the eventual outcome. Section 6.5 discusses possible implications of the TFA experience for multilateral cooperation in the WTO looking forward. Section 7 concludes.

6.1 Why Negotiate on Trade Facilitation?

Since the mid-1980s governments around the globe have greatly reduced tariffs and removed quantitative restrictions on imports. Today the international flow of products is mainly constrained by other factors. These reflect a mix of discriminatory policies that inhibit the entry and operation of foreign firms and regulatory policies that apply equally to local and foreign firms and products. The latter increase costs more for foreign than domestic suppliers simply because regulations differ across countries, but more important is that the policies raise costs across the board and thus the price of goods and services. On average it takes three times as many days, nearly twice as many documents, and six times as many signatures to trade in many African countries than in high-income economies (Djankov, Freund, and Pham 2010). Every extra day it takes in Africa to get a consignment to its destination is equivalent to a 1.5 percent additional tax (Freund and Rocha 2011).

The genesis of trade facilitation discussions in the WTO was the global business community's concern that inefficient border management procedures and controls were becoming an increasingly important impediment to global trade. WTO members put the subject of trade facilitation on the agenda of the Singapore ministerial meeting in 1996, along with investment policy, competition policy, and transparency in government procurement. Working groups were formed to discuss the three latter subjects, while the WTO Council for Trade in Goods addressed trade facilitation, given that the subject matter was already covered by WTO disciplines. The aim of the deliberations was to determine whether to launch negotiations to establish new rules of the game.

When the DDA was launched in 2001, many countries did not believe enough progress had been made to agree on a negotiating agenda for these issues. It was left to the 2003 Ministerial Conference in Cancun to determine if and how to launch negotiations. However, it proved impossible for participants to agree on how to proceed on these matters at Cancun. When WTO members regrouped in Geneva in July 2004, it was decided that negotiations would only be launched on trade facilitation,[3] focusing on five broad areas identified by the WTO Council for Trade in Goods: documentation requirements; official procedures; automation and use of information technology; transparency and consistency; and modernization of border-crossing administration (Hoekman and Kostecki 2009).

Achieving a significant reduction in trade costs is a complex challenge. The agenda goes beyond administrative practices and border clearance procedures. The quality of domestic transport and communications infrastructure and the degree of competition on services markets also matter. The multidimensionality of trade facilitation is reflected in differences in what the concept is understood to mean in different organizations. At the WTO, trade facilitation refers primarily to the reform of border management processes in order to make import and export transactions more transparent, predictable, and efficient. In the Asia Pacific Economic Cooperation (APEC) context, trade facilitation refers to a broader set of measures that may have an impact on trade costs, including policies that affect the efficiency of transport and logistics services. An even broader view of trade facilitation is to include any measure that promotes trade. For example, the International Finance Corporation regards programs that expand access to trade finance as a trade facilitation activity. From an economic perspective trade facilitation might be defined as actions to reduce the difference between domestic farm or factory gate prices and the price obtained in a foreign market (i.e., the difference between the export and import price).

Empirical research has found that lower trade costs can give a significant boost to bilateral trade, support diversification along the extensive margin of trade, and increase aggregate welfare. Trade facilitation is invariably found to benefit both locals and foreigners, although the distribution of the gains is a function of market structure, the type of products concerned, and so on. There will be losers—import-competing industries and agents who benefit from complexity and burdensome procedures (e.g., customs brokers) will lose rents—but overall both importers and exporters should benefit.[4] One important source of benefits is a reduction in uncertainty for traders regarding market entry conditions. This is particularly important for small firms, which find it more difficult to overcome the fixed costs of dealing with administrative requirements at the border, the unpredictable variable costs generated by delays, and the differences in regulations across markets.

For most economists trade facilitation is a "no-brainer" and the puzzle is why a country should need to include this in an international trade agreement. The economic literature has identified several possible motivations for trade agreements, including the internalization of terms-of-trade spillovers created by national policies (Bagwell and Staiger 1999); as a mechanism to address credibility problems (a commitment device—Maggi and Rodríguez-Clare 1998); and to overcome domestic political economy constraints that prevent a government from pursing welfare-increasing reforms (Bhagwati 1988; Hillman and Ursprung 1988; Ethier 2007). Trade facilitation is difficult to fit into the formal terms-of-trade theories of trade agreements because a lack of trade facilitation simply increases the domestic prices of imports *and* reduces the profitability of exports (for a given world price the exporter gets a smaller share due to costs arising from such factors as red tape, corruption, and delays). Not taking action to facilitate trade results in a deterioration of the terms of trade. Moreover, from a growth perspective, high trade costs will lock a country out of participation in the supply-chain trade that is accounting for an ever increasing share of world trade, without generating benefits for local producers because often there will not be local demand for the specialized inputs that would otherwise be imported as part of supply-chain trade production.

The puzzle therefore is that a government can unilaterally take actions that will improve its terms of trade without in the process creating an adverse impact on its trading partners. While the foreign country will benefit from a trading partner's trade facilitation, it does not do so at the expense of the country concerned. There is therefore no prisoner's dilemma situation of the type that often drives cooperation on trade policy. The TFA cannot be motivated by the terms-of-trade rationale that has become the staple of the formal economic literature on trade agreements. Instead, the TFA reflects domestic political economy and international coordination/collective action considerations.

The political economy drivers revolve around the rents that accrue to government officials that are in charge of customs and other border agencies, with the TFA negotiations providing a mechanism to mobilize importers, exporters, and groups in favor of better economic governance around an agenda to enhance the efficiency of border management. The pursuit of concerted action by trading partners increases the gains and thus the incentives of traders to support trade facilitation reforms. The TFA can also be seen as an effort to help solve a coordination problem that is created by countries pursuing different approaches and/or imposing redundant costs on business and traders in the pursuit of very similar objectives. As will be discussed, one dimension of this coordination problem is to address asymmetric implementation costs and capacity through technical and financial assistance.[5] But much more important are the mechanisms and processes that will be created or bolstered in implementing the TFA, which will enhance the ability of domestic actors (importers, exporters, distributors) to defend their interests through domestic enforcement mechanisms.

Before proceeding, it is useful to address two claims. First, some analysts have argued that trade facilitation is a national matter and that there is therefore no need to negotiate it. While much can and should be done unilaterally, in many areas international cooperation can increase gains and reduce trade costs. This is most obviously the case for landlocked countries that depend on what neighbors do to facilitate trade. But more generally, given the redundancy in documentary requirements, information demanded, inspections undertaken, and so on, there is significant scope to reduce overall trade costs through international cooperation to adopt common approaches toward customs and related matters.

Second, trade facilitation is often equated with trade liberalization by advocates of activist industrial/trade policy interventions and objected to on the grounds that it will lower protection for domestic industries. While a lack of trade facilitation will increase domestic prices and thus benefit domestic import-substituting industries, the two areas of policy are quite distinct. Trade facilitation involves removing policies that generate social waste. A country that makes active use of trade policy to protect national industries should also pursue trade facilitation as it will reduce the cost of whatever volume of imports it deems desirable. Using measures that raise the cost of trade is a very inefficient way of pursuing a protectionist policy—much better to directly support a desired domestic activity. Trade facilitation does not imply a country cannot use trade policies to support domestic industries. Arguments that trade facilitation should be opposed because it is disguised liberalization are therefore misguided.

6.2 Assessing the Impacts of Trade Facilitation

Trade costs drive a wedge between export and import prices. As a result of this wedge, producers export less than they would in a world with lower trade costs, and consumers purchase less of each traded product, as well as a narrower range of products, than they otherwise would. Trade facilitation reduces the size of the wedge. The big difference with textbook trade liberalization—removal of tariffs or quotas—is that a large part of the equivalent of tariff revenue or quota rents is not captured by customs officials or domestic industries but instead constitutes social waste.

How large are these costs? And to what extent could they be reduced by trade facilitation measures? What are good practices in this regard? What specific measures would have the biggest benefit-cost ratio? How much can be achieved through unilateral action? How much more could be realized through international cooperation and concerted action? When is cooperation a necessary condition for achieving trade facilitation gains? Are the benefits of trade facilitation equally distributed between countries? What about distributional effects within countries? These were the types of questions confronting negotiators and more generally, economic policymakers.

Much was already known in the customs and border management community on good practices through work done by the World Customs Organization (WCO). Much knowledge also existed in international development organizations such as the World Bank, the regional development banks, and the United Nations Conference on Trade and Development (UNCTAD), which had extensive experience in the design and implementation of trade facilitation projects. However, less was known about the relative impact of different forms of trade facilitation and their distributional effects. Negotiators could draw on a policy research literature that analyzes trade costs, but it was only during the course of the TFA negotiations that research focused specifically on the effects of trade facilitation. Prior to the launch of the TFA talks, economic research in this area was relatively sparse and primarily motivated by economic development concerns, with a focus on what national governments could do to enhance the competitiveness of domestic firms and industries. An important contribution of the epistemic community that emerged around trade facilitation was to provide objective professional expertise and advice on good practices and areas in which cooperation would benefit everyone (see e.g., McLinden et al. 2010).

Estimating the Benefits of Trade Facilitation Writ Large

Economic analysis of trade facilitation has tended to involve empirical assessments of the magnitude of prevailing trade costs and their impacts on bilateral trade flows at a disaggregated product level.[6] Empirical estimates of trade costs have also been incorporated into multi-country-computable general equilibrium models that focus on industry-level and economy-wide impacts. The empirical literature has relied heavily on the World Bank's *Doing Business* database for indicators of trade costs (the "trading across borders" indicators). A representative example is Djankov, Freund, and Pham (2010), who use export time as reported in the database as an indicator of national trade facilitation performance. This measure includes the time needed for document preparation, internal transport, passage through customs and other border agencies, and port and terminal handling. They find that the time to export measure is a statistically significant determinant of bilateral trade flows, with each day's delay associated with a reduction in bilateral trade of at least 1 percent. In the case of Africa, Freund and Rocha (2011) find the number is 1.5 percent.

Extensive research of this type has been undertaken, all of which comes to similar conclusions: a lack of trade facilitation reflected in observed (differences in) trade costs is an important determinant of overall trade performance. For example, Iwanow and Kirkpatrick (2007, 2009) estimate a gravity model augmented with trade facilitation, regulatory quality, and infrastructure indicators to assess the impact of trade facilitation and other trade-related constraints on export performance. They find that a 10 percent improvement in trade facilitation would yield an increase in exports of about 5 percent, whereas identical percentage improvements in the regulatory environment and in quality of infrastructure would result in increases of 9–11 and 8 percent, respectively. Spence and Karingi (2011) show that trade facilitation in Africa, defined as improvements in the types of indicators used in the literature, increases total-factor productivity and exports, but that the quality and quantity of physical infrastructure are also important.

Dennis and Shepherd (2011) conclude that improving trade facilitation helps promote export diversification by making it easier for countries to expand exports along the extensive margin—new products or existing products to new markets. A 10 percent reduction in the costs associated with the aspects of trade facilitation considered by Djankov, Freund, and Pham (2010) is associated with a 3 percent increase in the number of products exported. In a paper focusing specifically on the potential effect of implementing the WTO TFA, Beverelli, Neumueller, and Teh (2015) conclude there will be significant positive impacts on diversification along the extensive margin, with the largest impacts for African countries—in large part a reflection of the fact that Africa has the lowest performance in terms of trade facilitation indicators (TFIs). They estimate that the TFA could support an increase of up to 16.7 percent in the number of products exported by sub-Saharan African countries and an increase of up to 14.1 percent in the number of export destinations by product. Trade facilitation therefore not only promotes greater bilateral trade between countries, but also makes it easier for countries to export a wider range of products.

A conclusion from this research is that trade facilitation can contribute to better export performance, but that improvements in the quality of the regulatory environment more generally and basic transport and communications infrastructure ("connectivity") are equally or more important, in supporting export growth. Thus, trade facilitation narrowly defined need not result in a significant improvement in export performance. Guidance on how specifically observed trade costs can be reduced and what types of interventions would have the biggest cost reduction payoff requires country-specific analysis of the type that is undertaken by the World Bank and other development agencies that routinely undertake analytical work to identify priority areas for reform. Such analysis is equally important for developed countries. For example, Gresser (2013) notes that excessive paperwork for exports from the United States is one reason why shipping a container through New York costs $300 more than in competing ports: the United States has some forty-six separate federal agencies that require forms to be filled in, depending on the types of the goods concerned.

The economy-wide impacts of trade facilitation on real income (GDP) or welfare can be assessed using computable general equilibrium models. Research using such models generally finds that the income gains from trade facilitation can be large. Francois, Van Meijl, and Van Tongeren (2005) conclude that the national income effects from improved trade facilitation can be two or three times greater than what would result from removing all tariffs on manufactured goods. WEF (2013) argues that the ratio is on the order of five or more, and that a concerted effort to raise national trade facilitation performance halfway to global best practice could increase global GDP by some 5 percent.[7] Hufbauer and Schott (2013), based on a review of extant literature, both empirical and CGE, conclude that significant improvements in trade facilitation could increase exports of developing countries by approximately $570 billion and exports of developed countries by $475 billion—for a total of over $1 trillion world export gains. As total world trade in 2013 was some $22 trillion, this implies a 5 percent increase in global trade. This is not particularly large in percentage growth terms and is comparable to the estimated trade impact of removing remaining import tariffs (World Economic Forum 2013). WTO (2015) estimates that full implementation of all TFA provisions will reduce global trade costs by an average of 14.3 percent. Feeding this into a CGE model generates global export gains from the TFA in the range of $750 billion to over $1 trillion dollars per annum, depending on the assumed timeframe for implementation and the extent to which countries implement all the provisions. Using a gravity model, the WTO argues that the trade gains from the TFA could range from $1.1 to $3.6 trillion. The countries that will benefit the most from trade facilitation are those with the highest trade costs—mostly African economies.

Such estimates may be too high given that the trade effects of facilitation depend on trade potential. A problem with these types of exercises is that they ignore the endogeneity of observed trade facilitation performance in high-performing countries: if there is significant trade potential, countries have greater incentives to invest in trade facilitation Thus, if Rwanda were to try to emulate what has been achieved by Singapore it would not realize the level of trade performance achieved by Singapore. Whatever the impacts in practice will end up being, what is distinct about trade facilitation relative to trade liberalization (tariff reduction/removal) is that the real income gains associated with a given reduction in trade costs is larger than what would be generated by an equivalent percentage reduction in tariffs because trade facilitation involves the removal of real costs as opposed to the redistribution of income from producers to consumers that is the primary result of tariff reductions.

From the perspective of negotiators the extant research suggested that trade facilitation, if pursued seriously, could account for a large share of the total potential net welfare gains that might be realized by concluding the DDA. At the same time the relevance of the research from a negotiator's perspective was reduced because the TFA negotiations spanned only a subset of the trade facilitation measures analyzed in most of the research literature. Moreover, most research focused on the benefits of *national* trade facilitation measures. During most of the negotiating period there was little research focusing specifically on the magnitude of the gains from concerted, coordinated action by two or more governments. Practitioners identified many areas where such cooperation is a necessary condition for realizing trade facilitation gains—for example, joint border posts; joint investment in infrastructure to ensure IT systems can "talk" to each other; sharing of data; adoption of common classification and risk management systems; and adoption of the same administrative documents. Negotiators had less research to draw on that identified where *international cooperation* (as opposed to national action) would have the highest net benefit. This reflects both the difficulty of doing such research and the focus of the suppliers of technical and other assistance, which is generally country specific and not geared toward supporting international cooperation.

Mapping Specific Measures to Trade Cost Reductions and Potential Welfare Gains

While economic analysis provided a strong basis for focusing policy attention on trade facilitation broadly defined, the economic literature was less helpful in identifying what specific trade facilitation measures more narrowly defined would have the biggest benefits. International organizations such as the WCO and the World Bank provided expert knowledge on good practices and cross-country experience with trade facilitation projects in developing countries, and provided information on what they deemed to be priorities. A recurring theme of the reports, briefings, and presentations by trade facilitation and customs experts was that the measures being proposed and considered in the TFA talks constituted good practices—in other words, they had been validated in practice and were endorsed by expert practitioners—but that identification of what needed to be done to most effectively facilitate trade required country-level analysis and diagnostics, and that priorities were endogenous—a function of many other factors (e.g., World Bank 2006). However, as discussed in Finger (2008), the expert community did generally agree on what types of trade facilitation measures deserved to be prioritized in terms of likely impact on trade costs and which of these would give rise to relatively low as opposed to high implementation costs—both financial and in terms of administrative complexity.[8]

Extensive diagnostic work was undertaken by the WTO, the WCO, the World Bank, regional development banks, the ITC, and UN bodies (UNCTAD, UN regional Economic Commissions) to assess the "gap" between the status quo prevailing in a developing country on customs and transit matters that were the main focus of TFA talks and what would need to be done to implement a given set of potential disciplines, including informed guesstimates of the cost of closing the gaps (i.e., implementation costs associated with a TFA). This generally suggested that implementation costs of a TFA would be relatively small—with estimates on the order of $7–11 million for a sample of representative developing countries (see, e.g., OECD 2012).[9] However, this detailed, technical work made no promises that implementation would generate gains of the order of magnitude suggested by the empirical research literature discussed earlier. The main focus of the various specialized international organizations was to provide information on best practice, lessons of experience, and tools to assess priorities and guide reforms.[10] Staff from international organizations echoed the findings of the empirical research that while trade facilitation measures of the type discussed in the TFA talks would contribute to better trade performance and generate welfare gains, improvements in the quality of the regulatory environment and trade facilitation-related soft and hard infrastructure ("connectivity") were equally or more important—areas not covered by the TFA talks. An important example is ensuring competition in the provision of transport, logistics/distribution, and communications services (e.g., Arvis, Raballand, and Marteau 2010; Borchert et al. 2015). A major focus of the trade facilitation diagnostics and projects undertaken by development agencies tended to be on transport and logistics, both infrastructure and services, areas not covered by the TFA talks.

The OECD was the only organization to attempt to map what was on the table in the TFA to estimates of trade costs and potential trade cost reductions, thus giving a sense of where the potential benefits were the highest. Moïsé and Sorescu (2013), based on a comprehensive dataset of trade facilitation indicators (TFIs) compiled by Moïsé, Orliac, and Minor (2012), estimated that implementing the various elements of what was emerging in the TFA talks would lower developing country trade costs by around 14 percent—similar to what was estimated by the WTO (2015) using the OECD TFIs. The policy areas covered by the TFA that are predicted to have the greatest impact on trade volumes and trade costs were the availability of trade-related information, simplification and harmonization of documents, streamlining of procedures, and the use of automated processes.[11]

The Cost Side of the Equation

Most of the economic literature on trade facilitation ignores the cost of reforms, reducing the usefulness of the policy research from a policymaking perspective. The response to this issue was threefold: (1) to explicitly consider the costs of trade facilitation; (2) to refer to expert opinion and data on actual trade facilitation projects undertaken by countries to assess how high implementation costs were likely to be; and (3) to limit analysis of potential impacts of trade facilitation to measures that do not involve major investments—in other words, to exclude infrastructure-related investments. All of these approaches indicated that the benefit-cost ratio of trade facilitation was always positive and often high. Buys, Deichmann, and Wheeler (2010), for example, found that improved road connectivity in Sub-Saharan Africa could expand overland trade by up to $250 billion over fifteen years. Using detailed World Bank data on road projects, they estimate that the initial investment cost required would be of the order of $20 billion, with an additional $1 billion annually for maintenance. Thus, the costs of this type of trade facilitation would be offset by the associated trade gains. Similarly, Mirza (2009) concluded that increasing Sub-Saharan Africa's logistics performance by 1 percent would involve an up-front investment of some $18 billion, but that this would generate a welfare gain of some $70 billion. More detailed, micro-econometric studies of the impact of projects to facilitate trade also found that the return on investment was high and that benefits exceed costs (e.g., Calì and te Velde, 2011; Busse, Hoekstra, and Königer 2012; Königer, Busse, and Hoekstra 2011; Portugal-Perez and Wilson 2012; Helble, Mann, and Wilson 2012; Hoekstra 2013).

6.3 The Trade Facilitation Agreement

Before the TFA, the WTO had no provisions dealing explicitly with trade facilitation. Instead, specific articles dealt with aspects of the customs clearance process: Article V of the GATT on the treatment of goods in transit; GATT Article VII on valuation of goods, Article VIII on fees and formalities; and Article X requiring transparency of national trade regulations. In addition, a number of specific agreements negotiated during the Tokyo and Uruguay Rounds addressed policies associated with customs clearance: the Agreement on Customs Valuation, the Agreement on Pre-Shipment Inspection (PSI),[12] the Agreement on Import Licensing, and the Agreement on Rules of Origin.[13] The Agreement on Trade Facilitation follows the precedent of the Agreement on Customs Valuation and other agreements (e.g., on antidumping and on subsidies and countervailing measures) by extending disciplines on matters addressed by existing GATT articles—in this case GATT Articles V, VIII, and X.

Deliberations in the Council for Trade in Goods on trade facilitation following the 1996 Singapore ministerial meeting revealed general agreement on the importance of trade facilitation, but also that many developing countries were not enthusiastic about launching negotiations on the subject. In part the concerns related to potential implementation costs. Some governments argued that they did not have the resources to modernize customs procedures. Many were reluctant to take on legal obligations that might increase their exposure to WTO disputes. While developed countries sought the establishment of binding norms in the WTO, many developing nations preferred to identify voluntary guidelines and an accord focused on capacity building.

After years of exploratory discussions, and the failure to launch negotiations on trade facilitation at the 2003 WTO Ministerial Conference in Cancun, it was agreed to commence negotiations in July 2004, on the basis of modalities contained in Annex D of a July 2004 WTO General Council Decision—the so-called "July package" (WTO 2004). Negotiations were to "aim to clarify and improve relevant aspects of" GATT Article V (Freedom of Transit), Article VIII (Fees and Formalities Connected with Importation and Exportation), and Article X (Publication and Administration of Trade Regulations) "with a view to further expediting the movement, release and clearance of goods, including goods in transit ... [and] enhancing technical assistance and support for capacity building in this area."

Much of Annex D addresses the implementation cost concerns of developing countries. Separate provisions specify that "the extent and timing of entering into commitments shall be related to the implementation capacities of developing and least-developed Members" (Art. 2); that "Members would not be obliged to undertake investments in infrastructure projects beyond their means" (Art. 2); that as "an integral part of the negotiations, Members shall seek to identify their trade facilitation needs and priorities ... and shall also address the concerns of developing and least-developed countries related to the cost implications of proposed measures" (Art. 4). Articles 8 and 9 call on international organizations (with specific mention of the IMF, OECD, UNCTAD, WCO, and the World Bank—what came to be known as the Annex D organizations) to make technical assistance and capacity building in this area more effective and operational, to ensure better coherence. Due account was to be taken of the work of the WCO and other relevant organizations in this area.

Article 6 of Annex D encapsulates a key challenge confronting TFA negotiators:

> "Support and assistance shall also be provided to help developing and least-developed countries implement the commitments resulting from the negotiations. ... In this context, it is recognized that negotiations could lead to commitments whose implementation would require support for infrastructure development on the part of some Members. In these limited cases, developed country Members will make every effort to ensure support and assistance directly related to the nature and scope of the commitments in order to allow implementation. It is understood, however, that in cases where the required

support for such infrastructure is not forthcoming, and where a developing or least-developed Member continues to lack the necessary capacity, implementation will not be required. While every effort will be made to ensure the necessary support and assistance, it is understood that the commitments of developed countries to provide such support are not open-ended."

The contours of a possible deal on substantive matters had become clear by 2008. This included an emerging consensus that a single and binding agreement was needed. It was expected that all WTO members would sign an agreement, with specific commitments detailed in an implementation plan (with varying timelines) based on three specific categories of commitments: those taking effect immediately; those requiring a transition period; and those requiring both additional time and technical assistance before entering into force. Examples of what might be embodied in an agreement included establishment of an enquiry point for information on trade regulations (drawing on precedents established in the WTO Agreement on Sanitary and Phytosanitary (SPS) Measures and the WTO Agreement on Technical Barriers to Trade (TBT); a requirement to provide advance rulings on tariff classification and valuation; creation of a formal border agency "cooperation mechanism" for the exchange of information among members; limits on inspection of goods in transit; and elimination of proscribed transit routes (WTO 2008; Eglin 2008). Much of this ended up being embodied in the TFA that was agreed in Bali in 2013, with much of the focus of discussions post-2008 centering on how substantive disciplines should be implemented by developing countries, and whether a TFA would constitute a stand-alone agreement or whether what was agreed would be limited to amending existing GATT provisions (Arts. V, VIII, and X).

The TFA has three parts. Section I lays out substantive disciplines; Section II specifies special and differential treatment (SDT) provisions and defines the approach taken to implementation of disciplines by developing countries; and Section III deals with institutional arrangements (WTO 2014). What follows briefly summarizes the main elements of the TFA, including an indicative judgment of the extent to which a provision is binding as opposed to setting out good practices that should be applied insofar is possible ("best endeavors"-type commitments). The latter is inherently subjective as there can be differences in view regarding whether best endeavors provisions are enforceable, and, indeed, how relevant this distinction is in practice.

Section I: Substantive Disciplines

Section I of the TFA includes provisions on the following:[14]

1. *Publication of information.* A requirement to publish regulations on trade procedures, taxes, fees, and so on; and best endeavors language on using the Internet (portals; websites) and creating national enquiry points (mix of binding and best endeavors language).
2. *Opportunity to comment.* Commitment to provide opportunities to comment on proposed new regulations relating to movement, release, clearance, and so on, of goods (mix of binding and best endeavors language).
3. *Advance rulings.* Binding commitment to provide traders with advance rulings on a timely basis when requested to do so regarding tariff classification and origin criteria; a best endeavors commitment to do the same for the criteria used to determine valuation, exemptions, and quotas, including tariff quotas (mix of binding and best endeavors language).
4. *Appeal or review of decisions.* Binding commitment on the right to either administrative or judicial review of decisions on a nondiscriminatory basis on customs matters; best endeavors commitment to offer the same for decisions of other border management agencies (mix of binding and best endeavors language).
5. *Other measures to enhance impartiality, nondiscrimination, and transparency.* Lays out procedures to be followed when implementing enhanced SPS-related border controls (binding).
6. *Fees and charges.* Requirements on transparency (publication), permitted level of fees and charges (to be cost based), and the basis/process for imposition of penalties (binding).
7. *Release and clearance of goods* (mix of binding and best endeavors language). This article includes provisions calling for

- pre-arrival processing (binding);
- use of electronic payment (best endeavors);
- procedures allowing for separation of release of goods from final determination of payment liability (binding);
- adoption and use of risk management systems for clearance control (best endeavors); adoption/use of post-clearance audits (binding);

- measurement and publication of average release times (best endeavors);
- providing at least three of seven possible types of additional facilitation measures for "authorized operators"—with eligibility to be determined on the basis of satisfying published criteria relating to risk and track record of compliance (binding);
- putting in place procedures allowing for expedited release of air cargo shipments and specifying the types of criteria that may be used to condition eligibility for expedited release (binding); and
- requirements pertaining to the release of perishable goods (binding).

8. *Border agency cooperation.* Call for cooperation between adjacent border posts (e.g., alignment of working times, procedures, common facilities, and so on) and exchange of information/data when requested (best endeavors).

9. *Formalities associated with cross-border movement of goods, including transit* (mix of binding and best endeavors language) calling for

- commitment to review and assess extant procedures from a trade facilitation perspective and to adopt the least trade-restrictive measure to achieve underlying policy objectives;
- acceptance of copies of documents already provided (mix of binding and best endeavors language);
- use of international standards (best endeavors);
- establishment of "Single Window" systems (one-stop shops) (best endeavors);
- a ban on mandatory PSI (pre-shipment inspection) for classification/valuation (binding);
- a ban on introduction of new requirements mandating the use of customs brokers (binding); and
- provisions on treatment of rejected goods and use of temporary admission programs for inward and outward processing of goods (binding).

10. *Freedom of transit.* Commitment to not impose non-transport-related fees or to seek voluntary restraints (binding); various disciplines on inspection and guarantee schemes (mostly binding).

11. *Customs cooperation*. Provisions calling for sharing of information on best practice and on cooperation between customs agencies to exchange information on consignments (best endeavors).

A number of these substantive disciplines build on work done in the WCO—in particular provisions on appeal and review (Art. 4 TFA) and release and clearance of goods (Art. 7 TFA) (ITC 2013). In the 1990s, WCO members negotiated a revision of the 1974 International Convention on the Simplification and Harmonization of Customs Procedures. An updated and completely revamped Kyoto Convention establishing "international standards and facilitative customs procedures for the twenty-first century" was completed in 1999 (WCO 2002). This comprises a set of principles and detailed annexes that lay out standards and recommended best practices for customs procedures and related administrative practices, including risk assessment, electronic data interchange, use of ex-post audit-based systems of control, import and export procedures, transit arrangements, and bonded warehousing. As of September 2014, 95 countries had signed the Revised Kyoto Convention, out of a total of 178 WCO member countries. Implementation of the TFA will imply that some areas covered by the Kyoto Convention will over time extend to larger number of nations.

As described earlier, some of the TFA provisions can in principle be enforced through the WTO dispute settlement system. Others are of a best endeavors nature. Many of the latter either address matters that will require investment in soft and hard infrastructure, or that are sensitive (e.g., customs cooperation and exchange of information, something on which there were concerns by developed countries as well as developing economies). Binding commitments tend to pertain to matters relating to transparency, fees, and procedures applied by customs authorities. The activities of other government agencies at the border, if addressed at all, tend to be of a best endeavors nature.

Several provisions in the TFA are of interest from a political economy perspective, including the ban on the use of PSI for classification and valuation purposes and the provision precluding the adoption of new regulations requiring mandatory use of customs brokers by countries that did not require this at the time. These provisions are noteworthy because the companies involved in providing the associated services are direct losers from the TFA. The bans reflect a drive by both traders and customs authorities. Customs brokers provide valuable services to customers, but not all firms need their services. Mandatory use of customs brokers imposes an effective tax on companies that have the capacity to deal with customs compliance requirements and can do so at a lower cost than what they are required to pay a customs broker. PSI programs involve governments outsourcing customs activities to private companies, often as part of an effort to reduce corruption and tax avoidance by traders through misclassification of goods and over-or under-invoicing of consignments. Not surprisingly, the customs community was not supportive of such programs as they imply members are not doing their job; traders often oppose PSI because they perceive it as imposing too much of a burden. More generally, experience with PSI programs has been mixed—PSI companies are also open to corruption, and the cost of PSI to traders and the national treasury can be significant.[15]

The prevailing view of the customs community and many traders was that PSI may be helpful in the short term to deal with corruption and tax avoidance, but that in the longer term what is required is serious customs reform and institutional strengthening to allow a government to manage the border itself (Hoekman and Kostecki 2009). The customs community used the TFA negotiations as an opportunity to reassert members' exclusive authority to determine the classification and valuation of goods for tariff revenue collection purposes, while traders used it to ensure that there would be no new instances of WTO members requiring the use of customs brokers and thus having to pay for services they did not need or desire.[16] The ban on PSI is not necessarily a feature of the TFA that is consistent with trade facilitation given that it may be an effective mechanism to address severe instances of corruption in customs.[17]

Section II: Special and Differential Treatment

Section I of the TFA contains a mix of binding disciplines and best endeavors commitments. These all apply to developed countries once the TFA enters into force. This is not the case for developing countries and the LDCs insofar as these countries invoke the TFA's SDT provisions. These are spelled out in Section II, which deals with the implementation concerns of developing countries by allowing them to determine unilaterally when they will apply the various provisions laid out in Section I.

Implementation is divided into three categories: (1) provisions that will be applied unconditionally upon entry into force of the TFA (or after one year in case of a LDC); (2) provisions that will apply after a transition period that will be determined by each country itself; and (3) provisions that will apply after an *indicative* transition period *and* acquisition of the necessary implementation capacity through assistance and capacity building. One year after that signatories are to establish and report definitive dates for implementation of category B commitments and to report on the arrangements made to obtain the assistance needed to implement category C commitments. LDCs have an extra year to undertake these actions.

There are no limits on the length of implementation periods that can be scheduled—the presumption is that countries will undertake a good faith effort to determine how much time they will realistically need and will not engage in games. There are detailed provisions on procedures to be followed if a country needs an extension of the transition period because its government does not think it can implement a provision by the definitive date it specified in its schedule, including reporting the reasons for this and whether it is because of the need for additional assistance or not having received the assistance needed.[20] If a country continues to report implementation difficulties after transition periods have expired, the TFA Committee is called to establish an Expert Group of five independent trade facilitation professionals to examine the situation and make recommendations. No recourse can be made to the WTO dispute settlement mechanism until the Expert Group's recommendation has been considered. In any event, there are long grace periods for dispute settlement: Category A provisions cannot be contested within six years of the entry into force of the TFA for LDCs; in addition, LDCs have an eight-year grace period following implementation of their Category B and C provisions. There is no grace period regarding Category B and C provisions of developing countries (Art. 20 TFA).

Donors are to provide assistance and capacity-building support, either bilaterally or through international organizations, on mutually agreed terms.[21] In the case of LDCs, there is a call for such aid to be additional—donors are to endeavor to provide aid in a way that does not compromise existing developmental priorities (Art. 21). A long list of principles are specified that aid should conform to, including taking into account existing programs of support and the importance of coordination between donors and use of existing in-country donor coordination mechanisms. Donors are also required to report annually on assistance provided, while international organizations will be invited to do so by the TFA Committee. In addition there is a call for the committee to hold at least one annual session to review and discuss problems regarding implementation, review delivery of assistance, and share experiences obtained—in other words, to engage in a process of deliberation and learning.

Thus, the response to implementation concerns was to permit each country to determine its own transitional periods and to identify which specific provisions require technical or financial assistance and capacity-building support. No mention is made of "infrastructure" as a potential necessary element of implementing the agreement as in the 2004 Annex D modalities; assistance is simply linked to "implementation." There is no binding (enforceable) commitment on any member to provide assistance, nor any language specifying whether assistance can have strings attached. Instances where a lack of assistance gives rise to implementation problems are to be resolved through a process of identifying willing donors and alternative sources of aid.

Section III: Institutional Provisions

In Section III the TFA establishes a Committee on Trade Facilitation in the WTO, with a mandate inter alia to maintain "close contact" with other international organizations in the field of trade facilitation such as the WCO (the only agency mentioned by name). The TFA also requires the establishment of national trade facilitation committees in each WTO member to ensure the required domestic coordination and implementation of the TFA.

6.4 Reflections on Process and Outcome

The TFA illustrated that new rule making is feasible in the WTO. For that reason alone it is a milestone. That said, negotiations on the TFA took a decade. While this constitutes good performance compared to other areas of the DDA, it is clearly a very long time, especially given the fact that the contours of the TFA were pretty clear already in 2008, and the basic principle of linking implementation by developing countries to assistance from developed nations had already been established in the 2004 negotiation modalities. At least five factors help explain the slow progress and the shape of the eventual agreement.

The first factor was the overall difficulty of moving the DDA negotiations forward. Trade facilitation was often singled out by WTO negotiators as one area where there was a constructive atmosphere in which good progress was being made, but the deadlock on the DDA post-2008 meant that there was less pressure on TFA negotiators to agree on a text in a more timely fashion. At the same time the deadlock itself can be partly explained by a desire on the part of some countries to extract a "payment" for a TFA deal. This is part and parcel of the modus operandi of the WTO. While there was arguably little negotiating leverage associated with trade facilitation for the reasons discussed in section 6.2, countries nonetheless sought to pursue issue linkage. India's refusal to adopt the TFA protocol in July 2014 was simply another—albeit extraordinary—instance of a strategy that was pursued throughout the negotiations by many countries.

Second, trade facilitation is a technical area, and much learning was required by trade officials who are not necessarily aware of what is involved in putting in place risk management systems, what is implied by a "single window" for border management and customs clearance, and so on. The WTO and Annex D organizations undertook a substantial effort to provide information and educate negotiators as well as stakeholders more generally. While effective in helping to address the initial skepticism on the part of many developing countries, the very length of the negotiations meant that there was regular turnover of negotiators, implying a need for repeated learning by a new set of officials regarding the substance of the many technical issues on the table.[20] This was a factor that also affected the "supply side"—sustaining the engagement and support of specialized agencies in a process that lasts many years without a clear prospect of resolution was difficult, especially for development-focused organizations where performance is assessed on the basis of the impacts of projects and activities in which resources are invested.

Third, a feature of the negotiations was to ensure that poor countries would be able to implement and benefit from an agreement. The challenges here were to figure out what would be needed for effective implementation, how to obtain a credible commitment from developed countries to provide assistance, and to address concerns by developing countries about being subject to implementation-related disputes. Although in principle the link between implementation and assistance had already been agreed in 2004, it proved difficult to craft an approach that was acceptable to everyone. Key elements of what was ultimately included in Section II of the TFA were only agreed a few days before the Bali conference.

Negotiators confronted substantial uncertainty as to what would be involved in implementing TFA provisions in their countries. The response to this uncertainty included an extensive process of national "needs assessments" by the WTO Secretariat and Annex D organizations as well as many seminars and workshops. The outcome of national needs and gap assessments were not made public, however, reflecting the perverse incentives associated with taking a "negotiation mindset" to the issue. This uncertainty created a problem for developed country providers of assistance, as they did not want to be confronted with open-ended financial commitments. Nor were they willing to create a fund with earmarked resources to support TFA implementation. In large part this reflected a desire not to create a precedent for countries to take a "pay me for reform" position in future negotiations. But it also reflected desire to abide by the 2005 Paris Declaration on Aid Effectiveness, under which donor countries committed to align support with the priorities established by developing countries (country ownership and alignment principles).

The TFA leaves it to developing country governments to determine when to implement provisions based on their own self-assessment and in that sense is consistent with the aid effectiveness principles. It is important to note, however, that the TFA does not have language regarding the "conditionality" that might be imposed by donors. While the implicit presumption is that assistance will be grant based, in practice grants are increasingly earmarked for the poorest countries. Middle-income countries—whether large nations such as Brazil or small island economies such as Barbados—may not be eligible for grant-based assistance. International development agencies consistently made clear that they stood ready to support developing countries, but what conditions would apply to assistance were left ambiguous.[21] The World Bank made it clear that assistance for TFA implementation would not be available to all countries, stating that it "will prioritize (1) International Development Association-eligible, low-income, and fragile and conflict affected countries; and (2) middle-income countries that act as gateways to LDCs and/or whose performance significantly impact on the performance of regional LDCs as well as those that are willing to co-finance technical assistance activities" (World Bank 2014).

Donors consistently argued that they would provide the assistance needed. Recall that expert assessments suggested that TFA implementation costs would be limited—in the range of $7–11 million for a representative sample of developing countries, ignoring investments in hard infrastructure (e.g., roads, bridges, warehouses, laboratories, etc.). If we assume a rather conservative $10 million and assume further that most developing country WTO members request assistance we are talking about some $1 billion. This is not a huge amount, especially considering that costs will be spread over several years and that some developing countries may not make Category C commitments. But it is a lot larger than the commitments associated with various grant facilities that have been set up by different international organizations. For example, the World Bank Trade Facilitation Support Program was launched with an initial funding commitment of $30 million. In practice the resources needed to pursue trade facilitation more broadly will be much greater than $10 million per country. Many developing countries will need to tap available resources under general development assistance programs or borrow needed funds from the development banks, or both. Given the high rates of return to trade facilitation identified in the research literature discussed earlier, this will be money well spent, but some countries may argue that having to borrow to address matters covered by the TFA is not what they were looking for.

To maximize the development/real income impacts, the focus of attention must go beyond the TFA provisions narrowly defined, whether binding or best endeavors, as the research literature and country experience makes very clear that lowering trade costs involves action on a broader front (e.g., logistics, transport service sector, etc.). This implies that much depends on the extent to which the process of implementation of the TFA will be integrated into national development trade strategies, and the extent to which the TFA Committee and the various facilities that are established to provide support take a broader perspective. If the TFA helps countries to focus on the broader trade facilitation agenda in the process of implementing the agreement, it can become an important focal point for deliberation and reform and add value to what development organizations are already doing. Even if this is not achieved, the TFA adds value by focusing attention on a number of areas where cooperation between countries will be beneficial (i.e., is a necessary condition for gains). If the TFA serves as a coordination device—between agencies within countries, across countries, and between providers of assistance—it will generate the greatest benefits for members. This is of course not assured by any means. The burden of coordination rests on the countries concerned, and depends on the ability of governments to identify priorities for action and how the various TFA provisions "fit" into the broader national (and regional) trade facilitation agenda.

Fourth, the TFA negotiations broke no new ground with regard to the criteria for eligibility for SDT. Developing country status is self-defined in the WTO, so that in principle SDT applies to Argentina or Brazil in the same way as it does to Armenia or Belize. The only formally defined group of developing countries in the WTO are the LDCs. How much of a difference the TFA will make in lowering global trade costs will depend significantly on what middle-income and emerging economies decide to do regarding the TFA, in other words, what they will implement immediately and what will be left for later. At the time of writing this remains unknown—less than half of all WTO members had ratified the TFA Protocol as of the end of 2015. From a systemic perspective the positive impact of the TFA will be enhanced if more advanced developing economies implemented all provisions under Categories A and B, and committed to short implementation periods. Doing so would not only generate benefits by lowering trade costs, but also, from a systemic perspective, would help address a major problem with the broad way SDT is defined in the WTO.

Fifth, and finally, negotiators were not just seeking to ensure that the TFA would be Pareto-improving in a self-balancing sense—that is, ensuring that the substantive rules constituted good practices for trade development and that implementation constraints would be addressed. They were also concerned about the distribution of the overall gains from trade facilitation. An illustration of this was the argument that global value chains (GVCs) tend to be dominated by large "lead" firms that are headquartered in developed nations and that trade cost reductions will be mostly appropriated by these companies because they have market power or their suppliers are locked into dealing with specific lead firms, or both (Mayer and Milberg 2013). Hoekman and Shepherd (2015) analyze available firm-level data for a large number of developing countries to assess the effects of observed changes in average trade-time costs and find that firms of all sizes benefit from improved trade facilitation—all firms export more in response to reductions in the time required to export goods. While suggestive, this does not address the question of how trade facilitation benefits are distributed, which requires information on profits (rents) as opposed to trade volumes. This is an area where more research would have been helpful.

6.5 Possible Implications for Cooperation Looking Forward

What does the TFA suggest for future rule making in the WTO? Four aspects of the TFA experience appear particularly relevant: (1) the feasibility/desirability of universal membership agreements as opposed to plurilateral cooperation among clubs of countries; (2) the balance between hard law and self-enforcing agreements versus "softer" forms of cooperation; (3) linkages between the implementation of new rules and aid for trade; and (4) the challenge of achieving "policy coherence" within governments, within the WTO, and across the development community. These issues are all interrelated.

More Universal Membership, Self-Balancing Agreements?

The TFA is noteworthy from a systemic perspective because it demonstrates that the WTO membership is capable of negotiating new rules of the game that apply to all countries *and* devising mechanisms to assist those members that need it to implement what all have agreed are good practices. This is an important precedent. There has been much discussion in the literature about the need for the WTO to do a better job in dealing with the diversity of its membership *and* to do more to agree to rules of the game for policies that can generate negative international spillovers. Numerous voices have suggested that greater consideration be given to the pursuit of plurilateral cooperation under the umbrella of the WTO (e.g., Hoekman and Mavroidis 2015a, 2015b).

In the post-2008 period, when it became clear the DDA was deadlocked, suggestions were made to consider a plurilateral TFA (e.g., Finger 2008). A plurilateral agreement among a subset of the WTO membership might have allowed a "tighter" agreement to be concluded, with less in the way of best endeavors language. However, much of what is categorized as best endeavors in the TFA might well have stayed that way in a plurilateral as OECD nations did not see eye to eye on a number of provisions that ended up being best endeavors, such as customs cooperation. There is much to be said for having multilateral agreement on a set of good practices, even if many members may take a significant length of time to implement them and many of these practices have a significant best endeavors dimension.

Looking forward, the real question is, to what extent are WTO members willing to pursue Pareto-improving deals on a stand-alone basis? This is a question that affects both plurilaterals and efforts to conclude universally applicable agreements. It is a function of both the feasibility of constructing a stand-alone deal and the willingness of countries to abstain from efforts to link agreement to other areas. The TFA experience illustrates that WTO members have strong incentives to pursue issue linkages and this may preclude the pursuit and successful conclusion of stand-alone agreements. This constraint applies most strongly to the plurilateral track. A potential response to the decision by India to block adoption of the TFA Protocol would have been for the majority of WTO members to pursue the TFA on a plurilateral basis. However, making the TFA a formal Annex 4 plurilateral WTO agreement would also require consensus (Hoekman and Mavroidis 2015a). For plurilateral agreements to become more feasible in the WTO the consensus constraint needs to be addressed. Note, however, that consensus may not be needed if a club of countries decides on new disciplines that are applied on an MFN basis to countries that decide not to join the agreement—in other words, free riding is permitted. In such cases a majority could move ahead and simply schedule new commitments by incorporating these into their schedule of concessions (Hoekman and Mavroidis 2016).[22] A recognition by India that the majority of WTO members could go ahead and implement the TFA through this route may have been a factor leading it to join the consensus and accept the TFA Protocol in December 2014.

Best Endeavors Commitments and the Self-Enforcing Nature of WTO Commitments

The TFA contains a mix of binding and best endeavors language. A simple count of best endeavors provisions (measured by the use of the word "should") in related WTO agreements (on customs valuation and import licensing) makes clear that the TFA has about twice as many such provisions than these comparators. An implication is that there is less emphasis on "hard law" and more of a focus on cooperation aimed at achieving a set of good practices that all governments support. Examples are not just the emphasis on aid for trade facilitation (Category C provisions), but also the provisions for early warning/notification of problems; the use of an Expert Group to assess the situation in a member country once notified implementation periods have expired; and the use of the TFA Committee as a forum for the exchange of experiences and deliberation. Clearly the DSU is (will be) applicable to all binding provisions over time, and some of the best endeavors provisions with conditional language such as "to the extent practicable" or "to the extent possible" may be enforceable in that a country could ask a panel to assess whether implementation by the country concerned has become practicable and possible. But it is clear that the TFA is an agreement with less emphasis on the standard mechanism to ensure compliance—it is much less of a self-enforcing agreement than is the case with other WTO agreements. One reason for this is that the standard remedy in cases of noncompliance—withdrawal of concessions—is not really available: why would a country reverse trade facilitation and increase its trade costs in retaliation for noncompliance by another nation? Thus, implicitly, and to some extent explicitly, different channels are foreseen to sustain cooperation. Much of the burden will be on *national* enforcement mechanisms.

Assessing whether the rather large number of best-endeavors commitments and the linkages to aid for trade constitute an effective and efficient approach to improving policies and practices as opposed to a more straightforward set of binding disciplines is impossible ex ante. In some areas of regulation that generate trade costs and negative spillovers it may be impossible for governments to agree on hard (binding) cooperation. What is needed is agreement on principles and processes to foster greater communication and exchange of information, to identify redundant and duplicative procedures, and to work together in implementing new norms. The many best endeavor provisions in the TFA can be criticized as being nonenforceable, but in practice they may work more effectively than binding norms would do to lower trade costs for traders over time insofar as the TFA provides a focal point for domestic stakeholders to hold governments accountable for better trade facilitation outcomes.

The extent to which the TFA will help countries around the world improve the operation and governance of national border management systems and reduce uncertainty and trade costs for traders will depend on what countries decide to do—how long transitional implementation periods will last and the extent to which assistance is successful in helping developing countries to implement the agreement. Arguably most important is the extent to which the norms contained in the TFA are seen to benefit traders and consumers. The effectiveness of the transparency and surveillance mechanisms associated with the TFA—both domestic and in the WTO—are likely to be particularly important in helping to converge toward the norms that are incorporated in the TFA.

Linkages between Policy Commitments and Aid for Trade

Finger (2014) argues the TFA is a repeat of what negotiators have done in the past under the GATT/WTO: to create the appearance of legal obligations for developing countries but at the same time avoid substantive disciplines. This is because the TFA's provisions are not made legally binding by developing countries accepting technical assistance and capacity-building support. If developing countries obtain assistance but end up not complying with TFA provisions, there is no mechanism in the agreement to force governments to return the equivalent of the resources that were provided for implementation assistance. Conversely, if a country makes commitments conditional on receiving assistance, there is no mechanism to force developed countries to provide the required resources. While in such cases there is no threat of dispute settlement and enforcement, nonimplementation implies no benefit from participating in the TFA.

These are important considerations and some of the TFA provisions suggest negotiators recognized them—for example, by calling for having an Expert Group determine what would need to be done to permit implementation in instances where a developing country ends up notifying it cannot meet the timetable it has scheduled. As noted previously, a key feature of the TFA is that it establishes norms that all WTO members agree make sense. Whether the approach that was adopted will work is an empirical question. The proof of the pudding will be in the eating—once the TFA is incorporated into the WTO we will learn whether such concerns are valid. Insofar as they are validated, it would prove the critics of embedding aid linkages in WTO agreements correct in that there are potentially serious opportunity costs associated with the approach that was taken. In practice there are no constraints on the availability of technical and financial support from the development agencies. Tapping those resources may involve borrowing, but as noted the return on investment will be high. Not investing because of perceptions or the reality of donors not providing grants makes no sense from an economic development perspective. But the extent to which governments will actively sustain implementation of the norms that are embodied in the TFA will depend more on how effective the TFA-related institutional features—especially the domestic ones—will be in dealing with situations where vested interests resist trade facilitation.

Coherence

Whether the aid for trade linkages in the TFA will have a positive impact on trade costs in low-income economies will be a function of the degree to which the TFA helps firms to pressure government agencies to implement its norms and principles. But it will also depend on the effectiveness of the assistance provided. Here one worry is that the TFA will lead to a proliferation of development assistance facilities and greater coordination challenges for governments. The new TFA facility that will be established in the WTO implies one more development assistance fund under the WTO umbrella, adding to the already existing Enhanced Integrated Framework (EIF) (for LDCs) and the Standards and Trade Development Facility (STDF). The WTO facilities are part of an increasingly crowded scene. There are already many funds and facilities to support trade facilitation.[23]

Low-income countries face a major problem in managing the plethora of donors and assistance providers given weak institutional capacity. In their Joint Statement (2014), the International Trade Centre (ITC), the OECD, the United Nations Economic Commission for Europe (representing the UN Regional Commissions), UNCTAD, the World Bank Group, and the WCO committed themselves to coordinate their support to developing and transition economies in implementing the TFA, in close collaboration with the WTO and the donor community. How this coordination is to be achieved is not spelled out. The joint statement only involves a subset of the international agencies providing support—for example, the regional development banks were not included. How the various national providers of funding and assistance will coordinate within their own governments the allocation of assistance so as to support their national trade policy objectives and their international trade commitments is another challenge. In practice, at the end of the day coherence will require developing country governments to determine their priorities and manage the complicated menu of options they are presented with.

The TFA deals with a rather narrow set of policies centered on border clearance processes and transit regimes. As discussed previously, the trade facilitation agenda goes far beyond the subjects dealt with by the TFA, which was constrained by the Doha ministerial mandate to issues captured by GATT Articles V, VIII, and X. Other relevant GATT disciplines—for example, on customs valuation, pre-shipment inspection, import licensing, product standards—also have a direct bearing on the costs associated with getting goods into foreign markets. The same is true of the GATS—which offers the opportunity to make specific commitments on important logistics-related services such as transport, distribution, and warehousing that research has shown often accounts for a major share of total trade costs confronting firms (Francois and Hoekman 2010). The TFA does not cover logistics or transport services. Some policy areas that matter for trade costs are not covered by the WTO—such as competition policy or restrictions on foreign investment in transport sectors.

A message that consistently comes from the research literature on trade costs is that a broad view of the trade facilitation agenda at the national, regional, and multilateral levels is needed. From this perspective a key question is whether the TFA will reduce the attention that is given by governments to the trade cost agenda broadly defined. The creation of national trade facilitation committees and the process of implementing the TFA may do so. In practice it will be inevitable that matters not covered by the TFA will arise in national deliberations and inform the design of trade facilitation projects. The extent to which such positive spillover effects will arise depends on the willingness of government agencies to look at the trade facilitation agenda more broadly. Here again this is primarily a domestic challenge. It does not help that there are so many different WTO agreements that have a bearing on trade facilitation, with committees serviced by different parts of the WTO Secretariat.

From the perspective of international business and consumers around the world, attention is needed within governments and in the WTO—and more generally in trade agreements—to address the potential "silo problem" that can lead to a focus on the trees instead of the forest. Fostering regular communication and interaction between the various committees dealing with different dimensions of trade facilitation can help governments to identify gaps and possible overlaps that are important from a trade cost reduction perspective. This could be addressed through periodic joint sessions of the various committees; by the TFA Committee considering matters with a direct bearing on trade facilitation that are covered in other agreements; and through complementary mechanisms that bring in the business community and take a "whole of the supply chain" view of assessing progress made in facilitating trade, without regard to whether policies are covered by WTO agreements (Hoekman 2014). A complementary mechanism to enhance coherence would be to expand the mandate of the Trade Policy Review Body to incorporate not just a focus on what countries are doing to implement the TFA, but also a complete supply-chain assessment of prevailing policies in WTO members, thereby helping governments to identify areas of greatest potential to lower trade costs.

6.6 Conclusion

The TFA: milestone, mistake, or mirage? Only time will tell. The TFA is innovative for the WTO by encompassing a set of rules that apply to all WTO members while allowing for extensive differentiation in terms of timing of implementation and explicitly addressing developing country concerns regarding their ability to implement specific provisions. If more such agreements can be crafted the TFA would be a milestone by demonstrating that new rule making is possible in the WTO. Whether this will prove so is very much an open question. The difficulty in getting to yes on a subject that so unambiguously will improve welfare for all countries suggests the scope for WTO members to agree on rules of the game for other policy areas may be quite limited, even if there is willingness to replicate the TFA precedent of self-defined implementation periods. Other policy areas are likely to entail much greater variance in the distribution and incidence of costs and benefits of proposed rules and greater differences in the preferences of governments regarding the substance of new norms. If so, even if there is continued willingness by developed countries to provide implementation assistance, there will be more limited prospects of getting to yes on a stand-alone basis.

For proponents of active pursuit of trade facilitation initiatives the TFA negotiations were rather depressing. Why negotiate about actions that unambiguously promote economic welfare? Why insist on strong commitments by developed countries to provide assistance for implementing trade facilitation measures that are often low cost and have very high rates of return for the countries concerned? Why pay governments to undertake actions that are to their own benefit? Development practitioners have a hard time justifying the convoluted deal that is the TFA, especially the aid for trade linkages. From a more conceptual perspective one can question whether an agreement that is not self-enforcing should be part of the WTO. Many would argue that this is an area where policymakers should figure out what makes sense and then just do it, with assistance from the development community if needed, which is there to do just that and does not need any help from the WTO. Given the social rates of return to trade facilitation are high, any resources needed for implementation are well spent. Those who take this view would argue that Section II of the TFA is a mistake.

These are all valid concerns, but it must also be recognized that the TFA does more than simply define a set of good practices that benefit the countries that adopt them no matter what their trading partners do. It also identifies areas where joint action will reduce trade costs—for example, through cooperation among countries' customs in areas like information exchange. The TFA creates a focal point for governments in an area that matters a great deal from a trade cost reduction perspective, and offers an opportunity for businesses and traders to get governments to engage on trade facilitation more broadly, thus providing a mechanism to help address the reasons why governments have not been able to address trade facilitation domestically. Important factors will be how effective the institutional mechanisms associated with the TFA are in ensuring that trade facilitation gets more attention by governments, and whether the TFA will help or hinder efforts by governments to coordinate the many suppliers of technical and financial assistance. The large potential gains in trade and welfare identified in research call for a focus on trade facilitation broadly defined. This is the bread and butter of multilateral development banks, which have the capacity and mandate to take a more holistic approach that considers logistics, distribution and transport services, and infrastructure, as well as matters covered by the TFA.

The TFA demonstrates the potential for and the challenge of constructing Pareto-sanctioned agreements that address substantive policy matters and apply on a stand-alone basis. One reason it took ten-plus years to negotiate the TFA is that a lot of examination and learning were required on why trade facilitation matters for income growth and economic development, what constitutes good practices, and what kinds of disciplines would benefit all WTO members. This process took time, and occurred with the support and active engagement of an epistemic community comprising the international customs community, trade facilitation practitioners in international development agencies, and research analysts.[24] But this was not sufficient. The issue linkages that were required to get agreement in at the Bali WTO Ministerial Conference puts into question the feasibility of (incentive to negotiate) stand-alone agreements in the WTO.

The TFA experience is particularly pertinent in this regard because the subject it addresses does not lend itself well to issue-linkage dynamics. Trade facilitation predominantly benefits firms and consumers in the country that takes measures to lower trade costs. In contrast to tariffs or subsidies that benefit domestic industries and that can shift the terms of trade in a nation's favor, a neglect of trade facilitation simply raises costs for all industries, domestic as well as foreign. The absence of terms of trade effects should imply that the "linkage value" associated with withholding agreement on trade facilitation is limited—nobody should be willing to "pay" much (i.e., make concessions in other areas like agriculture) to get a deal done. Nonetheless, many developing countries tried to pursue issue-linkage tactics in the trade facilitation talks because they wanted other things that mattered more to them. This is rational in the context of the dynamics that drive WTO negotiations, but it was not very effective because of the "win-win" nature of trade facilitation. This allowed the TFA to be negotiated as a stand-alone agreement. But the July 2014 decision by India reveals the strength of issue-linkage incentives and how these can result in blocking of an agreement that all WTO members regard as Pareto-improving.

Both the Indian strategy in much of 2014 and the efforts of a number of developing countries during the negotiations to link the TFA to other issues of importance to them suggests doubts whether the TFA will be the first of more stand-alone agreements in the WTO. The Indian action may induce other countries to pursue similar tactics in the future. Even the prospects of such behavior may have a chilling effect on the willingness of governments to engage in efforts to negotiate stand-alone compacts. The end result may be to further increase the incentives to negotiate preferential trade agreements. Alternatively, it may lead WTO members to pursue more club-based cooperation and negotiate agreements that apply to only a subset of WTO members, or to go back to the drawing board and work on crafting a broad agenda that offers better prospects of a single undertaking to be negotiated than was the case with the DDA—something that many analysts and commentators have been advocating for some time.[25]

The 2015 WTO ministerial meeting in Nairobi effectively put an end to the DDA, creating a possibility for WTO members to consider alternative approaches in moving forward on both old and new issues. This may induce policymakers to explore new plurilateral agreements under the WTO as a way of addressing the difficulty of crafting new policy disciplines that make sense for all 160-plus WTO members. Often it will not be desirable to negotiate one-size-fit-all rules of the game on regulatory matters given the heterogeneity of the WTO's membership.[26] But even where it is desirable, the first twenty years of the WTO have made many observers increasingly pessimistic about the prospects of negotiating agreements on rules among the membership as a whole. The TFA proves the pessimists wrong, but developments in the two years following the Bali deal make clear that building on this precedent will be a challenge.

Notes

Earlier versions of this chapter were presented at the Italian Trade Study Group workshop, EUI, November 2013; the Second Biannual Trade Conference on Contemporary Challenges to World Trade, Stanford Center for International Development, April 2014; the DG Trade Chief Economist seminar, European Commission, September 29, 2014; and the Columbia University/John Hopkins University conference on Challenges Facing the World Trade System, October 2, 2014. I am grateful to Kyle Bagwell, Jagdish Bhagwati, Lucian Cernat, Mike Finger, Caroline Freund, Gary Hufbauer, Anne Krueger, Patrick Low, Petros

Mavroidis, Costas Michalopulos, Nora Neufeld, Jayanta Roy, Kamal Saggi, and Robert Wolfe for helpful comments and discussions.

1. Para. 47 of the DDA makes allowance for "early harvests" such as the TFA without prejudicing the ability of a WTO member to assess the overall balance of whatever eventually might emerge from the DDA as a whole.

2. The Indian government buys food staples from domestic farmers at administered prices. The resulting public stockholdings are used to supply consumers with food staples at highly subsidized prices.

3. See Eglin 2008 and Neufeld 2014 for discussions by WTO Secretariat staffers that were involved in the genesis, design, and process of TFA negotiations at different points in time.

4. Research suggests that the effect of trade facilitation is not very different for exports than for imports, and if anything, it favors the former. See, e.g., Hoekman and Shepherd 2015 and Hillberry and Zhang 2015.

5. Such side payments are provided by high-income countries. As the transfers are time bound and linked to implementation they cannot be used as an enforcement mechanism for sustained application of the TFA's disciplines over time. Once implemented, enforcement is left to the standard WTO mechanisms, including greater transparency for domestic consumers, the operation of the TFA Committee, and so forth.

6. The empirical literature is extensive and includes works by Hoekman and Nicita (2010, 2011), Hoekstra (2013), Iwanow and Kirkpatrick (2007, 2009), Martinez-Zarzoso and Márquez-Ramos (2008), Nordås, Pinali, and Grosso (2006), Persson (2008, 2013), Portugal-Perez and Wilson (2012), Saslavsky and Shepherd (2014), Shepherd (2013), Spence and Karingi (2011), Wilson, Mann, and Otsuki (2003, 2005), and Zaki (2015). Maur and Wilson 2011 collects some of the relevant research.

7. Other papers assessing the effects of trade facilitation using CGE models include Balistreri, Tarr, and Yonezawa 2014, Decreux and Fontagné 2015, and Zaki 2014.

8. Finger (2008) summarizes compilations of professional assessments and expert opinion on what types of interventions would have the greatest positive impacts. The experts generally ranked measures to adopt and use international standards; to ensure transparency, including online publication of trade regulations and procedures; risk management systems; and advance rulings on tariff classification as being among the highest priorities. See also Duval 2006, Grainger and McLinden 2013, and McLinden et al. 2010.

9. Surveys of professionals suggested that a major cost component associated with implementing trade facilitation measures is not related to regulatory reform, training or equipment costs, but is political—the required engagement at political level is often substantial given the rents that may be associated with the status quo (Duval 2006).

10. Significant resources and effort were devoted to this. For an illustratation of the kinds of materials that Annex D and other organizations generated on the

nuts and bolts of trade facilitation, see the reports and toolkits listed on the website of the Global Facilitation Partnership for Transport and Trade, http://www.gfptt.org/documents.

11. Updated estimates published in OECD 2014 indicate that the largest impacts for low-income countries would stem from a reduction in documentary requirements, automation, and improved information availability (3 percent, 2.4 percent, and 1.7 percent respectively). In contrast, the top three impacts for upper middle-income countries would come from fewer procedures, automation, and measures pertaining to advance rulings (2.8 percent, 2.3 percent, and 1.3 percent).

12. As the name suggests, PSI consists of inspection of goods by specialized firms before they are shipped to the country of importation.

13. This agreement aims to foster the harmonization of the rules used by WTO members for their nondiscriminatory (MFN) trade; i.e., it excludes rules that apply in the context of preferential trade agreements. Notwithstanding almost twenty years of discussion in a Technical Committee (serviced by the WCO, which acts as the secretariat for the committee) tasked with pursuing a harmonization work program, the WTO Committee on Rules of Origin has yet to agree on a common set of nonpreferential rules of origin.

14. What follows is a selective summary. Figures refer to the corresponding article number of the TFA; not all TFA articles are referenced.

15. An Agreement on Preshipment Inspection was negotiated in the Uruguay Round as a result of exporters' concerns regarding the methods used by inspection firms. The agreement requires countries using PSI to ensure that this is done in an objective, transparent, and nondiscriminatory manner, and that verification of contract prices satisfy certain methodological criteria. Research on the impact of PSI programs has found that they can make a significant improvement in customs clearance times but that they can also be costly—companies may charge the government on the order of 1 percent of the value of goods imported (Low 1995).

16. The ban on PSI for purposes of classification and origin concerns activities that are in the ambit of customs. Other TFA articles relating to these activities (transparency, review, appeal, etc.) are binding and can be contested through the DSU.

17. Evaluations of PSI programs suggest they can be effective mechanisms to improve tariff revenue collection. Yang (2008) concludes that PSI programs are associated with increases in tariff revenue collection and on average revenue increases exceed the costs of PSI programs by a factor of two or more.

18. To help address the possibility of some countries "falling through the cracks" as a result of coordination problems, the WTO set up a Trade Facilitation Agreement Facility in 2014. The aims of the facility are to enhance the WTO's technical assistance programs, support coordination between donors and recipients, and provide a source of funding for countries that are not able to access assistance through other channels for TFA implementation. It will do so by providing up to \$30,000 for project proposal preparation (to submit to a

donor agency for funding) and up to $200,000 for "soft infrastructure" projects if a country cannot find a donor to fund it (examples of potential projects include payment of consulting services for modernization of customs laws, in-country workshops, and training of officials). The Trade Facilitation Agreement Facility will become operational following the adoption of the TFA Protocol. See WTO 2015.

19. Footnote 16 of the TFA specifies that assistance and support for capacity building "may take the form of technical, financial, or any other mutually agreed form of assistance provided." The inclusion of the word "financial" was a negotiating objective of many developing countries, whereas some developed countries preferred to leave the type of assistance undefined.

20. The many seminars and workshops arguably were less effective in changing attitudes toward the TFA *negotiations* than they were in increasing understanding of the salience of the subject from a national development perspective.

21. A joint statement issued by the ITC, OECD, UNCTAD, the UN Regional Economic Commissions, the World Bank, and the WCO on July 22, 2014, says nothing about this (Joint Statement 2014).

22. GATT schedules are primarily designed to list tariff-specific and related product-specific commitments, but the way they are constructed also allows for nontariff policy commitments and concessions. See Hoekman and Mavroidis 2016.

23. Global programs include the EIF (WTO), the Trade Facilitation Support Program (World Bank), and the UNCTAD-ITC Partnership on Trade Facilitation. In addition there are many regionally focused programs, e.g., the Trade Facilitation Programme (EBRD); the Africa Trade Fund (AfDB); TradeMark East Africa (DFID); the Support to West African Regional Integration Programme (DFID); the West Africa Customs Administration Modernization project (WCO); the South Asia Subregional Economic Cooperation Trade Facilitation Program (Asian Development Bank); and numerous bilateral trade support programs funded by national donor agencies and the EU.

24. See Haas 1992 for a discussion of the role of epistemic communities in international negotiations and cooperation.

25. See, for example, Evenett 2014 and Wolfe 2015.

26. See Hoekman and Mavroidis 2015a and 2015b for discussion and references to the literature.

References

Arvis, J., Raballand, G., and Marteau, J. 2010. *The Cost of Being Landlocked: Logistics Costs and Supply Chain Reliability*. Washington, DC: World Bank.

Bagwell, K., and R. Staiger. 1999. "An Economic Theory of GATT." *American Economic Review* 89 (1): 215–248.

Balistreri, E., D. Tarr, and H. Yonezawa. 2014. "Reducing Trade Costs in East Africa: Deep Regional Integration and Multilateral Action." World Bank Policy Research Working Paper 7049, Washington, DC.

Beverelli, C., S. Neumueller, and R. Teh. 2015. "Export Diversification Effects of the WTO Trade Facilitation Agreement." *World Development* 76:293–310.

Bhagwati, J. 1988. *Protectionism*. Cambridge, MA: MIT Press.

Borchert, I., B. Gootiiz, A. Grover, and A. Mattoo. 2015. "Landlocked or Policy Locked? How Services Protection Deepens Economic Isolation." *The World Economy* . doi: 10.1111/twec.12327.

Busse, M., R. Hoekstra, and J. Königer. 2012. "The Impact of Aid for Trade Facilitation on the Costs of Trading." *Kyklos* 65 (2): 143–163.

Buys, P., U. Deichmann, and D. Wheeler. 2010. "Road Network Upgrading and Overland Trade Expansion in Sub-Saharan Africa." *Journal of African Economies* 19 (3): 299–332.

Calì, M., and D. te Velde. 2011. "Does Aid for Trade Really Improve Trade Performance?" *World Development* 39 (5): 725–740.

Capaldo, J. 2013. "The Uncertain Gains from Trade Facilitation." Global Development and Environment Institute Policy Brief 13-02, Tufts University, Medford, MA.

Decreux, Y., and L. Fontagné. 2015. "What Next for the DDA? Quantifying the Role of Negotiating Modalities." *World Trade Review* 14 (1): 29–43.

Dennis, A., and B. Shepherd. 2011. "Trade Facilitation and Export Diversification." *World Economy* 34 (1): 101–122.

Djankov, S., C. Freund, and C. Pham. 2010. "Trading on Time." *Review of Economics and Statistics* 92 (1): 166–173.

Duval, Y. 2006. "Cost and Benefits of Implementing Trade Facilitation Measures under Negotiations at the WTO: An Exploratory Survey." Bangkok: Asia-Pacific Research and Training Network on Trade Working Paper No. 3, January.

Eglin, R. 2008. "The Doha Round Negotiations on Trade Facilitation." In *Global Enabling Trade Report 2008*, ed. R. Lawrence et al., 35–40. Geneva: World Economic Forum.

Ethier, W. 2007. "The Theory of Trade Policy and Trade Agreements: A Critique." *European Journal of Political Economy* 23:605–623.

Evenett, S. 2014. "The Doha Round Impasse: A Graphical Account." *Review of International Organizations* 9 (2): 143–162.

Finger, J. M. 2002. *The Doha Agenda and Development: A View from the Uruguay Round*. Manila: Asian Development Bank.

Finger, J. M. 2008. "Trade Facilitation: The Role of a WTO Agreement." European Centre for International Political Economy Working Paper, Brussels.

Finger, J. M. 2014. "The WTO Trade Facilitation Agreement: Form without Substance Again?" http://papers.ssrn.com/sol3/papers.cfm?abstract_id=2489038 (accessed April 22, 2016).

Francois, J., and B. Hoekman. 2010. "Services Trade and Policy." *Journal of Economic Literature* 48 (3): 642–692.

Francois, J., H. Van Meijl, and F. Van Tongeren. 2005. "Trade Liberalization in the Doha Development Round." *Economic Policy* 20 (42): 349–391.

Freund, C., and N. Rocha. 2011. "What Constrains Africa's Exports?" *World Bank Economic Review* 25 (3): 361–386.

Grainger, A., and G. McLinden. 2013. "Trade Facilitation and Development." In *Handbook of Trade Policy for Development*, ed. A. Lukauskas, R. Stern and G. Zanini, 877–892. Oxford: Oxford University Press.

Gresser, E. 2013. "Trade Facilitation as a Growth Tool." July 16. http://progressive-economy.org/papers/trade-facilitation-as-growth-tool/ (accessed April 22, 2016).

Haas, P. 1992. "Introduction: Epistemic Communities and International Policy Coordination." *International Organization* 46 (1): 1–35.

Helble, M., C. Mann, and J. Wilson. 2012. "Aid for Trade Facilitation." *Review of World Economics* 148 (2): 357–376.

Hillbery, R., and X. Zhang. 2015. "Policy and Performance in Customs: Evaluating the Trade Facilitation Agreement." World Bank Policy Research Working Paper 7211, Washington, DC.

Hillman, A., and H. Ursprung. 1988. "Domestic Politics, Foreign Interests, and International Trade Policy." *American Economic Review* 78 (4): 719–745.

Hoekman, B. 2014. *Supply Chains, Mega-Regionals and Multilateralism: A Road Map for the WTO*. London: CEPR Press.

Hoekman, B., and M. Kostecki. 2009. *The Political Economy of the World Trading System*. 3rd ed. Oxford: Oxford University Press.

Hoekman, B., and P. C. Mavroidis. 2015a. "Embracing Diversity: Plurilateral Agreements and the Trading System." *World Trade Review* 14 (1): 101–116.

Hoekman, B., and P. C. Mavroidis. 2015b. "WTO à la Carte or WTO Menu du Jour: Assessing the Case for Plurilateral Agreements." *European Journal of International Law* 26 (2): 319–343.

Hoekman, B., and P. C. Mavroidis. 2016. "MFN Clubs and Scheduling Additional Commitments in the GATT: Learning from the GATS." Forthcoming in *European Journal of International Law*.

Hoekman, B., and A. Nicita. 2010. "Assessing the Doha Round: Market Access, Transactions Costs and Aid for Trade Facilitation." *Journal of International Trade & Economic Development* 19 (1): 65–80.

Hoekman, B., and A. Nicita. 2011. "Trade Policy, Trade Costs and Developing Country Trade." *World Development* 39 (12): 2069–2079.

Hoekman, B., and B. Shepherd. 2015. "Who Profits from Trade Facilitation Initiatives: Implications for African Countries." *Journal of African Trade* 1 (2): 51–70.

Hoekstra, Ruth. 2013. "Boosting Manufacturing Firms' Exports? The Role of Trade Facilitation in Africa." Ruhr Universität Bochum, IIE Working Paper 197.

Hufbauer, G., and J. Schott. 2013. "Payoff from the World Trade Agenda 2013." *ICC Research Foundation Report*. Washington, DC: Peterson Institute for International Economics.

ITC. 2013. *WTO Trade Facilitation Agreement: A Business Guide for Developing Countries*. Geneva: ITC.

Iwanow, T., and C. Kirkpatrick. 2007. "Trade Facilitation, Regulatory Quality and Export Performance." *Journal of International Development* 19:735–775.

Iwanow, T., and C. Kirkpatrick. 2009. "Trade Facilitation and Manufactured Exports: Is Africa Different?" *World Development* 37 (6): 1039–1050.

Joint Statement. 2014. "Coordinated Assistance for Implementation of the WTO Trade Facilitation Agreement," July 22. http://www.oecd.org/regreform/facilitation/trade-facilitation-agreement-2014.htm (accessed April 22, 2016).

Königer, J., M. Busse, and R. Hoekstra. 2011. "The Impact of Aid for Trade Facilitation on the Costs of Trading." *Kyklos* 65 (2): 143–163.

Low, P. 1995. "Preshipment Inspection Services." World Bank Discussion Paper 278, Washington, DC.

Maggi, G., and A. Rodríguez-Clare. 1998. "A Political-Economy Theory of Trade Agreements." *American Economic Review* 97 (4): 1374–1406.

Martinez-Zarzoso, I., and L. Márquez-Ramos. 2008. "The Effect of Trade Facilitation on Sectoral Trade." *B.E. Journal of Economic Analysis & Policy* 8 (1): article 42. https://www.degruyter.com/dg/viewarticle.fullcontentlink:pdfeventlink/$002fj$002fbejeap.2008.8.1$002fbejeap.2008.8.1.1927$002fbejeap.2008.8.1.1927.pdf/bejeap.2008.8.1.1927.pdf?format=INT&t:ac=j$002fbejeap.2008.8.1$002fbejeap.2008.8.1.1927$002fbejeap.2008.8.1.1927.xml (accessed November 1, 2015).

Maur, J. C., and J. Wilson, eds. 2011. *Trade Costs and Facilitation. Open Trade and Economic Development*. Cheltenham, UK: Edward Elgar.

Mayer, F., and W. Milberg. 2013. "Aid for Trade in a World of Global Value Chains: Chain Power, the Distribution of Rents, and Implications for the Form of Aid." Duke University working paper, Durham, NC.

McLinden, G., E. Fanta, D. Widdowson, and T. Doyle, eds. 2010. *Border Management Modernization*. Washington, DC: World Bank.

Mirza, T. 2009. "Infrastructure and Trade in Sub-Saharan Africa." Global Trade Analysis Project Resource 3127, Purdue University, Purdue, IN.

Moïsé, E., and S. Sorescu. 2013. "Trade Facilitation Indicators: The Potential Impact of Trade Facilitation on Developing Countries' Trade." Trade Policy Paper 144, OECD, Paris.

Moïsé, E., T. Orliac, and P. Minor. 2012. "Trade Facilitation Indicators: The Impact on Trade Costs." Trade Policy Paper 118, OECD, Paris.

Neufeld, N. 2014. "The Long and Winding Road: How WTO Members Finally Reached a Trade Facilitation Agreement." WTO Economic Research and Statistics Department Working Paper 2014-06, Geneva.

Nordås, H., E. Pinali and M. Grosso. 2006. "Logistics and Time as a Trade Barrier." Mimeo., OECD, Paris.

OECD. 2012. *The Costs and Challenges of Trade Facilitation Measures*. Paris: OECD.

OECD. 2014. "The WTO Trade Facilitation Agreement—Potential Impact on Trade Costs." Trade and Agriculture Directorate, February.

Persson, M. 2008. "Trade Facilitation and the EU-ACP Economic Partnership Agreements." *Journal of Economic Integration* 23 (3): 518–546.

Persson, M. 2013. "Trade Facilitation and the Extensive Margin." *Journal of International Trade & Economic Development* 22 (5): 658–693.

Portugal-Perez, A., and J. Wilson. 2012. "Export Performance and Trade Facilitation Reform: Hard and Soft Infrastructure." *World Development* 40 (7): 1295–1307.

Saslavsky, D., and B. Shepherd. 2014. "Facilitating International Production Networks: The Role of Trade Logistics." *Journal of International Trade & Economic Development* 23 (7): 979–999.

Sebenius, J. 1983. "Negotiation Arithmetic: Adding and Subtracting Issues and Parties." *International Organization* 37 (2): 281–316.

Shepherd, B. 2013. "Trade Times, Importing, and Exporting: Firm-Level Evidence." *Applied Economics Letters* 20 (9): 879–883.

South Centre. 2013. "WTO Negotiations on Trade Facilitation: Development Perspectives." http://www.southcentre.int/south-centre-report-15-november-2013/ (accessed April 22, 2016).

Spence, M., and S. Karingi. 2011. "Impact of Trade Facilitation Mechanisms on Export Competitiveness in Africa." African Trade Policy Centre Working Paper 85, Addis Ababa.

WCO. 2002. International Convention on the Simplification and Harmonization of Customs Procedures (as amended). (Revised Kyoto Convention.) Brussels: WCO.

Wilson, J., C. Mann, and T. Otsuki. 2003. "Trade Facilitation and Economic Development: A New Approach to Quantifying the Impact." *World Bank Economic Review* 17 (3): 367–389.

Wilson, J., C. Mann, and T. Otsuki. 2005. "Assessing the Benefits of Trade Facilitation: A Global Perspective." *World Economy* 28 (6): 841–871.

Winters, L. A. 2007. "Coherence and the WTO." *Oxford Review of Economic Policy* 23 (3): 461–480.

Wolfe, R. 2015. "First Diagnose, Then Treat: What Ails the Doha Round?" *World Trade Review* 14 (1): 7–28.

World Bank. 2006. “Needs, Priorities and Costs Associated with Technical Assistance and Capacity Building for Implementation of a WTO Trade Facilitation Agreement: A Comparative Study Based on Six Developing Countries.” http://siteresources.worldbank.org/INTTLF/Resources/Needs_and_Priorities.pdf (accessed April 22, 2016).

World Bank. 2014. “Trade Facilitation Support Program.” http://www.worldbank.org/content/dam/Worldbank/Highlights%20&%20Features/WesternEurope/Geneva/2014/06/TFSP_Factsheet_FINAL.pdf (accessed April 22, 2016).

World Economic Forum. 2013. *Enabling Trade: Valuing Growth Opportunities*. http://www3.weforum.org/docs/WEF_SCT_EnablingTrade_Report_2013.pdf (accessed April 22, 2016).

WTO. 2004. “Doha Work Programme: Decision Adopted by the General Council.” WT/L/579, August.

WTO. 2008. “WTO Negotiations on Trade Facilitation: Compilation of Members Textual Proposals.” TN/TF/W/43/Rev.14, March 12.

WTO. 2013. “Bali Ministerial Declaration and Decisions.” http://wto.org/english/thewto_e/minist_e/mc9_e/bali_texts_combined_e.pdf (accessed April 22, 2016).

WTO. 2014. “Agreement on Trade Facilitation.” WT/L/931, WTO, Geneva.

WTO. 2015. *World Trade Report 2015: Speeding Up Trade: Benefits and Challenges of Implementing the WTO Trade Facilitation Agreement*. Geneva: WTO.

Yang, D. 2008. “Integrity for Hire: An Analysis of a Widespread Customs Reform.” *Journal of Law & Economics* 51 (1): 25–57.

Zaki, C. 2014. “An Empirical Assessment of the Trade Facilitation Initiative: Econometric Evidence and Global Economic Effects.” *World Trade Review* 13 (1): 103–130.

Zaki, C. 2015. “How Does Trade Facilitation Affect International Trade?” *European Journal of Development Research* 27 (1): 156–185.

7

Agriculture: Food Security and Trade Liberalization

Stefan Tangermann

7.1 The Doha Round: Agriculture Again at Center Stage

It seems paradoxical. Agriculture accounts for a small and declining share of global trade, less than 10 percent in 2013. Yet, in trade negotiations agriculture continues to cause immense trouble. The cast of combatants changes and the acute issues debated are somewhat variable, but the sector is continuously in the headlines. Agriculture remains an Achilles heel of the world trade system.

In the Uruguay Round the most prominent opponents in the talks on agriculture were the United States and the EU, and on a number of occasions their inability to find common ground came close to breaking the neck of the negotiations overall.[1] It was not before a compromise on agriculture was found between the United States and the EU at Blair House that the Uruguay Round could be brought to a successful conclusion. The Agreement on Agriculture (AoA) then concluded was a turning point in the history of dealing with farm trade in the GATT. It established firm rules and clearly specified quantitative reduction commitments. It also called for another round of negotiations, to deal with the "continuation of the reform process." The rather large amount of water the Uruguay Round results had left in the new disciplines would then be wrung out of the reduction commitments, and—who knows—in the end agriculture could perhaps be integrated fully into the WTO regime, without any sectoral exceptions.

It turned out that these agricultural negotiations could be integrated into the Doha Round—where agriculture began to cause trouble again right from the start. It took a major effort to agree on the precise wording of the objectives for agriculture in the Work Program for the new round. But the real difficulties began when the negotiations turned to the details of new modalities for agriculture. Encouraged by emphasis on the "development dimension" of the Doha Round, developing and emerging economies raised their voices. At the 2003 Cancún ministerial meeting of the WTO the newly created (agricultural) G20 countries began to play a major role. Often led by Brazil, and frequently represented jointly by Brazil, China, India and South Africa, the G20 pushed emphatically for agricultural reforms in the developed countries, arguing strongly that it was a matter of fairness and social justice to allow farmers in the poorer countries to compete on an equal footing with those in rich nations.

As the Doha Round continued there were several occasions when agricultural matters caused significant difficulties. A culmination point was reached in July 2008 when time appeared increasingly ripe to reach closure on the modalities, in an informal meeting of the WTO's Trade Negotiations Committee at Geneva, with many countries represented at ministerial level. Though agreement on most other issues was in sight already, the mini-ministerial meeting collapsed over the impasse in agriculture. The possibility of calling a ministerial meeting in December 2008 was explored, in the hope that it might finalize the modalities. The chairmen of the agriculture and the negotiations on non-agricultural market access (NAMA) issued revised texts of draft modalities, reflecting results of both the July mini-ministerial and subsequent negotiations. However, gaps among negotiating positions remained so wide that risk of yet another failure appeared too high, and the ministerial meeting was postponed. In the absence of any significant further progress in the Doha negotiations, the draft modalities of December 2008, in WTO jargon referred to as "Rev.4" in reference to the number of the respective WTO document (TN/AG/W/4/Rev.4), documented for a long time what had, or had not, been achieved in the DDA negotiations on agriculture.

During the December 2013 WTO ministerial meeting at Bali, negotiations were tough and agreement hung by a thread, but the meeting could be saved from collapse and a "Bali package" was approved. It contained a number of elements. Most important, agreement was reached on the trade facilitation package that had been negotiated over the years. In agriculture, the most hotly debated and most notable outcome was a Ministerial Decision on "Public Stockholding for Food Security Purposes," an item for which India had fought vigorously. The decision established some sort of a temporary peace clause and mandated negotiations on a permanent solution.

After the Bali ministerial meeting, negotiations were resumed in a relatively positive spirit. In agriculture it was discussed whether the draft modalities of December 2008 could continue to serve as a reference for further negotiations. Some delegates felt that was definitely the case. Others argued that so many things had changed since 2008 that there was a need to take stock and see where the world has arrived meanwhile, before continuing to negotiate the details of any modalities. Before the 2014 Geneva summer break the gap between these diverging views had not yet been closed.

However, a much more dramatic hiatus then struck the WTO. The much heralded Bali achievement fell apart when it proved impossible to find a way of bringing all WTO members to adopt the protocol on the Trade Facilitation Agreement (TFA) by July 31, 2014, the deadline agreed by ministers at Bali. India would not let the trade facilitation package go forward as it felt there was not sufficient progress toward a permanent solution that would address its concerns regarding public stockholding of food. Once again disagreement over agricultural matters immobilized the WTO. Yet, a little later a compromise was found that papered over the diverging views, and the Doha Round was saved from a sudden death. In the first half of 2015 the negotiations appeared to gain a little dynamism again. But this slightly more positive mood soon dissipated when it turned out, in the second half of 2015, that it was extremely difficult to put together a meaningful, if not substantive, package of results that could potentially be achieved by the tenth ministerial conference of the WTO, to be held in Nairobi in December 2015. In fact, a number of major participants were hesitant to even agree to any reference to a continuation of the Doha Round negotiations at Nairobi. At the time of writing (October 2015), it was not clear whether the Doha Round would survive the Nairobi ministerial meeting.

In negotiations after Nairobi, two agricultural issues are likely to receive priority attention. First, how has the agricultural world changed since 2008, and what are the implications, if any, for the modalities envisaged in December 2008? Second, what should the response be to the concerns regarding public stockholding of food raised by India (and some other countries)?

This chapter primarily will discuss these two issues. Section 7.2 takes a look at the significant changes that have occurred in recent years on world markets for agricultural products. The evolution of agricultural policies in major countries since 2008 is considered in section 7.3. Section 7.4 discusses implications these developments might have for negotiations as based on Rev.4. Then section 7.5 turns to the "Indian problem." Conclusions are drawn in section 7.6.[2]

7.2 New Conditions on World Markets for Agricultural Products

International markets for agricultural commodities are notoriously volatile.[3] Most of the time volatility on agricultural commodity markets is essentially symmetric. Once in a while, however, such "normal" (though pronounced) volatility is interrupted by an extreme price spike, usually accompanied by particularly high volatility. This typical phenomenon of asymmetric price movements on agricultural commodity markets is closely related to stock changes. For storable commodities, stock variations can contribute to evening out some part of price volatility. However, once stocks are depleted they can no longer compensate for a decline of output. In that situation an output shortfall can drive up prices to very high levels.

Such episodes of extreme price spikes typically don't last very long. Output recovers, stocks are replenished, and prices return to their usual levels. This was, for example, the nature of the pronounced price spike on international cereals markets in the mid-1970s. After the extreme price spike was over, markets calmed down again and continued their secular decline in real terms (figure 7.1). More recently, in 2007 and subsequent years the world experienced another extreme price spike on international

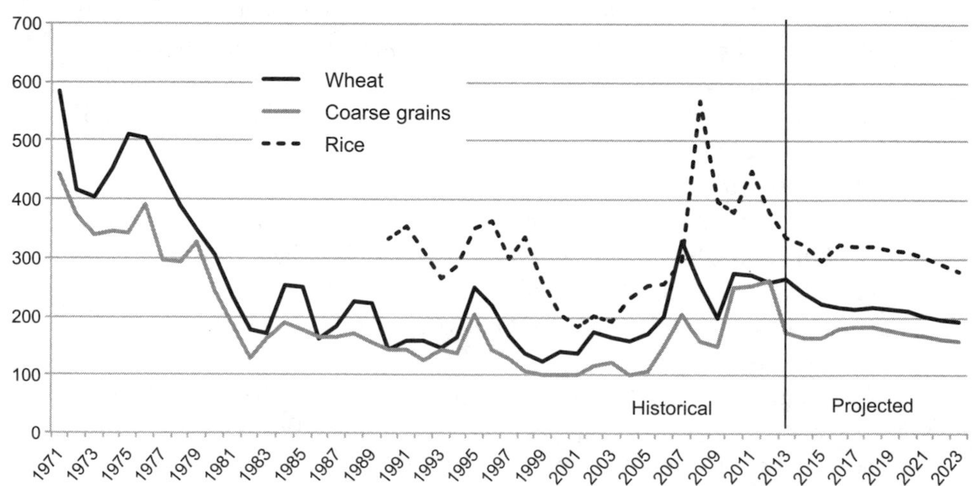

Figure 7.1
International market prices of cereals in real terms, 1971–2023.
Source: Database of OECD-FAO 2014.

markets for cereals. This time, however, the subsequent development of markets differed notably from the usual episode of a transitory price spike. After the original extreme price spike was over, prices did not revert to their pre-spike level. On the contrary, the first price spike was followed by more peaks, prices continued to exhibit much volatility, and even though they declined again from their extremely high levels of 2007–2008, prices remained for the time being at a level significantly higher than before 2007, even in real terms (figure 7.1).

More recently, international market prices for agricultural commodities have declined again. However, most observers agree that this is a transitory phenomenon and that the price level overall will have a tendency to rise again and remain in the foreseeable future higher than it was before the price peaks in 2007 and subsequent years. Market projections for the coming years differ somewhat between authors and institutions. The OECD-FAO Outlook projects real prices of cereals to decline again slightly over the whole of the 2014–2023 period, but even at the end of that projection period they would still be considerably higher than before the 2007–2008 price spike (figure 7.1). Real prices for most other agricultural commodities are also projected to attain a level significantly above that known in the past. Prices for the average of the ten-year period 2014–2023 are projected to be higher than those prevailing on average in the 1992–2006 period by some 15 percent to 35 percent in real terms for cereals, oilseeds, and sugar; by 40 percent to 60 percent for poultry meat and dairy products; and by 25 percent for beef/veal (figure 7.2). Relative to the base period 2000 to 2006, which does not include the above-noted trend prices of the mid-1990s, the projected increase of real prices in the coming ten-year period is even larger, for some products as much as 50 percent or even 80 percent (figure 7.2).

It thus appears that in 2007 and subsequent years the world has not only experienced an extreme price spike and hefty volatility, but also a notable step increase in the price level of agricultural commodities. This is a remarkable departure from past trends on world markets for agricultural commodities. Real prices for agricultural commodities have trended downward for a long time.[4] Around the year 2000 that downward trend slowed down, and then it was interrupted by what appears to have been an upward step in the price level, an increase in the order of magnitude, roughly speaking, of one third. A number of factors are cited that may explain that step increase. A major influence is attributed to high and rising energy prices and the resulting cost push in world agriculture, both

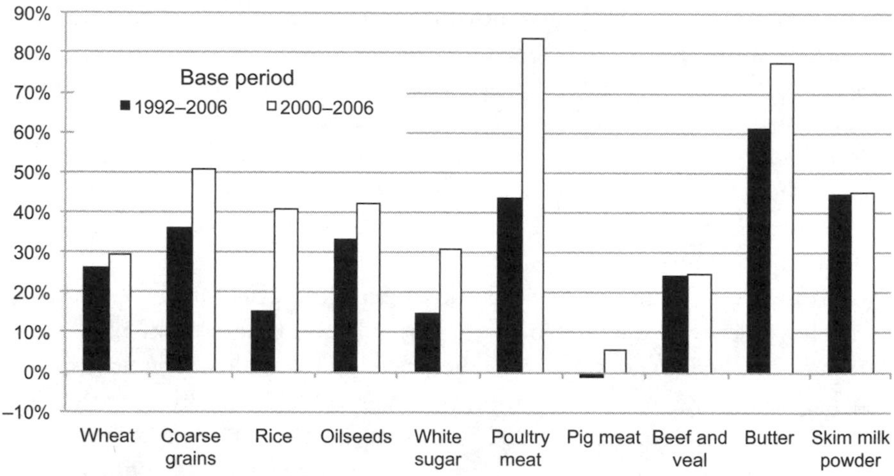

Figure 7.2
Price projections for selected agricultural commodities for the average of years 2014–2023 (percentage change of real prices relative to averages in two alternative base periods).
Source: Database of OECD-FAO 2014.

through direct energy consumption (e.g., tractor fuel) and through their impact on other input prices, in particular fertilizer. Another factor on the supply side is what appears to be a slowdown in yield growth and productivity improvement on a global scale. Moreover, resource constraints, specifically regarding the availability of water and land, become increasingly felt. On the demand side, food consumption continues to be stimulated by population growth and rising incomes, in particular in emerging economies. Growing use of agricultural commodities as feedstocks for the production of biofuels is also contributing to demand expansion. All of these factors appear to be of lasting nature for the foreseeable future. Thus it seems that the step increase in the level of real agricultural commodity prices that has occurred after 2006 is not just a transitory short-term phenomenon.

7.3 Evolution of the Policy Landscape

Producer Support

In its annual "Agricultural Policy Monitoring and Evaluation" (M&E), the OECD provides estimates of producer support for a total of forty-seven countries. Included are the thirty-four members of the OECD, six non-OECD member countries of the EU, and seven emerging economies.[5]

On aggregate, these forty-seven countries cover almost 80 percent of value added in world agriculture and thus provide a good impression of the global picture (OECD 2014). It should, therefore, be useful to take a look at developments in these countries while the DDA negotiations were going on, comparing 2012 with the average of the six-year period 2002–2007, the period before the Doha negotiations on agriculture ground to a halt. Over that time, the share of the Producer Support Estimate (PSE) in gross farm receipts, that is, the %PSE, for the aggregate of all forty-seven countries declined from 20.3 percent in 2002–2007 to 16.7 percent in 2012. The decline began in 2007 and continued in 2008, after which the support rate increased again somewhat, suggesting that much of the decline was a result of the rise of international market prices in 2007–2008 (figure 7.3).

Within this aggregate the evolution of producer support in different country groups has diverged notably. In the OECD area[6] the %PSE has declined significantly since the beginning of the century, while the %PSE for the aggregate of the emerging economies included has increased equally significantly. In fact, as it happens in both country groups the %PSE has changed by about 15 percentage points since around the year 2000—but in the OECD area downward and in the emerging economies group upward (figure 7.3). As a result the shares of these country groups in aggregate producer support for the forty-seven countries have shifted

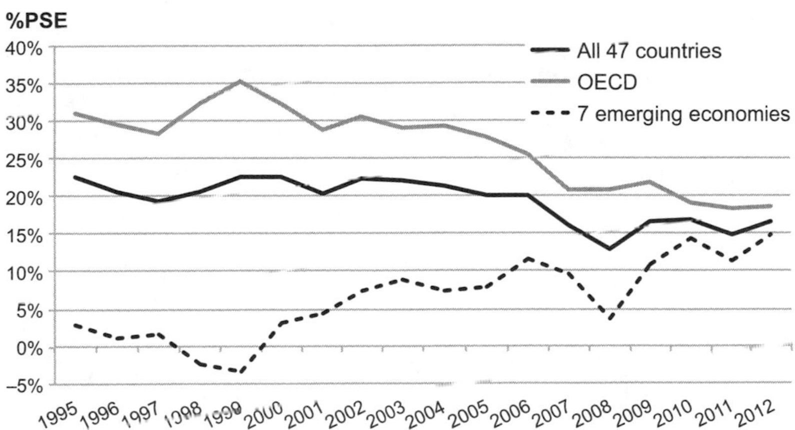

Figure 7.3
Producer support estimate as a share of gross farm revenue, 1995–2023.
Source: PSE database of OECD.

fundamentally. While the group of seven emerging economies made up for no more than 17 percent of the total in 2002–2007, its share had grown to 45 percent by 2012 (figure 7.4a,b).

Behind these averages for country groups there is a large variation across individual countries. While in the OECD area overall the %PSE declined by 9 percentage points from 2002 to 2007 to 2012, it decreased by 17 percentage points in Iceland and went up by 2 percentage points in Japan during that period (figure 7.5). Among the emerging economies covered, changes of the %PSE during that period range from -4 percentage points in South Africa to +10 percentage points in Indonesia. Given these large differences in the evolution of

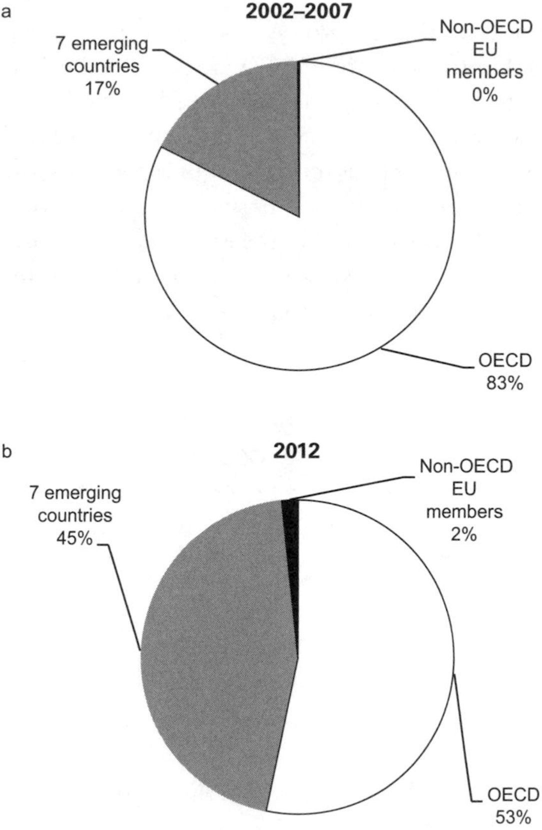

Figure 7.4
Shares of country groups in aggregate producer support of all 47 countries covered in the OECD's M&E. a: Average of 2002–2007; b: 2012.
Source: PSE database of OECD.

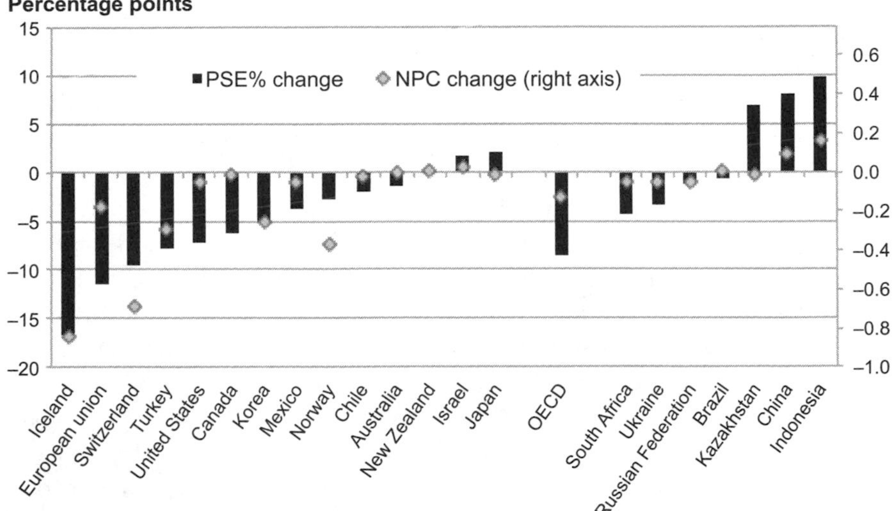

Figure 7.5
Change of %PSE and producer NPC from 2002–2007 to 2012 (percentage points for %PSE, absolute for NPC).
Source: PSE database of OECD.

producer support across countries all of which faced similar developments of international market prices it is clear that in several of the countries covered changing conditions on world markets can explain only some part of the observed changes in producer support. The remainder must have been due to exchange rate movements and the evolution of policy settings. The same conclusion can also be drawn from the wide variation in changes of the producer Nominal Protection Coefficient (NPC) during the period considered here (figure 7.5). In most countries where the %PSE has declined, the producer NPC has also been reduced and vice versa, indicating that a reduction in support based on commodity output has contributed to the decline in overall producer support.[7] In the OECD area overall, the NPC declined by 0.13, from 1.23 in 2002–2007 to 1.10 in 2012. This means that the gap between domestic producer prices (inclusive of payments per unit of output) and international market prices was reduced by 13 percentage points. In the seven emerging countries the (unweighted) average of NPCs increased slightly from 1.07 to 1.08 during this period.

The change in NPCs is one indication of the evolving composition of producer support. Another indicator is the share of potentially the most distorting support in the PSE, consisting of support based on commodity output and payments based on variable input use without input constraints. This indicator exhibits much variation across OECD member countries, in terms of both its level and its change over the period considered here (figure 7.6). The composition of support has improved (in the sense of becoming less distortive) in nearly all OECD countries, with the exception of Israel and Canada.[8] For the OECD area overall, the share of the most distorting support in overall producer support has declined from 63 percent in 2002–2007 to 52 percent in 2012. In the emerging countries covered, the (weighted average) share of the most distorting policies in all producer support not only is higher than in the OECD area, it also increased during the period considered here, from 68 percent in 2002–2007 to 75 percent in 2012.

The overall picture then is that since the beginning of the Doha Round negotiations the evolution of producer support has diverged notably between the OECD area and the emerging economies covered in the OECD's M&E. In the OECD area producer support as a share of gross revenue declined, while it increased for the aggregate of the emerging economies. The result was that the emerging economies' share

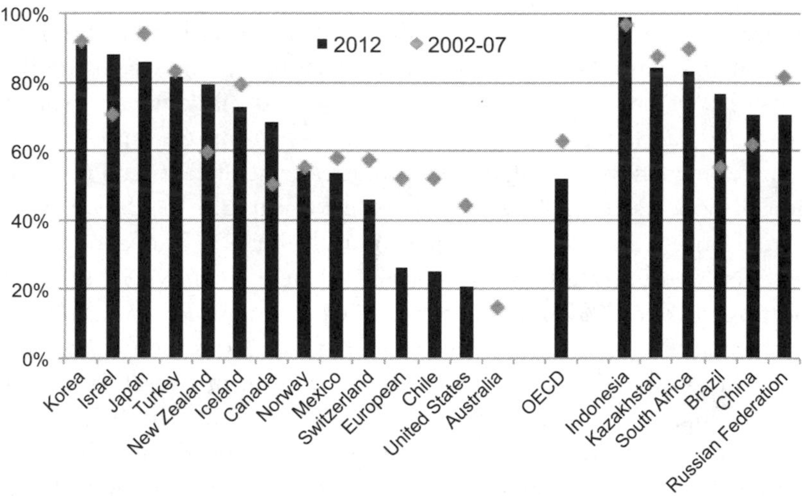

Figure 7.6
Share of potentially most distorting support in all producer support, 2002–2007 and 2012.
Source and notes: PSE database of OECD. Potentially most distorting support is defined as support based on commodity output and payments based on variable input use without input constraints. The Ukraine is not included in this figure as its share of most distorting support in the PSE was negative due to negative support based on commodity output.

of producer support in the aggregate of all countries covered has grown significantly. Also, while the composition of support has changed in the direction of less distorting measures in the OECD area, the opposite was the case in the group of emerging economies.

However, this picture does not include the most recent developments in agricultural policies. In particular, it does not yet reflect the implications of the 2014 U.S. Farm Bill, which reversed the trend toward decoupling support from production. The now much-increased reliance on "risk management" in U.S. farm policy has a tendency to lock in a level of domestic prices that will appear generous when international market prices decline. The results may well be a growing level of support in the United States measured in economic terms, meaning, through the OECD's PSE. With lower world market prices the United States may also experience a significantly higher level of domestic support to be notified to the WTO according to the rules of the Agreement on Agriculture.[9]

Import Measures

The level of tariffs in agriculture, averaged across all agricultural tariff lines (unweighted), differs very much across the countries covered here (figure 7.7).[10] In 2012, averages of MFN applied tariffs ranged from

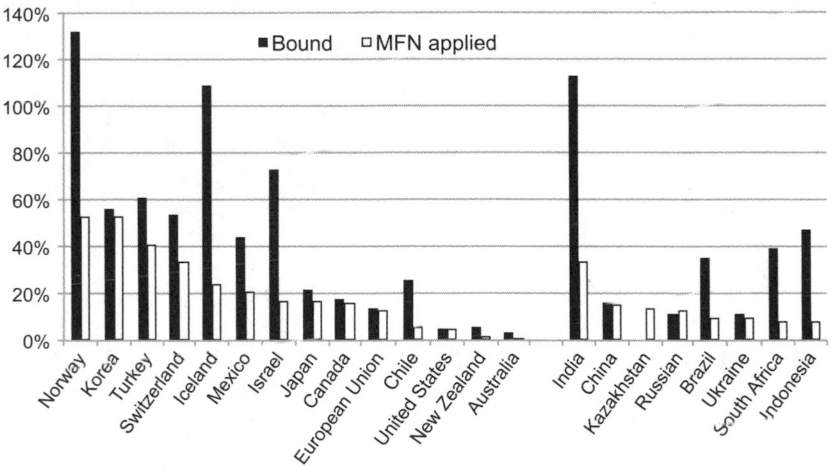

Figure 7.7
Bound and MFN applied tariffs for agricultural products, 2012 (simple average of all agricultural tariff lines).
Source and notes: WTO 2014a. For some countries, data relate to 2011. In the WTO database, agricultural products are defined as under the WTO Agreement on Agriculture, and specific tariffs are converted to ad valorem equivalents.

1.2 percent in Australia to 53.2 percent in Norway. Among the emerging countries covered here, India's MFN applied tariff level in agriculture is highest, at 33.5 percent. It is also notable that in many countries the tariffs actually applied (MFN) are far below the tariffs bound. The "binding overhang" is largest in Norway and India where in both cases it amounts to nearly 80 percentage points. Contrary to what is sometimes suggested, large margins of binding overhang exist not only in emerging and developing countries.

In most countries, tariffs for individual agricultural products vary widely across tariff lines. In many cases the maximum duty for any agricultural tariff line is very far above the average tariff level, often as high as several hundred percent, and in the cases of Norway and Switzerland even above a thousand percent (figure 7.8). Only Chile has a schedule of uniform tariffs, 6 percent for all agricultural products. Among the countries covered here, in only three other cases the maximum tariff is less than five times as high as the average, in China, India, and New Zealand.

From 2007 to 2012, average applied tariffs in agriculture declined in all OECD countries with the exception of Korea (figure 7.9). Tariff averages also declined in all emerging economies covered here with the exception of a minor increase in Kazakhstan. Since tariff bindings did not change much after the end of the implementation period of the Uruguay

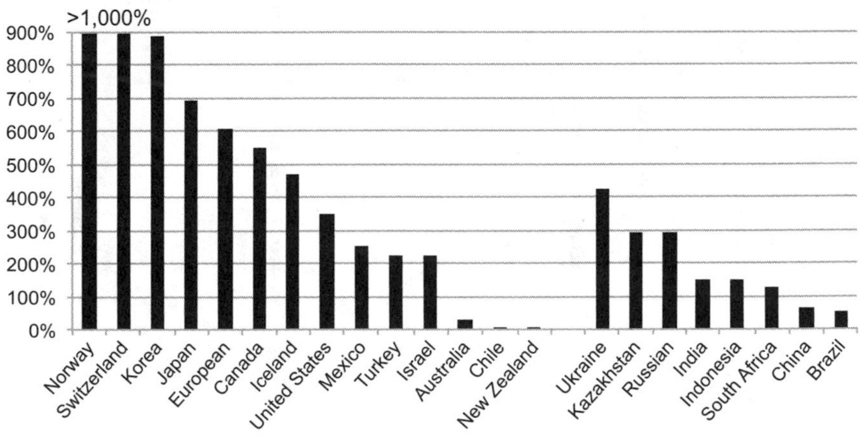

Figure 7.8
Maximum duty (MFN applied) among all tariff lines for agricultural products, 2012.
Source and notes: See figure 7.7.

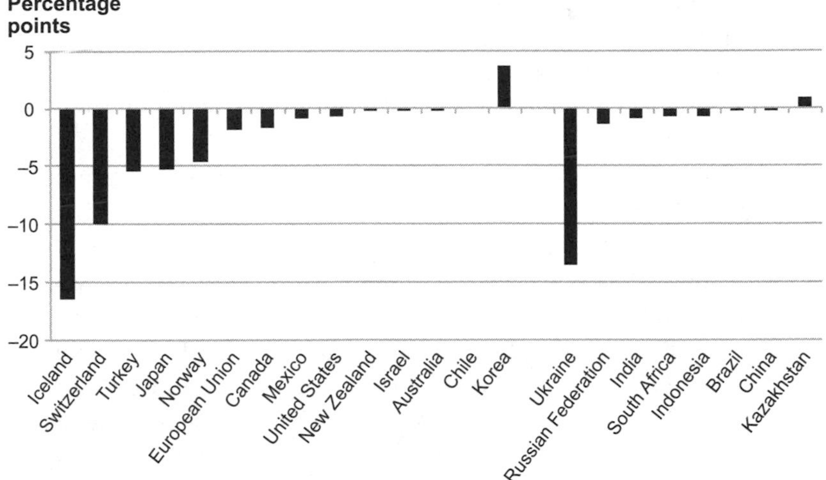

Figure 7.9
Change of average tariffs (MFN applied) for agricultural products from 2007 to 2012.
Source and notes: See figure 7.7 and WTO, ITC, UNCTAD 2008, 2013.

Round (except where countries acceded later to the WTO), reductions in applied tariffs went along with an increase of binding overhang.

Tariffs constitute only one category of the host of "traditional" border measures (as opposed to nontariff measures such as sanitary and phytosanitary restrictions). Another category of import barriers in agriculture is frequent use of tariff rates quotas (TRQ), many of which have resulted from the process of tariffication in the Uruguay Round. All WTO members taken together maintained 1,094 TRQ for agricultural products in 2011 (WTO 2013a). This number, which still stood at 1,430 in 2002, has remained nearly unchanged since 2007. Fill rates of these TRQ vary across countries, products, and methods of administration. On average (unweighted) the fill rate over the 2002–2011 period was 61 percent, with rather little variation from year to year.[11]

Export Measures

An important exception for agriculture in the WTO is that *export subsidies* are still legal, though only within the country and product-specific constraints agreed in the Uruguay Round. In the Doha Round negotiations, one aim is to eliminate that exception. At the Bali Ministerial Conference of the WTO, ministers reaffirmed their commitment to the elimination of all forms of export subsidies and parallel disciplines on all export measures with equivalent effect. Following that declaration, the WTO secretariat sent questionnaires to all members, in order to collect information on export competition policies. The results were compiled in a secretariat background document (WTO 2014b and addenda) that provides up-to-date information on export subsidization.

Actual use of export subsidies has declined notably in recent years, in part as a result of high prices on international markets, but in part also due to policy reforms. Of the eighteen WTO members (counting all EU member countries as one) that had agreed to non-zero export subsidy commitments in the Uruguay Round, ten countries[12] have not used export subsidies in all years notified since the beginning of the Doha Round in 2001.[13] Two countries have not submitted notifications since the Doha Round began.[14] The remaining six WTO members can be grouped in three classes. Three of them have continued to make ample use of their scope for granting export subsidies, using in the most recent years notified (up to 2011 or 2012), as much as about 20 percent (Canada and Switzerland-Liechtenstein) or even about 50 percent (Norway) of the sum of their aggregate budgetary outlay commitments (across all commodities). The United States has made zero or only marginal use of its commitments since 2003 (2010 being the last year notified). The EU, finally, is the WTO member that, when the Uruguay Round implementation period began, held by far the largest share of all export subsidy commitments in the WTO, amounting in 1995 to nearly 70 percent of all "rights" to budgetary outlays, and granted the overwhelming share of all export subsidies paid, accounting for nearly 90 percent of the total in 1995 (Tangermann 2002). In the first years of the Doha Round, the EU still utilized about 40 percent of its outlay commitments. Since 2004 the EU's export subsidies declined, and in 2011, the most recent year for which the EU notified export subsidization, it used no more than 2 percent of its outlay commitments. In 2013 the EU stopped using export subsidies, and under its new policy framework for the 2014–2020 period it has given up on using export subsidization as a systematic tool of its market policy, though it can still use export subsidies as an "exceptional measure." Under its 2014 Farm Bill the United States has repealed the Dairy Export Incentive Program.

While use of direct export subsidies has declined significantly, the picture is less clear regarding other export measures "with equivalent effect," such as export financing, food aid, and state trading enterprises. In particular, in the absence of data on the subsidy equivalent of export measures that are not direct subsidies it is not possible to gain an impression of the overall magnitude of the measures concerned and their evolution over time.

In the past, relatively little attention was paid to *export restrictions*, though there have always been occasional instances of governments blocking exports so as to maintain domestic food supplies in moments of acute shortages. Moreover, for a long time already some countries have tended to tax exports of raw materials in order to support availability to domestic consumers and processors, to collect fiscal revenue, or for a host of other reasons.[15] However, when agricultural product prices on world markets spiked in 2007–2008 and a number of exporting countries imposed export restrictions, placing priority on domestic food security, the international community began to pay much more attention to the implications of export restrictions in the food sector, and the issue of how to deal with them in the international trading regime became an agenda item in various forums. There is no doubt that export restrictions as well as ad hoc tariff reductions introduced in several countries to protect domestic consumers have exacerbated the recent price explosions on world food markets and thus caused significant hardship in other parts of the world, in particular among the poorest countries (Anderson, Ivanic, and Martin 2014). In other words, at the same time when export support through export subsidies and equivalent measures was declining there was significant activity in the domain of export-restrictive measures.

7.4 Implications for Agricultural Trade Negotiations Post-Bali

The point at which the negotiations on agriculture had arrived before Bali, after seven years into the Doha Round, is still essentially represented by the draft modalities for commitments in agriculture tabled by the then chair of the agricultural negotiating group in December 2008, the so-called Rev.4. Rev.4 is extensive and highly detailed; it specifies all sorts of qualitative provisions and contains all the quantitative parameters needed to define reduction commitments regarding market access, domestic support, and export competition. To the outsider these Rev.4 modalities may appear very close to what might become a final agreement. Yet, the negotiations in 2008 and after, including at Bali, have made it abundantly clear that WTO members are still rather far from agreeing on this text or any modified version of it.

From a purely factual perspective it could be argued that the fundamentally changed market conditions should now make it easier than in

2008 to find agreement on the core of the modalities, in other words, the parameters for reduction commitments suggested in Rev.4. The negotiations from which these parameters resulted were conducted in the years before 2008, at a time when the price spike on world markets for food and agricultural products had not yet occurred and, more important, when it had not yet transpired from market projections that the world appears to have entered into a phase where prices will remain at a higher level for some time to come. The food price spike began in the fall of 2007 and prices reached a first peak in 2008. However, it appears that these changes in market conditions were not really reflected in the reduction parameters considered at the time. This is at least the impression one can gain if one compares, for example, the tariff reductions suggested in the successive draft modalities tabled in 2006, 2007, and 2008 (figure 7.10). By 2006 the approach considered for tariff reductions in

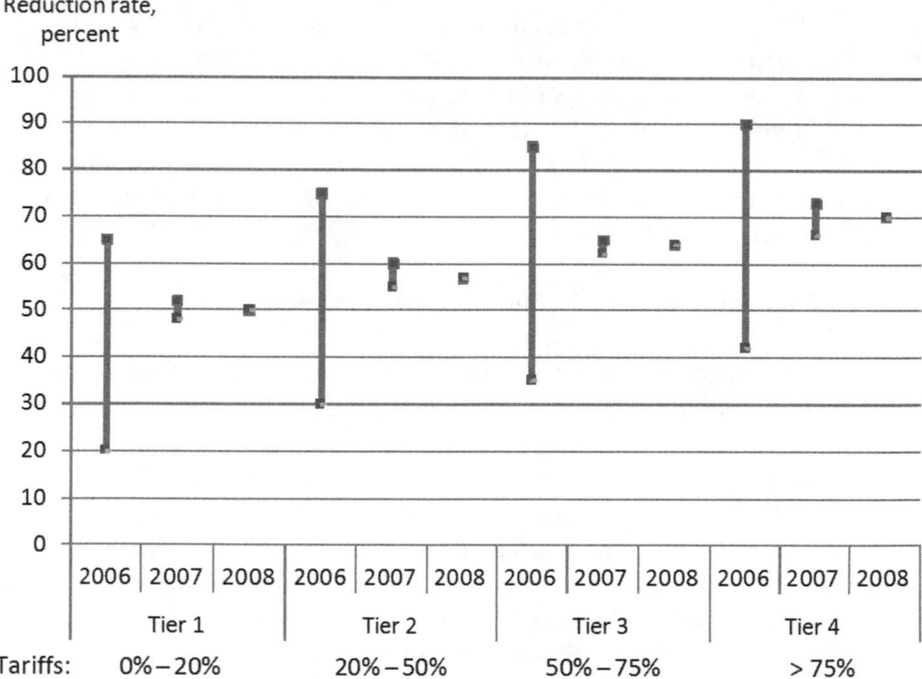

Figure 7.10
Ranges of reduction rates for agricultural tariffs in developed countries suggested in the successive draft modalities of 2006, 2007, and 2008.
Source: WTO documents TN/AG/W/3; TN/AG/W/4; TN/AG/W/4/Rev.4. In the 2006 document TN/AG/W/3, the tariff ranges suggested for tiers 1 to 4 were still 0%-[20–30%]; [20–30%]-[40–60%]; [40–60%]-[60–90%]; >[60–90%].

agriculture had stabilized to a tiered formula, with four tiers. The draft modalities tabled in 2006 still contained possible ranges of reduction rates for each of the tiers (in squared brackets). In the 2007 draft, these ranges were narrowed down considerably, and the 2008 Rev.4 had advanced to the point where only one reduction rate was still suggested for each of the four tiers. In terms of the negotiating dynamics, this evolution indicated good progress toward a common view. However, the orders of magnitude considered for tariff cuts did not change in response to market developments going on at the time. As reflected in figure 7.10, there was perhaps a slight increase in the magnitude of cuts considered between 2006 and 2007, but the reduction rates suggested in Rev.4, tabled in 2008 at a time when the price spike had already caused much excitement in the "real world" outside the negotiating rooms, were precisely the mid-points of the ranges considered already in July 2007, that is, before food prices began to rise dramatically.

Tariffs generate a given margin between domestic and international prices. Yet, from the perspective of pursuing a set of well-defined agricultural policy objectives that margin appears less relevant than the absolute level of domestic prices in relation to other domestic variables (such as farm incomes compared to incomes in the rest of the economy). On that basis it could be argued that a higher level of international prices should reduce the perceived "need" for tariff protection—and hence facilitate agreement on tariff cuts.

The same argument holds for export subsidies and equivalent measures. The higher the level of world market prices, the less the "need" for supporting exports. The decline in export subsidization actually observed in recent years (discussed earlier) is in line with that view. It should, therefore, be easier now than it was in 2008 to find agreement on an elimination of export subsidies and equivalent measures.

The situation is different for the market price support (MPS) element of domestic support commitments. As MPS is defined under the Agreement on Agriculture (AoA) relative to fixed external reference prices, the increase in actual world prices has not reduced the calculated level of MPS. It is only where countries use deficiency payments toward a given target price (or other payments of a similar nature) that the level of domestic support is related inversely to movements of world prices. Where governments raised applied administered prices in response to rising international market prices, the MPS to be considered relative to WTO commitments has actually increased even if the administered prices were raised less than the increase in world market prices. This is an issue of concern, for example, to India and is reflected in the Bali decision on public stockholding for food security purposes, as will be discussed.

In addition to the effects of market developments, the position that countries adopt relative to the parameters embodied in Rev.4 can also reflect the evolution of their national farm policies. The situation in the United States is a case in point. The 2014 Farm Bill adopted by the United States and its significantly more pronounced reliance on "risk management" likely imply that the level of U.S. domestic support to be notified to the WTO rises, potentially quite significantly, as world market prices decline. Hence there is the possibility that the United States may be in difficulty honoring its domestic support constraint agreed in the Uruguay Round, let alone the more restrictive constraints that would follow from the 2008 modalities considered in the Doha Round. This may well be reflected in the position taken by the United States in the most recent Doha Round talks on agriculture where the United States is reported to have exhibited a reluctance to accept the Rev.4 parameters for domestic support—while at the same time requesting commitments by the emerging countries to reduce their domestic support to farmers.

Another issue of relevance in the DDA negotiations on market access in agriculture is the large binding overhang of tariffs that has accumulated in several countries. On a global scale, tariffs applied for agricultural products have come down to about half of the tariffs bound (Bureau and Jean 2013). Tariff cuts that do not go beyond 50 percent would, therefore, in many cases not result in any actual improvement of market access, but only eliminate the binding overhang. An additional reason that speaks in favor of considering relatively large tariff cuts in the DDA negotiations is the growing significance of RTAs. A disadvantage of these preferential arrangements is their discriminatory nature, potentially resulting in trade diversion at the cost of third parties. The danger of this happening is less the lower the level of nonpreferential tariffs.

In short, it is true that the world has changed considerably since the last draft modalities for agriculture were tabled in December 2008 (Rev.4). However, the nature of the most important changes that have taken place in world agriculture and agricultural policies was such that it should now be easier, politically and economically, than it may have been in 2008 to implement the reductions in tariffs, domestic support, and export subsidization suggested at the time. A notable exception, though, may be the situation of the United States where the policy changes introduced by the 2004 Farm Bill appear to have resulted in growing reluctance to accept the domestic support parameters suggested in Rev.4. From a global perspective, though, larger reduction rates than considered in 2008 may now be appropriate, in particular regarding tariffs. On the other hand, experience with a significant use of export restricting measures in agriculture during the episode of food price spikes after 2006 suggests that more attention needs to be paid now to disciplines on export restrictions than what is reflected in Rev.4.[16]

7.5 Public Stockholding for Food Security: The "Indian Problem"

In the Doha Round negotiations, the G33 had for some time already demanded a relaxation of WTO constraints on government policies regarding stockholding of food. India spearheaded that request and made a solution to this issue a *conditio sine qua non* for overall agreement at the Bali ministerial meeting. It could proudly declare victory when a corresponding arrangement was indeed adopted in the last minute, in the form of a Ministerial Decision. The decision is essentially an interim peace clause in which WTO members have agreed not to bring disputes against a developing country that violates certain commitments. Under the Ministerial Decision, WTO members also agreed to work toward a permanent solution, to be achieved by the 11th Ministerial Conference of the WTO, by 2017. As already mentioned, in July 2014 India then argued that work toward this permanent solution had not made sufficient progress, and it therefore blocked adoption of the protocol on the Trade Facilitation Agreement, jeopardizing the validity of the whole Bali package.

The decision on food stocks is generally considered the most notable outcome of the Bali ministerial as far as agricultural matters are concerned. When discussing that decision, two dimensions need to be distinguished. First, what is its political and economic background? Second, what does it mean from the perspective of WTO rules for agriculture?[17]

As far as the political and economic dimension is concerned, it is interesting to note that India and the G33 were surprisingly successful in making political use of the revived concerns regarding global food security triggered by developments on world food markets in recent years. As discussed, food prices in international trade spiked in 2007–2008 and subsequent years, and meanwhile appear to have experienced a lasting step increase. There is no doubt that this has aggravated food security problems in a number of developing countries. Though food insecurity has always been a serious issue in given parts of the world where more than 800 million people suffer from chronic hunger, the exciting developments on global food markets since 2007 have lifted the issue of food security to a new and higher level of political attention, quite rightly so. Governments engaging in action to improve food security of their people can, therefore, count on sympathy in political circles and the media. India played that card very successfully at Bali. When addressing the plenary session of the ministerial, India's then Commerce and Industry Minister Anand Sharma made the point that "food security is essential for over four billion people of the world. For India, food security is non-negotiable. Need of public stockholding of foodgrains to ensure food security must be respected. Dated WTO rules need to be corrected. ... A trade agreement must be in harmony with our shared commitments of eliminating hunger and ensuring the right to food. These are an integral part of the Millennium Development Goals" (The Hindu 2013).

At Bali, when media and commentators referred to the increasingly dramatic negotiations on India's request they generally used terms such as "food security" or "food stock subsidies." The corresponding Ministerial Decision reached in the end is entitled "Public Stockholding for Food Security Purposes" (WTO 2013b). Yet, when one looks at the actual substance of that decision and considers the economics involved, this title is largely a misnomer.[18]

What the Ministerial Decision allows governments of developing countries to do, under certain conditions, without being challenged through a WTO dispute is to exceed their domestic support commitments under the Agreement on Agriculture "in relation to support provided for traditional staple food crops in pursuance of public stockholding programmes for food security purposes." What is not explicitly said in that wording, but what it means without any doubt is that the support referred to is support to farmers producing the staple food crops concerned, not support to food consumers. The level of producer support is constrained under WTO rules, and the Decision lets developing country governments off that hook when they pay higher than otherwise allowable prices to their domestic farmers in acquiring food for stockholding aimed at improving food security.

Do governments need to pay domestic farmers a supported price when they intend to acquire food for stockholding? Not at all, except under one very specific twofold condition: if domestic output of the relevant food product at market prices is less than the amount the government means to acquire, and if, moreover, the government wants to procure only domestically produced food, rather than imported produce. This condition does not apply in India, which has become a large exporter of both wheat and rice (indeed the world's largest rice exporter), the two relevant staple foods. The government of India can, therefore, definitely find sufficient supplies of these crops on the domestic market, without having to generate them through price support for domestic farmers. If it still wants to provide price support to farmers this cannot be justified by the intention to procure sufficient quantities for stockholding of food.

Price support for farmers is also not an effective way to overcome malnutrition. To improve food security what is needed is to provide poor families better access to food. Two major options can be considered to achieve this.[19] The first and most efficient is to enhance incomes of the families concerned, in the longer term through better employment opportunities and more immediately through social safety net policies. The less efficient but still effective option is to subsidize food. Neither of these policy options involves price support to farmers producing staple food. Of course it can also be the case that the poor who suffer from food insecurity include many farmers. One could then be tempted to argue that price support enhances their incomes, allowing them to acquire more food. However, higher prices for food products enhance real incomes only for families who are net sellers of the food concerned—in which case these families are unlikely to suffer from inadequate consumption of this food. Among rural people, the food insecure primarily refers to those families who do not have a sufficient resource base to produce enough for their own food consumption needs. These families are net buyers of the food concerned—and therefore suffer rather than benefit from higher prices. Agriculture can play an important role in reducing poverty and overcoming food security in rural areas, but policies that interfere with the market mechanism, such as price support or input subsidies, are far from optimal in fostering that role.[20]

In other words, what India (and the G33) wanted to achieve was more scope for providing price support to domestic farmers. The food security argument sounded good and was effective in persuading the international community to provide that scope. But this argument is not underpinned by economic logic.

But then the "Indian problem" also has the obvious dimension relating to concerns regarding legal rules under the WTO AoA. To cut a long story short, and in nonlegal terms, the provisions governing public stockholding for food security purposes are found among the rules defining the Green Box, which exempts certain types of government expenditure from the constraints on domestic support. This applies to expenditure on the accumulation and holding of food security stocks as long as the food is purchased at current market prices and sold not below the current market prices of the products concerned. While this rule applies to all countries, there is an additional rule for developing countries, allowing them to deviate from the requirement to purchase at current market prices. They may acquire and release food security stocks at "administered prices," but then must account for the difference between the acquisition price and the "external reference price" in their Aggregate Measurement of Support (AMS), that is, in the constrained Amber Box.[21] Thus developing countries can acquire food security stocks at administered prices only if they have sufficient room in their domestic support commitment.

Where a country had no or only minimal AMS support in the base period and hence has a zero commitment in its schedule, as is the case for India and many other countries, it can provide AMS support only within the *de minimis* levels defined under the AoA. For a developing country the *de minimis* constraint for product specific support (which is relevant when given products are acquired for food security stocks) is equivalent to 10 percent of the total value of production of the product concerned.[22] The G33 and India felt that these provisions constrained their scope for acquiring food security stocks too much.[23] Hence they requested, and received at Bali, the interim peace clause that saves them from being challenged through WTO disputes when they do not comply with these constraints. And the Bali decision promised that WTO members would "negotiate on an agreement for a permanent solution" of this issue.

To understand the *problématique* of these AoA provisions on the acquisition of food security stocks in developing countries it is necessary to say a few words about the two prices involved: the "administered price" and the "external reference price." The meaning of the term "administered price" is not defined in the AoA. In the practice of notifying the market price support (MPS) element of the AMS it is interpreted as a price officially announced by the government, typically before the respective crop year, and maintained through some form of government intervention, in particular through buying into public storage (or into government-supported private storage) or through export subsidization. It appears that the precise meaning of the term has also not been clarified very much in WTO jurisprudence. There is, though, wording in one panel report, to the effect that "for the type of price support contemplated in Annex 3 of the Agreement on Agriculture, ... a direct form of government control over domestic prices is required, in the form of a fixed, administered price."[24] In any case, experience has demonstrated that the term is sufficiently vague to allow governments to play around with it. There are a few notable cases where governments have changed the wording, if not the nature, of the definition of their market policy such that the "administered price" was abandoned without any effect on the economic level of support actually provided—but with the implication that their domestic support level measured and notified to the WTO was greatly reduced.[25]

The "external reference price" is much more clearly defined in the AoA. It is the border price actually observed on average in the years 1986 to 1988.[26] This benchmark for calculating MPS under the AoA remains constant and has still to be used. It is, therefore, also referred to as the fixed external reference price (FERP). There is also no doubt about the concrete FERPs to be used in any country's domestic support notifications as all WTO members had to specify these reference prices in calculating their base period AMS for their schedules. The MPS element of domestic support as defined under the AoA has, then, to be calculated "using the gap between [the] fixed external reference price and the applied administered price multiplied by the quantity of production eligible to receive the applied administered price."[27]

These AoA rules for calculating MPS based on FERPs involve a number of issues that are relevant in discussing the "Indian problem." One of them is that inflation may drive up domestic prices and hence the gap toward the FERPs. As a consequence, countries may see their policy space increasingly constrained even though they may not have changed their policy settings in real terms. Yet, two options can be used to counteract this effect. First, when their commitments were originally established countries had the option to specify the FERPs in a currency different from their own—for example, in U.S. dollars. Where they did so their domestic support constraint eroded not by the rate of inflation of their domestic currency, but only by inflation of the U.S. dollar. In its original base period submission to the WTO, India had used the Indian rupee. Later, though, in its domestic support notifications it switched to the dollar. This helped to reduce the impact of rupee inflation, but according to Gopinath (2011) successive increases of the applied administered prices brought them close to (in the case of wheat) or even above (in the case of rice) the FERPs in 2007–2008 and 2008–2009 even in dollar terms. Moreover, it is questionable whether switching notifications to a different currency from that used for the base period is legally acceptable.[28]

Another option is to take recourse to the AoA provision that due consideration shall be given "to the influence of excessive rates of inflation on the ability of any Member to abide by its domestic support commitments."[29] Hoda and Gulati (2013) have presented a calculation with inflation-adjusted FERPs according to which India's MPS for rice and wheat was negative in all years between 2007–2008 and 2010–2011, except for rice in the year 2009–2010. They found that even when product-specific investment and input support was added, total product-specific support for rice and wheat was negative in all years, except for rice in 2009–2010, when it remained far below the 10 percent *de minimis* constraint. It should be noted, however, that how to interpret the "excessive inflation" provision has not yet been tested in WTO jurisprudence.[30]

Another issue involved in the AoA rules for calculating MPS is the relationship between the "applied administered price" and the actual market price. In economic terms, there is no price support as long as the administered price is below the international market price. However, under the AoA the benchmark for calculating MPS is not the international market price but the FERP. Hence, even where the administered price remains below the prevailing world market price, the AoA rules require a country to notify MPS whenever the administered price exceeds the FERP, and requests it to keep that "virtual" price support within the limits of its domestic support commitments.

In the case of India, this creates a paradoxical situation. As shown by Hoda and Gulati (2013), India's minimum support prices for rice and wheat, based on recommendations of the Commission for Agricultural Costs and Prices (CACP) and maintained through purchase operations by the Food Corporation of India (FCI), have remained below the relevant international market prices in most years from 2000–2001 to 2011–2012 (see figure 7.11a,b). Thus in economic terms India has not provided effective price support for rice and wheat in most years, and only marginal support in some years. Yet, as estimated by Brink (2014), when applying strict AoA rules for calculating MPS India's product-specific support for rice and wheat exceeded the *de minimis* constraint of 10 percent of the value of production in all these years, mostly by a large margin.[31]

A couple of thoughts follow from this brief discussion of the background to the "Indian problem" and the corresponding Bali decision,

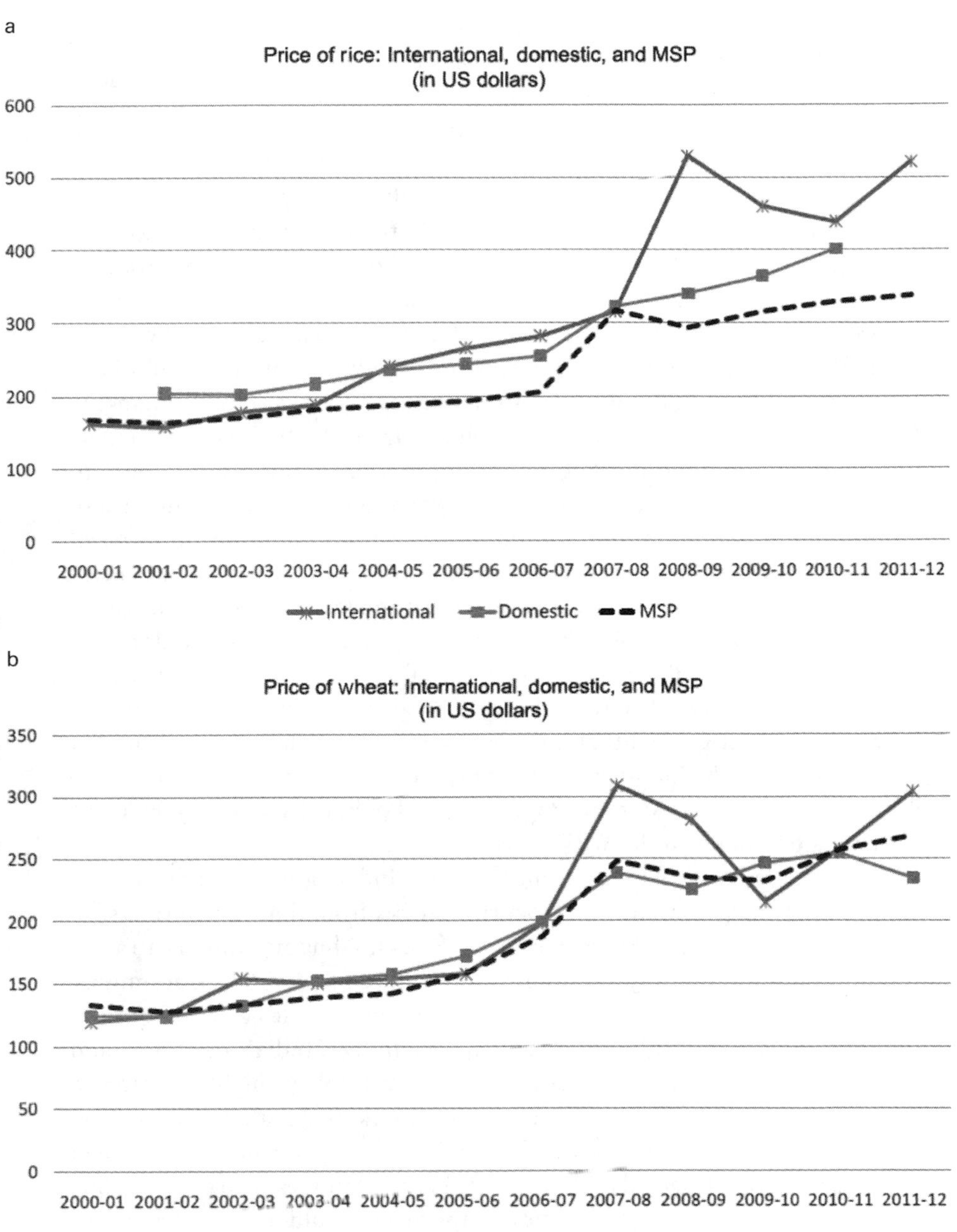

Figure 7.11
Price developments in India: International and domestic market prices and minimum support prices (MSP) for (a) rice and (b) wheat, U.S. dollar per tonne.
Source: Reproduced from Diaz-Bonilla 2014 who used data from Hoda and Gulati 2013.

some related to India's position in the WTO negotiations, some to the future of WTO rules for domestic support in agriculture.

Regarding India's position it would be interesting to know why the government decided, along with governments of other G33 countries, to pursue the issue of food security stocks so vigorously in the WTO, pushing the Bali ministerial meeting to the brink of collapse and sinking the trade facilitation package (and potentially the rest of the Doha Round) on July 31, 2014. After all, India could have tried alternative approaches that might have yielded the same outcome in terms of policy space for procuring food security stocks. It could have invoked the "excessive inflation" clause. Did India feel this was too legally insecure? It could have abandoned the notion of administered prices, without actually changing its purchase operations, thereby freeing it from the WTO constraint on MPS. Did the government reject that option because it feels it needs to create some degree of certainty for farmers by announcing minimum support prices, even though the purchase operations based on these prices have little if any effect on actual market prices? Somewhat more controversial, India could also have simply continued its policies and disregarded a potential violation of its WTO commitments on domestic support, crying foul when challenged in a dispute, on the grounds that its opponents prevented it from fighting food insecurity. After all, it was precisely that argument that India employed with such political success at Bali. Why did the Indian government decide not to try any of these more subtle options, but rather to stage a big and politically visible fight, causing major trouble in the WTO?

At a different level one may also ask why India's government is so keen on maintaining its policy of procuring stocks from domestic farmers, so as to provide food to families in need. Stockholding not only is a rather costly operation, it also can do little to stabilize prices.[32] Stock accumulation involves the danger that one day the government has to dispose of surplus stocks through subsidized exports. In fact, India's neighbors and competitors are rather concerned that India's policy might threaten to cause massive distortions of international markets. An alternative option to improve food security would be for the Indian government to move in the direction of targeted cash transfers to poor families who can then buy food in the market place. This policy approach would not only be unconstrained by the WTO, it would also be more effective and efficient from a domestic perspective.

Regarding the future of WTO rules for domestic support in agriculture, the "Indian problem" has brought a number of issues to the forefront. The wisdom of including MPS in the AoA's constraints on domestic support has been questioned from the beginning, on a number of grounds (Josling, Tangermann, and Warley 1996). The scope for governments to provide MPS depends on their ability to prevent arbitrage between the domestic market and international trade through border measures, meaning, tariffs or export subsidies or both. Since the Uruguay Round, all tariffs in agriculture are bound and export subsidization is constrained. Hence there is, in principle, no need to impose an additional constraint on MPS through the domestic support provisions. In each individual market, only one of the three constraints on MPS is effective at any time, either the domestic support commitment or the tariff binding or the limit on export subsidization. To be sure, in many cases the tariffs applied are below the bindings (as discussed earlier), and hence the domestic support commitments are often more restrictive than the tariff bindings. This is also the case for India. However, where a country is a net exporter (as is the case for rice and wheat in India), tariffs are not needed to prevent arbitrage, and hence the scope for domestic prices is limited only by the maneuvering room for providing export subsidies. Thus, it would appear to make sense in the WTO to negotiate appropriate adjustments in tariff bindings and export subsidization and then to drop MPS from the domestic support provisions.

This would also do away with all uncertainties resulting currently from the vagueness of the AoA definitions of "administered price" and "eligible quantity." Above all, abandoning MPS from the domestic support provisions would eliminate the need to rely on the strange concept of fixed external reference prices, still dating back to the 1986–1988 base period. The economic implications of using these FERPs have always been questionable. FERPs were introduced to the AoA as negotiators felt that governments could not commit, in a legally binding way, to disciplines whose quantitative parameters depended on something they could not control, that is, volatile world market prices. Understandable as that may have been from an operational point of view, the approach adopted in the AoA has never made economic sense. The longer the 1986–1988 base period recedes, and the more actual prices in international trade have moved away from these FERPs, the less reasonable is continued reliance on that approach. The situation becomes completely paradoxical where a country bumps against WTO constraints even though the (administered) prices at which it buys into public stocks are below the prevailing international market prices, as might be the case in India if the government were to notify domestic support for recent years under a strict interpretation of AoA provisions.

In the discussion on a "permanent solution" to the food security stock issue as evoked in the respective Bali decision, various options are being suggested. Some of them might also (or would even have to) be applied more generally to calculating all MPS under the AoA. In particular, an update of the FERPs to a more recent base period is sometimes considered, or a switch to a moving average of external reference prices.[33] However, such fixes would not do away with the fundamental problems involved in making MPS a part of domestic support under the AoA. In the longer term it would make sense to reduce the concept of domestic support, as a binding constraint under the AoA, to government expenditure only (and revenue forgone) and rely on the commitments regarding border measures (tariffs and export subsidies) for constraining MPS. Of course that would require adjustments of the numerical values of domestic support commitments, and ideally also of tariff bindings, over and above those considered in relation to improving market access.[34] All this would require negotiations on complex issues. Such more fundamental changes to the nature of AoA provision on domestic support will, therefore, most likely not be achievable in the Doha Round. But negotiators should not lose sight of the desirability of eliminating, at some point, the unconvincing elements of the AoA provisions on domestic support.

What could then constitute a "permanent solution" of the "Indian problem"? One possibility would be to agree that government-set prices are only considered "administered prices" (in the AoA sense of generating MPS) if they exceed the border price equivalent.[35] This approach would largely do away with the problem India might have with its notifications. It would also eliminate the paradoxical situation that a country that is not effectively providing price support is still considered, under WTO rules, to do so. This solution would have the advantage of responding to the "Indian problem" constructively without acting as an invitation for developing countries to provide price support to their domestic farmers. It would thus avoid waste of resources and trade distortions. And it would constitute a first step in the direction of eliminating MPS altogether from the AoA provisions on domestic support.

7.6 Conclusions

Despite the important achievements on agriculture reached in the Uruguay Round, agricultural matters continue to cause major trouble in the

Doha negotiations. On a number of occasions, inability to agree on items related to agriculture retarded or blocked progress in the Doha Round. A rather dramatic incidence was a temporary refusal by India and a few other countries to let the trade facilitation package go forward, on the grounds that they considered progress in negotiations on food security stocks insufficient. Another indication of the problems faced in agriculture was the difficulty of putting together a meaningful and substantive package for the December 2015 WTO Ministerial Conference at Nairobi. How this will affect the future of the Doha Round remains to be seen.

In the first half of 2014 and again in the first half of 2015, what appeared to have been some sort of a breakthrough at Bali had revived spirits in Geneva, including in the agricultural negotiations. Negotiators were in the process of taking another look at the December 2008 draft modalities for agriculture and engaged in discussions on whether they could still serve as the vantage point for further negotiations, or whether the world had changed so much that a new framework was needed.

Against this background this chapter has looked, in its first part, at the changes in world agriculture since 2008. Prices of agricultural commodities in international trade have exhibited large volatility, but perhaps more important they also appear to have experienced a lasting step increase, by around one third. Agricultural policies in major countries have also changed. In the OECD area, the level of producer support in agriculture has declined, and policy structures have changed in the direction of less distorting instruments. Major emerging economies, though, have raised levels of producer support and resorted to somewhat more distorting policies. An important fact is that in many countries, in particular in the South, agricultural tariffs exhibit a large binding overhang. A phenomenon that also requires attention is the frequent use of export restrictions in the food sector observed when international market prices spiked after 2006.

In other words, the world has indeed changed since the agricultural negotiations of the Doha Round ground to a halt in 2008. However, the changes that took place have not made obsolete the draft modalities for agriculture tabled in December 2008. Given the changes observed on markets and in policies, the reduction rates suggested in those modalities (in Rev.4) are now even more important than they were at the time, and they should also be easier to implement in both political and economic terms. If anything, larger reductions could be considered now, in particular for tariffs. At the same time, disciplines on export restrictions are more important than they may have appeared in 2008.

The second theme that played a role in the agricultural negotiations during the first half of 2014 was public stockholding for food security purposes. This issue, so much emphasized by India, raises a number of interesting questions. From one perspective one can ask why India felt it needed to push this issue so hard. The economic rationale of the relevant policies in India is debatable. And in terms of mechanics, under the AoA India potentially could have chosen different avenues. Whether the issue was worth the possible failure of the trade facilitation package, and even that of the Doha Round, is questionable.

However, at the same time one can also argue that India has pointed to a notable deficiency in the WTO provisions for commitments on domestic support in agriculture. Constraints on market price support, in addition to disciplines for tariffs and export subsidies, and in particular the use of fixed external reference prices dating back some three decades, coupled with a vague definition of "administered prices," don't make good economic sense. This element of the AoA should be revisited in the longer term. However, this probably will not be possible in the current negotiations. Hence a different "permanent solution" to the issue of public stock acquisition for food security purposes will have to be found. It could come in the form of agreeing that procurement prices below prices prevailing on international markets are not considered "administered prices" and hence do not count in calculating the market price component of domestic support.

Whether a pragmatic decision of this nature has any chance of being realized in the Doha Round will depend on the fate of the negotiations overall. It is conceivable that frustration over the failure to move forward in 2014 and 2015 is so pronounced and so widespread that the Doha Round may face tremendous difficulty in gaining traction again. If that is the case, it may turn out that a unique chance has been lost to complete the agricultural reform process that began in the Uruguay Round.

Notes

Chapter based on article prepared for the conference on "Challenges Facing the World Trade System" organized by Jagdish Bhagwati, Pravin Krishna, and Arvind Panagariya, Columbia University, New York, and Johns Hopkins University, Washington DC, September 29–October 2, 2014. The author gratefully acknowledges comments on an earlier draft received from Lars Brink and Bernard Hoekman.

1. The treatment of agriculture in the multilateral trade regime, including the Uruguay Round negotiations, is discussed extensively in Josling, Tangermann, and Warley 1996. For an analysis of the fifty years history of U.S.-EU conflict in agriculture, and potential resolution through TTIP, see Josling and Tangermann 2015.

2. Some parts of sections 7.2–7.4 overlap with Tangermann 2015.

3. The nature, determinants, and policy implications of volatility on agricultural commodity markets are discussed more fully in Tangermann 2011 and the literature referenced there.

4. For a statistical analysis of the long-term movement of commodity prices, see Jacks 2013.

5. The seven emerging economies included in the OECD's M&E are Brazil, China, Indonesia, Kazakhstan, the Russian Federation, South Africa, and Ukraine.

6. Note that the OECD area does not include the six non-OECD member countries of the EU, even though they are covered by the EU's Common Agricultural Policy.

7. It should be noted that the producer NPC as defined by OECD includes not only market price support, but also payments per unit of current output (e.g., deficiency payments).

8. The increase of this indicator in New Zealand is irrelevant given that New Zealand's %PSE is below 1 percent.

9. See Josling and Tangermann 2015 and the references cited there.

10. In addition to the countries included above in the section on producer support, India is included here in the review of tariff levels.

11. It should, however, be noted that for many TRQ (accounting for around 40 percent of all TRQ between 2002 and 2008; more recent years may not be representative due to late notifications) no imports are notified, for various reasons.

12. Australia, Brazil, Colombia, Iceland, Indonesia, Mexico, New Zealand, Panama, South Africa, and Uruguay.

13. The source of the data used in this paragraph is WTO 2014b.

14. The most recent export subsidy notification for Turkey was 2000 and for Venezuela 1998.

15. Lists of rationales for imposing export restrictions are provided in box 1 of Kim 2010 and table 7 of Fliess and Mård 2012.

16. For a discussion of disciplines regarding export restrictions in agriculture, see Anania 2013 and Tangermann 2013.

17. For an extensive discussion of the Bali decision on food security stocks and potential responses, see Diaz-Bonilla 2014.

18. To be fair it must be mentioned that the title of the decision is precisely the same as the heading of the respective provision in the Agreement of Agriculture.

19. For a more extensive discussion of policy options to improve food security, see OECD 2013.

20. Policies that can unleash the potential of agriculture to contribute to reducing poverty are discussed in OECD 2006 and Brooks 2012.

21. AoA Annex 2, paragraph 3 and footnote 5. Footnote 5&6 also allows developing countries to provide "foodstuffs at subsidized prices with the objective of meeting food requirements of urban and rural poor in developing countries on a regular basis at reasonable prices" without having to include the related expenditure in their AMS.

22. AoA Article 6.4(a)(i) and (b).

23. Häberli (2014) has commented that "the main driver was India which had just raised the minimum producer price for rice and foresaw that this subsidy risked exceeding its Amber Box limit for 2013," and added the observation that "somewhat ironically, the massive devaluation of the Indian Rupee seems to have brought Indian farm support back below the AMS limit just at the time of the Bali Conference."

24. Panel Report on China—GOES, para. 7.87.

25. Japan's rice policy and the EU's policy for fruit and vegetables are cases in point; see for example Orden, Blandford, and Josling 2011.

26. AoA Annex 3, para. 9: "The fixed external reference price shall be based on the years 1986 to 1988 and shall generally be the average f.o.b. unit value for the basic agricultural product concerned in a net exporting country and the average c.i.f. unit value for the basic agricultural product concerned in a net importing country in the base period. The fixed reference price may be adjusted for quality differences as necessary."

27. AoA Annex 3, para. 8.

28. For a discussion of that legal question, see Brink 2014 and Diaz-Bonilla 2014.

29. AoA Art. 18.4.

30. See the discussion by Brink 2014 and Diaz-Bonilla 2014.

31. According to India's WTO notifications, its price gaps for rice and wheat, expressed in U.S. dollars, and hence its sums of product-specific market price support were negative in all years from 1998 to 2003; see Brink 2014.

32. For a discussion of policy options to deal with volatility on food markets, see Tangermann 2011.

33. See, for example, Montemayor 2014.

34. As there appears to be general agreement that export subsidies (and equivalent measures) should be eliminated in the Doha Round there is no need to adjust them in response to eliminating MPS from the domestic support provisions.

35. This option is also discussed by Diaz-Bonilla 2014 and Matthews 2014.

References

Anania, Giovanni. 2013. "Agricultural Export Restrictions and the WTO: What Options Do Policy-Makers Have for Promoting Food Security?" ICTSD Programme on Agricultural Trade and Sustainable Development, Issue Paper No. 50. Geneva: International Centre for Trade and Sustainable Development.

Anderson, K., M. Ivanic, and W. J. Martin. 2014. "Food Price Spikes, Price Insulation, and Poverty." In *The Economics of Food Price Volatility.* ed. J.-P. Chavas, D. Hummels, and B. D. Wright, 311–344. Chicago: University of Chicago Press for the National Bureau of Economic Research.

Brink, L. 2014. "Support to Agriculture in India in 1995–2013 and the Rules of the WTO." IATRC Working Paper #14-01. St. Paul: International Agricultural Trade Research Consortium.

Brooks, J., ed. 2012. *Agricultural Policies for Poverty Reduction.* Paris: OECD.

Bureau, J., and S. Jean. 2013. « Do Yesterday's Disciplines Fit Today's Farm Trade? Challenges and Policy Options for the Bali Ministerial Conference." Draft Issue Paper for the E15 Expert Group on Agriculture and Food Security. Geneva: International Centre for Trade and Sustainable Development.

Diaz-Bonilla, E. 2014. "On Food Security Stocks, Peace Clauses, and Permanent Solutions after Bali." Working Paper, June. Washington, DC: International Food Policy Research Institute.

Fliess, B., and T. Mård. 2012. "Taking Stock of Measures Restricting the Export of Raw Materials: Analysis of OECD Inventory Data." OECD Trade Policy Papers, No. 140. Paris: OECD.

Gopinath, M. 2011. "India." Chapter 8 in *WTO Disciplines on Agricultural Support—Seeking a Fair Basis for Trade*, ed. D. Orden, D. Blandford and T. Josling, 277–309. Cambridge, UK: Cambridge University Press.

Häberli, C. 2014. *After Bali: WTO Rules Applying to Public Food Reserves.* Geneva: World Trade Institute.

The Hindu. 2013. Article on "Food Security Non-negotiable: Anand Sharma." 4 December 4. http://www.thehindu.com/business/Industry/food-security-nonnegotiable-anand-sharma/article5420830.ece (accessed August 9, 2014).

Hoda, A., and A. Gulati. 2013. "India's Agricultural Trade Policy and Sustainable Development." ICTSD Issue Paper No 49. Geneva: International Centre for Trade and Sustainable Development.

Jacks, David S. 2013. "From Boom to Bust: A Typology of Real Commodity Prices in the Long Run." NBER Working Paper Series No. 18874. Cambridge, MA: National Bureau of Economic Research.

Josling, T., S. Tangermann, and T. K. Warley. 1996. *Agriculture in the GATT.* Houndmills, London, and New York: Macmillan Press.

Josling, T., and S. Tangermann. 2015. *Transatlantic Food and Agricultural Trade Policy: Fifty Years of Conflict and Convergence.* Northampton, MA: Edward Elgar.

Kim, J. 2010. “Recent Trends in Export Restrictions.” OECD Trade Policy Papers, No. 101. Paris: OECD.

Matthews, A. 2014. “Food Security and WTO Domestic Support Disciplines Post-Bali.” ICTSD Programme on Agricultural Trade and Sustainable Development, Issue Paper No. 53. Geneva: International Centre for Trade and Sustainable Development.

Montemayor, R. 2014. “Public Stockholding for Food Security Purposes Scenarios and Options for a Permanent Solution.” ICTSD Programme on Agricultural Trade and Sustainable Development, Issue Paper No. 51. Geneva: International Centre for Trade and Sustainable Development.

OECD. 2006. *Trade, Agriculture and Development: Policies Working Together, The Development Dimension*. Paris: OECD.

OECD. 2013. *Global Food Security: Challenges for the Food and Agricultural System*. Paris: OECD.

OECD. 2014. *Agricultural Policy Monitoring and Evaluation 2013: OECD Countries and Emerging Economies*. Paris: OECD.

OECD-FAO. 2014. *OECD-FAO Agricultural Outlook 2014–2023*. Paris: OECD.

Orden, D., D. Blandford, and T. Josling, eds. 2011. *WTO Disciplines on Agricultural Support: Seeking a Fair Basis for Trade*. Cambridge, UK: Cambridge University Press.

Tangermann, S. 2002. “Agriculture on the Way to Firm International Trading Rules.” In *The Political Economy of International Trade Law: Essays in Honor of Robert E. Hudec*, ed. Daniel L. M. Kennedy and James D. Southwick, 254–282. Cambridge, UK: Cambridge University Press.

Tangermann, S. 2011. “Policy Solutions to Agricultural Market Volatility: A Synthesis.” ICTSD Programme on Agricultural Trade and Sustainable Development, Issue Paper No. 33. Geneva: International Centre for Trade and Sustainable Development.

Tangermann, S. 2013. “A Post-Bali Food Security Agenda: Report for the E15 Initiative ‘Strengthening the Multilateral Trading System.’” Bali: ICTSD and World Economic Forum.

Tangermann, S. 2015. “Are Past OECD Analyses of Agricultural Policy Reforms Relevant to Current Policy and Market Settings?” In OECD, ed., *Issues in Agricultural Trade Policy: Proceedings of the 2014 OECD Global Forum on Agriculture*, 25–68. Paris: OECD Publishing.

WTO. 2013a. “Tariff Quota Administration Methods and Fill Rates 2002–2011.” Background Paper by the Secretariat. Document TN/AG/S/26/Rev.1, March 28. Geneva: WTO.

WTO. 2013b. “Public Stockholding for Food Security Purposes.” Ministerial Decision of December 7, 2012. Document WT/MIN(13)/38, December 11. Geneva: WTO.

WTO. 2014a. *Tariff Profiles, Summary Tables Download Facility*. Geneva: WTO. http://stat.wto.org/TariffProfile/WSDBTariffPFReporter.aspx?Language=E (accessed September 20, 2014).

WTO. 2014b. "Export Subsidies, Export Credits, Export Credit Guarantees or Insurance Programmes, International Food Aid and Agricultural Export State Trading Enterprises—Background Document by the Secretariat." Documents G/AG/W/125 and addenda 1, 2, 3 and 4, May 21. Geneva: WTO.

WTO, ITC, and UNCTAD. 2008. *World Tariff Profiles 2008*. Geneva: WTO.

WTO, ITC, and UNCTAD. 2013. *World Tariff Profiles 2013*. Geneva: WTO. http://stat.wto.org/TariffProfile/WSDBTariffPFHome.aspx?Language=E (accessed September 20, 2014).

Part II

Regional Perspectives

8

The Trans-Pacific Partnership: Perspectives from China

Dimitar D. Gueorguiev and Mary E. Lovely

Heads turned in May 2013, when the White House formally extended invitations for China to join in negotiations over a proposed Trans-Pacific Partnership (TPP), a twenty-first century regional trade agreement poised to be the world's largest and most advanced.[1] Up until this point, the TPP was widely seen as an "anyone-but-China club," especially by the Chinese who saw it as a deliberate attempt to contain their economic rise.[2] To be sure, it did not help that prominent U.S. officials went on record describing the TPP as a "centerpiece" in America's "pivot" toward Asia.[3] Unsurprisingly, many dismissed America's invitation as a hollow courtesy—extended precisely because China would not and could not accept. Yet, when, on May 30, 2013, China's Ministry of Commerce (MOC) announced that it would "analyze the pros and cons of joining the Trans-Pacific Partnership (TPP)," the idea of a TPP that included China suddenly transformed from a pie in the sky to a real and very tantalizing prospect.[4]

The year following America's invitation inspired hopeful speculation on both sides of the Pacific. In the United States, prominent organizations like the US China Business Council and The Heritage Foundation voiced robust support for including China in the negotiations. In China, prominent economists laid out strong arguments for why the TPP needed China, as well as why China needed the TPP. Former World Bank senior vice president Justin Yifu Lin, for example, argued that the TPP would be "fundamentally incomplete without China."[5] Likewise, China's chief economist, Ma Jun, argued the TPP could "augment China's GDP by up to two percent."[6] Even within the Chinese leadership, the mood for cooperation was in high spirits. As one MOC official put it, "We know it's difficult, but the key point is we have to change minds and stick to opening-up to the world. Once we are determined on the TPP, everything else will be solved."[7] Such statements encouraged many to conclude that political sentiments in China had unambiguously shifted toward joining in on the TPP. As Beijing University's Huang Yiping put it, "an increasing number of policy advisers are now urging the government to join TPP negotiations as early as possible."[8]

Not everyone, however, agreed. In the first draft of this chapter, delivered in September 2014, we argued that it would be extremely unlikely for China to join the TPP. In particular, we argued that the arguments in favor of China's joining the TPP fail not only to demonstrate a clear economic benefit for China, but also to appreciate the strategic concerns and options entertained by China's leaders with respect to both international trade and domestic politics. Specifically, we argued that by endorsing parallel agreements, China could join in on the benefits of TPP without actually acceding TPP. Moreover, we argued that doing so would allow China to better navigate a gradual entry into a TPP-like regime, so as to maximize domestic political objectives.

Our initial skepticism has so far been confirmed in at least three ways. First and foremost, China to date has not joined any TPP-related negotiations. Second, China has made lightning progress on at least two TPP alternatives, the Regional Comprehensive Economic Partnership (RCEP) and the Free Trade Agreement of the Pacific (FTAAP).[9] Finally, with *fast-track* authority in hand, the Obama administration has successfully negotiated with its partners a TPP configuration that has no mention of China and will attempt to shepherd the deal through the U.S. Congress in 2016.[10]

And yet, speculation remains that China may still play a part in the TPP. Most recently, prominent western media groups, think tanks, and consultancies have outlined why China *should* be included in the TPP and why it is in fact, eventually, likely to join.[11] Likewise, on October 26, 2015, the *Study Times*, a mouthpiece for the Central Party School, expressed China's continued interest in the TPP, "the rules of the TPP and the direction of China's reforms and opening up are in line. ... China should, at an appropriate time, join the TPP."[12]

For our part, we continue to maintain that such speculations are unwarranted. However, the fact that key TPP players, like John Kerry, are still holding out an open palm to China, means that this conversation is far from over.[13] In this chapter, we review our initial misgivings about the prospects for China joining the TPP in an attempt to move forward a more fruitful discussion concerning China's evolving response to a TPP, for which it has deep concerns but few prospects for joining.

We begin by outlining the various arguments made by proponents of a TPP-plus-China formation. In particular, we address three common claims for why China is likely to join. The first is economic, which, simply stated, argues that China has the most to gain from tariff reductions associated with TPP membership and the most to lose from trade diversion should it not join. A second common argument is that China's failure to join will undermine its reputation as an open and peaceful economic giant, giving regional economies further incentive to invest in economic and security relations with the United States. Finally, proponents point to China's domestic political environment, arguing that joining the TPP could help the current administration push through declared reform objectives, much like WTO accession did for China's previous administration in the early 2000s.

In combination, these three arguments described are compelling and suggest a clear TPP-bound trajectory for China. Individually, however, each is open to reinterpretation. With respect to the economic logic, we show that the gains from trade, as well as the potential losses from trade diversion, are actually less substantial than might be expected. As for China's international reputation, while we agree that joining negotiations would provide a credible signal of China's peaceful aspirations and a better bargaining position on trade and investment, we also point out that China has alternative means by which to influence its neighbors and their negotiations, namely, by offering attractive parallel alternatives to the TPP. Finally, with regard to domestic politics, we agree that joining the TPP would help the regime coordinate reform objectives. But, after examining the actual reform strategies employed by the current leadership, we conclude that comprehensive reform is not China's goal, at least not in the short term. Instead, the push for localized Free Trade Zones (FTZs) and selective restructuring of state-owned assets suggests a more gradual and politically calculated strategy—a strategy that would be severely compromised under TPP obligations.

The chapter proceeds as follows. In section 8.1, we review existing international political economy (IPE) and international relations (IR) arguments on regional integration and how they apply to China's relationship with the TPP. In section 8.2, we address the economic rationale for Chinese TPP membership by estimating the benefits China would enjoy by joining the TPP and inferring the costs it would incur should it not join. In section 8.3, we assess the international reputation argument by contrasting the TPP with the RCEP and FTAAP trade arrangements, for which China has expressed strong support. In section 8.4, we engage the domestic politics argument by evaluating China's current reform strategy from both an economic and political perspective. Based on this three-part analysis, we conclude that China is unlikely to join the TPP, not for economic or geopolitical reasons, but because TPP requirements would undermine the current administration's domestic reform strategy. Instead, we argue that China is most likely to continue promoting alternatives to the TPP in the hope of maintaining good faith with the regional partners. In section 8.5, we summarize our logic and offer our predictions for China's future, indirect involvement with the TPP through alternative regional trade arrangements.

8.1 The TPP and the China Possibility

The TPP is set to become the most substantial free trade agreement (FTA) of the twenty-first century, encompassing items that have largely been excluded from previous agreements, namely, nontariff barriers, investment standards, and intellectual property. Since negotiations first launched in 2002,[14] the TPP's formal negotiating partners have expanded from three to twelve nations. Once concluded, the TPP trading bloc will encompass nearly 40 percent of global trade and produce gains estimated at about $295 billion for members of the pact (Petri, Plummer, and Zhai 2014). In its entirety, the TPP hopes to tackle a litany of trade-relevant issues neglected by previous arrangements along with an array of nontrade issues such as protections for foreign capital, environmental quality, and even cloud computing. The TPP also takes aim at unfair competition from state-owned enterprises and government procurement practices. Combined with a potential twin agreement between the United States and Europe, the Transatlantic Trade and Investment Partnership (TTIP), the TPP is poised to achieve much of what WTO negotiations failed to achieve during the Doha Round of negotiations (2001–2008).

Despite the significant prospects, successful negotiation on the TPP seemed a distant possibility for over eight years. This is understandable. Generally speaking, the size and scope of a union is inversely related to the degree of heterogeneity between the countries inside it (Alesina, Angeloni, and Etro 2001), and the TPP pushes the limits in both respects. As currently defined, the TPP includes twelve economies: Australia, Brunei Darussalam, Canada, Chile, Japan, Malaysia, Mexico, New Zealand, Peru, Singapore, the United States, and Vietnam. As shown in table 8.1, these twelve differ in terms of size, income level, and technological

Table 8.1
Country characteristics, TPP-12 countries and China, 2012

	Country	GDP in billions of 2012 USD	GDP per capita (2012 USD)	Merchandise export (2012 USD)	Service export (2012 USD)	Total exports of goods and services (2012 USD)
High	Australia	1532	67436	256	53	309
	Brunei Darussalam	17	41127	13	1	14
	Canada	1821	52409	455	84	539
	Chile	266	15245	79	13	92
	Japan	5938	46548	799	134	933
	New Zealand	171	38680	37	13	50
	Singapore	287	54007	408	119	527
	United States	16245	51755	1547	650	2197
Upper-middle	China	8229	6093	2049	196	2245
	Malaysia	305	10432	227	38	265
	Mexico	1186	9818	371	16	387
	Peru	193	6424	46	4	50
Lower-middle	Vietnam	156	1755	145	10	155

Source: World Bank, World Development Indicators 2013.

capacity, meaning that the TPP was a hard sell for nearly everyone. Some general points of contention have included IPR (intellectual property rights) provisions that may make pharmaceuticals much more expensive in the poorer countries and language that will make it possible for companies and multinationals to sue governments if they believe their market access is unfairly restricted.[15] Even more contentious, perhaps, provisions aimed at eliminating competition from state-owned enterprises posed serious threats to countries with large state sectors, like Vietnam, Singapore, and Malaysia.

China's ambivalent position on TPP served to complicate negotiations even further, by raising the prospect of a much larger and more lucrative

TPP that included China or simply a larger version of the TPP that included more of the regional economies and fewer American conditions. For instance, countries like Malaysia and Vietnam, which have their own bloated state sectors, welcomed Chinese criticism toward restrictions on government procurement and state-owned enterprises under the TPP. Similarly, Chinese resistance to strict IPR and limits on exchange rate management found support among developing economies in the group (Malaysia, Mexico, Peru, Vietnam).[16] Most important, the prospect of China entering the mix gave all parties reason to hold out for a more substantial regional FTA. Here it is important to remember that China is already the largest regional importer of parts and components and a major importer of commodities. China also is emerging as a primary source of outward FDI (foreign direct investment) to the region, recently surpassing the United States as the region's second largest investor after Japan (see table 8.2).[17] Moreover, an agreement including China promises the region greater peace of mind that China would remain open to trade into the future, when its economy slows down and its imports begin to overtake its exports (Panagariya 1999).

Two important developments over the past year have fundamentally altered the playing field. First, in December of 2014, a snap election in Japan gave the ruling LDP a powerful mandate with which to ram

Table 8.2
ASEAN FDI inflows, by source, in million USD

	2011	2012	2013
European Union (EU)	29693.3	18084.9	26979.6
Japan	9709.0	23777.1	22904.4
ASEAN	15228.4	20657.6	21321.5
China	7857.7	5376.8	8643.5
Hong Kong	4273.8	5029.9	4517.3
United States	9129.8	11079.5	3757.5
Republic of Korea	1742.1	1708.4	3516.2
Australia	1530.2	1831.0	2002.3
Taiwan, Province of China	2317.0	2242.3	1321.7
India		2233.4	1317.5

Source: ASEAN, Foreign Direct Investment Statistics Database.

through the TPP. Likewise, although President Obama continues to face stiff opposition from both Republicans and fellow Democrats, his win on fast-track negotiation authority in the summer of 2015 means there is little the U.S. Congress can do to derail or delay the bid by early 2016, by which time it must vote on ratification. These two events made it possible for a successful conclusion to TPP negotiations in October 2015, and now leave China with a choice. Either it begins to inch its way into the partnership or it doubles up on efforts to establish parallel arrangements. To predict its ultimate course of action, we break down China's calculus on the TPP, as well as what appears to be its preferred strategy.

8.2 China's Economic Stake in the TPP

Whether China will actually join the TPP is still unclear, and there are several compelling arguments for why it should. The most prominent of these is the economic argument, the basic claim of which is that China stands to lose out on potential trade benefits and trade volume if it does not join. In particular, given China's role as the dominant exporter in the region, it has an incentive to join any agreement that could potentially expand its trade and investment flows or that prevents it from losing volume as a result of trade diversion. But how large are the potential trade-related benefits? Similarly, how large are the potential trade diversion losses to not joining? Answering these questions is essential for gauging the strength of the economic argument.

Much of the gain from an FTA comes from trade creation, as originally identified by Viner (1950). Trade creation occurs when a member of the FTA begins to import from an FTA partner a good that it previously produced for itself. Since it would do so only if the partner produces it more cheaply than it can itself, both it and the partner benefit from this exchange in terms of the cost of the country's total consumption (Deardorff 2013). Offsetting the gains to FTA members from trade creation are losses from trade diversion. Trade diversion occurs when a member country imports from a partner a good that it previously imported from a third (nonmember) country. Because both countries previously faced the same tariff, we can assume that imports from the third country were due to lower cost. Sourcing from the partner country rather than the third country, therefore, means purchasing a higher cost good. As Deardorff (2013) notes, this loss to the importing country is not obvious to consumers, who find the higher-cost product cheaper due to the absence of tariff. The absence of the tariff instead accrues as lost tariff revenue for the state. Bhagwati and Panagariya (1999) define trade creation and diversion succinctly in what they term the original Vinerian sense: a shift from an inefficient to an efficient source under trade creation and a shift from an efficient to an inefficient source under trade diversion.

Petri, Plummer, and Zhai (2012, 2014) use a computable general equilibrium (CGE) framework to gauge the magnitude of possible welfare gains from conclusion of a TPP agreement. The model they use is novel, specially developed by Zhai (2008) to incorporate firm-level differences in productivity, detailing twenty-four regions and eighteen sectors and modified for the specific trade agreements in the Asia-Pacific. Without China, countries joining the TPP will benefit through the creation of trade among its members, enhancing average productivity, expanding consumer variety, and increasing price competition. For the TPP-12, Petri, Plummer, and Zhai (2014) estimate total income gains of $223 billion (in 2007 dollars) by 2015. Given the relative size of their economies, about four-fifths of the gains are predicted to accrue to the United States and Japan. The United States has FTAs with half the expected TPP members, but not with Japan. The largest effect of the TPP-12 will be through the U.S.-Japan relationship, with Japan's gains estimated to exceed those accruing to the United States. The estimated gains for Malaysia and Vietnam exceed those for Singapore and Mexico, despite the almost similar shares of manufactures in each country's total merchandise trade (see table 8.3).

Nonmember countries are not affected at all by trade creation, at least not directly. However, as a nonmember of the TPP-12, China may lose as a result of trade diversion. As Deardorff (2013) notes, "One does not need subtle theoretical analysis to realize that outside countries are harmed by an FTA, to the extent that the markets for their exports are reduced. This effect of an FTA is arguably more important than any loss to partner countries, since it is both inevitable and potentially large." Petri, Plummer, and Zhai (2014) estimate welfare losses on the magnitude of $34 billion by 2025 for China under TPP-12 alone. These losses are large relative to the total gains to the members: an estimated 15 percent of total gains are offset by trade diversion costs estimated for China. Yet, these losses are small when viewed in the context of China's economy: by 2025 they are only an estimated 0.2 percent of China's baseline GDP of $17.2 trillion.[18] Petri, Plummer, and Zhai also estimate net losses for Hong Kong, Indonesia, Thailand, and the Philippines.

Table 8.3
Manufactures as share of merchandise trade, TPP-12 countries and China, 2012

Country	Manufactures imports (% of merchandise imports)	Manufactures exports (% of merchandise exports)
Australia	73	16
Brunei Darussalam	73	4
Canada	76	47
Chile	67	14
Japan	48	90
New Zealand	69	20
Singapore	60	70
United States	70	63
China	55	94
Malaysia	69	62
Mexico	78	74
Peru	73	15
Vietnam	74	69

Source: World Bank, World Development Indicators 2013.

One explanation for the small size of potential losses to China of not joining the TPP initially is that it already has preferential agreements with some of the TPP-12 countries. China has FTAs with the AFTA (Malaysia, Singapore, Brunei, and Vietnam) countries as well as with Chile, New Zealand, and Peru. Nearly all exports and imports to those members are already subject to zero tariffs, so no tariff-related trade diversion will occur.

But this leaves Australia, Canada, Japan, Mexico, and the United States as TPP members with whom China has no FTA and where it can expect a decline of exports due to trade diversion. By 2007, the United States was the most important individual-country market for Chinese exports and Japan the third largest (Dean, Lovely, and Mora 2009). These important bilateral flows suggest that China would experience major losses from trade diversion as a nonmember of the TPP. However, as shown in figure 8.1, average MFN tariffs in all TPP countries on

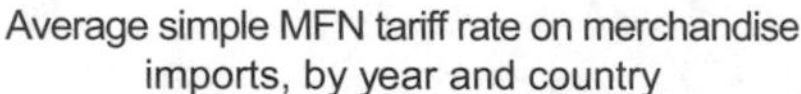

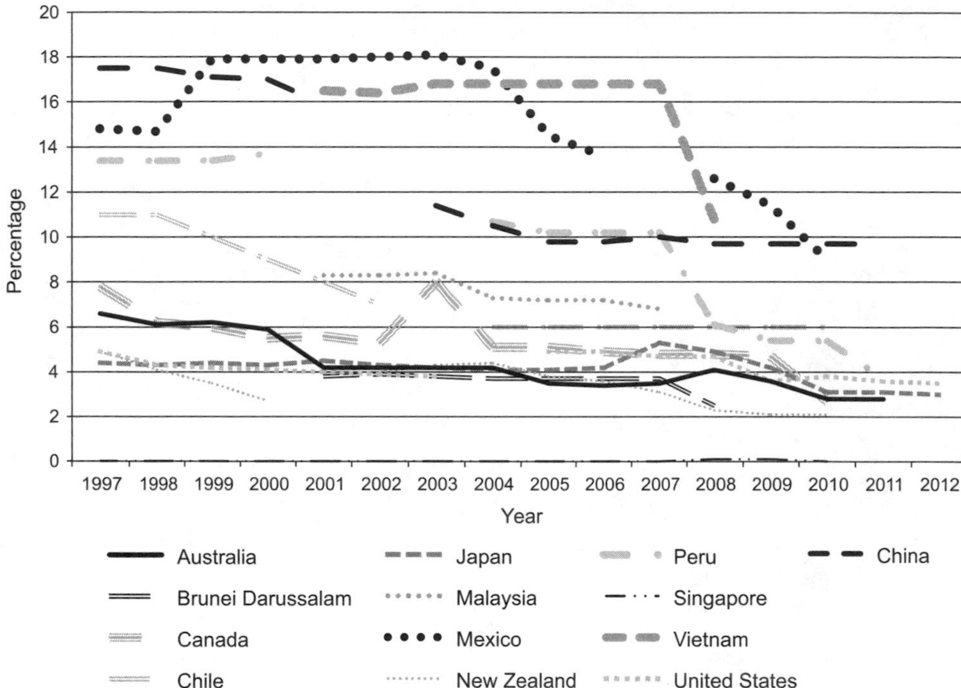

Figure 8.1
MFN tariff rates of TPP negotiating parties and China.
Source: World Bank, World Integrated Trade System, 2014.

merchandise trade are already low and this partly accounts for the small estimated losses to China through trade diversion. Nevertheless, the small magnitude of the trade diversion estimated by Petri, Plummer, and Zhai (2014) is surprising given that the TPP reduces barriers on trade in agriculture and services, two areas where China still faces significant barriers.

Although many aspects of the complex TPP agreement had not yet been fully defined, Petri, Plummer, and Zhai (2014) used their model to estimate the additional gains accruing from the expansion of the TPP-12 to a TPP-17 by the inclusion of China, Indonesia, Korea, the Philippines, and Thailand. They found that global benefits would rise enormously by the inclusion of these four members, expanding from $223 billion to $1908 billion by 2015. Over half of the additional gains would accrue to China, with the estimated welfare effect changing from a $35 billion loss for TPP-12 to a gain of $808 billion by 2015. Remarkably, over 40 percent of the estimated global gain is expected to accrue to China alone. But the TPP-12 partners would also experience larger gains through the inclusion of these five Asian economies in the FTA, as predicted benefits triple, from $285 billion to $893 billion by 2025.[19]

The Possibility of Foreign Direct Investment Diversion

The inclusion of investment provisions is not new to the TPP. Beginning with the North American Free Trade Agreement and then into the TRIMs provisions of the Uruguay Round of the GATT, trade agreements have explicitly acknowledged the link between multinational investment and trade flows. Foreign investment is a priority for the United States in its negotiations, especially the right of establishment by foreign goods and service providers in the partner-country territory. Although the details have yet to emerge, issues under discussion include nondiscriminatory treatment of foreign investments and investors; minimum standard of treatment; rules on expropriation; transfer of payments of the foreign investor out of the host territory; state-to-state and investor-state dispute settlement procedures; and prohibition on performance requirements such as mandatory export levels and local content stipulations (Fergusson et al. 2013, 40).

Beginning in initial openings through Special Export Zones in 1979, foreign direct investment (FDI) has played an important role in China's development. It remains important today, as a conduit for foreign technology and as the base for deep linkages into global supply chains. As shown in figure 8.2, net foreign direct investment inflows to China have grown rapidly since China's entry into the World Trade Organization in 2001. Remarkably, net FDI inflows to China have exceeded those into the United States since 2009. While the largest share of foreign capital comes from Hong Kong and other ethnically Chinese economies, Japan and the United States have been the most important investors from the developed economies.

It is difficult to overstate the importance of production fragmentation and foreign-invested enterprises (FIEs) to Chinese trade flows. Processing trade—the import of intermediates for assembly and transformation in China and their subsequent re-exporting—lies behind much of the growth in China's imports and exports (Hammer 2006). Although China's reliance on processing trade has fallen over time, in 2007 half of its total exports were processing exports.[20] Production fragmentation and regional specialization is especially important in China's trade with the United

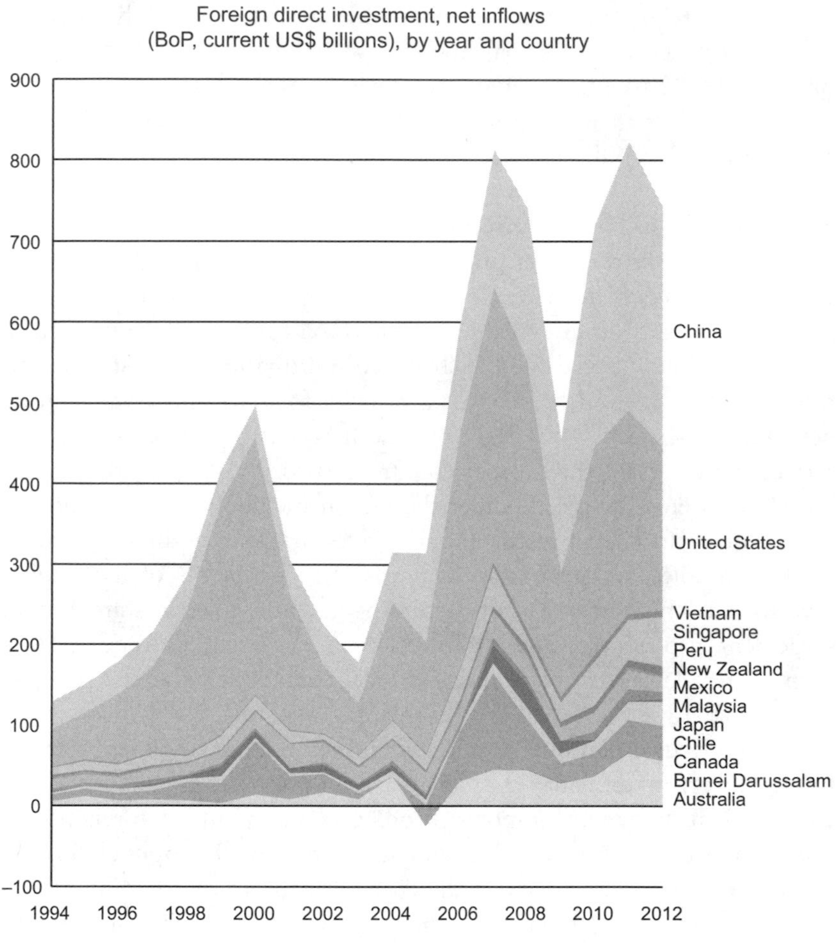

Figure 8.2
Foreign investment inflows to China.
Source: World Bank, World Development Indicators 2013.

States and Japan. In 2007, 62.5 percent of China's exports to the United States and 56.6 percent of its exports to Japan were processing exports. Much of these processing exports were mediated through FIEs. From 1998 to 2007, American foreign direct investment in China averaged $3.9 billion per year, while Japanese foreign direct investment averaged somewhat more, $4.3 billion per year. In 2007, 86.2 percent of China's total processing exports to the United States came from FIEs, with a very similar share (86.9 percent) of total processing exports to Japan coming from FIEs.

In some respects, the investment and intellectual property provisions of the TPP are more important than its promised reduction in tariffs. From this perspective, investment-related provisions of the TPP have the potential to further expand and deepen the production fragmentation, regional specialization, and wealth creation unleashed by the IT revolution and the liberalization of trade and investment policies in the developing world. Further support for the view that the TPP is important to China's continual receipt of foreign direct investment comes from studies of the determinants of FDI flows. Among other studies, Büthe and Milner (2008) analyze FDI flows into 122 developing countries over the period 1970–2000 and conclude that joining international trade agreements allows developing countries to attract more investment and, thus, to increase economic growth. They argue that international commitments regarding the treatment of foreign investors are more credible than domestic policy choices because they raise the cost of backsliding.

If China fails to join TPP, it may see FDI diverted away from its shores toward middle- and low-income countries that are TPP members. Already, there has been substantial movement of foreign investment in labor-intensive industries such as footwear, apparel, and sporting goods away from coastal China. The main driver of this movement of footloose industries is believed to be the steady increase in Chinese real wages, which have grown an average of 10 percent per year over the past decade. The greater investor protections and enhanced dispute resolution procedures offered by the TPP may simply amplify this ongoing trend by making alternative locations even more attractive.

However, while some sectors have migrated away from China, a second look at figure 8.2 suggests that this investment diversion cannot be large relative to the total inflow. First, the size of foreign investment flows into China dwarfs flows into any middle- or low-income country in the TPP-12. Second, the size of these alternative economies is small relative to the size of potentially deflected investment flows. As shown earlier in table 8.1, only Mexico has a gross domestic product that exceeded $1 trillion in 2012, in comparison to FDI inflows to China in the same year of almost $300 billion. Moreover, Mexico is an unlikely alternative for production that will receive further processing in East Asia since it is not within the region. Finally, Mexico's manufacturing wages exceed those of China.

In addition to investor protections, through the TPP the United States seeks intellectual property rights (IPR) protections that "reflect a standard of protection similar to that found in U.S. law" and that exceed those provided for in the WTO Agreement on Trade-Related Aspects of Intellectual Property (TRIPS) (Fergusson et al. 2013, 34). Because such "TRIPS plus" provisions are seen as investor friendly, there is again concern that a failure by China to join the TPP negotiations will diminish its attraction as a location for export-processing investment.

Such concerns may be overstated, however, when we consider two features of the current investment landscape. First, since joining the WTO, FDI inflows to China have soared, as previously discussed. This trend suggests that the TRIPS provisions provide a level of protection that has increased investor confidence substantially. Second, a comparison of China's existing level of IPR to those in place in other TPP-12 countries suggests that China is hardly an outlier in this regard. The well-known Park index of patent protection is provided for the TPP-12 countries plus China in table 8.4. By 2005, China's score of 4.08 on the Park index exceeds all other middle- and low-income TPP countries as well as the

Table 8.4
Park index of patent rights, TPP-12 countries and China, selected years

Country	Average 1960–1990	1995	2000	2005
Australia	2.96	4.21	4.33	4.33
Brunei Darussalam	n.a.	n.a.	n.a.	n.a.
Canada	3.00	4.34	4.67	4.67
Chile	2.04	3.91	4.28	4.28
Japan	2.93	4.42	4.67	4.67
New Zealand	2.67	4.01	4.01	4.01
Singapore	1.64	3.88	4.01	4.21
United States	4.14	4.88	4.88	4.88
China	1.33	2.12	3.09	4.08
Malaysia	1.70	2.70	3.03	3.48
Mexico	1.19	3.14	3.68	3.88
Peru	0.59	2.73	3.32	3.32
Vietnam	1.38	2.90	2.92	3.03

Source: W. G. Park, "International Patent Protection: 1960–2005," *Research Policy* 37 (2008): 761–766.

score given to New Zealand. Through this lens, China is making significant progress on patent protection without the "hard law" provisions of the TPP (Park 2008).

A final, and important, reason to argue against significant FDI diversion if China fails to join the TPP is the impending Bilateral Investment Treaty (BIT) between China and the United States. BIT talks began in 2008 and the partners have engaged in twenty-one negotiating rounds to date. The U.S.–China BIT breaks with China's traditional BIT model in at least two significant respects.[21] First, China has agreed that it will negotiate on the basis of a "negative list." This approach allows the BIT negotiations to move forward with exchanges of "negative lists," which detail sectors closed to foreign investors and typically leads to broader liberalization since it requires "opting out" of liberalization rather than "opting in."[22] Second, in 2013 the two countries agreed to talks on the basis of pre-establishment national treatment (PENT). PENT means that foreign investors will be accorded national treatment in the pre-establishment phase of their businesses, affording greater certainty for investments in various sectors. This arrangement represents a major departure from the current Chinese national investment approval system and it creates an environment for foreign investors that provides many of the disciplines sought through the TPP.

While the TPP contains other provisions that go beyond existing and proposed agreements to which China is party, evidence suggests that China's economic losses from not joining the TPP are unlikely to be other than negligible. Current barriers to trade between the TPP-12 and China are already low and trade flows are already enormous. China receives the lion's share of foreign direct investment into the developing world, reflecting in part substantial progress already made in the policy environment facing foreign investors. Last, China has other mechanisms, such as the Bilateral Investment Treaty, that provide selected liberalization in Sino trade and investment regimes.

8.3 International Reputations

Another common argument for why China is likely to join the TPP is that it needs to signal its commitment to free trade and a peaceful rise as a regional superpower. This need is especially pressing given recent spats between China and some of its neighbors, including Japan and Vietnam, both of which are party to the TPP negotiations. In particular, relations between China and Japan were strained in 2012, when the Japanese government purchased the disputed Senkaku (or Diaoyu in Chinese) islands from their private Japanese owner.[23] China responded with a new Air Defense Identification Zone (ADIZ) over the area and a ramp-up in nationalistic rhetoric, both of which have further undermined good faith between the two economies.[24] Similarly, in May 2014, China parked a portable oil drilling station in disputed waters within Vietnam's Exclusive Economic Zone (EEZ). The move prompted street protests from Vietnamese citizens who directed their anger toward local Chinese businesses (though many turned out to actually be Taiwanese). Most recently, assertive land reclamation efforts in the South China Sea have added to regional concerns that China's economic pragmatism has given way to geopolitical realism.

Under this tense backdrop, China has been struggling to convince neighbors that, while it remains resolute in pressing territorial claims, it is nevertheless committed to economic cooperation. One of the clearest examples of China's softer side is the One Road One Belt initiative, a multidimensional logistics and investment platform, financed by China, that promises billion-dollar prospects for China's neighbors, particular in South and Southeast Asia.[25] While this strategy ultimately may pan out quite favorably, it is still too early to tell. Indeed, already we have seen parts of the strategy, such as deep-water ports in South Asia, fall into disarray.[26]

Arguably, joining in on the TPP would be the best way for China to signal its regional benevolence and commitment to economic cooperation. However, the TPP is not the only option China has for sending such signals. Since the mid-1990s China has entertained the possibility of a regional free trade agreement in the Asia Pacific. In 2004, China concluded the China ASEAN Free Trade Agreement (CAFTA) and is poised to adopt a larger and more significant Regional Comprehensive Economic Partnership with the ASEAN states in 2015. Underneath these regional arrangements lies a tangle of Chinese bilateral trade agreements (BTAs), which offer China various avenues through which to maintain existing trade relations.[27] The TPP is, by far, a "higher quality" agreement than anything China already has in place. However, it is not clear whether China is interested in, or even capable of, subscribing to such high standards. Chinese trade representatives, for example, have already criticized the "one size fits all" approach to the TPP negotiations, arguing that there are "developed" as well as "developing" countries at the negotiation table and that no single menu could satisfy everyone.

What China is offering is options and it has been busy marketing several alternatives, some of which appear to be resonating with ASEAN members. During the inaugural 2013 U.S.-ASEAN summit, Malaysian Prime Minister Najib Razak stated that a more flexible approach was needed in future trade negotiations, as ASEAN members were not simply "yes men" in the TPP initiative.[28] In a rare case of common opinion, Anwar Ibrahim, the Malaysian opposition leader, has also come out in criticism of the TPP as an attempt by the United States "to impose its brand of economic model" on unwilling partners. More recently, Japan's chief TPP negotiator remarked that the TPP provides a blank check on monetary policy but imposes strict restrictions on exchange rate policy, terms that seem to benefit the United States at the expense of exporters.[29]

China's push for TPP alternatives, or "complements," as it prefers to call them, has a simple sales pitch, namely, "TPP-like trade coordination without the TPP level of stringency." In short, China hopes to advance a "win-win" approach to integration that focuses on breadth of membership, not depth of partnership. For example, China has even argued that there are too many overlapping trade arrangements in the region (even though a large portion of them involve China) and that a new mega-FTA would actually simplify matters.[30] This is all fair and good, but what exactly is China putting its weight behind?

First, China is actively promoting the RCEP for East Asia, which would include the ten ASEAN members, as well as Australia, India, Japan, Korea, New Zealand, and of course China. Much more than the TPP, RCEP is very much a regionally inspired idea, not a meeting of like-minded economies. China, for instance, stresses that RCEP is grounded in ASEAN centrality and that "close neighbors are better than distant relatives." This message is likely to resonate with those in Southeast Asia who feel left behind by the selective annexation of some ASEAN economies into the TPP. RCEP's regional focus also allows for the inclusion of India, which has so far been left out of regional arrangements, including the TPP.

China's proposals offer several other enticing features. For example, China has called for the adoption of flexible rules of origin (ROOs) for RCEP, which would allow products to circulate seamlessly across countries during their production cycle. RCEP would also allow members to ease into liberalization by allowing sector-specific reductions. For example, RCEP members could focus initial efforts on sectors, such as tourism and textiles, which are relatively easy to expose and tend to generate quick returns. Such provisions, even if they are unlikely to materialize any time soon, complicate the TPP process, which promises to adopt strict ROOs and blanket tariff reductions.

In addition to RCEP, China has also expressed interest in speeding up negotiations on the FTAAP, which poses to be the largest RTA in history, both in terms of geography and economic size. Under the "Yokohama Vision," articulated during the 2010 APEC summit, FTAAP was seen as a natural progression from TPP and RCEP that would eventually encompass all the APEC member countries, accounting for about 60 percent of the global economy. What China essentially is proposing is to skip the warm-up acts and go straight to the main show. Until recently, negotiations were not even supposed to begin until 2020,[31] but again China's leaders have upped the ante by announcing intentions to push toward an FTAAP agreement under the current Chinese administration.[32] Interestingly, the APEC economies, with reservations from the United States, welcomed the idea, announcing in their 2014 communiqué that the FTAAP arrangement could be established within the next two years, potentially earlier than the TPP![33]

Finally, it is important to note that although these alternative arrangements are more flexible and less stringent than what is being offered under the TPP, China has nonetheless moved to improve its intellectual and physical investment environment. As mentioned earlier, China is in the final stages of negotiating a U.S.–China BIT, which will greatly improve investment conditions for foreign firms operating in China, first by opening up previously opaque investment sectors and by offering much stronger intellectual property rights for firms operating in China. Chinese interest in reaching a final bilateral investment deal was affirmed by its latest formal offer in the marathon negotiations, which included a reduced list of industry sectors it wants to keep off limits to foreigners.[34] Beijing reportedly regards this investment treaty as a top priority, as it will signal American confidence in the Chinese economy.[35]

This is all in China's interest as it tries to upgrade its industrial profile and move up the technological production ladder. As the United States is a core source of high-tech investment in China, the U.S.–China BIT will go a long way in achieving these goals.[36] China is also improving its physical investment environment, enacting labor and environmental standards that even U.S. and European business groups describe as "too stringent."[37] The Labor Contract Law, adopted in 2007 and revised in 2012, for example, greatly strengthens the collective bargaining rights of Chinese workers and makes it harder for businesses, foreign and domestic, to exploit inconsistencies in wage requirements. Similarly, the recently adopted amendment to China's Environmental Protection Law makes it much harder for polluting firms to get operating licenses and includes stiffer penalties that accrue daily for any uncorrected environmental violations.[38] Already, American business authorities are noting that Chinese authorities are turning away polluting investors.[39]

8.4 Domestic Politics and the TPP

One of the great ironies surrounding the TPP negotiations is that the United States, despite serving as lead architect and advocate for the agreement, has been one of the main obstacles toward a negotiated treaty.[40] Indeed, for nearly eight years, domestic U.S. opposition has obstructed bargaining at the international negotiations table. In this respect, at least, the prospect of China joining in the TPP probably complicates the ratification process further, since both houses of Congress have a long-standing "anti-China" record, and representatives believe that China got an easy pass when it joined the WTO in 2001.[41] Obama's victory in winning fast-track negotiations authority in June 2015 have put many of these concerns to rest, however.

Now that the ball is China's court, it is just as important to consider its domestic political constraints, which unfortunately are often overlooked. As a single-party leadership—unimpeded by a formal opposition or the prospects of upcoming elections—it is convenient to conclude that China's leaders face few such constraints.[42] However, China's one-party leadership is not a monolithic force. The country is highly fragmented, both administratively and geographically (Lampton and Lieberthal 1992; Montinola, Qian, and Weingast 1995; Xu 2011), as well as along factional lines (Cai and Treisman 2006; Nathan 1973; Shih 2004). Increasingly, scholars are starting to include the role of Chinese state-owned enterprises (SOEs) as a major interest group in Chinese domestic politics (Minxin 2006; Steinfeld 1998).

When it comes to free trade, these forces have rarely been in alignment. SOEs and the local governments that depend on them, for instance, have much to lose and little to gain from further liberalization, either in trade or investment. As a consequence, we can expect SOEs to resist any comprehensive trade liberalization, especially the TPP, which carries specific provisions aimed at countering unfair competition from SOEs. This resistance will not manifest the same way it does in the United States. That is, provincial delegates are unlikely to challenge a TPP initiative in the National People's Congresses (NPCs), nor are SOE workers likely to organize demonstrations against trade policy. The pressure of domestic politics in China works its way behind the scene, making it extremely difficult to predict how local politics or special interests would pressure the leadership, should it choose to enter negotiations to join the TPP. What can be said, however, is that these forces have prevented China's leaders from implementing much needed reforms in the past (Minxin 2006). For example, the Hu-Wen administration (2002–2012) was expected by many to be the most reform-minded administration in the PRC's history. By the end of 2012, however, most anticipated reforms, such as SOE liberalization and bank reform, had made zero, perhaps even negative, progress—leading many China scholars to bill the Hu-Wen period a "Lost Decade" for reform.[43]

The current Xi-Li administration appears considerably more assertive and consolidated than its predecessor, suggesting that if the leadership wanted TPP it might stand a better chance of forcing it through subnational opposition and the SOEs. Some even argue that joining the TPP would help the regime achieve its reform objectives. For example, during the Chinese Communist Party's 3rd Plenum, held in November 2013, President Xi Jinping made it clear that he envisions market forces to play a leading role in the future of China's economy, in other words, that SOEs will play a smaller role. From this perspective, at least, joining the TPP could be instrumental in forcing SOEs out of lucrative market position. Zhu Rongji, for instance, is believed to have leveraged WTO accession to push through (Zweig 2001) and lock in (Fewsmith 2001) economic reforms in the late 1990s and early 2000s. Could the TPP serve a similar purpose under Xi Jinping and Li Keqiang? This is a compelling thesis, but it is not one that is supported by the regime's current approach to reform.

Rather than calling for far-reaching reforms, as Zhu did in 1998, the current administration has proposed a more nuanced approach toward easing SOEs out of the production economy, not by selling them off, but by reorienting their interests toward investment.[44] In particular, as outlined in the sixty-point addendum to the Third Plenum Communiqué, the leadership wants SOEs to reorient assets away from manufacturing and distribution and toward investing in private businesses operating within their sectors.[45] This politically tactful approach allows SOEs to preserve much of their wealth and to further cultivate their sectoral patronage networks while also discouraging them from production, where they have proven to be increasingly inefficient (Song, Storesletten, and Zilibotti 2011). Whether large SOEs will buy into this strategy and whether or not it will lead to improvements in private sector productivity is still unknown. What is clear, however, is that this approach would be compromised by a TPP-style trade agreement that would require China to expose sectors to unfettered foreign investment, thereby undercutting the appeal of the reorientation strategy for SOEs. Moreover, since many of China's largest SOEs operate in politically sensitive industries, like telecom, media, finance, and energy, it is unlikely that the regime will allow foreign investors in any time soon, especially if the regime believes it can liberalize them internally.

The desire to move incrementally and selectively is even more visible in China's approach to internal Free Trade Zones. In September 2013 China established its first FTZ in Shanghai, a twenty-nine-square kilometer stretch of land on the outskirts of Shanghai's financial Pudong district. The Shanghai FTZ provides three functions. First, it removes tariff barriers to imports. Second, it expands the number of sectors open to foreign investment. Third, it encourages policy and legal innovation within the zone. These features would be welcome in most of China, yet there is no intention to scale the policy nationwide. Instead, twelve additional FTZs are anticipated across a number of provinces, including Zhejiang, Shandong, Liaoning, Henan, Fujian, Sichuan, Guangxi, and Yunnan, and cities such as Suzhou, Wuxi, Hefei, Guangzhou, and Tianjin, but the process has been slow and opaque.[46] One interpretation of the piecemeal FTZ approach is that it is a gradualist attempt at opening up China's economy. An alternative interpretation is that liberalization is part of a more complicated political strategy, in which FTZs are selectively rewarded to important subnational political actors in exchange for support on other reform dimensions. If this were indeed the case, the leadership would, as in the case of SOE reforms, lose a valuable political resource if it were to agree to blanket TPP standards on trade and investment.

To help understand why the TPP conflicts with China's current reform strategy, it is helpful to look back at the Deng Xiaoping's approach to reform during the 1980s. At the time, Deng faced an entrenched bureaucracy that survived on the planning model, resistant to any attempt at reforming it. Deng, could have, if he had wanted to, taken the bureaucracy head-on. Instead, he chose to encircle it through what Susan Shirk calls "particularistic contracting" (Shirk 1993, 15). This involved cutting deals with particular parts of the bureaucracy in exchange for support on further reforms. In the case of price reform, for example, Deng offered dual-track pricing that allowed prices to rationalize while giving select portions of the bureaucracy access to below-market rates. While it was obvious this setup would incentivize corruption through arbitrage, it nevertheless allowed Deng to build and dismantle reform coalitions with limited resistance.

Deng's particularistic contracting was even more pronounced in the designation of Special Economic Zones (SEZs) in Shenzhen, Tianjin, Dalian, and Xiamen. As with price reforms, Deng selectively handed out SEZ status as a way of building support and preempting opposition to further reform (Crane 1990; Shirk 1993). Moreover, by focusing on these select locations, Deng was able to channel central resources to specific SEZs and ensure their success, thereby fostering envy among those who had not been selected (Shirk 1993). Had Deng chosen to open the economy in one broad stroke he would very likely have faced much stiffer opposition. More important, had he chosen to open the economy broadly, Deng would have had far fewer supporters on other aspects of his reform strategy.

Parallels between Xi's political strategy and Deng's are hard to ignore. Take, for example, Xi Jinping's inaugural tour of Shenzhen, a tribute to a city with deep affection for Deng Xiaoping, who fathered its economic miracle by making it China's first SEZ. Similarly, opening the Shanghai FTZ was clearly tactical. Shanghai is seen as the base of former president Jiang Zemin's faction, long considered the informal opposition to the Hu administration and, more recently, an existential threat to Xi Jinping. Shanghai is also, to the surprise of many, one of the China's SOE strongholds, with over 60 percent of output coming from some of China's most prominent SOEs, like SAIC, China's largest automobile manufacturer, and China Unicom, the country's second-largest telecom provider. As such, choosing Shanghai for China's first FTZ sends two messages, that Xi intends to retake the city and that SOEs will be targeted. A year into the FTZ, the strategy appears to be paying dividends. Han Zheng, the current Shanghai Party Secretary and long-time associate of Jiang Zemin, appears to have shed his old patron and pledged allegiance to Xi Jinping.[47] Several of Shanghai's prominent SOEs are also starting to toe the line by selling off stakes to private equity funds.[48] It is unlikely that the leadership will abandon this apparently effective strategy by signing on to the TPP.

Another political strategy that might be compromised by joining a rigid TPP is China's Western Development Initiative, sometimes referred to as the "Go West" policy, intended to accelerate development in western provinces by shifting investment, production, and education resources to the region. Part of this policy involves building up infrastructure connecting China's western hinterlands with the dynamic coastal cities in the East. The policy also entails various efforts at creating preferential investment opportunities for both domestic and foreign firms that invest in the West, including tax breaks, fast-track registration, and, unfortunately, weaker regulation.[49] There are political and economic reasons for the CCP's push toward the West. Politically, the western provinces, especially Xinjiang, Tibet, Gansu, and Sichuan, contain some of the more restive regions in the country. While oppressive government policies are partly to blame, so is excessive poverty, which is much more prevalent in the western provinces. Economically, this is also an opportunity as wages in western China are still low, about 70 percent of wages in the East.[50] Things were much worse, however, before the western development policy came into effect and policymakers can take some credit for that. For example, poverty in western China has fallen by more than half (over thirty million people) since 2000. State-led investment and policy incentives also appear to have been successful in attracting increasing amounts of foreign investment. Observing rates of change from 2005 through 2012, we see that western provinces had the fastest growth across China (see figure 8.3). While it is unclear how this picture would have differed based on purely market-led investment, it is unlikely that China's leaders are ready to give up these powerful policy levers just as they appear to be bearing fruit.

Political strategy aside, China also has some unique economic reservations about the TPP. Unlike its potential TPP counterparts, who are primarily concerned with direct costs of foreign competition, China is concerned about the opportunity costs from foreign competition on sectors that have yet to emerge. China's domestic consumption economy is growing rapidly and it is expected to grow even faster once the leadership implements reforms on land use and household registration. Foreign investment will certainly play a role in this expansion. Indeed, Premier Li Keqiang has emphasized, on a number of occasions, the need for foreign investment in all types of industry. Yet, unfettered foreign investment today may preclude Chinese producers from competing in this emerging domestic market tomorrow. A clear example of this risk is visible in China's automobile industry where foreign investment is restricted to joint ventures. Although foreign partnership is helping Chinese firms innovate, it is not making them more competitive as Chinese consumers still flock to the foreign branded version of domestically produced vehicles.[51]

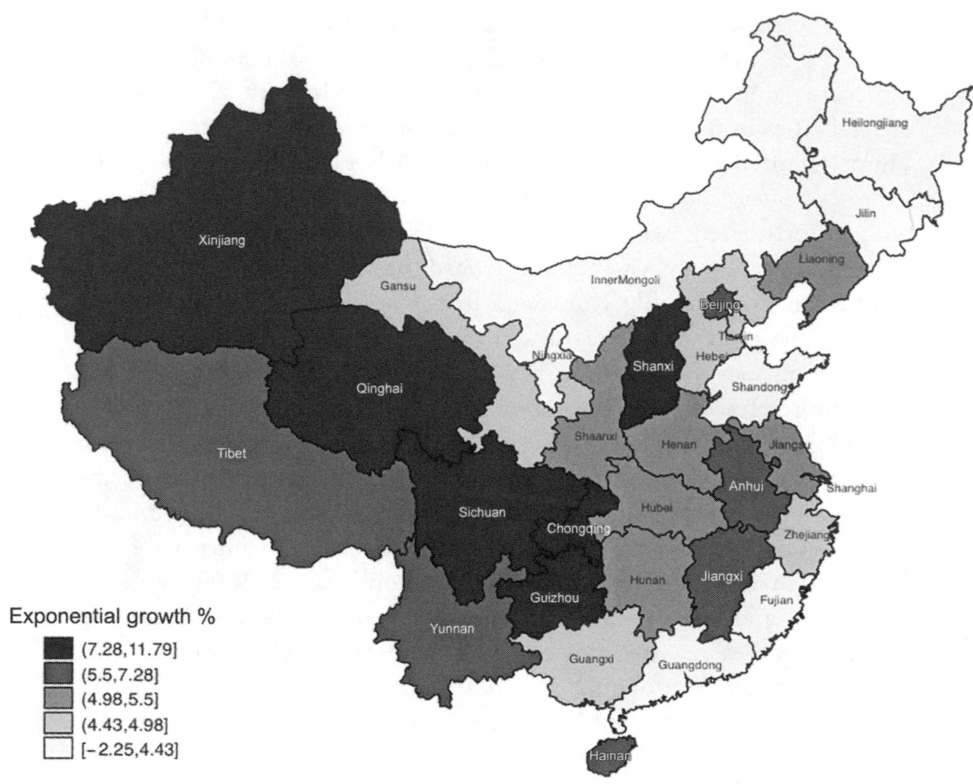

Figure 8.3
Growth of provincial foreign investment inflows.
Source: Chinese Statistical Yearbook, 2013.

Similar concerns exist about China's budding services sector. In the first quarter of 2014, for example, services accounted for over 60 percent of China's GDP growth.[52] Services are also employing an increasing share of the Chinese labor market, surpassing both primary and manufacturing sector employment in 2010 (see figure 8.4). Unfortunately, China's service sector is less productive than the manufacturing sector and therefore more vulnerable to foreign competition (Nabar and Yan 2013). For example, financial services in China have long been seen as inefficient and in need of reform. TPP standards would certainly go a long way in strengthening this sector, but it might mean an early loss in domestic market share that will be hard to make up.

As in most countries, economic interests in China at times overlap with political ones. Take for example China's media market, which is the

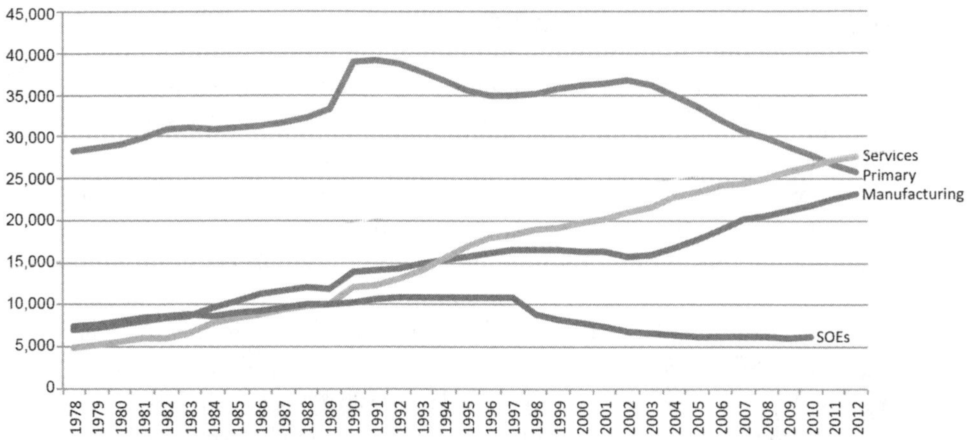

Figure 8.4
Chinese employment by sector (unit: 10,000 workers).
Source: Chinese Statistical Yearbook, 2013.

largest in the world. A genuine implementation of the TPP would require not only opening media to foreign investment, currently restricted to a limited range of advertising and distribution, but also curtailing censorship and editorial oversight, neither of which seem likely any time soon. If anything, investment into Chinese media is getting harder, with only a handful of foreign content providers operating in the country. If Vietnam, which has had a bilateral trade and investment agreement with the United States since 2001, is any comparison, these politically sensitive sectors will remain heavily restricted well into the future (Malesky, Gueorguiev, and Jensen 2014).

8.5 Summary and Perspectives

Without indulging in the broader merits of the TPP as yet another regional trade agreement, on which opinions are hotly divided, this chapter assesses the narrow prospect of China joining into the mix. China's potential entry into the TPP would vastly alter and augment the impact of the pact. In particular, Chinese involvement would expand the TPP's economic girth to roughly 55 percent of global GDP and offer the current TPP partners what may be the ultimate bounty, preferential access to China's budding domestic market. There are good reasons to suspect that China might eventually join. In particular, in its role as primary exporter to the region, joining the TPP would be economically rational for China's terms for trade. Similarly, joining the TPP architecture would be diplomatically prudent for China's international reputation, which has suffered as of late. Finally, just as joining the WTO was instrumental in helping China's leaders push through much-needed and liberalizing domestic economic reforms, joining the TPP today would go a long way in helping the current administration upgrade China's economic profile by stimulating a still nascent services and high-tech sector.

For each of the arguments we have outlined, we concede that while extant claims are compelling, they are far from convincing. In particular, we argue that China's trade losses from not joining are predictable and negligible while its short-term opportunity costs and political liabilities are indeterminate and potentially quite large. With respect to diplomacy, we concede that China's failure to join the TPP may undermine China's reputation as a *free-marketer*, but we also point out that China has alternative avenues through which to define its position on free market politics. Finally, while we agree that joining the TPP would serve as a powerful weapon in the current administration's economic reform efforts, we cannot ignore the valuable patronage and policy space the administration would forfeit should it forgo a piecemeal approach to reform and adopt the TPP's blanket provisions on trade and investment.

While we arrive at an unambiguous conclusion—China will not join the TPP—we should also point out that, from our perspective, this is not a big deal. China is so deeply embedded in the global supply chain, including most of the TPP partners, that it will be indirectly included in the TPP whether or not it is a formal member. As Ikenberry (2008) points out, "The United States cannot thwart China's rise, but it can help ensure that China's power is exercised within the rules and institutions that the United States and its partners have crafted." In the case of the TPP, even though China is not party to the institutions, it is moving along a similar path as it tries to market its own parallel agreements. This does not mean that the TPP partners are better off without having China as a member. They are not. However, losses from trade creation and trade diversion are unlikely to last for long, since China is actively pursuing alternative arrangements with virtually all the TPP member states.

The end game outcome of all this may in fact turn out to be a broader, albeit less stringent, free trade area that includes many important but currently excluded economies, like India, Indonesia, Thailand, and Russia. India, for one, has never before been invited to regional summits. China changed this unfortunate pattern by inviting Indian Prime Minister Narendra Modi to the 2014 APEC summit in Beijing and has since strongly supported India's inclusion in ongoing RCEP negotiations. India's inclusion in a regional trade agreement, just like China's, compromises the United States' vision of a higher standards trade arrangement. This is perhaps why China has been so eager to push for RCEP. Indeed, China's best-case scenario is not a world without TPP, but rather a world where the TPP makes a slow and soft entry.

Slow and soft, however, is not in the interest of the United States. Indeed, China's apparent efforts to complicate the TPP negotiations have been more than matched by an increased urgency in Washington to settle disagreements with the other TPP partners and secure fast-track negotiations authority at home. Importantly, however, competing interests have not boiled over into outright competition. On the contrary, U.S. negotiators have been surprisingly effective at keeping China positively engaged by keeping an invitation open. Likewise, Chinese counterparts have tactfully raised hopes that they might join the TPP. China's suggestive approach was on full display during Xi Jinping's visit to the United States in September 2015, during which he promised cooperation on intellectual property rights and cybersecurity.[53] Whereas some have interpreted these corresponding overtures as evidence of a possible "TPP plus China" arrangement, we contend that such configurations are unlikely because they fail to internalize the complex political and economic calculus currently in Beijing.

Now that TPP negotiations have been concluded, however, the pressure is back on China. Assuming that the agreement is ratified by the U.S. Congress, which is highly likely, the TPP will represent a major win for the United States and Japan. First, a successful TPP means that China's parallel RTA efforts will have to further converge toward America's vision of free trade in order to be viable. Second, a successful TPP raises the likelihood that Shinzo Abe, Japan's hardline prime minister, will make good on his promise to revive the Japanese economy, thereby bolstering his country's ability to balance China's influence in the region. Third, a ratified TPP will highlight China's lack of progress domestically. It has now been two years since China announced its first Free Trade Zone in Shanghai. Unfortunately, this effort, along with eleven other zones under construction, has failed to attract much excitement or investment.[54] To make matters worse, China's summer stock market woes have knocked the wind out of the current administration's preferred marketization strategy, which was heavily reliant on shareholder discipline.[55]

While these developments do not raise the prospects of a Chinese entry into the TPP, they do put pressure on Beijing to make tangible progress on its various TPP countermeasures. In particular, these include the Bilateral Investment Treaty (BIT) with the United States and two regional trade pacts, RCEP and FTAAP. At their September 2015 summit, President Obama and Premier Xi reiterated that a "high-quality" BIT is the most important item of the bilateral economic agenda.[56] Similarly, members of the RCEP negotiations have expressed a "new urgency" in completing a joint agreement by the end of 2015.[57] Much as the United States felt compelled to make several notable concessions to TPP partners in its final push for agreement in 2015,[58] we speculate that added pressure will encourage China to make similar concessions and peaceful overtures to the United States and ASEAN partners in the proximate future.

Notes

1. The first invitation arguably came from Hillary Clinton in 2012, but it was not until May 2013 that the White House formally announced its willingness to accept China at the TPP roundtable.

2. Sanchita Basu Das, "The Trans-Pacific Partnership as a Tool to Contain China: Myth or Reality?" *East Asia Forum*, June 8, 2013, http://www.eastasiaforum.org/2013/06/08/the-trans-pacific-partnership-as-a-tool-to-contain-china-myth-or-reality/,accessed August 18, 2014; Donald Gross, "Welcoming China to the Trans-Pacific Partnership," *Huffington Post*, July 9, 2013; Zeyu Shao, "America Uses TPP to Contain Chinese Manufacturing '美国利用TPP遏制中国制造,'" *E-Manufacturing* 5, no. 71 (2013): 8.

3. Thomas Donilon, "National Security Advisor to President Obama Discusses U.S. Policy in the Asia-Pacific Region in 2013," *Asia Society*, March 11, 2013, http://asiasociety.org/new-york/complete-transcript-thomas-donilon-asia-society-new-york, accessed November 9, 2015.

4. Ministry of Commerce, "China to Rigorously Study the TPP Possibility" [商务部:中方会认真研究分析加入TPP利弊和可能], http://www.chinanews.com/gn/2013/05-30/4875990.shtml, accessed August 15, 2014.

5. Justin Yifu Lin, "Justin Yifu Lin Says China Should Join TPP/Faculty Viewpoints—National School of Development," *Beijing University National School of Development—Faculty Viewpoints*, 2014, http://en.nsd.edu.cn/article.asp?articleid=7332, accessed September 26, 2014.

6. Ma's projection should be seen as an upper bound as it assumes having sixteen countries in the TPP including the additions of China, South Korea, Thailand, and Indonesia. See http://www.bloomberg.com/news/2014-06-24/pboc-s-ma-urges-joining-tpp-to-boost-growth-report-shows.html, accessed August 15, 2014.

7. Qingfen Ding and Joseph Boris, "'Positive' Sign on Free Trade Pact," *China Daily*, July 3, 2013.

8. Huang Yiping, "The U.S. and China Should Avoid an Economic Cold War," *Caixin*, February 21, 2014, http://english.caixin.com/2014-02-21/100641687.html, accessed November 9, 2015.

9. Gordon Chang, "TPP vs. RCEP: America and China Battle for Control of Pacific," *The National Interest*, October 6, 2015, http://nationalinterest.org/feature/tpp-vs-rcep-america-china-battle-control-pacific-trade-14021, accessed November 9, 2015.

10. Jordan Fabian, "Obama to Sign Fast-Track Trade Legislation," *The Hill*, June 29, 2015, http://thehill.com/homenews/administration/246418-obama-to-sign-fast-track-trade-legislation, accessed November 9, 2015.

11. Felipe Caro and Christopher Tang, "Leaving China Out of the TPP Is a Terrible Mistake," *Fortune*, October 6, 2015, http://fortune.com/2015/10/06/leaving-china-out-trans-pacific-partnership-terrible-mistake/; Editors, "China Belongs in the TPP," *Bloomberg News—Editorial Board*, 2015, http://www.bloombergview.com/articles/2015-10-08/china-belongs-in-the-tpp; Joshua Meltzer, "Why China Should Join the Trans-Pacific Partnership," *Brookings*, September 21, 2015, http://www.brookings.edu/blogs/order-from-chaos/posts/2015/09/21-us-china-economic-integration-tpp-meltzer; Jing Yang, "What China Stands to Gain by Joining US-Led Trade Pact TPP," *Southern China Morning Post*, September 17, 2015, http://www.scmp.com/comment/insight-opinion/article/1859033/what-china-stands-gain-joining-us-led-trade-pact-tpp., accessed November 9, 2015.

12. Chengjin Xu, "如何面对 TPP (How to Deal with the TPP)," *学习时报* (*Study Times*), 2015, http://www.studytimes.cn/zydx/SCJJ/XIANYJJ/2015-11-11/1408.htm, accessed November 8, 2015

13. John Kerry, "Interview With Askar Alimzhanov of Mir TV," Astana, Kazakstan, 2015, http://www.state.gov/secretary/remarks/2015/11/249070.htm, accessed November 8, 2015.

14. At the time, negotiations centered on the "Pacific Three Closer Economic Partnership" or TCEP framework, which evolved into the current TPP formation in 2011.

15. David Pilling and Shawn Donnan, "Trans-Pacific Partnership: Ocean's Twelve," *Financial Times*, September 22, 2013, http://www.ft.com/intl/cms/s/0/8c253c5c-2056-11e3-b8c6-00144feab7de.html-axzz3ETrOQWV7, accessed September 27, 2014.

16. "Developing economy" status based on International Statistical Institute classification.

17. "Foreign Direct Investment in ASEAN—Key Findings," *ASEAN Business News*, 2014 http://www.aseanbriefing.com/news/2014/04/22/foreign-direct-investment-asean-key-findings.html, accessed September 27, 2014.

18. Estimates drawn from Petri, Plummer, and Zhai 2014, table 1, and expressed in 2007 U.S. dollars.

19. Ibid.

20. Statistics on processing trade shares in this paragraph are drawn from Dean, Lovely, and Mora 2009.

21. Marney Cheek, "Why a U.S.–China Bilateral Investment Treaty Matters," *Investment Policy Central*, 2012, http://www.investmentpolicycentral.com/content/why-us-china-bilateral-investment-treaty-matters, accessed November 9, 2015.

22. "China, U.S. to Start Negative List BIT Negotiation," *Xinhuanet*, July 10, 2014, http://news.xinhuanet.com/english/china/2014-07/10/c_133472362.htm, accessed November 9, 2015.

23. The Japanese government's decision was intended to avert a potentially more controversial move by Tokyo's nationalistic governor Shintaro Ishihara. For further reading, see Jane Perlez, "China Accuses Japan of Stealing Disputed Islands." *New York Times*, September 11, 2012 http://www.nytimes.com/2012/09/12/world/asia/china-accuses-japan-of-stealing-disputed-islands.html, accessed November 9, 2015.

24. James Fallows, "How to Think about the Chinese Air-Defense News," *The Atlantic*, November 25, 2013, http://www.theatlantic.com/china/archive/2013/11/how-to-think-about-the-chinese-air-defense-news/281871/, accessed November 9, 2015.

25. Ruan Zongze, "What Kind of Neighborhood Will China Build?" *China Institute of International Studies* 45 (March/April) (2014): 26–60.

26. Dimitar D. Gueorguiev and Janeen Fernando, "Fish Out of Water: China's Economic Diplomacy in Sri Lanka," Syracuse Working Paper, presented on November 2, 2015, Moynihan Center, Syracuse University.

27. As of early 2012, China signed BTAs with ten countries/regions: Thailand, Hong Kong, Macau, Taiwan, Pakistan, Chile, New Zealand, Singapore, Peru, and Costa Rica, and is negotiating with Australia, Iceland, South Korea, Norway, and Switzerland, as well as the Gulf Cooperation Council (GCC), and the Southern African Customs Union (SACU).

28. Tsuru Etsushi and Igarashi Makoto, "China Asserts Self at ASEAN, Seeks Alternative to TPP," *Asahi Shimbun*, October 10, 2013, http://ajw.asahi.com/article/asia/china/AJ201310100071, accessed November 3, 2015.

29. Obe Mitsuru, "Japan TPP Negotiator Wonders Why Pact Excludes Monetary Policy," *Wall Street Journal*, July 17, 2014, http://blogs.wsj.com/economics/2014/07/17/japan-tpp-negotiator-wonders-why-pact-excludes-monetary-policy/, accessed November 3, 2015.

30. Jiabao Li, "China Mulls 'Mega' FTA," *China Daily*, May 2, 2014, http://fta.mofcom.gov.cn/enarticle/enrelease/201405/15661_1.html, accessed November 3, 2015.

31. Michael G. Plummer, "A Vision of Global Free Trade? The New Regionalism and the 'building Blocs' Debate," *Asia Pathways*, 2013, http://www.asiapathways-adbi.org/2013/12/a-vision-of-global-free-trade-the-new-regionalism-and-the-building-blocs-debate/.

32. Karl Lee, "Making Sense of China's Asia-Pacific FTA Agenda," *The Sun Daily*, May 5, 2014, http://www.thesundaily.my/news/1036063, accessed September 22, 2014.

33. "2014 Leaders' Declaration, Beijing Agenda for an Integrated, Innovative and Interconnected Asia-Pacific," Beijing, November 11, 2014, http://www.apec.org/Meeting-Papers/Leaders-Declarations/2014/2014_aelm.aspx, accessed September 27, 2014.

34. William Mauldin and Mark Magnier, "U.S., China Make Progress toward Trade and Investment Deal," *The Wall Street Journal*, September 25, 2015, http://www.wsj.com/articles/u-s-china-make-progress-toward-trade-and-investment-deal-1443208549, accessed September 25, 2015.

35. Minxin Pei, "US–China Summit: It's Time for Some Cautious Optimism," *Fortune*, September 28, 2015, http://fortune.com/2015/09/28/china-us-obama-xi-jinping-meeting/, accessed September 27, 2014.

36. Manisha Singh, 2015 "Forget the TPP, Let's Talk about the BIT with China," *Forbes*, http://www.forbes.com/sites/realspin/2015/06/24/forget-the-tpp-lets-talk-about-the-bit-with-china/, accessed January 4, 2015.

37. EUCCC, "Re: Comments of the European Union Chamber of Commerce in China on the Draft Labour Contract law, April 18, 2006; USCBC, "Comments on the Draft Labor Contract Law of the People's Republic of China" (Draft of March 20, 2006), https://www.uschina.org/public/documents/2006/04/uscbc-comments-labor-law.pdf, accessed September 13, 2014.

38. Yang Yi, "China's Legislature Adopts Revised Environmental Protection Law," *Xinhua News Agency*, April 24, 2014, http://news.xinhuanet.com/english/china/2014-04/24/c_133287570.htm; "Environmental Protection: Green Teeth," *The Economist*, May 17, 2014, http://www.economist.com/news/china/21602286-government-amends-its-environmental-law-green-teeth, accessed May 15, 2014.

39. "2013 Investment Climate Statement—China," U.S. Department of State, Bureau of Economic Affairs and Business, http://www.state.gov/e/eb/rls/othr/ics/2013/204621.htm.

40. The TPP did not originate with the United States, but it has, since January 2008, adopted and restructured the proposed pact as a U.S.-driven trade initiative. See Chris Daniels, "First Step to Wider Free Trade," February 10, 2008, *New Zealand Herald*, http://www.nzherald.co.nz/business/news/article.cfm?c_id=3&objectid=10491556, accessed February 9, 2014.

41. David Pilling and Shawn Donnan, "Trans-Pacific Partnership: Ocean's Twelve," *Financial Times*, September 22, 2013, http://www.ft.com/intl/cms/s/0/8c253c5c-2056-11e3-b8c6-00144feab7de.html-axzz3ETrOQWV7.

42. For further reading on domestic political constraints and international bargaining, see Putnam 1988.

43. Ian Johnson, "China's Lost Decade," *New York Review of Books*, 2012, http://www.nybooks.com/articles/archives/2012/sep/27/chinas-lost-decade/, accessed September 27, 2014.

44. Arthur R. Kroeber, “Xi Jinping’s Ambitious Agenda for Economic Reform in China,” *Brookings*, November 17, 2013, http://www.brookings.edu/research/opinions/2013/11/17-xi-jinping-economic-agenda-kroeber, accessed August 18, 2014.

45. “The Decision on Major Issues Concerning Comprehensively Deepening Reforms in Brief,” *China Daily*, November 16, 2013, http://www.china.org.cn/china/third_plenary_session/2013-11/16/content_30620736.htm, accessed September 26, 2014.

46. Zhu Ningzhu, “China Approves 12 More Free Trade Zones,” *Xinhua*, January 22, 2014, http://news.xinhuanet.com/english/china/2014-01/22/c_133066293.htm, accessed December 9, 2014. The government has retracted from this position a little, but most believe the information was valid, albeit premature.

47. Zheng Han (韩正), “Leaders and Study” (韩正为‘解放书单’撰文: 上海领导干部必须静心读书), July 25, 2014, *Liberation Daily (解放日报)*, July 25, 2014, http://cpc.people.com.cn/n/2014/0725/c64094-25339446.html (accessed September 26, 2014).

48. Daniel Inman, Chao Deng, and Shen Hong. “Shanghai Leads the Way in Revamp of China State Enterprises,” *Wall Street Journal*, September 17, 2014, http://www.wsj.com/articles/shanghai-leads-the-way-in-reform-of-china-state-enterprises-1410989402 (accessed September 26, 2014).

49. For further background, see Tian 2004 and Ziran 2002.

50. “Western China: Enhancing Industrial Competitiveness and Employment,” UNIDO Technical Report US/CPR/03/051. Available at Juergen Reinhardt, “Western China Enhancing Industrial Competitiveness and Employment: Technical Report,” in *United Nations Industrial Development Organization* (Vienna: United Nations Industrial Development Organization, 2005), https://www.unido.org/fileadmin/user_media/Publications/Pub_free/Western_China_enhancing_industrial_competitiveness_and_employment.pdf, accessed November 9, 2015.

51. Angelo Young, “For Chinese Automakers, Profitability Comes from Partnerships,” *International Business Times*, March 15, 2013, http://www.ibtimes.com/gm-ford-vw-dominate-chinas-auto-industry-why-cant-chinese-companies-saic-dongfeng-1130893, accessed September 26, 2014.

52. Ryan Rutkowski, “China Chart of the Week: Services Lead Growth as Industry Slows,” *China Economic Watch*, September 19, 2004, http://blogs.piie.com/china/?p=4058, accessed November 9, 2015.

53. “President Xi Jinping’s State Visit to the United States,” White House, Office of the Press Secretary, September 25, 2015, https://www.whitehouse.gov/the-press-office/2015/09/25/fact-sheet-president-xi-jinpings-state-visit-united-states, accessed November 13, 2015.

54. Gabriel Wildau, “Shanghai Free-Trade Zone Struggles for Relevance,” *Financial Times*, 2015, http://www.ft.com/intl/cms/s/0/8cec0faa-6364-11e5-9846-de406ccb37f2.html-axzz3quOPMggX, accessed November 9, 2015.

55. Blade Oliver Barron, "Did China's Stock Market Crash Just End Economic Reform?" *Forbes*, 2015, http://www.forbes.com/sites/oliverbarron/2015/07/05/did-chinas-stock-market-crash-just-end-economic-reform/, accessed November 9, 2015.

56. Minxin Pei, "US–China Summit: It's Time for Some Cautious Optimism," *Fortune*, September 28, 2015, http://fortune.com/2015/09/28/china-us-obama-xi-jinping-meeting/, accessed November 26, 2015.

57. Jack Kim, "China-Backed Trade Pact Playing Catch-up after U.S.-Led TPP Deal," *Reuters*, October 10, 2015, http://www.reuters.com/article/2015/10/11/us-trade-tpp-rcep-idUSKCN0S500220151011-ofdSHpjUPIB8AlLY.97, accessed November 12, 2015.

58. William Mauldin, "U.S. Reaches Trans-Pacific Partnership Trade Deal With 11 Pacific Nations," *Wall Street Journal*, October 5, 2015, http://www.wsj.com/articles/u-s-reaches-trade-deal-with-11-pacific-nations-1444046867, accessed November 13, 2015.

References

Alesina, Alberto, Ignazio Angeloni, and Federico Etro. 2001. "The Political Economy of International Unions." NBER Working Paper No. 8645. Cambridge, MA: National Bureau of Economic Research.

Bhagwati, Jagdish, and Arvind Panagariya. 1999. "Preferential Trading Areas and Multilateralism—Strangers, Friends, or Foe." In *Trading Blocs: Alternative Approaches to Analyzing Preferential Trade Agreements*, ed. Jagdish Bhagwati and Arvind Panagariya, 33–100. Cambridge, MA: MIT Press.

Büthe, Tim, and Helen V. Milner. 2008. "The Politics of Foreign Direct Investment into Developing Countries: Increasing FDI through International Trade Agreements?" *American Journal of Political Science* 52 (4): 741–762.

Cai, Hongbin, and Daniel Treisman. 2006. "Did Government Decentralization Cause China's Economic Miracle? " *World Politics* 58 (04): 505–535.

Crane, George T. 1990. *The Political Economy of China's Special Economic Zones*. Armonk, NY, and London: M. E. Sharpe.

Dean, Judith M., Mary E. Lovely, and Jesse Mora. 2009. "Decomposing China–Japan–U.S. Trade: Vertical Specialization, Ownership, and Organizational Form." *Journal of Asian Economics* 20 (6): 596–610.

Deardorff, Alan V. 2013. "Trade Implications of the Trans-Pacific Partnership for ASEAN and Other Asian Countries." Discussion Paper No. 638, Research Seminar in International Economics. Ann Arbor, MI: Gerald R. Ford School of Public Policy.

Fergusson, Ian F., William H. Cooper, Remy Jurenas, and Brock R. Williams. 2013. "The Trans-Pacific Partnership: Negotiations and Issues for Congress." CRS Report for Congress, August 21.

Fewsmith, Joseph. 2001. "The Political and Social Implications of China's Accession to the WTO." *China Quarterly* 167:573–591.

Hammer, Alexander B. 2006. "The Dynamic Structure of US–China Trade, 1995–2004." Washington, DC: United States International Trade Commission.

Ikenberry, G John. 2008. "The Rise of China and the Future of the West." *Foreign Affairs* 87 (1): 23–37.

Lampton, David M, and Kenneth G Lieberthal. 1992. "The 'Fragmented Authoritarianism' Model and Its Limitation." In *Bureaucracy, Politics, and Decision Making in Post-Mao China*, ed. Kenneth G. Lieberthal and David M. Lampton, 1–3. Berkeley: University of California Press.

Malesky, Edmund J., Dimitar D. Gueorguiev, and Nathan M. Jensen. 2014. "Monopoly Money: Foreign Investment and Bribery in Vietnam, a Survey Experiment." *American Journal of Political Science* 59 (2): 419–439.

Minxin, Pei. 2006. *China's Trapped Transition: The Limits of Developmental Autocracy*. Cambridge, MA: Harvard University Press.

Montinola, Gabriella, Yingyi Qian, and Barry R. Weingast. 1995. "Federalism, Chinese Style: The Political Basis for Economic Success in China." *World Politics* 48 (01): 50–81.

Nabar, Malhar, and Kai Yan. 2013. *Sector-Level Productivity, Structural Change, and Rebalancing in China*. Washington, DC: International Monetary Fund.

Nathan, Andrew J. 1973. "A Factionalism Model for CCP Politics." *China Quarterly*, no. 53: 34–66.

Panagariya, Arvind. 1999. "The Regionalism Debate: An Overview." *World Economy* 22 (4): 455–476.

Park, Walter G. 2008. "International Patent Protection: 1960–2005." *Research Policy* 37 (4): 761–766.

Petri, Peter A., Michael G. Plummer, and Fan Zhai. 2012. *The Trans-Pacific Partnership and Asia-Pacific Integration: A Quantitative Assessment*. Washington, DC: Peterson Institute for International Economics.

Petri, Peter A., Michael G. Plummer, and Fan Zhai. 2014. "The TPP, China and the FTAAP: The Case for Convergence." *SSRN Electronic Journal*.

Putnam, Robert D. 1988. "Diplomacy and Domestic Politics: The Logic of Two-Level Games." *International Organization* 42 (3): 427–460.

Shih, Victor. 2004. "Factions Matter: Personal Networks and the Distribution of Bank Loans in China.' *Journal of Contemporary China* 13 (38): 3–19.

Shirk, Susan L. 1993. *The Political Logic of Economic Reform in China*. Berkeley: University of California Press.

Song, Zheng, Kjetil Storesletten, and Fabrizio Zilibotti. 2011. "Growing Like China." *American Economic Review* 101 (1): 196–233.

Steinfeld, Edward S. 1998. *Forging Reform in China: The Fate of State-Owned Industry*. Cambridge: Cambridge University Press.

Tian, Qunjian. 2004. "China Develops Its West: Motivation, Strategy and Prospect." *American Economic Review* 13 (41): 611–636.

Viner, Jacob. 1950. *The Customs Union Issue*. New York: Oxford University Press.

Xu, Chenggang. 2011. "The Fundamental Institutions of China's Reforms and Development." *Journal of Economic Literature* 49 (4): 1076–1151.

Zhai, Fan. 2008. "Armington Meets Melitz: Introducing Firm Heterogeneity in a Global CGE Model of Trade." *Journal of Economic Integration* 23: 575–604.

Ziran, Zhong. 2002. "The Chinese Western Development Initiative: New Opportunities for Mineral Investment." *Resources Policy* 28 (3–4): 117–131.

Zweig, David. 2001. "China's Stalled 'Fifth Wave': Zhu Rongji's Reform Package of 1998–2000." *Asian Survey* 41 (2): 231–247.

9

Transatlantic Free Trade: The Viewpoint of Germany

Gabriel Felbermayr and Rahel Aichele

Among industrialized countries, Germany is a relatively open economy. In 2012, exports of goods and services amounted to almost 52 percent of GDP. Trade with countries in the European Union (EU) amounted to about 27 percent of GDP; with countries outside of the EU to 25 percent. This is a striking difference from the United States, where exports totaled about 14 percent of GDP.[1] In Germany, in 2012, exports directly and indirectly supported twelve million jobs, almost a third of total jobs (full-time equivalents), more than ever since records started. This is in spite of the fact that, over the last decades, German firms have begun to massively source inputs from foreign suppliers: as of 2011, domestic value added accounts for about 70 percent of the gross value of exports. In fact, many observers believe that the comparative industrial strength of Germany is due to the country's increasing engagement in global and regional production chains (Marin 2010; Aichele, Felbermayr, and Heiland 2013).

Therefore, it is only natural that German governments of different colors have always stressed the importance of unrestricted access to export and import markets. Globally active businesses have pushed this agenda, and their international success has reinforced their political influence. The traditional orientation of German trade policy was staunchly multilateralistic. However, with international trade (and, since the Lisbon treaty of 2009, also investments) being an exclusive competence of the European Union, trade policy topics have gradually lost importance in the German political debate. This has changed abruptly with the transatlantic trade and investment partnership (TTIP) that the EU and the United States are currently negotiating: the proposed agreement has come under fierce attack from many civil society stakeholders.[2] This is not so much due to the changed orientation of the EU Commission which, since 2006, has actively pursued bilateral free trade agreements (European Commission 2006), but to a dramatically different political economy of trade policy. Traditional agreements were almost exclusively about lowering tariffs as much as possible to the advantage of consumers and to the detriment of some producers; the proposed TTIP is also about optimal regulation which is supposed to avoid unnecessary costs for producers, but consumers resist for fear of losing protection.

In this complex environment, the German government, opposition parties, various lobby groups, and the wider public have been trying to influence the negotiations that are conducted by the European Commission on behalf of all EU member states on the basis of an explicit negotiating mandate. While very few observers deny the possibility of welfare gains from a TTIP, the debate is about the size of these gains and how they compare to the risks that the agreement could entail. Very broadly, the debate relates to the tension between democratic decision making, the need to provide efficient and effective governance for global markets, and the still-prevailing reality of the nation state (Rodrik 2011).

Advocates of a TTIP have defended their case by pointing out that the multilateral system has not delivered since the creation of the World Trade Organization in 2005. While this has been acknowledged by the WTO Director-General Roberto Azevedo in the aftermath of the 2013 Bali Summit,[3] it clearly is an exaggeration. While the Doha Round has run aground, the WTO has added thirty-six new members, among them heavyweights such as China and Russia. It also helped to avoid a protectionist backlash in the 2008–2009 global trade collapse. And the WTO has developed an excellent track record in competence building and training in poorer economies.

Having said this, it is true that the existing rules of the WTO have been shaped during negotiations in the Uruguay Round from 1986 to 2004. During the first six years of this period, the Soviet Union still existed and the other BRICS countries have only started to open up. The new information and communication technologies (ICT) had just started to penetrate the business world. The combination of unilateral liberalization in countries such as China together with the ICT revolution have led to the development of complex international production networks, in which countries specialize in different stages of the value chain. The establishment of these networks requires foreign direct investment, and it also relies heavily on international trade of services. Also, increased trade of components implies that the value added embodied in them may be subject to the payment of tariffs several times when components, processed parts, and final goods cross borders. Moreover, the smooth functioning of production networks requires compatibility of regulatory regimes. For these reasons, the post-1995 world has different international governance needs than the world before. Nontariff measures, investment, services, and regulatory cooperation are, thus, seen as the key areas of modern trade policy (Baldwin 2011). Also, there are substantial doubts over the desirability of common global standards in these areas, and about the ability of the multilateral regime to establish them. The German government, the EU Commission, and major stakeholders such as the BDI (Federation of German Industries) have all defended bilateral negotiations on these grounds (BDI 2014).

Moreover, with low average growth in the EU, the German government hopes that an ambitious TTIP could spur economic dynamism and incentivize further reform in EU member states. Since a TTIP would cover about 46 percent of world GDP, it can be expected to have substantial economic effects.

For these reasons, the High-Level Working Group (HWLG) on Jobs and Growth, set up by the so called Transatlantic Economic Council (TEC), in its final report of February 2013, has recommended that the EU and the United States engage in "a comprehensive, ambitious agreement that addresses a broad range of *bilateral trade* and *investment issues*, including *regulatory issues*, and contributes to the development of *global rules* [that] goes *beyond* what the United States and the EU have achieved in previous trade agreements" (italics added).

As this quote shows, the TTIP is not only about the classical market access questions (i.e., tariffs, or quantitative restrictions), but also about a number of "new" issues as well that are only partly covered by the WTO and raise a number of new questions. For example: Is bilateral cooperation in regulatory affairs discriminatory for third countries? How can legitimate regulatory burdens be separated from protectionist motives? What is the right level for international regulatory governance—global or regional?

In this chapter, we address these (and other questions) with a special emphasis on Germany. We start with describing Germany's trade and investment relationship with the United States relative to other trading partners. In doing this, in section 9.1 we start by drawing attention to a couple of facts that are often overlooked—such as the strong intra-industry nature of bilateral trade or the huge importance of horizontal foreign direct investment (FDI)—but that matter for a correct understanding of the expected impact of the TTIP on Germany and of the ongoing public debate. In section 9.2, we review different studies that have tried to quantify the economic effects of the agreement for Germany and its relationship to other EU countries and the world. Section 9.3 focuses on the political debate on the TTIP in Germany. We address a number of contentious points, such as the inclusion of an investment chapter, the establishment of a regulatory cooperation council, mutual recognition of standards, and the "level playing field" problem. We explain how intra-European heterogeneity matters for Germany's stance on the TTIP, how different political forces and stakeholders view the project, and how they are shaping the debate. In section 9.4, we provide our conclusions.

9.1 How Important Is Transatlantic Trade and Investment for Germany?

The Macroeconomic Context

Two of the most important stylized facts on the German economy are its overall openness and its persistent and substantial current account surpluses. Another fact that has attracted international attention is that Germany has been able to maintain a comparatively important role for manufacturing in total value added.

The upper panel of figure 9.1 presents the evolution of a widely used openness measure—total gross exports of goods and services relative to GDP—since German reunification. In Germany, that ratio has gone up from about 24 percent in 1992 to almost 52 percent in 2012. Now, this ratio has increased in many other countries as well, but by less: while it has more than doubled in Germany it has gone up by less than 40 percent in the United States.

Similarly, while both the United States and Germany have experienced a decline in the relative importance of manufacturing in total value added (GDP), the decline has been about 4 percentage points in the United States but only about 2 percentage points in Germany (1998–2011). The difference between the two countries has increased to almost 9 percentage points. During the same period, however, the share of manufactures in total exports has remained rather similar in both countries.

German Trade Partners: The United States and the Others

As shown in table 9.1 for the year of 2009,[4] German gross exports to the United States amounted to about $98 billion; this is approximately 8.5 percent of total exports of goods and services ($1.15 trillion). Imports

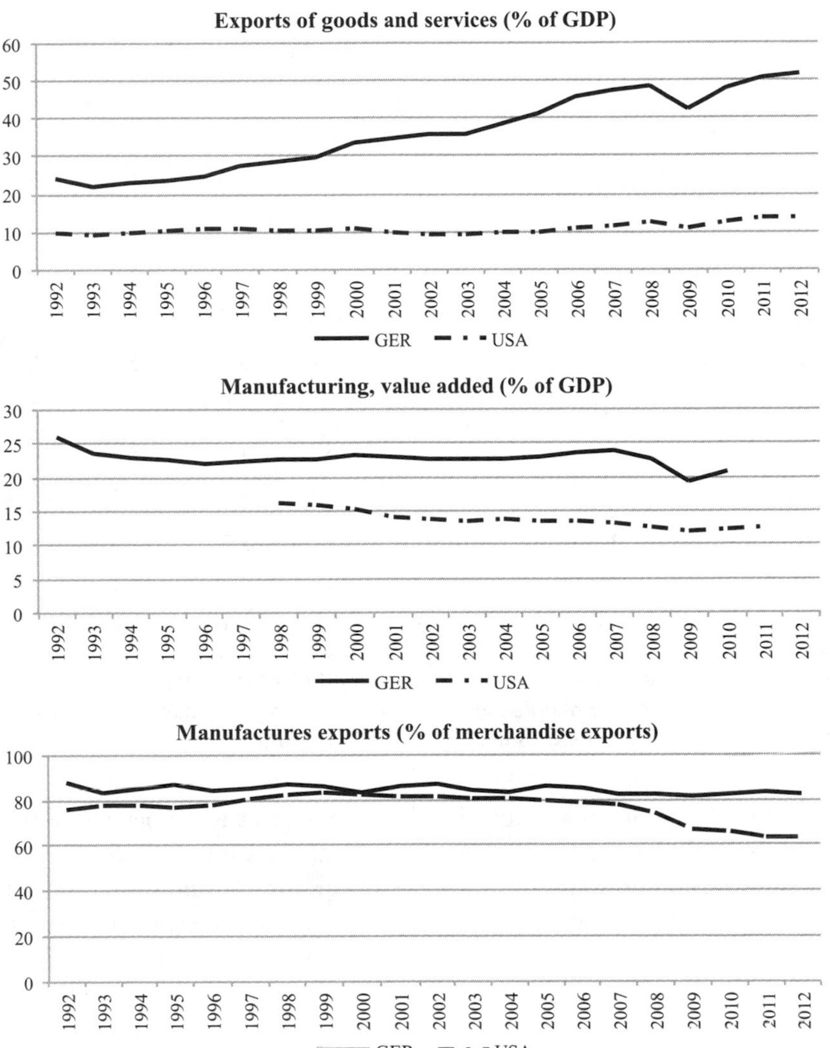

Figure 9.1
Openness and deindustrialization in Germany and in the United States.
Source: World Bank, World Development Indicators 2013

Table 9.1
Total German exports and imports in gross and value added (VA) terms, in $U.S. billions and %, 2009

	Exports				Imports			
Partner	Gross	Share	VA*	Share	Gross	Share	VA**	Share
FRA	99.1	8.6	64.9	8.0	80.9	8.1	48.1	7.4
USA	98.0	8.5	95.3	11.7	74.4	7.5	62.9	9.7
ITA	77.0	6.6	55.2	6.8	62.6	6.3	41.3	6.4
GBR	76.7	6.6	59.0	7.2	59.4	6.0	40.4	6.2
CHN	63.3	5.5	40.8	5.0	68.8	6.9	46.1	7.1
CHE	60.0	5.2	29.0	3.6	45.2	4.6	23.3	3.6
AUT	53.0	4.6	26.5	3.3	48.9	4.9	24.0	3.7
NLD	52.3	4.5	27.0	3.3	67.0	6.7	32.7	5.0
ESP	43.4	3.7	32.7	4.0	38.1	3.8	25.5	3.9
BEL	34.9	3.0	20.1	2.5	30.5	3.1	15.2	2.3

Source: Trade in Value Added (TiVA) statistics, OECD (May 2013).
*German value added embodied in partner country's final demand; **partner country value added embodied in German final demand.

from the United States amounted to $74 billion, this is 7.5 percent of the total ($990 billion). According to these data, the United States was the second most important single trade partner for Germany, both as an exporter and as an importer. Gross exports refer to the transaction value at the border; they do not measure the domestic value added embodied in these transactions. In a world where trade in intermediate inputs amounts to at least two thirds of total trade, expressing trade data in value added terms leads to different conclusions than using the official data expressed in gross terms. This is particularly important for Germany: according to recent estimates, one euro of gross exports contains only 69 cents of German value added; the rest is mostly made up by imported components that are reexported in the final goods (Aichele, Felbermayr, and Heiland 2013). However, the role of imported intermediates varies strongly across trade partners.

Indeed, when looking at the amount of German value added embodied in U.S. final demand as a share of total German value added embodied in foreign demand, the United States ranks first with a share of 11.7 percent.

Also, when asking which partner country's value added matters most in total foreign value added embodied in German final demand, the United States occupies a share of 9.7 percent, which also puts it ahead of France and China. Hence, the official trade statistics, which are based on gross transaction values, underestimate the relative importance of trade with the United States for German value added, meaning, for wages, corporate profits, and taxes. Also, the data reveal that the bilateral trade balance of $24 billion that Germany has registered with the United States is about a third larger ($32 billion) when expressed in value added terms.

Figure 9.2 illustrates the role that Germany and the United States play for each other as markets. It shows that about 0.45 percent of U.S. income (measured by the share of U.S. value added "sold" to Germany) depends on German final demand. Should Germany disappear, everything else equal, U.S. GDP would be lower by this amount. German value added embodied in U.S. final demand makes up 0.69 percent of total U.S. demand (measured by U.S. GDP). In turn, due to the asymmetry in market sizes between the United States and Germany, the United States is much more important for Germany: About 2.89 percent of total German income (GDP) is realized through sales to the United States; 1.91 percent of total German demand (GDP) is spent on U.S. services (labor, capital).

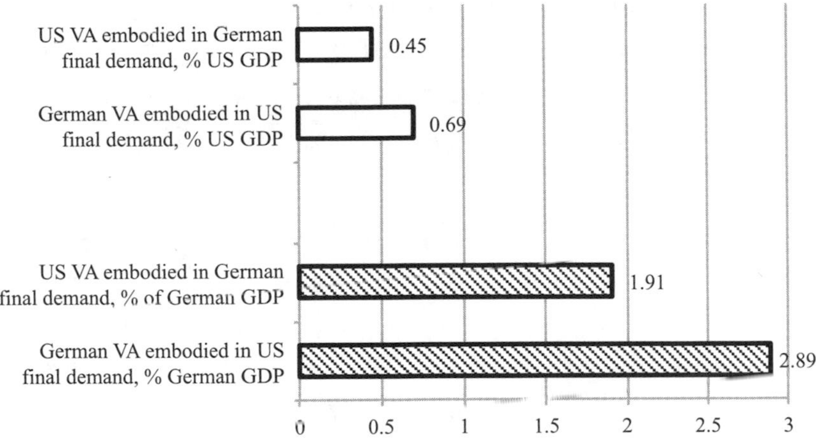

Figure 9.2
Exported and imported value added in final demand, percent of total value added (GDP). *Source and notes:* OECD-WTO Trade in Value Added (TiVA) Statistics, authors' calculations. VA refers to value added.

The Sectoral Trade Structure

Table 9.2 informs about the sectoral structure of German trade with the United States. It refers to data from 2007 (which is the base year of the current version of the GTAP database),[5] but it reveals patterns that have remained fairly stable over the last ten years. It shows that just about 18 percent of German exports lie in the area of services, less than 2 percent in agriculture and food products. Manufacturing still accounts for more than 80 percent of total exports; and the machinery and equipment, automotive, and chemical sectors make up more than 60 percent of this.

On the import side, the pattern is similar, but it is less pronounced. The three main manufacturing sectors together account only for 42

Table 9.2
Main sectors of U.S.-German trade, 2007, in $U.S. billions

	German Exports		German imports		Grubel-Lloyd Index
	$U.S. billions	Share	$U.S. billions	Share	
Manufacturing	**87.0**	**80.3%**	**50.2**	**65.8%**	**0.73**
Machinery and equipment	29.9	27.6%	11.6	15.3%	0.56
Cars and car parts	24.9	23.0%	7.1	9.3%	0.44
Chemicals, rubber, plastic	13.9	12.8%	13.6	17.8%	0.99
Electronics	2.8	2.6%	6.4	8.4%	0.61
Other transportation goods	2.6	2.4%	5.1	6.7%	0.68
Metals	2.5	2.3%	1.6	2.1%	0.77
Services	**19.7**	**18.2%**	**24.0**	**31.5%**	**0.9**
Services	6.2	5.7%	8.6	11.3%	0.83
Public procurement	4.4	4.0%	2.1	2.8%	0.66
Agriculture and Food	**1.6**	**1.5%**	**2.0**	**2.7%**	**0.88**
Food	0.7	0.7%	0.5	0.7%	0.81
Alcoholic beverages and tobacco	0.6	0.5%	0.2	0.3%	0.56
Total	**108.4**	**100.0%**	**76.3**	**100.0%**	

Source: Global Trade Analysis Project 8.0.

percent of total German imports from the United States. Imports of electronics from the United States to Germany are relatively important. Services exports (mostly business services, but also tourism) amount to almost a third of total U.S. exports. Also, the agricultural sector is relatively more important, even if the absolute amount of U.S. exports to Germany is very similar to the amount of imports. These data reveal the structure of comparative advantage between the United States and Germany: the United States has a slight advantage in the services and agri-food areas; Germany has a small advantage in the classical manufacturing sectors.

The last column in table 9.2 sheds light on an important fact in German-U.S. trade: that it occurs mainly within the same broad industries rather than across them. The Grubel-Lloyd index measures the importance of this phenomenon:[6] it takes values from 0 to 1, where a high value indicates that trade is strongly intra-industry. Clearly, the more disaggregate the industry classification is, the lower the index. Nonetheless, the table shows that at the two-digit level, the index is usually above 50 percent in the relevant industries.[7]

This fact has important implications: it suggests that any reallocation effects from a TTIP will occur within industries rather than between them. For example, if a chemical plant in Germany closes down due to increased competition from the United States, another chemical plant can be expected to expand, so that many laid-off workers can find employment without switching occupation. This means that both the speed of transition to a new competitive situation will be higher and the associated adjustment costs will be lower than in other agreements, where inter-industry reallocation effects are likely to dominate (such as, e.g., in the proposed EU-India agreement).

Trade Barriers

As figure 9.3 shows, import tariffs on both sides of the Atlantic are already low. Their trade weighted average is between 2 and 3 percent. However, due to the increasing fragmentation of production it is possible that final products have been effectively taxed several times when parts and components have crossed international borders. Moreover, in several industries, the height of tariffs is still considerable. Most important, for Germany, the EU imposes a 10 percent import tax on cars—this provides substantial protection to firms in this industry. The U.S. import levy on autos is only 2.5 percent, but due to high volumes of trade in this area this is a noticeable barrier. Moreover, in specialized product categories,

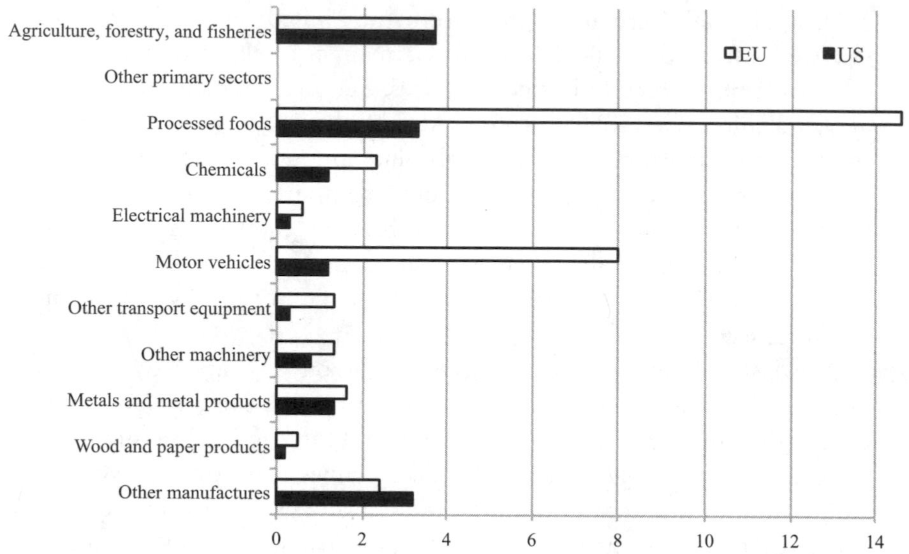

Figure 9.3
Ad valorem tariffs in transatlantic trade, industry averages, 2012.
Source: Francois et al. 2013.

U.S. import tariffs can be very high: for example, on small trucks they amount to 25 percent. Similar arguments apply to the chemical sector, where U.S. import tariffs amount to a weighted average of 1.7 percent, but the volume of German exports is about $14 billion. In the area of processed foods, EU import tariffs are particularly high; they average more than 14 percent. While the United States has more costly nontariff barriers, tariffs for certain products are quite high: dairy products (19 percent), sugar (16 percent) or beverages (15 percent).

Virtually all observers agree that the bulk of trade barriers between Germany and the United States comes in the form of nontariff measures (NTMs). These arise from partly incompatible domestic regulations that may have legitimate origins but may nonetheless operate like trade barriers. Estimates of such barriers are difficult, and they are very likely to differ massively across EU member states as the single market program is still not fully completed and substantial differences continue to exist (e.g., in the services area). Available evidence, such as that provided by Berden et al. (2009), ignores this heterogeneity. Nonetheless, it suggests that several sectors of major importance for the German-U.S. trade relationship are strongly affected.

Figure 9.4 shows that, across industries, the ad valorem equivalent of NTMs is estimated to be at least one order of magnitude higher than prevailing tariffs. They are highest in the food and beverages industries. However, they are also high in sectors, such as motor vehicles, where they take mostly the form of technical barriers, amounting to about 25 percent. Even a partial reduction of those costs in the key German export industries would amount to a massive cost reduction for suppliers.

The problem with NTMs is that their existence, in contrast to tariffs, is often not motivated by a desire to discriminate against foreign suppliers. Differences in regulation across Germany and the United States can reflect differences in preferences, such as those pertaining to risk aversion. This is mostly relevant in the agri-food sector and, partly, also in chemicals or pharmaceuticals, where the so-called precautionary principle practiced in the EU is in conflict with a U.S. approach that relies more on liability law. However, in many industries—such as automotive, machinery, electronics—differences in regulation are mainly due to historical reasons. There, some convergence—in the form of mutual recognition of standards—appears feasible. Finally, even in the sensitive agri-food sector, partial initiatives can be successful, and there is some encouraging

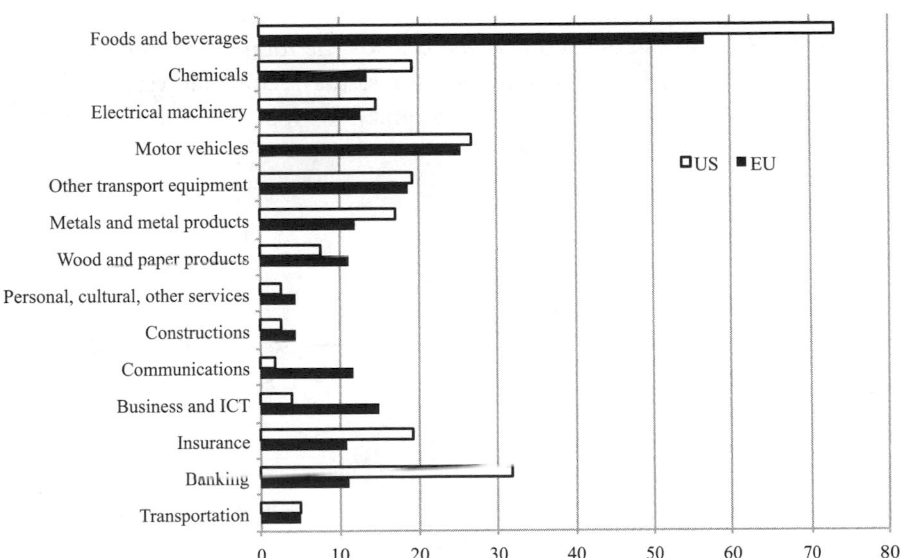

Figure 9.4
Ad valorem equivalents of nontariff measures.
Source: Berden et al. 2009.

evidence from past efforts: since an EU-U.S. agreement on organic food labels has entered into force in 2012, German trade in this segment with the United States has increased substantially.

U.S.-German Investment Ties

Since World War II, U.S. firms have held many large subsidiaries in Germany, such as General Motor's subsidiary Opel. But by the end of the last century, German investments in the United States have soared. Figure 9.5 shows that the value of the stock of German foreign direct investment (FDI) in the United States is about $265 billion in 2012 and that it has almost increased ten-fold since 1992.[8] U.S. FDI in Germany, in 1992 very similar to the German level in the United States, has also grown, but much less dynamically. In 2012, it stood at about $54 billion. The patterns in the figure are driven by several facts. First, Germany traditionally supplies capital to foreign countries mostly through FDI and bank loans, while the United States uses portfolio investment (minority shareholdings) much more frequently. Therefore, the picture underestimates the amount of U.S. capital for the German economy. Second, the boom in the late 1990s occurred in a procyclical fashion, and was driven by a few very large transactions (such as the acquisition of Chrysler by Daimler in 1998).

Table 9.3 shows that about 22 percent of the total German outward FDI stock is invested in the United States; the second largest non-EU destination is China, but it only amounts to 4 percent of the total.

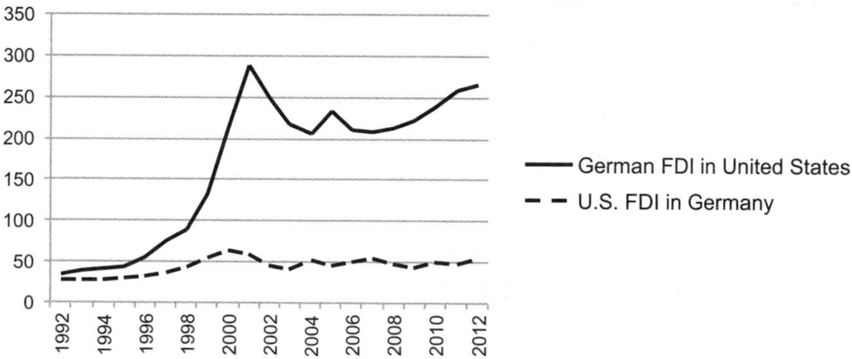

Figure 9.5
Stocks of foreign direct investment, in $U.S. billions.
Source: Deutsche Bundesbank and U.S. Department of Commerce, valued at historical cost basis.

Table 9.3
Structure of FDI stocks between the United States and Germany, 2012, in $U.S. billions

	German direct investment abroad		Foreign investment in Germany	
	Value	Share	Value	Share
EU	634	53%	454	80%
USA	263	22%	57	10%
China	48	4%	0	0%
Rest of Europe	96	8%	51	9%
Rest of the world	156	13%	6	1%
Total	1197	100%	567	100%

Source: Deutsche Bundesbank Bestandserhebung über Direktinvestitionen, April 2014. Consolidated stocks.

Concerning inward FDI, the United States amounts to 10 percent of the total in Germany.

It is often argued that the EU-U.S. relationship is characterized more by very deep capital market integration rather than by trade. This is broadly true in general; and it is a particularly accurate description in the case of the U.S.-German link. Figure 9.6 contrasts German exports (in $ billions) to the United States with sales of affiliates of German multinationals in the United States. The diverging pattern of these series is striking: in 2012, affiliate sales of $519 billion were about five times higher than exports. These sales vary strongly with the U.S. business cycle, but—at least until 2006—they have also exhibited an upward trend that has much outperformed exports. The annual growth rates in nominal volumes were 10 percent and 7 percent, respectively. Interestingly, while German exports to the United States have recovered their historical maximum from 2008, affiliate sales still are below the 2007 maximum.

German firms employ about 762,000 workers in the United States; this number is somewhat lower than the all-time high of 827,000 workers in 2001, but it is about 70 percent higher than the employment at the time of German reunification (1989).

Comparing the relative importance of the United States and European (EU plus Switzerland, Norway, Iceland, Liechtenstein) markets for German multinational activities, figure 9.7 shows that—despite the

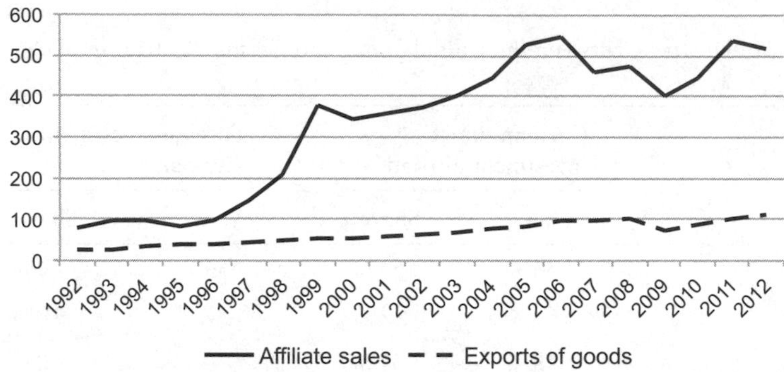

Figure 9.6
German exports to the United States and U.S. sales of affiliates of German multinationals, USD.
Source: COMTRADE and German Bundesbank, own calculations.

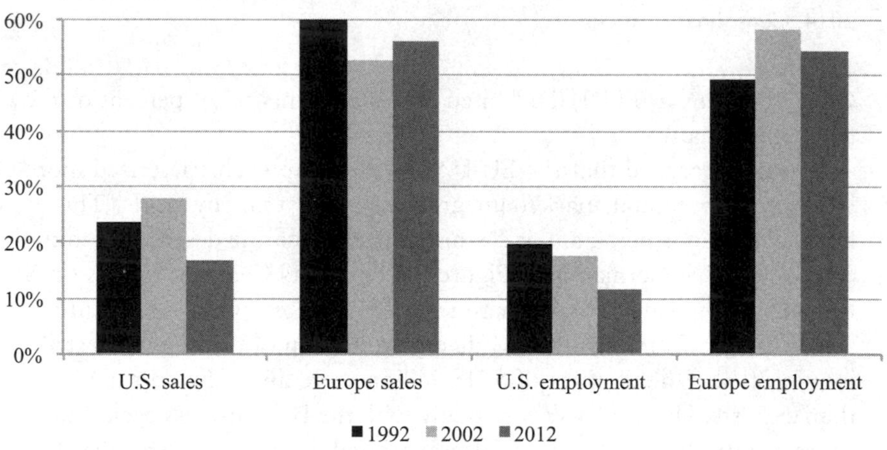

Figure 9.7
Activities of German multinationals in the United States and Europe, percent of total sales and employment.
Source: German Bundesbank, author's calculations.

impressive trends in figure 9.6—the United States has gradually lost importance since 1992. The share of employment of German affiliates in the United States has fallen from about 20 percent to 12 percent, and the share of sales has come down from 23 to 17 percent.

The largest part of German FDI in the United States is horizontal, that is, market seeking. It is strongly motivated by the desire to avoid exchange rate risk, tariffs, or other trade barriers, and to shorten delivery times. Vertical, that is, cost seeking, FDI has been modest, since wage costs are not systematically lower in the United States than in Germany. With energy prices strongly diverging over the last years, cost-seeking FDI could, however, become more important.

9.2 What Economic Benefits Can Germany Expect from a TTIP?

Trade Potential Utilization Rates

The volume of German trade with the United States is impressive in absolute terms. However, it is difficult to interpret the data without putting it into perspective. For this reason, figure 9.8 relates observed bilateral trade in goods and services (in value added terms) to the amount of trade that one would expect in hypothetical textbook circumstances. Assuming that there are no trade frictions of whatever form, that consumers have identical preferences in all countries, and that trade results from national product differentiation (such as Anderson and van Wincoop 2003 or Krugman 1980 models; see, e.g., Feenstra 2004, chapter 5), one can easily

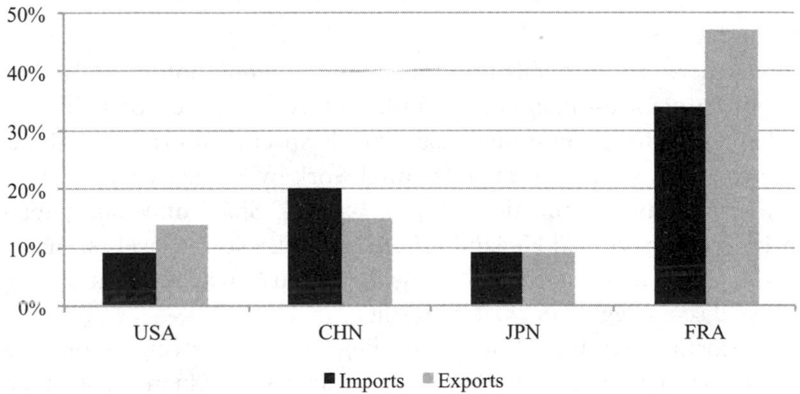

Figure 9.8
Utilization rates of German bilateral trade, percent, value added, 2009.
Source: OECD-WTO TiVA statistics, author's calculations.

derive an estimate of the potential bilateral trade volume. German exports to the United States amount to about 14 percent of this friction-free benchmark; this is one percentage point lower than the corresponding utilization rate in exports to China, and much below the 47 percent achieved with France. German imports from the United States fall even shorter from the potential.

The very large gap between actual and hypothesized trade must arise due to a violation of the preceding assumptions because: (1) preferences between the countries may differ; (2) the assumption of specialization driven by product specialization may fail; or most obviously (3) there are substantial frictions to trade. As we have shown before, trade between the United States and Germany is predominantly intra-industry in nature, so product differentiation seems consistent with the facts. Also, since per-capita income levels and the internal distribution of income are not too different between the United States and Germany, differences in preferences cannot plausibly explain much of the gap. Consequently, trade costs must still play a substantial role in U.S.-German trade.

Clearly, trade costs take many forms—tariffs and nontariff barriers make up only a limited part. For trade among OECD countries, Anderson and van Wincoop (2004) estimate total trade costs, expressed in ad valorem terms, to amount to about 74 percent, only 8 percent thereof being attributable to policies. However, as we have argued, estimations of nontariff measures are fraught with uncertainties. Not only is it difficult to ascertain their level, but it also is hard to come up with plausible estimates of how they could realistically fall in a TTIP.

Different Studies

By now, there are a number of quantitative simulation models that attempt to provide estimates of the trade and welfare effects of a TTIP. In this chapter we focus on studies that provide specific information about Germany. Thus, we refer to the influential work by Francois et al. (2013) for the European Commission only in passing. Since only one paper, Aichele, Felbermayr, and Heiland (2014), provides sector-level estimates for Germany, we provide a full-fledged comparison of estimates only when we discuss aggregate welfare results.

The existing studies differ regarding the underlying economic model. Felbermayr et al. (2014) use a single-sector Krugman (1980)-type ("macro") model with an extensive margin; Aichele, Felbermayr, and Heiland (2014) use an Eaton and Kortum (2002)-type model with multiple sectors and input–output linkages;[9] Egger et al. (2015) use a multi-sector model with input–output linkages that features Krugman (1980)-type modeling for some sectors and the Armington setup for others. Fontagné, Gourdon, and Jean 2013 is a more conventional CGE model with perfect competition.

For the treatment of nontariff measures, Fontagné, Gourdon, and Jean (2013) employ a bottom-up approach (also used in Francois et al., 2013) whereas the other studies use a top-down approach, as will be discussed. While all studies refer to long-run effects, meaning, the numbers assume that all adjustment has already taken place, they use different base years (for reasons of data availability). Fontagné, Gourdon, and Jean (2013) use forecasts for the year 2025; Aichele, Felbermayr, and Heiland (2014), Egger et al. (2015), and Felbermayr et al. (2014) use the observed situation of 2007, 2011, and 2012, respectively. The later the base year, the smaller are the welfare effects because the shares of both the EU and the United States in world GDP have been falling over time and are predicted to fall even further. There are numerous other modeling differences, from different levels of regional aggregation, to the overall treatment of trade costs, to different assumed or estimated trade elasticities. Thus, a balanced comparison of studies is very difficult and beyond the scope of this chapter.

Bottom-Up versus Top-Down Estimates of NTMs in Quantitative Models of a TTIP

It is not our objective here to discuss advantages and disadvantages of different modeling approaches. However, some explanation is required because different quantitative assessments come to different conclusions regarding the expected trade and welfare effects of a TTIP. Models differ with respect to several dimensions, but the most important distinction rests on the treatment of trade costs.

One strand of research works with the available *bottom-up* estimates of the level of NTMs and assumes some reduction (i.e., by 25 percent). Another strand works with a very generic definition of trade costs and assumes that a TTIP would result in a reduction by the same amount that can be inferred from other, already existing, trade agreements. This *top-down* approach is usually embedded into a structurally estimated general equilibrium model of international trade (as described by Costinot and Rodríguez-Clare 2014), while the *bottom-up* approach usually is implemented in a more traditional computable general equilibrium (CGE) model of the GTAP type whose calibration uses external parameter estimates. Kehoe (2005) has compared the ex ante predictions for several trade agreements obtained under the latter approach with econometric ex post evaluations and finds that standard "models drastically underestimated the impact of NAFTA on North American trade."

Two major reasons for this failure lie in the inadequate treatment of trade costs (NTMs are largely ignored) and in the definition of scenarios that ignore dynamic effects of trade agreements on trade costs (i.e., changed incentives for private and public agents to invest in a further reduction of bilateral trade costs).

The existing quantifications of the economic effects of a TTIP go more or less far in remedying these problems. For example, the studies by Francois et al. (2013) or Fontagné, Gourdon, and Jean (2013) allow for NTMs along with tariffs and incorporate econometric estimates of their ad valorem tax equivalents, but they do not allow a TTIP to affect other types of trade costs. Moreover, their scenarios are based on expert opinions about what is achievable in a TTIP. Egger et al. (2015), Felbermayr et al. (2014), and Aichele, Felbermayr, and Heiland (2014), in contrast, allow a TTIP to potentially affect a broad class of trade costs. Moreover, these papers use econometric estimates of the average ex post effect of existing agreements on trade costs to define the TTIP scenario. The latter approach leads to much larger trade and welfare effects of a TTIP. Moreover, basing the TTIP scenario on the observable effects of existing agreements logically implies a different treatment of trade costs among non-TTIP countries or between non-TTIP countries and the EU or the United States. While Francois et al. (2013) assume that these trade costs fall by 20 percent and 30 percent, respectively, of the assumed trade cost reduction within the TTIP, the other studies do not assume such spillovers (in their default scenarios), mostly because there is no clear empirical evidence for their existence (discussion follows).

In the following, we briefly discuss potential trade and welfare effects obtained by different studies for Germany. Since Francois et al. (2013) and Fontagné, Gourdon, and Jean (2013) do not provide country-level results for the EU, we focus on the results reported by Felbermayr et al. (2014) and Aichele, Felbermayr, and Heiland (2014).[10] The latter study provides an analysis for a TTIP that is assumed to be as deep and comprehensive as the deepest and most comprehensive trade agreements that exist (according to the analysis of Dür, Baccini, and Elsig 2014). This means that the TTIP is assumed to be as ambitious as an average over NAFTA, the EU, and a couple of smaller preferential trade agreements.

Trade Effects of a TTIP

In all studies that provide information on the effect of TTIP on overall openness, a substantial increase in the ratio of exports over GDP is predicted. In Felbermayr et al. 2014, it goes up by approximately 10 percentage points. It goes up by about 5.5 percent in Francois et al. 2013 for the whole of Europe and by about 2 percent in Fontagné et al. 2013 in Germany. These are substantial effects that would make a relatively open economy even more open.

Aichele, Felbermayr, and Heiland (2014) provide more detailed information; so we draw on that study in the following discussion. Table 9.4 presents baseline and counterfactual German exports without and with a TTIP. The baseline refers to the observed data from year 2007. The counterfactual analysis asks: what would the world economy have looked like if—in the year of 2007—the EU and the United States had had a deep preferential trade agreement that has had time to unfold all its effects?

The table shows total exports (of goods and services) of Germany to different destinations. Over the long run, the value of exports to the United States as measured at customs is predicted to increase by more than 200 percent, from about $111 billion to $351 billion. This is a spectacular increase. Exports to other destinations, in contrast, are bound to fall. This demonstrates the possibility of trade diversion. Total exports, however, go up by slightly less than 12 percent.

German gross exports may contain value added from other countries (including the United States itself) and German firms may export to the United States indirectly as they deliver intermediate inputs to producers in other countries that export to the United States. Also, the United States may not be the place where the recorded trade flow is finally consumed or invested. Accounting for these possibilities, we report the value added exports (i.e., the transfer of German value added to U.S. consumers) and show how it would change under TTIP. Aichele, Felbermayr, and Heiland (2014) find that VA exports would increase less than exports. This reflects changes in the structure of value chains: Under the TTIP Germany would source more inputs from the United States, in particular, and consequently the German value added share in German goods goes down. For the same reason, the model also predicts that German value added exports to *third countries* falls more than the exports, with two notable exceptions. German value added exports to Canada and Mexico go up, presumably because the U.S. exports to these countries contain more German value added than before TTIP. So, in value added terms, trade diversion is even

Table 9.4
The effect of TTIP on German Exports, Aichele, Felbermayr, and Heiland (2014), in $U.S Billions

	Exports			Value added exports		
	Base	TTIP	Change (%)	Base	TTIP	Change (%)
EU27	807	743	-8	514	462	-10
USA	111	351	216	106	249	136
EFTA	65	63	-3	37	35	-5
China	54	51	-6	40	37	-7
Eurasian Customs Union	48	47	-3	39	37	-6
East Asia	47	43	-9	36	33	-8
ASEAN	25	24	-7	17	15	-7
Middle East and North Africa	25	24	-4	21	20	-6
Oil exporters	25	24	-4	19	18	-5
Turkey	21	20	-4	17	15	-8
Mercosur	15	14	-5	13	13	-5
Pacific Alliance	15	14	-7	12	12	2
South Asia	15	14	-5	15	14	-6
Canada	11	10	-9	10	11	12
Australia and New Zealand	11	11	-4	10	10	-5
Central Asia	11	11	-3	9	8	-6
Southern African Customs Union	11	10	-3	8	7	-6
Rest of Europe	10	10	-1	9	8	-6
Sub-Saharan Africa	9	9	-4	9	9	-6
Latin America and Caribbean	4	4	-4	4	4	-1
Rest of World	1	1	0	1	1	-4
Oceania	1	0	-6	1	0	-8

Source: Aichele, Felbermayr, and Heiland 2014. Regional aggregates are GDP-weighted averages of country-level estimates. See Aichele, Felbermayr, and Heiland 2014 for a definition.

magnified unless the third country has close trade ties with the United States.

Table 9.5 shows that imports from the United States are bound to increase even more strongly so that they exceed imports from China by a wide margin. Nevertheless, the bilateral trade surplus (measured at customs values) that Germany has with the United States goes up.[11] Germany's imports from the EU are expected to shrink by something around 5 percent; imports from Turkey, China, and East Asia could fall by similar amounts. Imports from other regions, however, are bound to increase. This reflects an income (or scale) effect: as production and incomes go up in Germany, demand for intermediate inputs, raw materials, and for consumption goods and services increases.

Interestingly, in value added terms, trade diversion is much weaker. With this metric, imports from China actually rise. This means that TTIP allows this region to export to Germany through the United States. Also the German trade surplus with the United States increases less in value added terms ($42 billion vs. $46 billion).

Other studies also find that a comprehensive TTIP would substantially increase bilateral trade across the Atlantic. The results of Aichele, Felbermayr, and Heiland (2014) are at the upper end of the known results. Felbermayr et al. (2013) use a macroeconomic one-sector setup. They report that German exports and imports to the United States could almost double (both go up by approximately 94 percent). The other studies have no Germany-specific trade effects. Francois et al. (2013) and Fontagné, Gourdon, and Jean (2013) find an EU-wide increase of exports to the United States by 28 percent and 49 percent, respectively, while imports would go up by 37 percent and 53 percent, respectively. Trade changes for Germany should be expected to be somewhat stronger. The more recent exercise by Egger et al. (2015) does not provide any detail on trade effects.

All studies report that within-EU trade will be redirected. This is to be expected as the trade diversion resulting from the EU customs union and the single market program is partly unwound. Again, studies differ with respect to the magnitude of this effect.

Figure 9.9 is taken from Aichele, Felbermayr, and Heiland 2014. It plots density estimates of the distribution of German bilateral trade changes with the EU in four key industries. It differentiates between changes in exports as recorded at the customs on the one hand and changes in value added exports on the other hand. These two distributions can but need not differ substantially from each other. In the

Table 9.5
The effect of TTIP on German imports, in $U.S billions

	Imports			Value added imports		
	Base	TTIP	Change (%)	Base	TTIP	Change (%)
EU27	665	631	-5	373	348	-7
China	78	75	-5	55	55	1
USA	77	271	253	60	162	169
EFTA	73	72	-1	40	39	-2
East Asia	56	51	-8	45	43	-3
Eurasian Customs Union	42	44	4	35	35	0
ASEAN	34	33	-3	24	24	0
Middle East and North Africa	22	23	3	19	20	2
Turkey	17	16	-3	12	11	-4
Mercosur	16	16	1	13	14	3
South Asia	14	14	1	11	12	2
Pacific Alliance	13	12	-3	11	13	18
Central Asia	7	8	2	6	6	-1
Southern African Customs Union	7	7	1	5	5	0
Sub-Saharan Africa	6	7	2	7	7	7
Rest of Europe	6	6	-1	4	4	-3
Oil exporters	6	6	6	12	12	5
Canada	6	6	6	6	9	42
Australia and New Zealand	5	5	5	6	6	3
Latin America and Caribbean	5	5	3	4	4	7
Rest of World	2	2	4	1	1	4
Oceania	1	1	7	1	1	3

Source: Aichele, Felbermayr, and Heiland 2014.
Notes: Regional aggregates are GDP-weighted averages of country-level estimates. See Aichele, Felbermayr, and Heiland 2014 for a definition.

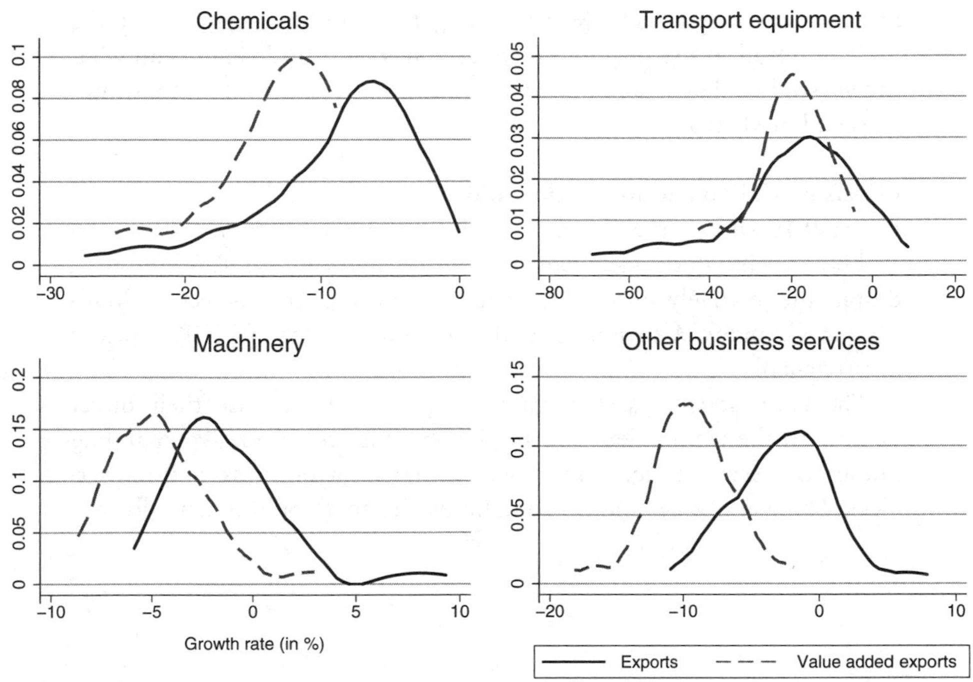

Figure 9.9
Trade with EU members: distribution of changes for selected industries.
Source and notes: Aichele, Felbermayr, and Heiland 2014. Univariate Epanechnikov kernel density estimates. Bandwidth varies across plots but is set optimally. Solid lines refer to exports as measured at customs; dashed lines to value added trade.

chemical sector, the entire mass of the distributions lies in the negative area: both bilateral exports and value added exports fall with all EU trade partners. However, the value added exports tend to fall more. The latter also capture indirect effects via sectors that use German chemicals as input. So the pattern can be explained by the fact that other sectors (in Germany or abroad) reduce the usage of German chemicals; or that sectors that rely heavily on German chemical inputs have adverse trade effects; or that more of the German chemical value added does not stay in the trade partner but is processed and shipped on (e.g., to the United States)—or all of the above. A similar pattern emerges for the machinery and other business services sector. In the transport equipment industry, the distributions have a similar peak, but the changes in value added exports are less dispersed. Indirect effects seem to be less important in this sector, presumably because German value added is concentrated in downstream products. Summarizing, these results suggest that the TTIP will lead to a stronger weakening of intra-EU trade links than what earlier studies that ignored inter- and intra-national input–output linkages had predicted.

Effects of TTIP on Sectoral Value Added

Figure 9.10 shows how selected sectors contribute to total GDP (bars) and how their value added contributions change with TTIP.[12] Note that, despite the relatively strong role of manufacturing, services sectors dominate in Germany. Also note that the sectoral impact of TTIP is rather heterogeneous.

The main services sectors gain, not so much because their direct exports to the United States go up, but because the strongly expanding automotive sector triggers additional demand for business or trade services. There are two manufacturing industries that could potentially lose

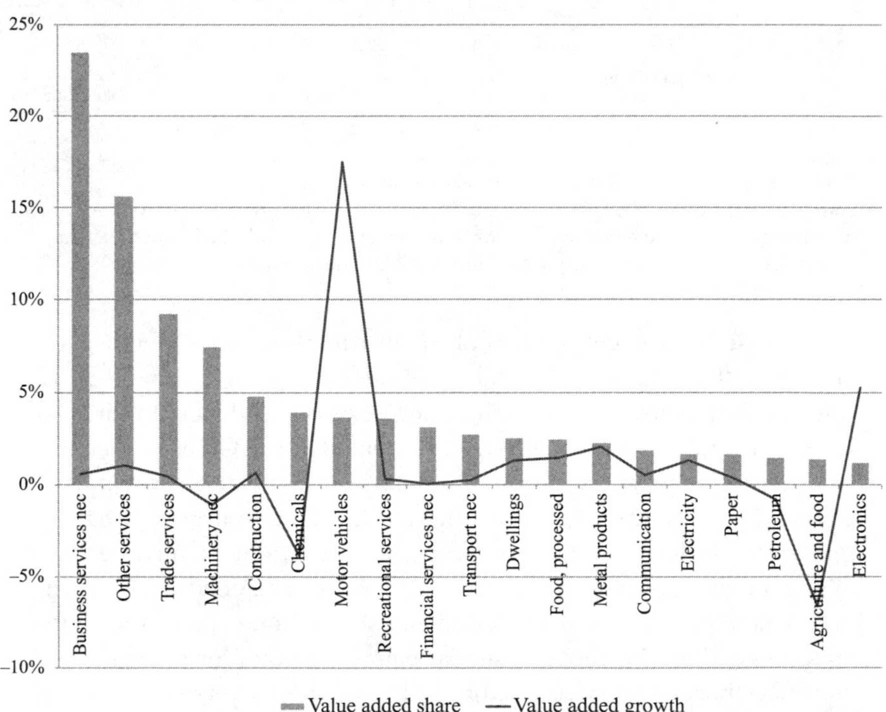

Figure 9.10
Sectoral value added shares and change due to TTIP (percent).
Source: Aichele, Felbermayr, and Heiland 2014.

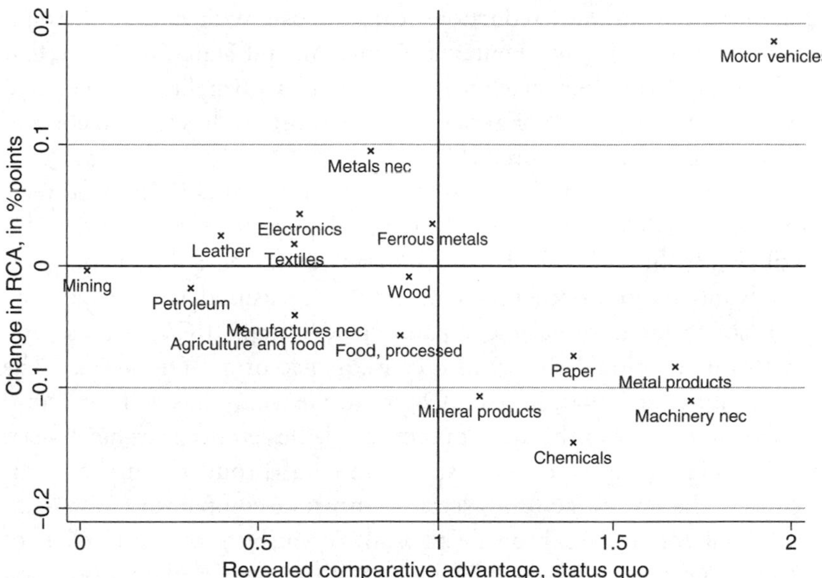

Figure 9.11
Change in Germany's structure of revealed *multilateral* comparative advantage (RCA) through a TTIP.
Source: Aichele, Felbermayr, and Heiland 2014.

out from a TTIP: these are the machinery and the chemical sectors. The former suffers only slightly. The reason is, mostly, that the strong expansion in the automotive sector increases the competition for resources and this drives up costs. The chemical sector, in contrast, could be more strongly affected, simply because this sector features a comparative advantage for the United States, which has even increased over the last years. The third sector that could be negatively affected is the agri-food industry. According to the calculations in Aichele, Felbermayr, and Heiland (2014), this sector could be hit quite strongly. Again, this response is due to the strong comparative advantage that the United States enjoys in this sector.

So far, the study by Aichele, Felbermayr, and Heiland (2014) is the only one to report general equilibrium consistent industry-level estimates of a TTIP for Germany. However, while quantitative impacts are generally much higher in Aichele, Felbermayr, and Heiland 2014, the results are qualitatively comparable to what Francois et al. (2013) find for the entire EU. In that study, the industries that are set to benefit most are transportation equipment and machinery. For electronics and optical equipment, the assumed reduction of trade costs with non-TTIP countries neutralizes any gains. Fontagné, Gourdon, and Jean (2013) also find that transportation and machinery are bound to benefit, however, and they find negative effects for agriculture. So, those studies tend to confirm the pattern depicted in figure 9.11.

The patterns visualized in figure 9.10 suggest that a TTIP could reinforce Germany's comparative advantage. Figure 9.11 investigates this possibility. It shows in which sectors Germany currently has a comparative advantage compared to the world (as measured by the Balassa–Samuelson index of revealed comparative advantage (RCA); x-axis), and how this index would change as a consequence of a TTIP (y-axis). The diagram illustrates that, in manufacturing, Germany has a strong comparative advantage in the areas of motor vehicles equipment, machinery, metal products, paper, chemicals, and mineral products. In the status quo, the other manufacturing sectors feature a comparative disadvantage, albeit often a weak one. The analysis suggests that a number of sectors could improve their RCA index with respect to the world: First and foremost, the motor vehicles sector would benefit. Some areas in the metal and the electronics industries would also be able to improve their RCA. If one abstracts from the motor vehicles sector, the picture suggests some convergence: areas with weak comparative advantage tend to see improvements, while those with strong comparative advantage see deterioration.

Welfare Effects of a TTIP for Germany

All available studies clearly suggest that the mere elimination of transatlantic tariffs would result in very minor welfare gains that range between 0.0 percent and 0.28 percent for Germany. Indeed, it is well known that reducing low tariffs even further cannot unlock large welfare gains as those are proportional to the square of the initial tariff rate. In contrast, nontariff barriers are different, in particular if they are assumed to waste resources. The evidence strongly suggests that the levels of NTMs are by an order of magnitude higher than those of tariffs. Moreover, their elimination does not entail the loss of government income but frees up resources for the production of additional goods and services.

Table 9.6 reports welfare results from different studies that provide details about Germany. The table also shows welfare effects for a number of other countries and regions. It presents results for the default scenarios proposed by the studies but adds results from alternative scenarios

Table 9.6
Welfare effects (%) from a TTIP for selected countries and regions

	Fontagné, Gourdon, and Jean (2013)	Egger et al. (2015)		Aichele, Felbermayr, and Heiland (2014)			Felbermayr et al. (2014)
	Default	Default	Spillovers	Default	Spillovers	TTIP+Doha	Default
Germany	0.4	1.1	1.3	2.6	3.0	2.8	3.5
EU27	0.3	1.1	1.5	2.1	2.6	2.3	3.9
USA	0.3	0.4	0.7	2.7	3.3	2.8	4.9
EFTA	n.a.	-0.4	0.5	0.1	0.5	0.5	-1.9
Rest of Europe	n.a.	0.0	0.2	0.3	0.7	0.5	1.3
MENA	n.a.	-0.1	0.2	0.1	0.4	0.7	-0.6
Japan	n.a.	-0.2	0.0	-0.1	0.0	0.3	-0.5
Turkey	n.a.	-0.4	0.8	0.1	0.4	0.3	-1.6
China	n.a.	0.3	-0.7	-0.2	0.2	0.4	-0.5
World	n.a.	n.a.	n.a.	1.3	1.7	1.6	1.6

Notes: The reported numbers are equivalent variation measures. They report the change in real per capita income after full phase-in of a TTIP relative to an observed or predicted (if referring to a future date) reference situation. MENA refers to "Middle East and North Africa" (in Egger et al. 2015: Mediterranean). EU27 average always includes Germany.

whenever sensible. From left to right, the studies find increasingly large effects. From most pessimistic to most optimistic, the estimates range from 0.4 to 3.5 percent. This shows that modeling assumptions and scenario definitions matter and that the findings of individual studies have to be interpreted with caution.

One question of particular interest in the EU is whether countries in the core of the continent—such as Germany and countries closely connected to it such as Austria or the Czech Republic—benefit more than countries in the periphery. The available studies suggest that, whenever intra-European production chains are fully accounted for (Fontagné, Gourdon, and Jean 2013; Aichele, Felbermayr, and Heiland 2014), Germany registers larger gains than the EU average. This would tend to increase income inequality within the EU. It appears that countries that are strongly integrated into the German value chain benefit more than those left outside. The single-sector perspective adopted in Felbermayr et al. (2014) comes to a more optimistic conclusion, as Germany wins slightly less than the EU average. Note that the single-sector view imposes less structure; it can be understood as a reduced form approach to a more complex model where the fundamental drivers of comparative advantage are not fixed. This interpretation implies that a TTIP could be less beneficial for peripheral countries in the short run, but may turn out to offer overproportional advantages for them in the long run.

Finally, the studies disagree about whether or not the TTIP will affect third countries negatively. The study of Francois et al. (2013) is the only one to assume that bilateral trade cost reduction between the EU and the United States always generates spillovers through which trade costs in the rest of the world fall, too, albeit by a lower rate. This is a topic of great political relevance, in particular regarding the multilateral system; see section 9.3 for further discussion.

Before turning to the policy debate in Germany, it is worth reiterating that the simulation results should all be taken with a grain of salt: whether the economic effects are large or small depends on, more than anything else, the supposed scenario. In Aichele, Felbermayr, and Heiland (2014), if the TTIP is not a deep agreement but only a "medium" one, the welfare benefits for Germany would be less than half the 2.6 percent presented in table 9.6. With this caveat in mind, the simulations are still informative about the qualitative impacts and should be interpreted accordingly.

9.3 Elements of the Public Debate in Germany

A TTIP is hotly debated in Germany. Economists have been stressing the possibility of welfare gains and have been warning that the project could harm multilateralism. While there is some debate about the size and importance of these effects, the discussion is well framed in mainstream trade models. Also, in protected sectors such as agriculture, the public sector, and some services industries, there is some fear of losing economic rents. Of course, this has always accompanied initiatives of trade liberalization from Ricardo's times to today. What is new is the fierce debate about regulatory cooperation and investment protection. The EU has just started to address these issues in its international agreements, broadly because member states had not given it the mandate to do so before. Since the Global Europe report of 2006 the EU Commission has become more assertive in using trade treaties to make the EU a more dynamic economy, and since the Lisbon Treaty of 2009 the EU has competence over foreign direct investment.

In this section, we start out with providing some explanation and discussion on this debate. We begin with regulatory cooperation, and then move to investment protection. The latter is linked to the former, since it could potentially limit the liberty of governments to regulate at will. We go on by providing some information on key industries, and close with some observations on multilateralism.

Regulatory Cooperation

In some areas, regulation of products and processes differs across the Atlantic. This means that market access is fully denied to certain foreign products, or that producers, who want to sell on both markets to double engineer goods, go through two testing procedures, and run the risk of market access denial twice. There are multiple ways to achieve greater regulatory convergence: formulate and impose joint standards, mutually recognize the other region's standards, recognize test results obtained in the other region, improve information and transparency on regulatory requirements. The German debate is mostly about the extent of regulatory cooperation, which consumer protection groups, environmentalists, animal right groups, and trade unions want to be as limited as possible.

Regulatory divergence has different reasons that give rise to different policy prescriptions. Some differences clearly have their roots in a more or less explicit desire to keep foreign competition out. This may be the case with the prohibition to import into the EU chicken that has been rinsed in chlorinated water. Among many others, the German Federal Institute for Risk Assessment (BfR) has argued that this simple and well understood treatment actually reduces rather than creates health hazards. Thus, the only party that obviously benefits from the regulation appears to be the European chicken industry, which, broadly, appears to be less competitive than the American one.

Maybe the largest part of regulatory divergence is a result of path dependence. At the time when standards were drawn up, the possibility of transatlantic trade appeared remote, and no attention to regulatory compatibility was paid. Often, while regulation differs, outcomes are very similar: for example, in the automotive industry standards differ, but cars are no less safe on either side of the Atlantic. In these cases, mutual recognition could be feasible.

Finally, and more controversially, regulatory differences result from different political preferences or philosophies. While the EU stresses the precautionary principle according to which the safety of a product needs to be proved before it is allowed on the market, the United States relies more on the responsibility of the producer and on ex post enforcement via liability law. However, differences are much more subtle, and the United States practically often respects the precautionary principle without making explicit reference to it. Wiener et al. (2011) show that, de facto, the United States does not apply precaution more rarely than the EU, and that an exchange of best practice has been common in the past. However, this applies to averages, and strong differences in certain industries do exist. The most prominent example is the chemical industry, to be discussed. There, mutual recognition of standards is out of question.

A trade agreement such as the TTIP is most likely not the right place for the development of joint standards, given the tremendous amount of legislation on both sides of the Atlantic. However, in the TTIP, it is planned that negotiators set up regulatory councils—institutions that provide a forum for the development of common standards for products or processes that do not exist today, such as in nanotechnology and biotechnology, developments in the sphere of the Internet, and so on. Rather, regulatory convergence in a TTIP will be limited to the mutual recognition of standards and test results where possible and to improve information exchange in other areas. The Canada-EU comprehensive economic and trade agreement (CETA) shows how difficult even small progress in regulatory cooperation is.

In the German debate, some take issue with the proposed design of regulatory councils. These consist of delegates of the EU Commission, of the U.S. administration, and of industry experts. Critics complain that parliaments have no say in these bodies, that lobbyists will gain too much influence, that the council meetings and decisions do not involve the public, and that the councils establish a parallel legislative. Some of this criticism could and should be addressed in the TTIP text.

Investor-State Dispute Settlement

With the entry into force of the Treaty of Lisbon on December 1, 2009, the European Union has gained exclusive competence with respect to FDI.[14] As of today, there is no EU trade agreement in force that has an investment chapter, but all major trade deals in negotiations are planned to include one. The text of the proposed Canada-EU agreement contains a substantial investment chapter.

And the High-Level Working Group has also recommended an investment chapter for the TTIP. It would include provisions that remove market access barriers for foreign investors and grant protection against discrimination and expropriation without compensation to foreign investors. If the agreement is breeched, foreign investors can sue the state (i.e., the EU or the United States) via a special investor-state dispute settlement (ISDS) mechanism that is separate from the normal public judicial system. While such ISDS clauses are written into many existing bilateral investment treaties (BITs), in the ongoing negotiations the ambition is to set the standard for a modern and more comprehensive investment chapter: it would go beyond traditional bilateral investment treaties by applying to preestablishment as well as postestablishment; it would cover a broader range of financial transactions, and it would go farther in ensuring transparency and impartiality of the decision process in the ISDS processes in line with recommendations put forward by the UNCTAD in its *Investment Policy Framework for Sustainable Development.*

Germany has the world's largest current account surpluses; therefore, it is the world's largest exporter of capital. One may argue that the country has a particularly strong interest in ensuring that foreign investments are well protected. Germany was the first country in history to sign a BIT: it did so in 1959 with Pakistan. Since then, it has concluded 155 treaties, 132 of which are still in force. Twenty-one agreements have been replaced by new ones (e.g., the agreement with China); two agreements have been unilaterally canceled (Bolivia, South Africa). Typically, the partners to the agreement are poorer, less developed countries, which are recipients of German FDI. In the case of the TTIP, Germany itself is a recipient of FDI—this has dramatically changed the public perception of BITs.

Moreover, under the umbrella of the Energy Charter, an agreement covering the energy sector that contains an ISDS mechanism, Germany has been sued twice by the state-owned Swedish energy firm Vattenfall, which purchased power plants in Germany in the 1990s. The more controversial of these cases relates to the German *Energiewende* project, which foresees shutting down all nuclear power plants by the year 2022. Vattenfall has access to the ISDS while other—Germany-based—electricity producers must go to the standard courts to seek compensation. Critics say this constitutes a parallel system that treats foreign investors differently from domestic ones and gives multinational corporations too much clout. Advocates of ISDS counter that it neutralizes various advantages that domestic companies may enjoy in domestic courts.

Other critics claim that an investor chapter is simply not needed because the degree of capital market integration is much deeper than the degree of integration on goods and services markets. This is particularly true for the U.S.-German relationship, where both countries are important sending and receiving countries of foreign direct investment from each other. Hence, critics claim, from Germany's point of view there is no particular need to include an investment chapter into a TTIP. Moreover, the sheer size of transatlantic FDI could result in numerous disputes being treated before investor-state tribunals, even more so if the investment chapter goes beyond FDI and includes a broader set of financial instruments.

Interestingly, in other EU member states, there is very little debate about the proposed investment chapter. Most new member states concluded bilateral investment treaties with the United States in the early 1990s, but these agreements do not respect the recent UNCTAD recommendations on best-practice BITs, nor do they contain preestablishment provisions (i.e., on liberalization of market access). Replacing those old BITs with an investment chapter in TTIP would offer the opportunity to modernize the rules and procedures; it would also substitute the EU for member state governments as the U.S. counterpart (to be discussed). Finally, there is also a geostrategic component to the debate: German multinational enterprises have built far-reaching global production networks and they have a vital interest in protecting their foreign direct investments. For this reason, the EU is currently negotiating a BIT with

China. Since such a BIT would of course be reciprocal, it would grant Chinese investors in Europe special rights that—in the absence of an EU BIT with the United States—would be denied to American investors. So, while an investment chapter in TTIP is no priority for Germany, it is important for other EU member states and plays a key role in the overall EU strategy in international investment protection.

A more relevant point of criticism is that investors may sue governments when the latter modify regulations that affect the profitability of firms' investments post-establishment. This can happen under the title of indirect expropriation, which occurs when the expected present value of the investment is reduced without compensation. Existing agreements often are rather unclear on the exact legal definition of indirect expropriation. This uncertainty may invite frivolous claims, which—even if they end up being turned down—cause substantial costs and make governments reluctant to envision regulatory changes in the first place. This regulatory chill need not be bad, in particular in a country such as Germany in which the density of regulation is already very high.

The last important question on ISDS of particular importance to Germany is this: Which legal entity—the EU or the member state—is the respondent to an investment dispute under the investment chapter in the TTIP? A recent EU regulation includes an attempt to clarify. In Article 5 it states:

> Where the Union, as an entity having legal personality, has international responsibility for the treatment afforded, it will be expected, as a matter of international law, to pay any adverse award and bear the costs of any dispute. However, an adverse award may potentially flow either from treatment afforded by the Union itself or from treatment afforded by a Member State. It would as a consequence be inequitable if awards and the costs of arbitration were to be paid from the budget of the Union where the treatment was afforded by a Member State, unless the treatment in question is required by Union law. It is therefore necessary that financial responsibility be allocated, as a matter of Union law, between the Union itself and the Member State responsible for the treatment afforded on the basis of criteria established by this Regulation.[14]

So, under an investment chapter the EU has legal responsibility, while the financial responsibility rests with the member states.

The regulation clarifies the allocation of financial responsibility. But what looks like a simple administrative procedure has deep economic implications. Under the investment chapter, political risks, which a foreign investor incurs in a specific member state, will, in case of damage, be dealt with at the union level. This implies that the risk premium that an investor requires will be the same in the entire EU. The equalization of risk premiums implies an implicit transfer of countries with low levels of risk to those with higher levels. By distorting the price system, it could incentivize investors from the United States to invest in countries with high underlying risk rather than, say, in Germany. This problem only now is emerging and has not been discussed much in the public debate so far. However, it deserves further scrutiny as it could preempt political configuration within the EU that many member states would probably resist.

Cross-Sector Heterogeneity

While the effects of a TTIP will be mostly felt within narrowly defined industries or sectors, there is, of course, a substantial amount of heterogeneity across them. It is beyond the scope of this chapter to provide a comprehensive analysis; however, some remarks on a number of key sectors are useful as they illustrate larger issues. For this reason, in the following we provide some discussion on the agricultural sector, the automotive sector, and the chemical sector.

Agriculture. Most regions within Germany are characterized by small farms; farms in Eastern Germany are an exception. The agricultural sector employs 646,000 persons who generate value added amounting to 0.86 percent of GDP.[15] Net incomes in the agricultural sector amount to about double this quantity due to various transfers (BELV 2013).

Germany is a net importer of raw agricultural goods, but a net exporter of processed food; these products amount to less than 1 percent and to 4 percent of total exports, respectively. Exports to the United States amounted to about 1 percent and 2 percent of total exports in raw and in processed goods, respectively. For imports, those numbers stand at 5 percent and 2 percent; see Bureau et al. 2014 for details. It is therefore safe to say that raw agricultural exports to the United States are almost nonexistent; exports of processed goods are more important. Among the most important goods, only four goods (at the six-digit level of disaggregation) amount to 74 percent of total exports—they are all alcoholic beverages (wine, sparkling wine, spirits).

Regarding imports of raw agricultural goods, Germany imports nuts (almonds, pistachios), and animal feed (soy beans, sunflower seeds) from the United States; alcoholic beverages (whiskies and wines) and seafood dominate imports of processed goods (see table 9.7).

Overall, the United States imports amount to less than 5 percent of Germany's agricultural imports; Brazil has overtaken the United States in

Table 9.7
Top 10 source countries, agricultural imports (ISIC Rev. 3 01–05), 2013

Rank	Country	Imports, $U.S. billions	Share
1	Netherlands	7.6	19.7%
2	Spain	3.8	9.8%
3	France	2.3	6.0%
4	Italy	2.1	5.5%
5	Brazil	2.0	5.1%
6	USA	1.9	4.9%
7	Poland	1.5	3.9%
8	Denmark	1.1	3.0%
9	Czech Republic	1.0	2.6%
10	Vietnam	0.7	1.9%
	Sum over top 10	24.0	62.3%
	Total	38.5	100.0%

Source: Destatis (database of the German Statistical Federal Office).

the last years, mostly by expanding its exports of soy beans, ethanol, and tropical fruits at the expense of the United States. But also Vietnam has emerged as an important supplier of agricultural goods to Germany. Both countries could be affected by trade diversion should a TTIP be concluded.

The agricultural sector has always been an important source of trade conflicts between the EU and the United States: while their bilateral trade does not account for more than 10 percent of world trade in much of the history of the GATT/WTO, the EU and the United States have been responsible for more than half of all trade disputes. The ongoing debate relates to long-lasting conflicts at the WTO about genetically modified organisms, hormone-treated beef, and poultry, to name only a few. While some in Germany argue that critical U.S. products should be admitted to the EU market as long as they are labeled, many others oppose this possibility and claim that labeling alone does not sufficiently protect the consumers.

Despite all the fundamental disagreements, over recent years, the transatlantic dialogue has nevertheless brought some progress on which negotiators could build. For example, as of 2006, the parties have accepted mutual recognition of wine-making practices and recognition of geographic indications for wine and spirits. Such dialogue has not solved all disagreements, though, and the United States still considers important European wine names as "semi-generic." They have concluded an agreement (in 2003) on sanitary measures to protect public and animal health in trade in live animals and animal products, including the progressive recognition of the equivalence of sanitary measures, the recognition of animal health status, the application of regionalization, and the improvement of communication and cooperation. However, the parties did not manage to overcome any of the issues that involved fundamental conceptions in risk analysis. Neither did negotiations solve the divergence regarding decontamination at the end of the processing chain (meat), rather than control at each step. In 2012, a mutual recognition agreement on organic products entered into force. As a result, organic products certified in either the EU or the United States can be sold as organic in either region as of June 1, 2012. The EU-U.S. banana agreement entered into force January 2013. Finally, there are other signs of a willingness to progress within the TTIP discussion, which, on the U.S. side, led to greater acceptance of regionalization for recognition of low risk of dissemination of the bovine spongiform encephalopathy status; and, on the EU side to accept lactic acid-based methods of pathogen control in beef.

All these efforts are steps on which the TTIP can build. It is also worth recalling that, by signing the WTO SPS agreement, both parties have agreed that all measures aimed at protecting human, animal, and plant health must be based on scientific principles. Furthermore, in all EU and U.S. free trade agreements concluded with third parties, both entities have made explicit references to WTO rules in the sections dealing with SPS and TBT standards, suggesting that they intend to comply to a common set of standards. Compliance to this global framework is important to ensure that bilateral agreements remain consistent. It should also ease the bilateral negotiations on these issues.

On the optimist side, one may also argue that regulatory divergence is sometimes overestimated. For example, in terms of food safety, critics often stress the differences between the EU and U.S. philosophy for risk management. The EU philosophy is said to rely on the idea that the whole process is monitored and traceable at each step. By contrast, the U.S. system is seen mostly as verifying safety of the end product. While there is some truth in this comparison, it ignores that both the EU and the

United States have adopted a compulsory Hazard Analysis at Critical Control Point approach in several food sectors, including meat.

Bureau et al. (2014) find that the main areas where Germany could expect additional exports to the United States are dairy products, processed products including wine and spirits, and possibly sugar and biodiesel. The TTIP could, however, have serious adverse consequences for the suckler cow sector (cows raised for meat production only). Ethanol, poultry, and cereals (corn and low-quality wheat) could also be affected by strong increases in imports from the United States.

Beyond the potentially negative impact for particular sectors, the main farmer association in Germany issues warnings on distortions that would result if trade is liberalized without regulatory convergence, for example concerning the use of pesticides, standards (such as minimum space requirements for pigs or chicken), or the treatment of meat in lactic acids. Consumer protection agencies, in contrast, fear that regulatory convergence would undermine significant sections of the EU policy, in particular in terms of risk management and precaution, but also on consumer information and dispute settlement.

Automotive industry. The most visible export industry of Germany is, beyond doubt, the automotive industry. Traditionally, this industry's leaders have doubted the advantages of further trade liberalization. Indeed, it is one of the most protected sectors, with EU import duties at 10 percent. However, in the current discussion about TTIP, the car industry has adopted a different, very welcoming, position. This is due to the fact that the industry already is very strongly integrated across the Atlantic. All major U.S. car manufacturers—General Motors Corporation, Ford Motor Company, and Chrysler—either have very sizeable European affiliates or are owned by a European firm. Similarly, the main German car makers—Volkswagen, BMW, and Daimler-Benz—have large production sites in the United States. Indeed, the BMW plant in Spartanburg, South Carolina, is the biggest exporter of U.S.-made cars to markets outside North America, beating any facility run by General Motors, Ford, or Fiat Chrysler Automobiles as well as the entire state of Michigan, the historic home of the American auto industry.[16]

U.S. car workers are about 40 percent less expensive than workers in highly unionized German plants, according to data from VDA, the German car lobbyist.[17] For this reason, the German car industry is increasingly interested in exporting U.S. made cars to Europe and to other destinations. Accordingly, the elimination of tariffs would be very welcome. Similarly, the car manufacturers would benefit greatly from a mutual recognition of standards such as bumper height, brake light color, side-mirror design, and emissions testing.

Without providing details for Germany, Francois et al. (2013) find that the elimination of tariffs and 25 percent of existing U.S. and EU nontariff barriers would increase EU vehicle and parts exports to the United States by 149 percent and increase U.S. vehicle and parts exports to the EU by 347 percent. Similar effects are found by Aichele, Felbermayr, and Heiland (2014) for Germany. For this reason, the industry has lobbied for comprehensive mutual recognition, where a vehicle certified as compliant with safety and environmental requirements in the United States is accepted as compliant in the EU, and vice versa. The underlying assumption, which is broadly supported by data, is that European and U.S. cars have very similar safety and environmental performance even if regulation differs.

Chemical industry. The chemical industry is an example of a highly sophisticated sector that is hardly visible in citizens' daily lives but evokes fears and worries, in particular in Germany. There are many concerns about a lowering of safety standards in this area.

In the chemical sector, differences in the regulatory environment across the Atlantic are deep. Both sides have different regulations for the safety of chemicals. REACH in the EU and the U.S. Toxic Substances Control Act (TSCA) cannot be compared because their underlying principles are very different (precautionary principle in the EU versus ex post application of sound science in the United States). This makes mutual recognition impossible until the legislation changes. The chemical industry in Germany has acknowledged this problem (VCI 2014). It has argued that a TTIP cannot and will not put into question the regulatory autonomy, neither of the EU nor of the United States. Regulatory autonomy does not preclude regulatory cooperation. A difference needs to be made between regulatory convergence in existing and future legislation: in fields where the goal of legislation is comparable or even identical, ideally both parties agree on mutual recognition. This will remain the exception in the chemical sector where the transatlantic gap has widened rather than closed in the past years. But it should be possible to approximate certain points—which have arisen under existing legislation and constitute trade obstacles, such as reporting requirements, exchange or recognition of data—without compromising the protection standards.

The German chemical industry has proposed concrete steps for reducing duplication and for achieving more convergence in the long term. These include (1) cooperating in the prioritization of chemicals that need to undergo assessment; (2) approximation of methods in chemical assessment; (3) intensive exchange of information and exploring possibilities for cooperation in newly arising topics (e.g., regulation of nanomaterials, combination effects of chemicals, endocrine active substances); and (4) cooperation and exchange of information for data between public agencies in charge of chemicals.

Moreover, for the energy-intensive chemical industry, it is important to benefit from the U.S. "shale gas revolution," for example by liquefying gas and exporting it to Europe. This would at least reduce the transatlantic differential in gas prices and improve the European industry's competitiveness.

Multilateralism and Discrimination of Third Countries

The stated objective of the TTIP, for example, according to the negotiating mandate that EU member states have given to the EU Commission, "is to increase trade and investment between the EU and the US"; creating trade between and within the group of third countries is not an objective. Rather, much of the political discussion about the TTIP puts forward the need to ascertain transatlantic leadership in the future world trade system. While a TTIP certainly would not be an open attempt to discriminate against third countries, containment of emerging powers such as China or Brazil does certainly play a role in the motivation of politicians.

It is obvious that most of the future demand growth will happen outside of the transatlantic economy. In 1995, about 60 percent of world demand (world income in USD) originated within the EU or the United States; in 2013 this share had already fallen to 46 percent and it is projected to fall to about less than a third of world demand by 2050 (OECD 2014). Moreover, the share of German exports to the EU27 and the United States has fallen from 75 percent in 2000 to 65 percent in 2012. A similar but somewhat less dramatic erosion of relative importance has happened with imports. And there is very little evidence that would suggest a reversal or even a slowing down of these trends.

These facts are, of course, well known to all relevant German decision makers. Representatives of several key lobbying groups have stated repeatedly that they do not wish to see an Atlantic Fortress or an Economic NATO established as such a development could endanger free access for German firms to emerging markets. However, so far, very few proposals have been made to ensure that a TTIP would not discriminate against outsiders. The BDI, the German Federation of Industries, has argued that a TTIP should be designed such that discriminatory disadvantages for third countries are minimized, for example by simplifying rules of origin, or by limiting the requirement to prove the origin of goods to a short list of sensitive sectors.

One may argue that a TTIP will not have substantial trade-diverting effects since both the EU and the United States have relatively low MFN tariffs relative to most trade partners. However, the TTIP is supposed to do much more than eliminate most tariffs. In many areas—for example the opening of public procurement markets, liberalization of investment, or reduction of quantitative restrictions—the TTIP will effectively discriminate against foreign suppliers. A key question is whether regulatory convergence between the EU and the United States also reduces trade costs between third countries and TTIP members or among third countries themselves, or both.

The evidence strongly suggests that preferential trade agreements do divert trade. Panagariya (2000) nicely motivates his discussion of trade creation and diversion by stating: "Any discussion of the welfare effects of PTAs must inevitably begin with the influential concepts of trade creation and diversion." Are these trade diversion effects substantial?[18] While Clausing (2001) finds little evidence for trade diversion for the Canada–United States Free Trade Agreement (CUSFTA),[19] Trefler (2004) and Romalis (2007) do find evidence for trade diversion for CUSFTA and NAFTA, respectively. While Trefler (2004) finds trade creation does still outweigh trade diversion to ensure that there are welfare gains from NAFTA in Canada, Romalis (2007, 417) concludes that "the more detailed data used in this paper reveals much more substantial trade diversion than Trefler, so much so that there appear to be essentially no welfare gains for any NAFTA member." However, Romalis (2007) not only finds no welfare gains for the NAFTA members, but also finds evidence for negative third-country effects for non-NAFTA members. His analysis of trade diversion reveals that a 1 percent drop in intra-North American tariffs leads to about a 2 percent fall in exports from other countries relative to the European Union.

Chang and Winters (2002) analyze the trade diversion effects of non-Mercosur exports to Brazil after inception of Mercosur. They find strong negative terms-of-trade effects for nonmember countries and conclude their analysis with the statement: "Our results give empirical backing to the well-known theoretical argument that even if external tariffs are unchanged by integration, nonmember countries are likely to be hurt by regional integration."

Regulatory cooperation can proceed in two main ways: by creating a joint standard, or by mutually recognizing standards. Establishing joint standards is hard, so that most progress has been made by negotiating mutual recognition agreements (MRAs). The problem with MRAs is that they do not create a single world standard to which third countries could adhere. Rather, they would have to abide by the national standards in the PTA countries, since the MRA does not extend to them. For this reason, MRAs are potentially as much trade diverting as tariff reductions are; joint standards, in contrast, could actually spur third country trade. What is the empirical evidence on this question?[20]

Chen and Mattoo (2008) use panel data to analyze the effects of PTAs that harmonize standards and find that while they increase trade between participating countries, the effects on outsiders are less clear cut. They depend on the ability of the outside countries to meet standards. As the standards more likely are met by developed than by developing countries, Chen and Mattoo (2008) conclude that specifically developing countries will be negatively affected by trade diversion from an MRA where they are not members. Additionally, the stringency of the rules of origin plays a crucial role for the effects on outsiders. If the rules of origin are very strict, then gains from the MRA are restricted to MRA member countries, whereas otherwise outside countries likewise potentially gain from harmonization of standards of other countries. Baller (2007) uses a gravity model accounting for heterogeneous firms to investigate the effects of MRAs on developed and developing countries. She distinguishes between MRAs for which she finds positive effects on the extensive (entering new markets) and intensive (volume of trade) margin, and harmonization of standards or technical regulations. For the latter she finds ambiguous effects. Specifically, in line with Chen and Mattoo (2008), she finds that developing countries' trade is affected by regional harmonization whereas trade with developed countries is increased.

Fink and Jansen (2009) focus on services trade and argue that the scope for MRAs is likely to be limited. The reason is that with regard to services, MRAs are mainly relevant for mode 4 movements.[21] However, mode 4 trade is hardly affected by trade liberalization, making large gains from MRAs unlikely. MRAs for services only apply to a small number of professional services sectors, like accounting, architecture, and engineering. In addition, most of the MRAs do not implement automatic recognition of qualifications (OECD 2003), limiting their effect further. There is also a recent paper by Cadot, Disdier, and Fontagné (2013) that highlights trade diversion effects for nontariff measures.

They show that North–South PTAs hurt trade between developing countries. If the harmonization is based on regional standards, exports of developing countries to developed countries also are predicted to be negatively affected.

Let us summarize these empirical findings in the words of the World Trade Organization (2012): "To sum up, evidence suggests that regional integration of TBT/SPS [Technical Barriers to Trade (TBT), Sanitary and Phytosanitary (SPS)] measures has trade-diverting effects, especially to the detriment of developing countries." The implication of all this is that Germany could be negatively affected if a TTIP ends up disrupting trade with emerging countries.

The Position of the German Government

In its 185-pages-long so-called coalition agreement between the conservative and market-friendly CDU/CSU and the social democratic SPD, the current government has committed itself to the TTIP. In a section entitled "Strengthening Free Trade and Trade Agreements," the pact first talks about the need to strengthen global trade governance through the World Trade Organization and to complete the Doha Round. Then, the agreement says that the coalition strives for the speedy conclusion of a free trade agreement with the United States and of further agreements with fast-growing emerging markets.

As to the much disputed protection of international investments, the government pushes for maintaining the high current levels of protection. It strives toward establishing "level playing fields" and international standards.

The coalition agreement sets forth that EU trade deals should enshrine the core labor provisions of the International Labor Organization (ILO), so that free trade does not lead to wage and social dumping. It insists that a TTIP must maintain the high European standards in the areas of consumer and data protection.

The German position in Europe recognizes "the special need for protection of cultural goods and media." In the negotiations about an EU-U.S. free trade agreement, this need must be respected and secured by means of exceptions.

The planned free trade agreement with the United States is central to deepening the transatlantic relations. We want the negotiations to be successfully concluded without compromising parliamentary control and judicial protection. Our objective is to eliminate as far as possible any existing barriers in the transatlantic trade and investment relations.

Justified exceptions must be part of the treaty for both sides. We will pay special attention on securing the European standards of protection in the areas of data, social, environmental, and food safety as well as consumer rights, public services, and culture and media.[22]

However, the social democratic party has increasingly expressed concerns about several dimensions of the TTIP. State secretary Brigitte Zypries (from the SPD) said on March 13, 2014 in German Parliament, as regards ISDS: "At present, we are in the consultation procedure, and we are speaking against an inclusion of the arbitration procedures in the agreement. We are working towards this, and we would be grateful for support."

Bernd Lange,[23] German socialist-democrat politician and chairman of the International Trade Committee in the European Parliament, sees the TTIP as an important contribution toward the reindustrialization of Europe—an important policy objective of his party. In particular, the areas of public procurement and the mutual recognition of technical standards would present interesting opportunities. He also stresses that tariffs, despite their low average levels, still matter for EU-U.S. trade because of the sheer volume of transactions. Finally, he also asks for a U.S. commitment to ratify a number of ILO norms relating to the recognition of trade unions or work councils.

He defines three "red lines," which, if transgressed, would lead to rejection of a TTIP by the social-democrat faction in the EU Parliament. First, he stresses the need for a parallel EU-U.S. framework agreement on data protection. Moreover, in his party's view, provisions on data protection have no place in a free trade agreement. In Europe, many citizens are very sensitive in this area, not least because of historical experiences with totalitarian regimes. Second, he opposes the inclusion of an investor-state dispute settlement mechanism in trade agreements between countries (such as the EU or United States) with reliable and developed judicial systems. He does recognize the importance of investment provisions in an agreement, and seems to accept ISDS in treaties with emerging countries. Finally, he formulates the opposition of his group against the speedy conclusion of a treaty that delegates responsibility about regulatory convergence to extra-parliamentarian bodies. If a comprehensive agreement turns out impossible, he proposes a smaller deal centering on the elimination of tariffs, the mutual recognition of technical standards, and public procurement. The red lines have been concocted into a joint position paper of the SPD and the trade unions, in which fourteen conditions are laid down that need to be met if the SPD is to accept the treaty. The core of these points is similar to Bernd Lange's demands.

At the same time, the conservative party is increasingly coming under pressure as well. Besides the small but powerful lobby of farmers, it is also exposed to criticism from both the Catholic and the Protestant churches. The President of the Commission of the Bishops' Conferences of the European Community (COMECE), the German cardinal Reinhard Marx, has stressed that a free trade agreement between the United States and Europe not only is an economic opportunity, but also constitutes a particular responsibility. A key question, in his mind, is whether the agreement serves the common—global—good, or whether it harms developing countries. He would oppose an agreement that does not create advantages for the world's weakest. He asks for TTIP to advance clear, ethically founded norms in the world economy. By this, he seems to mean labor or environmental standards.[24]

Summarizing, the German government supports a TTIP. But there is a substantial degree of skepticism in both coalition parties and the final position of the government is not yet fully clear.

9.4 Conclusions

Germany is a country that has hugely benefitted from globalization. Its strong and efficient redistributive welfare state has cushioned adverse effects for individuals with low incomes. Germany has successfully secured a rather advantageous spot in the global production chain in what one may call "old economy" sectors (automotive, chemical, machinery) as it has specialized on relatively value added-intensive activities.

TTIP carries great promise for Germany. All available quantitative studies predict that the country could register a substantial increase in its real per capita income. However, not all sectors will benefit from the agreement. Most important, the agricultural sector will come under pressure. Moreover, the TTIP goes beyond a traditional free trade agreement. In particular, the inclusion of an investment chapter containing an investor-state dispute settlement mechanism has raised concerns from many sides.

The TTIP will affect the economic and political relations of Germany with other EU member states. First of all, the available quantitative studies all predict that the relative importance of traditional German trade partners such as France, Italy, and the UK will decline to the advantage of the United States. This is a natural consequence of the fact that a TTIP would unwind the discriminatory effects that the EU customs union and the EU single market have had on the United States. However, the erosion of links within the EU will further limit the readiness of Germans to invest into the EU unification project. Second, certain aspects of the TTIP could lead to a socialization of liabilities between EU member states, as the EU would act as the respondent in investment disputes. This could be seen as an additional step toward a liability union in Europe.

The TTIP will also affect Germany's economic and political links with third countries. Quite clearly, it will shift the trade pattern away from emerging economies and toward the United States. This could endanger Germany's close economic links with China, and it could also push Asian and African developing countries closer to China. While Germany remains officially committed to multilateralism, it remains to be seen which steps are taken in order to avoid that a TTIP leads to new opposing blocks in world trade—a situation that Germany more than many other participants to the TTIP would suffer from.

Notes

We thank Matthias Matthijs for his comments and suggestions.

1. Data from World Development Indicators 2013, http://data.worldbank.org/data-catalog/world-development-indicators/wdi-2013, accessed April 29, 2016.

2. The same is true for the Comprehensive Economic and Trade Agreement (CETA) that the EU has negotiated with Canada and on which a final text has been agreed upon (but not yet ratified).

3. "I am delighted to say that, for the first time in our history: the WTO has truly delivered." Roberto Azevedo, from concluding remarks to the WTO's Ninth Ministerial Conference in Bali on December 7, 2013.

4. We look at data for 2009, which is the most recent year for which the OECD reports the bilateral value added content of trade.

5. We use GTAP here, because bilateral trade in services and manufacturing is reported in a consistent manner. Moreover, much of the quantitative literature is based on these data.

6. The Grubel-Lloyd index is defined as $1-|X-M|/(X+M)$, where X denotes exports and M imports in a certain industry.

7. Clearly, moving the calculation of the Grubal-Lloyd index to lower levels of aggregation reduces its magnitude. However, compared to many other bilateral trade relationships outside the EU, the U.S.-German one is particularly strongly intra-industry.

8. Foreign direct investment is defined by the fact that an investor holds at least 10 percent of the equity of a foreign company.

9. The model is the one by Caliendo and Parro (2015) extended to capture nontariff barriers and free trade agreements.

10. Note that Felbermayr et al. 2014 is an update of Felbermayr et al. 2013.

11. The model assumes that the multilateral trade balances of countries remain fixed at the baseline equilibrium, but it does allow that the bilateral structure of balances adjusts.

12. We show the twenty (out of thirty-two) sectors with the highest contributions to overall value added. Together, they account for about 94 percent of GDP.

13. Point (e) of Article 3(1) of the Treaty on the Functioning of the European Union (TFEU).

14. Regulation (EU) No 912/2014 of the European Parliament and the Council of 23 July 2014 establishing a framework for managing financial responsibility linked to investor-to-state dispute settlement tribunals established by international agreements to which the European Union is party.

15. Most recent data (2013), Destatis.

16. Reported by Bloomberg, http://www.bloomberg.com/news/articles/2014-07-10/bmws-made-in-america-surging-as-biggest-auto-export-cars.html, accessed April 29, 2016.

17. Ibid.

18. Panagariya 1999 is a nice survey discussing the likely effects of PTAs including the potential trade diversion effects.

19. Note that Clausing (2001) uses prices rather than quantities in the welfare analysis, which is problematic (see Feenstra 2004). Additionally, the results from Clausing 2001 may be driven by the rapid growth of imports that would have occurred if CUSFTA was not in place (see Romalis 2007).

20. For a detailed discussion, see the World Trade Report prepared by the World Trade Organization (2012).

21. Mode 4 movements are services supplied by nationals of one country in the territory of another. This includes independent services suppliers and employees of the services supplier of another country, for example a doctor going from his home country to the patient's country to treat him there.

22. Coalition agreement, page 168, translation of the author. Full agreement at http://www.bundesregierung.de/Content/DE/_Anlagen/2013/2013-12-17-koalitionsvertrag.pdf?__blob=publicationFile&v=2, accessed April 29, 2016.

23. Bernd Lange, "Die roten Linien von TTIP," Internationale Politik und Gesellschaft, 2014, http://www.ipg-journal.de/kommentar/artikel/die-roten-linien-von-ttip-559/, accessed April 29, 2016.

24. Press release by the German Bishops' Conference, 10.06.2014-Nr. 099.

References

Aichele, Rahel, Gabriel Felbermayr, and Inga Heiland. 2014. "Going Deep: The Trade and Welfare Effects of TTIP." CESifo Working Paper Series No. 5150, December 30. http://papers.ssrn.com/sol3/papers.cfm?abstract_id=2550180, accessed April 29, 2016.

Aichele, Rahel, Gabriel Felbermayr and Inga Heiland. 2013. "Neues aus der Basarökonomie." *ifo Schnelldienst* 66 (6): 17–28.

Anderson, James, and Eric van Wincoop. 2003. "Gravity with Gravitas: A Solution to the Border Puzzle." *American Economic Review* 93 (1): 170–192.

Anderson, James, and Eric van Wincoop. 2004. "Trade Costs." *Journal of Economic Literature* 42 (3): 691–751.

Baldwin, Richard. 2011. "21st Century Regionalism: Filling the Gap between 21st Century Trade and 20th Century Trade Rules." Staff Working Paper ERSD-2011-08, World Trade Organization, Geneva.

Baller, Silja. 2007. "Trade Effects of Regional Standards. A Heterogeneous Firms Approach." *World Bank Policy Research Working Paper* 4124. Washington, DC.

BDI. 2014. *Transatlantische Handels- und Investitionspartnerschaft (TTIP).* Berlin: Mythen, Fakten, Argumente.

BELV. 2013. *Die wirtschaftliche Lage der landwirtschaftlichen Betriebe: Buchführungsergebnisse der Testbetriebe, Wirtschaftsjahr 2011/12.* Berlin: Bundesministerium für Ernährung, Landwirtschaft und Verbraucherschutz.

Berden, K. G., J. Francois, M. Thelle, P. Wymenga, and S. Tamminen. 2009. "Non-Tariff Measures in EU-US Trade and Investment—An Economic Analysis." Study commissioned by the European Commission, Directorate-General for Trade, Rotterdam.

Bureau, J. C., A.-C. Disdier, C. Emlinger, J. Fouré, G. Felbermayr, L. Fontagné, and S. Jean. 2014. "Risks and Opportunities for the EU Agri-Food Sector in a Possible EU-US Trade Agreement." Study commissioned by the European Parliament, European Union, Brussels.

Cadot, Olivier, Anne-Célia Disdier, and Lionel Fontagné. 2013. "North-South Standards Harmonization and International Trade. " *World Bank Economic Review* 29 (2): 327–352.

Caliendo, L., and F. Parro. 2015. "Estimates of the Trade and Welfare Effects of NAFTA." *Review of Economic Studies* 82 (1): 1–44.

Chang, Won, and L. Alan Winters. 2002. "How Regional Blocs Affect Excluded Countries: The Price Effects of MERCOSUR." *American Economic Review* 92 (4): 889–904.

Chen, Maggie Xiaoyang, and Aaditya Mattoo. 2008. "Regionalism in Standards: Good or Bad for Trade?" *Canadian Journal of Economics: Revue Canadienne d'Economique* 41 (3): 838–863.

Clausing, Kimberley A. 2001. "Trade Creation and Trade Diversion in the Canada-U.S. Free Trade Agreement." *Canadian Journal of Economics. Revue Canadienne d'Economique* 34 (3): 677–696.

Costinot, A., and A. Rodríguez-Clare. 2014. "Trade Theory with Numbers: Quantifying the Consequences of Globalization." In *Handbook of International Economics*, vol. 4, ed. Gita Gopinath, Elhanan Helpman and Kenneth Rogoff, 197–261. Oxford, UK, and Amsterdam: North-Holland.

Dür, Andreas, Leonardo Baccini, and Manfred Elsig. 2014. "The Design of International Trade Agreements: Introducing a New Database." *Review of International Organizations* 9 (3): 353–375.

Eaton, Jonathan, and Samuel Kortum. 2002. "Technology, Geography, and Trade." *Econometrica* 70 (5): 1741–1779.

Egger, Peter, Joseph Francois, Miriam Manchin, and Douglas Nelson. 2015. "Non-Tariff Barriers, Integration, and the Trans-Atlantic Economy." *Economy Policy* 30 (83): 539–584.

European Commission. 2006. "Global Europe: Competing in the World. A Contribution to the EU's Growth and Jobs Strategy." http://trade.ec.europa.eu/doclib/docs/2006/october/tradoc_130376.pdf, accessed April 29, 2016.

Feenstra, Robert. 2004. *Advanced International Trade*. Princeton, NJ: Princeton University Press.

Felbermayr, Gabriel, Mario Larch, Finn Krüger, Lisandra Flach, Erdal Yalcin, and Sebastian Benz. 2013. *Dimensionen und Auswirkungen eines Freihandelsabkommens zwischen der EU und den USA*. ifo Forschungsberichte 62. Munich: ifo Institut.

Felbermayr, Gabriel, Benedikt Heid, Mario Larch, and Erdal Yalcin. 2014. "Macroeconomic Potentials of Transatlantic Free Trade: A High Resolution Perspective for Europe and the World." *Economic Policy* 30 (83): 491–437.

Fink, Carsten, and Mario Jansen. 2009. "Services Provisions in Regional Trade Agreements: Stumbling Blocks or Building Blocks for Multilateral Liberalization?" In *Multilateralizing Regionalism: Challenges for the Global Trading System*, ed. R. E. Baldwin and P. Low. Cambridge, UK: Cambridge University Press.

Fontagné, L., Gourdon, J. and S. Jean. 2013. "Transatlantic Trade: Whither Partnership, Which Economic Consequences?" CEPII Policy Brief No. 1, CEPII, Paris, September.

Francois, J., M. Manchin, H. Norberg, O. Pindyuk, and P. Tomberger. 2013. "Reducing Transatlantic Barriers to Trade and Investment: An Economic Assessment." Report for the European Commission, London.

Kehoe, T. 2005. "An Evaluation of the Performance of Applied General Equilibrium Models of the Impact of NAFTA." In *Frontiers in Applied General Equilibrium Modeling*, ed. T. Kehoe, T. Srinivasan and J. Whalley, 341–378. Cambridge, UK: Cambridge University Press.

Krugman, Paul. 1980. "Scale Economies, Product Differentiation, and the Pattern of Trade." *American Economic Review* 70 (5): 950–959.

Marin, Dalia. 2010. "Germany's Super Competitiveness: A Helping Hand from Eastern Europe." *VoxEU* (June). http://www.voxeu.org/article/germany-s-super-competitiveness, accessed April 29, 2016.

OECD. 2003. "Service Providers on the Move: Mutual Recognition Agreements." *OECD Papers* 3 (2): 237. http://www.oecd-ilibrary.org/docserver/download/0203021e.pdf?expires=1445336626&id=id&accname=ocid56012597&checksum=0A2B197D576875362822BE245E166899, accessed April 29, 2016.

OECD. 2014. *World Economic Outlook* (May). http://www.oecd-ilibrary.org/docserver/download/1214011e.pdf?expires=1445346078&id=id&accname=ocid56012597&checksum=F9304B660D2343BEECF6381EF89B7982, accessed April 29, 2016.

Panagariya, Arvind. 1999. "The Regionalism Debate: An Overview." *World Economy* 22 (4): 477–512.

Panagariya, Arvind. 2000. "Preferential Trade Liberalization: The Traditional Theory and New Developments." *Journal of Economic Literature* 38 (2): 287–331.

Rodrik, Dani. 2011. *The Globalization Paradox: Democracy and the Future of the World Economy*. New York; London: W. W. Norton & Company.

Romalis, John. 2007. "NAFTA's and CUSFTA's Impact on International Trade." *Review of Economics and Statistics* 89 (3): 416–435.

Trefler, Daniel. 2004. "The Long and Short of the Canada-U.S. Free Trade Agreement." *American Economic Review* 94 (4): 870–895.

VCI (Verband der Chemischen Industrie). 2014. "TTIP: Questions & Answers from the Chemical Industry." https://portal.vci.de/Downloads/PDF/Questions%20and%20Answers%20from%20the%20chemical%20industry%20regarding%20an%20EU-US%20free%20trade%20agreement.pdf, accessed April 29, 2016.

Wiener, Jonathan B., Michael D. Rogers, James K. Hammitt, and Peter H. Sand. 2011. *The Reality of Precaution: Comparing Risk Regulation in the United States and Europe*. Washington, DC: RFF Press.

World Trade Organization. 2012. *World Trade Report 2012—Trade and Public Policies: A Closer Look at Non-Tariff Measures in the 21st Century*. Geneva: WTO. https://www.wto.org/english/res_e/booksp_e/anrep_e/world_trade_report12_e.pdf.

10

The Abolition of Antidumping Measures in the EU: An Example and Inspiration for the TTIP

Jonas Kasteng

Overview

In recent years, there has been a proliferation of regional trade agreements. This could be a consequence of as well as a contributing factor to the lack of progress in the World Trade Organization (WTO) negotiations. Regional trade agreements require the elimination of trade barriers between the parties. However, the use of antidumping measures is normally not considered in this respect; most parties to regional trade agreements, accordingly, maintain the right to use antidumping measures against each other.

There are a number of regional trade agreements that have eliminated the use of antidumping measures—and some of them have replaced the use of the antidumping instrument with competition rules. The European Union (EU) and the European Economic Area (EEA) might be the most successful examples of regional trade agreements that have eliminated the use of antidumping measures between the integrating parties. The EU is unique as a regional trade agreement in abolishing antidumping measures currently in force. The EU is also an example of a regional trade agreement that remains open to parties joining later. In the EEA, thirty-two countries have eliminated antidumping measures against their main trading partners. This chapter analyzes the effects on trade of imposing, as well as abolishing, antidumping measures in the EU. It also analyzes the experiences of the EU and the EEA in eliminating antidumping measures, something that might be of relevance to the Transatlantic Trade and Investment Partnership (TTIP) negotiations.

Section 10.1 focuses on the effects on trade of imposing and abolishing antidumping measures in the EU based on empirical evidence. The imposition of antidumping measures in the EU is analyzed from the points of (1) effectiveness, that is, if the protection is effective as regards

EU producers, the exporters of allegedly dumped products and third country exporters; and (2) efficiency, that is, the cost of protection for EU user industry and consumers. The abolition of antidumping measures in the EU is analyzed from the point of (1) injury to EU producers when it comes to price undercutting and loss of market shares; and (2) possible changes in the use of the antidumping instrument against third countries.

Section 10.2 focuses on antidumping measures between the EU and the United States, as well as the experiences with abolishing antidumping measures in the EU and the EEA as an inspiration for the TTIP negotiations. This section provides an overview of regional trade agreements that have eliminated antidumping measures. It also provides an overview of the use of antidumping measures in regional trade agreements negotiated by the EU and the United States. By way of conclusion, the section provides an analysis of the antidumping measures currently in effect between the EU and the United States, as well as the experiences of the EU and the EEA in eliminating antidumping measures, as a source for inspiration for the TTIP negotiations.

If major regional trade agreements—sometimes referred to as "mega-regionals"—such as the TTIP follow the examples of the EU and the EEA and eliminate antidumping measures, regional trade agreements might serve as a "stepping stone" to a new multilateral regime in this field, in other words, as a way of "multilateralizing regionalism."

Objective and Limitations

One of the main challenges facing the world trade system is whether regional trade agreements—a reality of today—might lead to a new multilateral regime. The overall objective of this chapter is to identify whether the abolition of antidumping measures in regional trade agreements might contribute to a new regime in the multilateral trading system. This chapter focuses on the analysis of the effects on trade of abolishing antidumping measures in the EU and the EEA and the possible learning of lessons for the TTIP, that is, the opportunity to abolish the use of antidumping measures in the TTIP.

The focus of this chapter is limited to the use of the antidumping instrument according to the current WTO provisions. The use of antisubsidy measures and safeguard measures are, accordingly, not considered for the purpose of this analysis. Antidumping measures are the most frequently used trade remedies by the EU and the United States, and they are also considered by most economists to be the most controversial among the trade remedies. The chapter, however, does not consider how the antidumping instrument could be improved, in terms of possible methodological concerns with the current proceedings.

This chapter is limited to the experiences of the EU and the EEA of imposing and abolishing antidumping measures, but comparisons with the United States and other regional trade agreements are made where the implications are relevant. The EU is one of two regional trade agreements where antidumping measures in force have been abolished (at its creation in 1958 and in its successive enlargements from 1973 to 2013). The other regional trade agreement that has abolished the use of antidumping measures in force is the free trade agreement between Australia and New Zealand in 1990. The EU enlargement in 2004 was its largest. This is why the EU enlargement in 2004 is used as an example in the analysis of the effects on trade of abolishing antidumping measures in force. This chapter is only considering the antidumping measures that were abolished by EU15 and not the antidumping measures by the ten accession countries against EU15.

This chapter is mainly based on previous research by the National Board of Trade, Sweden, in the field of antidumping policy. This implies that this chapter is based on research and reports prepared and presented at different moments in time with slightly different methodologies, and so on.

Finally, this chapter aims to be explorative and not exhaustive as regards the initiative to abolish antidumping measures in the TTIP. It argues that it might be possible to abolish antidumping measures in the TTIP if certain preconditions are fulfilled (even though, in reality, this is more of a political decision than anything else). The chapter presents useful background information on the use of antidumping measures between the EU and the United States. However, it is mainly qualitative with regard to the analysis of the effects on trade of imposing and abolishing antidumping measures in the TTIP.

This chapter might, accordingly, be used as a reference document in initial discussions or negotiations or both on the opportunity to abolish the use of antidumping measures in the TTIP. It might also serve as an inspiration for future research in this field.

10.1 The Effects on Trade of Imposing and Abolishing Antidumping Measures: The Experience of the EU

The Effects on Trade of Imposing Antidumping Measures in the EU

The European Union (EU) currently has some 122 antidumping measures in force (on average during 2008–2012). The EU is the world's fifth largest user of the antidumping instrument (European Commission 2014). These measures aim to protect EU producers from alleged price-dumped imports—products that are believed to cause economic injury to EU producers through being exported at prices below their domestic sales prices. The measures are expected to reduce imports from countries that export at allegedly dumped prices and to increase EU producers' sales volumes and prices on the EU market.

Are EU Antidumping Measures Effective? The economic effects on EU trade (in terms of import value, import volume, and import unit price) of imposing antidumping measures are analyzed by examining data from antidumping cases investigated from 2000 until 2008 (see annex 1 for a detailed description of the methodology used in the analysis).

The effects on *import values* of imposing antidumping measures seem to be immediate (see figure 10.1). The effect on imports from targeted countries can already be seen in the year the antidumping investigations are initiated (year "0"), which indicates that the market interprets that an antidumping investigation will result in measures being imposed. The year the provisional antidumping measures are imposed (year "1"), the imports from targeted countries decrease by 20 percent on average compared to the previous year. Imports from intra-EU trade increase by 19 percent on average, and imports from nontargeted countries increase by 23 percent on average. In the following two years, imports from targeted countries continue to decrease, albeit at a slower pace. Imports from intra-EU trade remain stable at the higher level, while imports from nontargeted countries continue to increase sharply.

The effects of imposing antidumping measures are also presented as the average changes in EU import market shares based on the import value (see figure 10.2). In this case, it provides an immediate picture of the level of competition in the EU import market. To a great extent, the figure for market shares is consistent with the figure for import values; it indicates that the antidumping action has an immediate effect on trade, reducing the import shares from targeted countries by 9 percentage points on average, and increasing import shares from nontargeted countries by

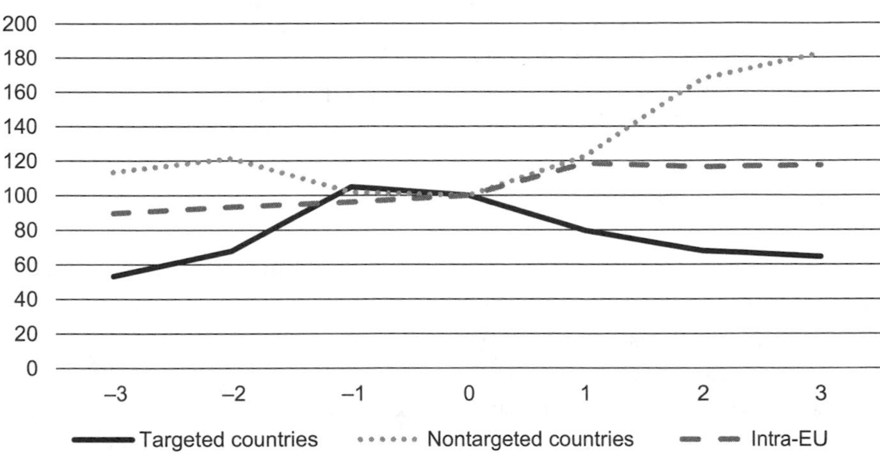

Figure 10.1
Average changes in import values (index 100 = year 0).
Source: Eurostat Comext database and the National Board of Trade 2012a.

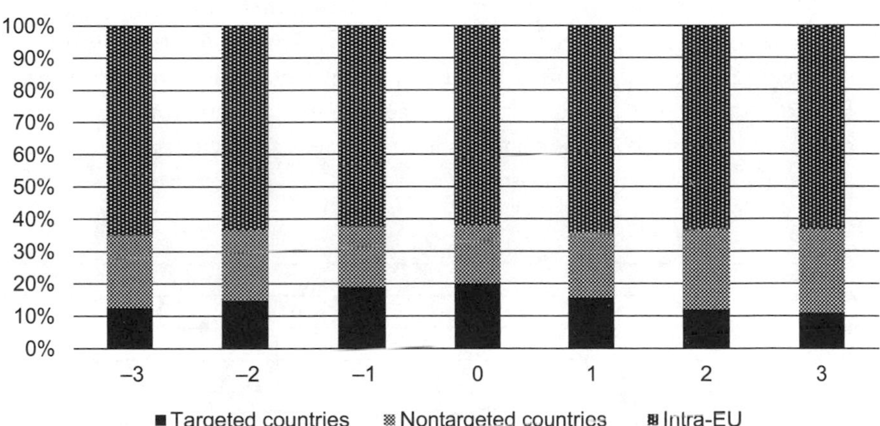

Figure 10.2
Average changes in import value market shares (percentage).
Source: Eurostat Comext database and the National Board of Trade 2012a.

an average of 8 percentage points. The market share of intra-EU imports also increases after the initiation of the antidumping investigation, indicating that EU producers benefit from the action. However, this increase is quite modest and considerably lower than the increases of the intra-EU import value. Three years after the initiation of the investigation, the intra-EU market shares have only increased by an average of 1 percentage point.

The average effects on *import volumes* of imposing antidumping measures—the average changes of import volume and the average changes in market shares of import volume—are almost identical to those for import values (see figures 10.3–10.4).

Three years after the initiation of the antidumping investigation, the unit value *import prices* from both extra-EU trade and intra-EU trade increased. Import prices from nontargeted countries increased by 5 percent on average; import prices for intra-EU trade increased by, an average of 10 percent; and import prices from targeted countries increased by 28 percent on average (see figure 10.5).

The large increase in the unit value price of imports from targeted countries may seem counter-intuitive, especially considering that the antidumping duty is not included in this price; meaning the actual price the EU consumers pay for imports increases even more since the average antidumping duty is 30 percent. In the case of a normal customs duty, the prices of imports will not normally increase. However, there are special

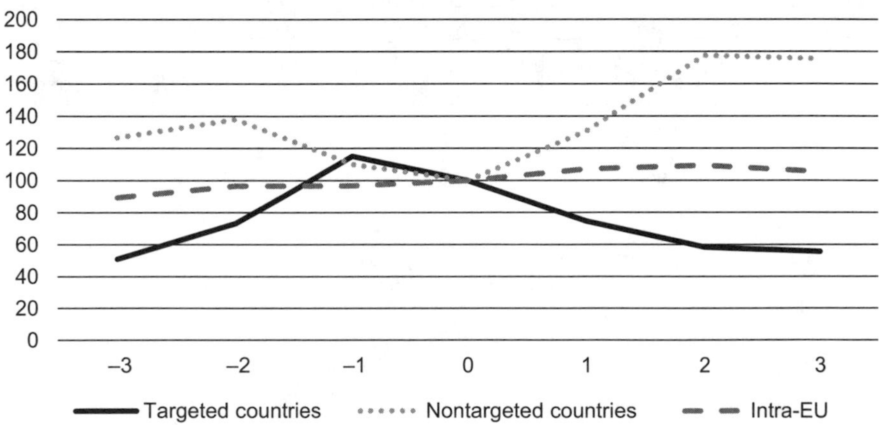

Figure 10.3
Average changes in import volumes (index 100 = year 0).
Source: Eurostat Comext database and the National Board of Trade 2012a.

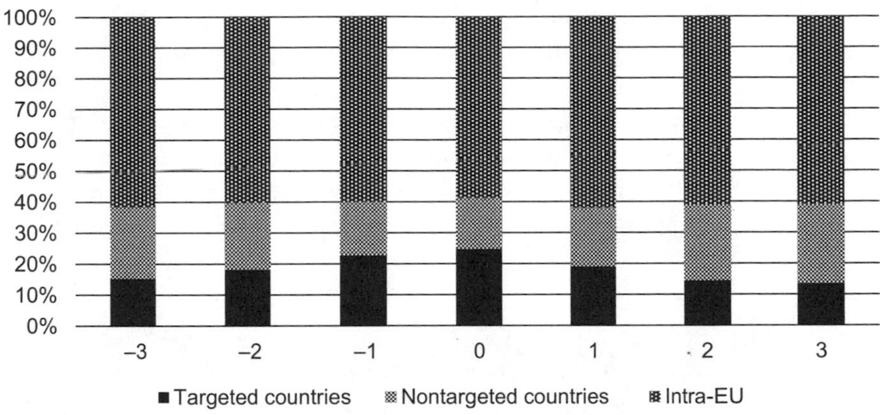

Figure 10.4
Average changes in import volume market shares (percentage).
Source: Eurostat Comext database and the National Board of Trade 2012a.

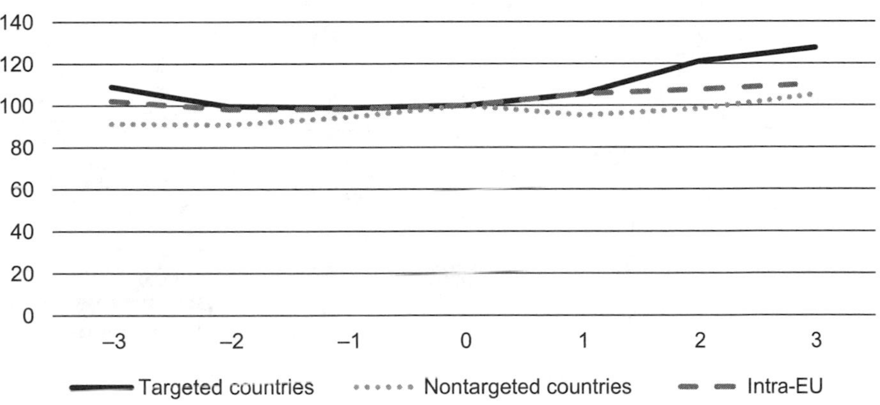

Figure 10.5
Average changes in import unit value prices (index 100 = year 0).
Source: Eurostat Comext database and the National Board of Trade 2012a.

features of antidumping measures that might provide companies targeted by antidumping duties with incentives to export at increased prices (see box 10.1).

The results of the statistical analysis suggest that the EU's antidumping actions, in general, have a restraining effect on imports from targeted countries and a positive effect on imports from nontargeted countries. The antidumping policy seems also to have some positive effects for EU

Box 10.1
Effects on import prices of imposing antidumping measures

The effect of antidumping duties on prices is different compared to normal customs duties. When antidumping duties are imposed, it appears that the (deflated) import prices—excluding the antidumping duties—tend to increase. This is contrary to the theoretical foundations of economics when it comes to normal duties. According to these theories, the import price (excluding duties) should decrease in order to ensure that the price (including duties) will not increase for the final consumer (see table A).

Table A. Price effect at the imposition of antidumping duties

Imposition of duties	**Import prices**		**Prices in the domestic market**
	Excluding duties	Including duties	
Normal duties	Decreases	Constant (or slight increase)	Constant or increases (due to limited competition)
Antidumping duties	Increases	Increases (due to price increase and imposed antidumping duties)	Constant or increases (due to limited competition)

Source: National Board of Trade 2013a.

There may be different explanations behind the price increases of products targeted for antidumping duties. One explanation could be that exporters increase their prices in order to counter the allegations of dumping. Another explanation could be that only products of a higher segment, namely, more expensive products, are exported when antidumping duties are imposed.

For the effects on import prices of abolishing antidumping measures, see box 10.2.

producers. The increase of the shares of intra-EU imports is modest, particularly in relation to the large increase in imports from nontargeted countries, but it should be seen in the light of the initially very high level of intra-EU imports. Moreover, it is important to bear in mind that there is no information on counter-factual scenarios. In the absence of antidumping measures, it is possible that the intra-EU share of the market, on average, would have decreased rather than increased slightly, as has been the case.

Are EU Antidumping Measures Efficient? The preceding analysis suggests that the imposition of antidumping measures seems to have some beneficial impact on EU producers when it comes to import volumes and prices; in that sense, the measures are effective. In this context, analyzing if antidumping measures are efficient, in terms of the costs that antidumping measures bring to the EU user industry and consumers, is relevant. This issue can be addressed by using an economic welfare approach to compare the losses with the gains of the antidumping policy for the EU as a whole.

Observations regarding the *price effects* show that intra-EU prices increase after the initiation of the antidumping investigation (see figure 10.5). This implies an economic gain for EU producers as they receive higher revenue for their products. For EU user industry and consumers, a higher price implies an economic loss.

The total increase in consumer costs as a result of the price increase is, however, somewhat smaller as consumers tend to substitute products that are relatively less expensive when prices increase. Consumers reduce their import volume from the targeted countries and increase their import volume from EU countries and, especially, from the nontargeted countries (see figure 10.3). Upon imposing antidumping measures, however, import prices increased from all sources.

For the EU as a whole, the increase of import prices is a net economic cost. The benefit for EU producers that results from the price increase for consumers buying EU products equals EU consumers' loss in buying EU products. The cost of duty for the consumers is equal to revenue for national customs authorities and the EU budget. The cost for consumers that arises from the price increase for extra-EU trade, however, constitutes only a cost for the EU as a whole. This cost can be interpreted as a negative terms-of-trade effect. In this case, the effect is quite strong as the unit value price from countries subject to antidumping measures increases sharply after the initiation of the antidumping investigation.

Observations regarding the *volume effects* show that EU producers gain when they are selling more products. If the antidumping policy results in a diversion from imports from targeted countries toward EU products, this would imply a large profit for EU producers, especially considering that prices have increased. For the sample used, the average increase in intra-EU import volume is 9 percent during the three-year period after the initiation of the investigation (see figure 10.3). EU import volume market shares also increase, albeit only by 1 percentage point, indicating that the diversion to imports from nontargeted countries does not completely mitigate the protective effect of the antidumping measure on EU producers.

The approach employed in this chapter allows for the calculation of average relative changes in imports and prices due to the imposition of antidumping measures. Consequently, the average relation between the EU producers' benefit and the EU consumers' loss is identified by analyzing the average change in producer surplus and the average change in consumer surplus for each of the antidumping cases. Such a welfare analysis suggests that the unweighted ratio between consumers' loss and producers' benefit is, on average, 4.5:1, namely, for every euro the producers gain, consumers lose 4.5 euro.

The results suggest that the antidumping measures come with rather high costs. Although estimates of this kind should be interpreted with caution, they are likely to provide a fair indication of the cost of imposing antidumping measures in the EU.

The Effects on Trade of Abolishing Antidumping Measures in the EU

The EU and its member states have traditionally been intensive users of antidumping measures against one another, but the successive enlargements have significantly changed this pattern. When the EU was enlarged in May 2004 with ten new member states (Cyprus, the Czech Republic, Estonia, Hungary, Latvia, Lithuania, Malta, Poland, Slovakia and Slovenia), the antidumping measures that EU15 had in place against the new member states were immediately abolished. These antidumping measures fulfilled the criteria of (1) dumping, (2) injury, (3) causality, and (4) the Union interest test as required by the EU antidumping regulation, but they were nevertheless terminated overnight. The EU is, accordingly, an example of a regional trade agreement that abolished antidumping measures previously in place.

Did Abolishing EU Antidumping Measures Cause Injury to Domestic Industry? The economic effects on EU15 trade (in terms of import value, import volume, and import unit price) of abolishing the antidumping measures in force at the EU enlargement in 2004 are analyzed by examining data from antidumping measures on the products concerned between 1998 and 2008 (see table 10.1). The data are also used to analyze whether the abolition of antidumping measures has caused injury to EU15 producers when it comes to price undercutting and lost market shares (see annex 2 for a detailed description of the methodology used in the analysis).

A comparison between 2004, the year when the antidumping measures from the EU accession countries were abolished, and 2008, the year when the economic crisis started, shows that the average *import values* increased from all sources (see figure 10.6).

In the years following the abolition of antidumping measures, intra-EU15 imports decreased in terms of market share by 9 percentage points. However, the drop in market share of EU15 producers was primarily due to the increase in market share of third countries other than the targeted accession countries (see figure 10.7). In 2008, the targeted accession countries gained a market share of only 1 percentage point on average, but the market share of the third countries increased by an average of 8 percentage points.

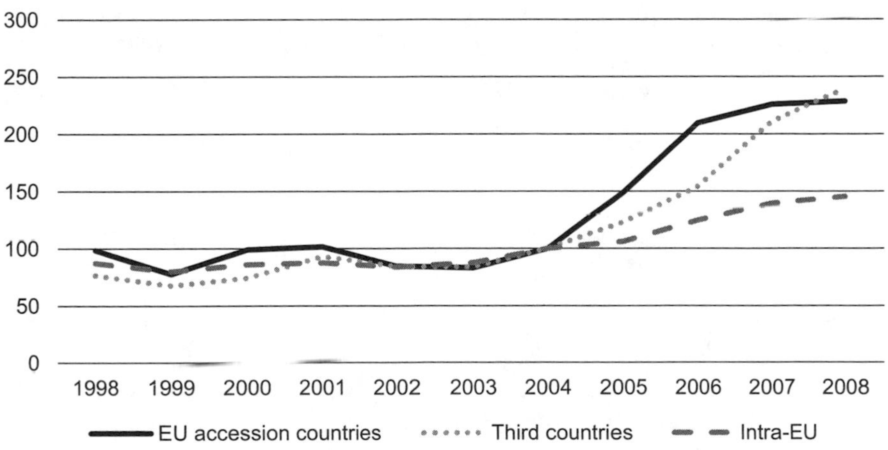

Figure 10.6
Average changes in import values (index 100 = year 2004).
Source: Eurostat Comext database and the National Board of Trade 2013a.

Table 10.1
Antidumping measures against accession countries, abolished as a result of the EU enlargement in 2004 (in alphabetical order)

Product	Targeted country	Initiation of antidumping investigation	Imposition of definitive antidumping measures	Countrywide duty level
Ammonium nitrate	Poland	1999	2001	26.91 EUR/tonne
Malleable tube or pipe fittings	Czech Republic	1999	2000	26.1%
Seamless pipes and tubes	Czech Republic	1996	1997	28.6%
	Poland	1991	1993	30.1%
	Slovakia	1996	1997	7.5%
Steel ropes and cables	Czech Republic	2000	2001	47.1%
	Hungary	1998	1999	28.1%
	Poland	1998	1999	48.3%
Urea	Estonia	2000	2002	11.43 EUR/tonne
	Lithuania	2000	2002	10.05 EUR/tonne
Urea ammonium nitrate solutions	Lithuania	1999	2000	3.98 EUR/tonne
	Poland	1993	1994	22.00 EUR/tonne
Tube and pipe fitting, of iron or steel	Czech Republic	2001	2002	22.4%
	Slovakia	2001	2002	15.0%
Welded tubes and pipes of iron or nonalloy steel	Czech Republic	2001	2002	52.6%

Source: National Board of Trade 2013a.

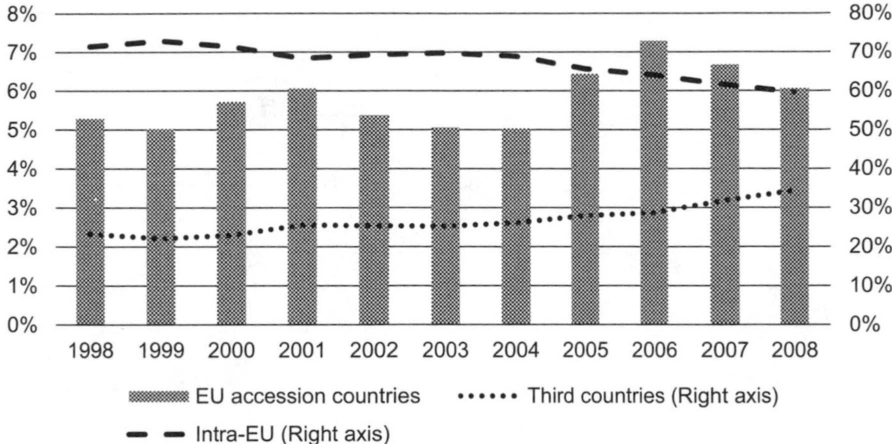

Figure 10.7
Average changes in market shares (import value), percentage.
Source: Eurostat Comext database and the National Board of Trade 2013a.

The average effects of abolishing antidumping measures on *import volumes*, in terms of total volume and in terms of share of total volume, are similar to the effects with regard to value (see figure 10.8 and figure 10.9).

Prior to the EU enlargement in 2004, the average (deflated) unit value *import prices* from the accession countries were generally lower than the average (deflated) unit value prices for intra-EU15 trade for most products (see figure 10.10). Subsequent to 2004 the import prices of the accession countries and the intra-EU15 import prices decreased slightly. In general, the import prices from the accession countries decreased less than the prices of intra-EU15 products (see box 10.2).

In the EU's antidumping investigations, price undercutting is defined as the difference between the EU producer's price and the price of imported products. Price undercutting could, accordingly, be used as a proxy for injury to EU producers, meaning, the *price effects* of the abolition of the antidumping measures.

According to the trade statistics, the average unit price level of the allegedly dumped exports from the accession countries remained below the average EU15 unit price level throughout the period studied (see figures 10.11–10.15). Trade statistics also indicate that the abolition of antidumping measures did not accelerate the alleged dumping practices of the accession countries. On the contrary, the level of price undercutting

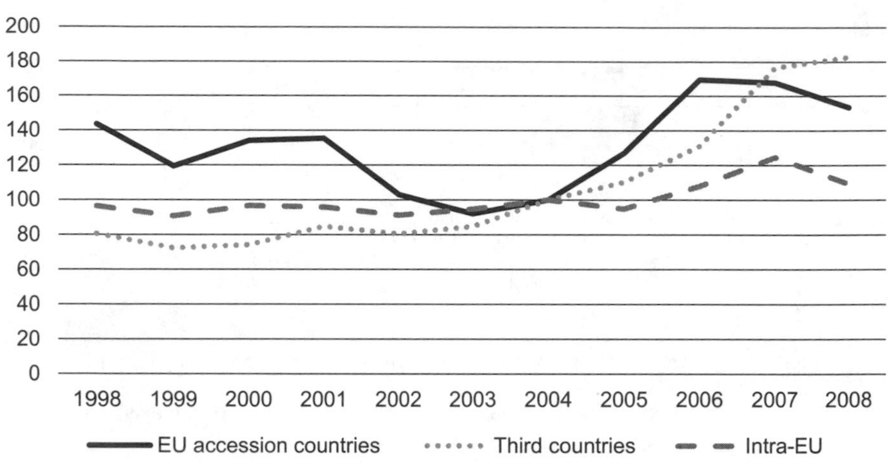

Figure 10.8
Average changes in import volumes (index 100 = year 2004).
Source: Eurostat Comext database and the National Board of Trade 2013a.

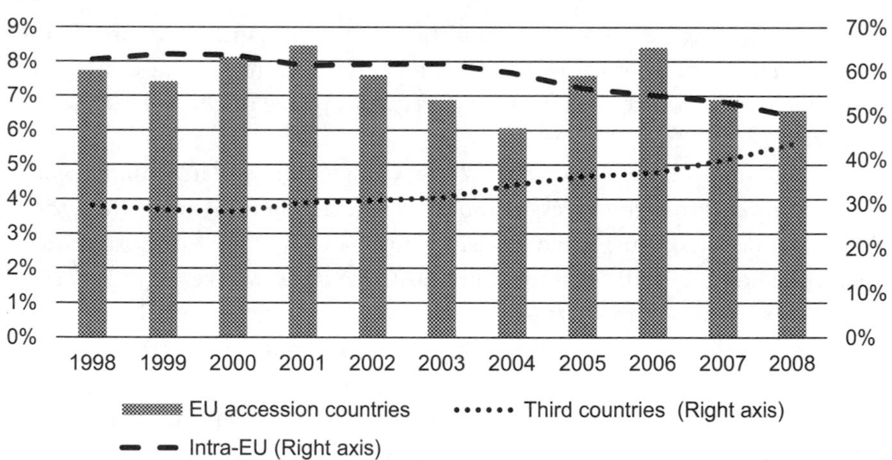

Figure 10.9
Average changes in market shares (import volume), percentage.
Source: Eurostat Comext database and the National Board of Trade 2013a.

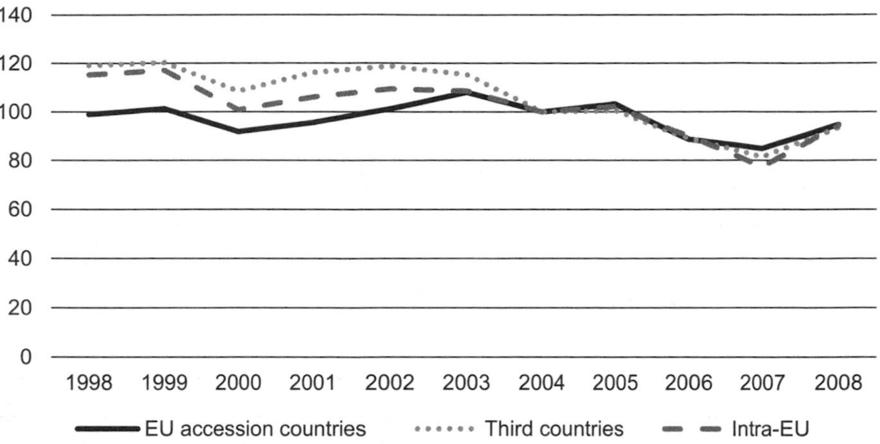

Figure 10.10
Average changes in import prices (index 100 = year 2004).
Source: Eurostat Comext database and the National Board of Trade 2013a.

Box 10.2
Effects on import prices of abolishing antidumping measures

The findings of this chapter indicate that abolishing antidumping duties produces effects that are reversed compared to the abolition of normal customs duties (see table B). The (deflated) import prices tend to decrease when antidumping duties are abolished. The explanations for the decrease in prices are likely to be the opposite of those at the imposition of antidumping measures.

Table B. Price effect at the abolition of antidumping duties

Abolition of duties	Import prices		Prices in the domestic market
	Excluding duties	Including duties	
Normal duties	Increases	Constant (or slight decrease)	Constant or decreases (due to increased competition)
Antidumping duties	Decreases	Decreases (due to price decrease and abolished antidumping duties)	Constant or decreases (due to increased competition)

Source: National Board of Trade 2013a.

For the effects on import prices of imposing antidumping measures, see box 10.1.

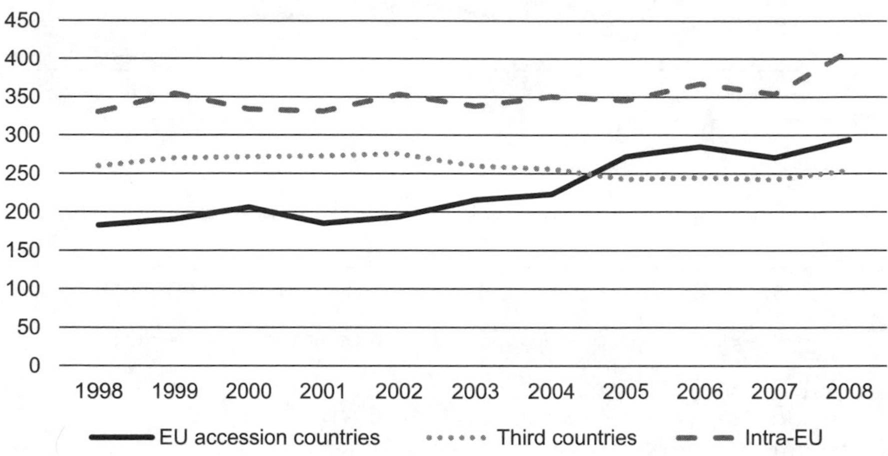

Figure 10.11
Malleable tube or pipe fitting, prices in euro (weighted average).
Source: Eurostat Comext database and the National Board of Trade 2013a.

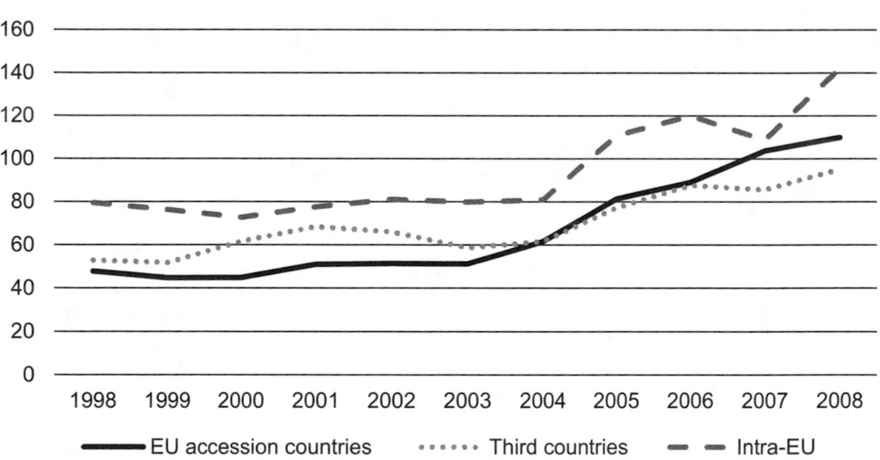

Figure 10.12
Seamless pipes and tubes, prices in euro (weighted average).
Source: Eurostat Comext database and the National Board of Trade 2013a.

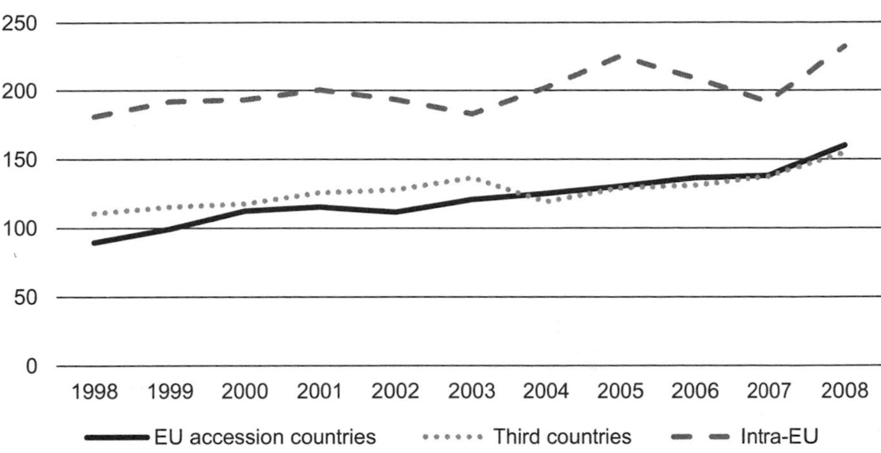

Figure 10.13
Steel ropes and cables, prices in euro (weighted average).
Source: Eurostat Comext database and the National Board of Trade 2013a.

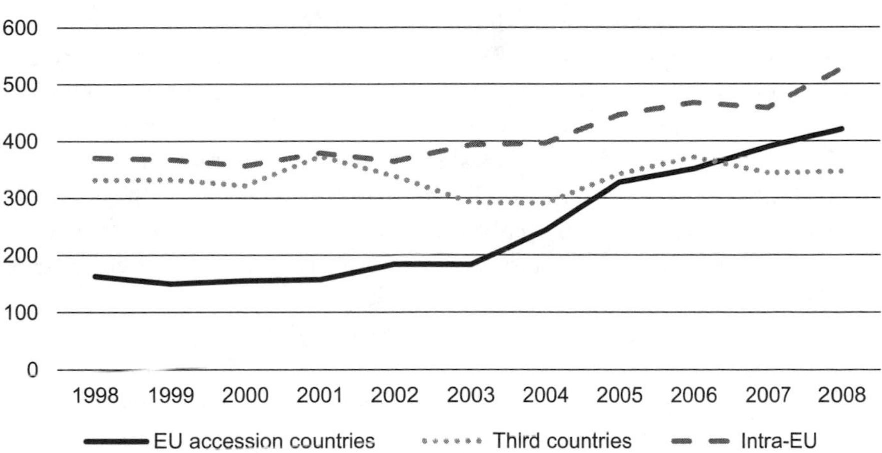

Figure 10.14
Tube and pipe fitting of iron or steel, prices in euro (weighted average).
Source: Eurostat Comext database and the National Board of Trade 2013a.

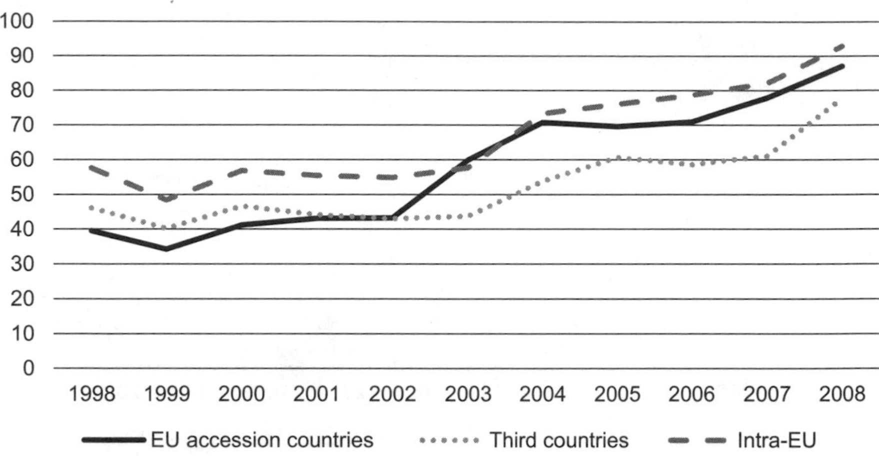

Figure 10.15
Welded tubes and pipes of iron or nonalloy steel, prices in euro (weighted average).
Source: Eurostat Comext database and the National Board of Trade 2013a.

decreased in most cases when the antidumping measures were abolished upon accession (see table 10.2). Accordingly, abolishing antidumping measures on imports from the accession countries does not seem to have affected EU15 producers negatively in terms of price undercutting.

In order to analyze whether abolishing antidumping measures against the accession countries has caused injury to EU15 producers, the change in market share of the allegedly dumped imports, that is, the *volume effects* of the abolition of antidumping measures, could be used as an indicator of injury.

In general, abolishing antidumping measures did not affect the accession countries' market share, in terms of import value, on the EU15 market (see figures 10.16–10.20). Immediately following the EU enlargement, the accession countries' market share increased, but then decreased to the preaccession level after about two years. Accordingly, the market share of the accession countries remained constant or increased only marginally after the EU enlargement.

This development following the abolition of antidumping measures implies that the imports from the accession countries did not cause injury to the EU15 producers as regards lost market share. On the contrary, the statistics indicate that the market share of EU15 producers decreased to an extent that corresponds to nontargeted third countries' increased share of the market, not because of the abolition of antidumping measures

Table 10.2
The development in price undercutting between 2003 and 2008 (in alphabetical order)

Product	Price in 2003		Price in 2008		Price undercutting (in percentage of the EU price)		Change in price undercutting between 2003–2008
	EU10	EU15	EU10	EU15	2003	2008	
Malleable tube or pipe fittings	215	338	294	410	36%	28%	-8%
Seamless pipes and tubes	51	80	110	142	36%	23%	-13%
Steel ropes and cables	121	183	160	232	34%	31%	-3%
Tube and pipe fitting, of iron or steel	183	393	421	527	53%	20%	-33%
Welded tubes and pipes	60	58	87	93	-4%	6%	10%

Source: National Board of Trade 2013a.
Note: The decrease in price undercutting was mainly due to the fact that the average (nondeflated) unit price levels of imports from the accession countries (EU10) increased more than the average (nondeflated) EU15 unit price levels.

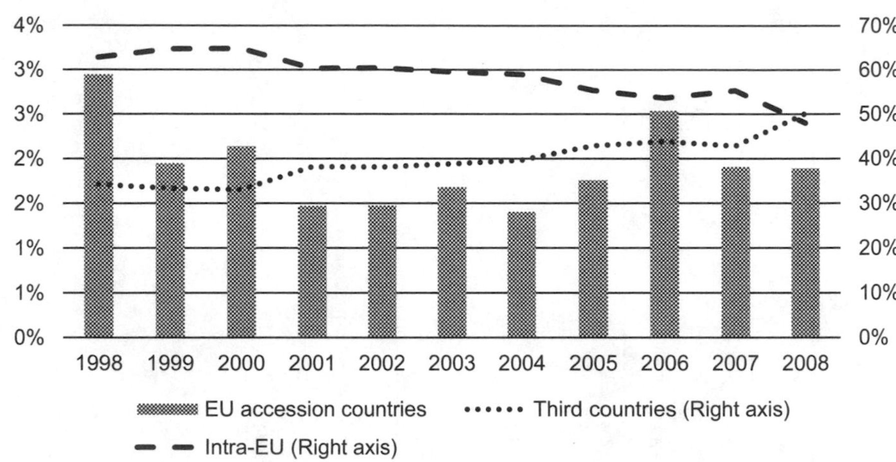

Figure 10.16
Malleable tube or pipe fittings, market share (import value), percentage.
Source: Based on Eurostat Comext database and the National Board of Trade 2013a.

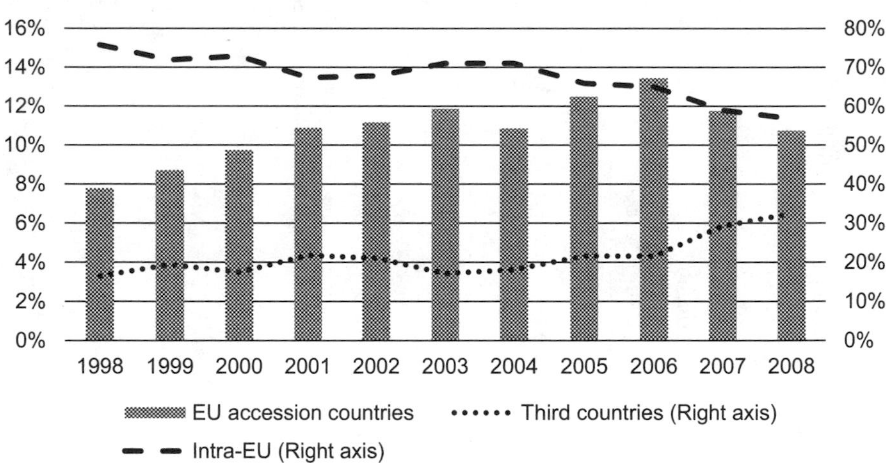

Figure 10.17
Seamless pipes and tubes, market share (import value), percentage.
Source: Based on Eurostat Comext database and the National Board of Trade 2013a.

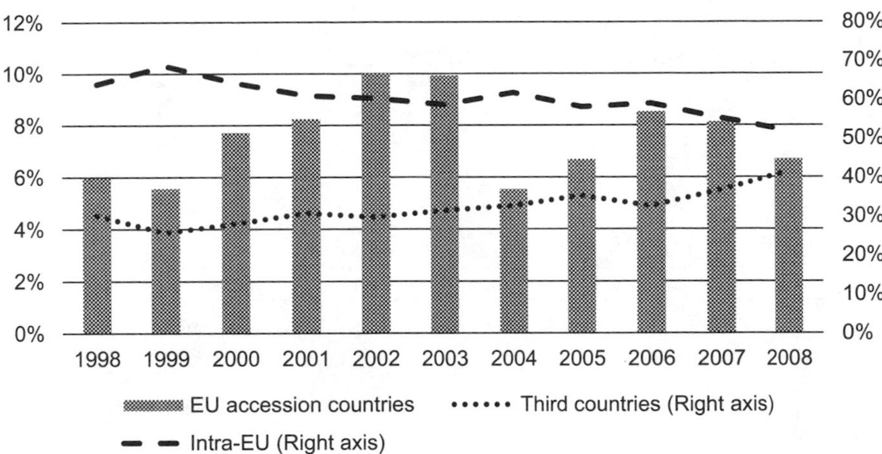

Figure 10.18
Steel ropes and cables, market share (import value), percentage.
Source: Based on Eurostat Comext database and the National Board of Trade 2013a.

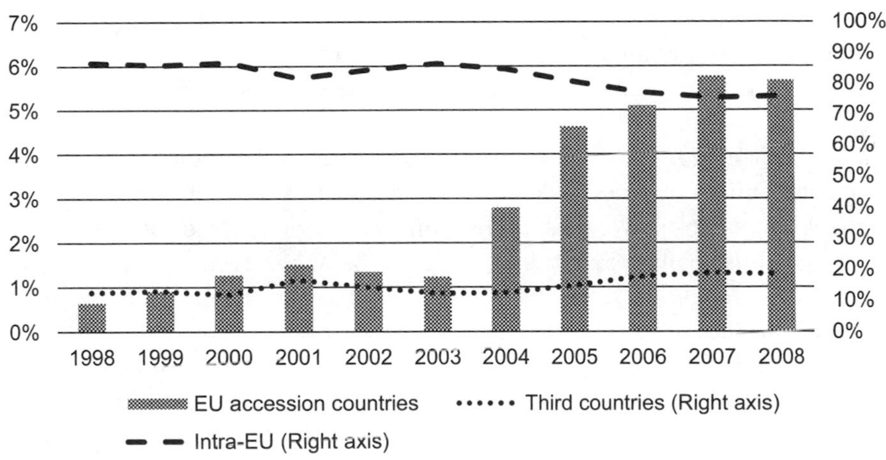

Figure 10.19
Tube and pipe fitting of iron or steel, market share (import value), percentage.
Source: Based on Eurostat Comext database and the National Board of Trade 2013a.

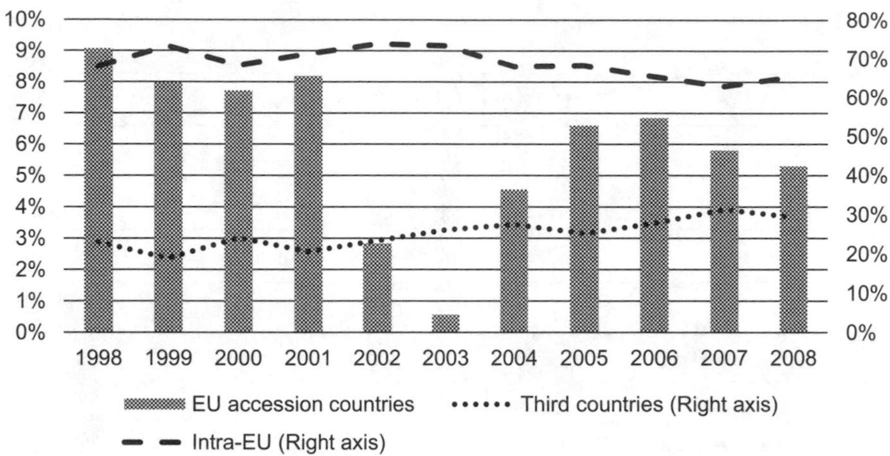

Figure 10.20
Welded tubes and pipes of iron or nonalloy steel, market share (import value), percentage.
Source: Based on Eurostat Comext database and the National Board of Trade 2013a.

against the accession countries. The increase in third country imports is not necessarily related to the abolition of antidumping measures, but might indicate a limited competitiveness of the EU producers.

Did Abolishing EU Antidumping Measures Increase Antidumping Action against Third Countries? A number of academic studies have examined the relationship between the establishment of regional trade agreements and possible changes in antidumping patterns. It has been argued (Bhagwati and Panagariya 1996; Prusa and Teh 2010) that the establishment of regional trade agreements gives partner countries the incentive to increase the number of antidumping measures targeting third countries. The WTO has also stated that the abolition of antidumping measures could result in "an increase in antidumping protection directed towards non-[regional trade agreement] members when in fact the injury to domestic industry mostly stems from imports from other [regional trade agreement] members" (WTO 2011).

The EU is one of the few regional trade agreements where there is empirical evidence—albeit limited—of the abolition of antidumping measures. According to the number of new antidumping measures of the products concerned following the EU enlargement in 2004, there is no clear evidence of such a development even though the imports from third countries—and their market shares on the EU market—increased.

Between 1998 and 2008, the EU had a large number of antidumping measures against imports of the products concerned from third countries, but most of these measures were imposed several years before the EU enlargement in 2004 (see table 10.3).

Antidumping measures were only imposed on three of the products concerned subsequent to the EU enlargement. The three products are steel ropes and cables (from Moldova, Morocco, and South Korea), tube and pipe fitting, iron or steel (from Indonesia, Sri Lanka, the Philippines, Russia, and Turkey), and welded tubes and pipes, iron or nonalloy steel (from Belarus, China, and Russia). These antidumping measures were, however, mainly anticircumvention measures against third countries that were targeted with antidumping measures prior to the abolition of the antidumping measures from the accession countries. As many as five of the seven antidumping investigations were initiated as anticircumvention investigations of measures already in force. The two new antidumping investigations, tube and pipe fitting, iron or steel (from Russia and Turkey). and welded tubes and pipes, iron or nonalloy steel (from Belarus, China, and Russia) were initiated several years after the EU enlargement in 2004.

10.2 The Opportunity to Abolish Antidumping Measures in Regional Trade Agreements: The TTIP as an Example

Use of Antidumping Measures by the EU and the United States in Regional Trade Agreements

According to WTO rules, it is possible to eliminate antidumping measures in regional trade agreements. In general, however, most regional trade agreements maintain the right to use antidumping measures against their partner countries. This is the case even though the measures were not frequently used either before the regional trade agreement entered into force or afterward. There are, however, seventeen regional trade agreements that have explicitly eliminated antidumping measures against partner countries. The EU has eliminated all three trade remedies (antidumping measures, antisubsidy measures, and safeguard measures) among its member states, and has also used WTO-plus provisions against certain free trade partners. The United States, on the other hand, has tended to maintain its right to use antidumping measures in all its free trade agreements.

Table 10.3
Exhaustive list of all countries targeted by antidumping measures for the products concerned (in alphabetical order)

Product	Targeted country	Initiation of antidumping investigation	Imposition of definitive antidumping duty	Termination of antidumping duty	Countrywide duty level
Ammonium nitrate	Russia	1994	1995	[2013]	47.07 EUR/tonne
	Poland	**1999**	**2001**	**2004**	**26.91 EUR/tonne**
	Ukraine	1999	2001	2012	33.25 EUR/tonne
Malleable tube or pipe fittings	**Czech Republic**	**1999**	**2000**	**2004**	**26.1%**
	Brazil, China, Japan, Korea, Thailand	1999	2000	2005	22.1–49.4%
	Argentina	2002	2003	2008	34.8%
Seamless pipes and tubes	**Poland**	**1991**	**1993**	**2004**	**30.1%**
	Czech Republic, Slovakia	**1996**	**1997**	**2004**	**7.5–28.6%**
	Hungary	1996	1997	2002	36.5%
	Romania, Russia	1996	1997	2006	26.8–38.2%
Steel ropes and cables	**Hungary, Poland**	**1998**	**1999**	**2004**	**28.1–48.3%**
	China, India, Mexico, South Africa, Ukraine	1998	1999	[2017]	30.8–60.4%
	Czech Republic	**2000**	**2001**	**2004**	**47.1%**

Table 10.3 (continued)

Product	Targeted country	Initiation of antidumping investigation	Imposition of definitive antidumping duty	Termination of antidumping duty	Countrywide duty level
	Russia	2000	2001	2012	50.7%
	Turkey, Thailand	2000	2001	2007	31–48.2%
	*Moldova**	*2003*	*2004*	*[2017]*	*51.8%*
	*Morocco**	*2004*	*2004*	*[2017]*	*60.4%*
	*South Korea**	*2009*	*2010*	*[2017]*	*60.4%*
Tube and pipe fitting, of iron or steel	China, Thailand	1994	1996	[2014]	58.6–58.9%
	Taiwan	1999	2000	[2014]	58.6%
	Czech Republic, Slovakia	**2001**	**2002**	**2004**	**15–22.4%**
	Russia	2001	2002	2007	43.3%
	Korea, Malaysia	2001	2002	[2013]	44–75%
	*Indonesia, Sri Lanka**	*2004*	*2004*	*[2014]*	*58.6%*
	*Philippines**	*2005*	*2006*	*[2014]*	*58.6%*
	Russia, Turkey	*2011*	*2013*	*[2018]*	*16.7–23.8%*
Urea	Russia (USSR)	1986	1987	2007	45.9%
	Estonia, Lithuania	**2000**	**2002**	**2004**	**10.05–11.43 EUR/tonne**

Table 10.3 (continued)

Product	Targeted country	Initiation of antidumping investigation	Imposition of definitive antidumping duty	Termination of antidumping duty	Countrywide duty level
	Bulgaria, Romania	2000	2002	2007	8.01–21.43 EUR/tonne
	Belarus, Croatia, Libya, Ukraine	2000	2002	2008	7.81–16.84 EUR/tonne
Urea ammonium nitrate solutions	**Poland**	**1993**	**1994**	**2004**	**22 EUR/tonne**
	Bulgaria	1993	1994	2007	22 EUR/tonne
	Lithuania	**1999**	**2000**	**2004**	**3.98 EUR/tonne**
	Algeria, Belarus, Russia, Ukraine	1999	2000	2007	6.88–26.17 EUR/tonne
Welded tubes and pipes of iron or nonalloy steel	**Czech Republic, Poland**	**2001**	**2002**	**2004**	**23–52.6%**
	Turkey	2001	2002	2008	6%
	Thailand, Ukraine	2001	2002	2013	35.2–44.1%
	Belarus, China, Russia	*2007*	*2008*	*[2013]*	*20.5–90.6%*

Source: National Board of Trade 2013a.
Note: The antidumping measures that are imposed at the same time are grouped together in the table. The antidumping measures against the EU accession countries are marked in bold. The antidumping measures that were imposed after the abolition of antidumping measures against the EU accession countries are marked in italics. The anticircumvention investigations are marked with.
*Brackets around certain years indicate when the antidumping measures are scheduled to expire but that the decision has not been formally taken (and that the measures may be prolonged).

WTO Member Use of Antidumping Measures in Regional Trade Agreements The primary economic objective of regional trade agreements (i.e., free trade agreements and customs unions) is to eliminate barriers to intra-regional trade between members. In this regard, it is reasonable to expect that partner countries eliminate antidumping measures in intra-regional trade. It is sometimes claimed that eliminating antidumping measures is a requirement according to Article XXIV of the General Agreement on Tariffs and Trade (GATT) (Teh, Prusa and Budetta 2007).

In Article XXIV:8(a) and (b) of the GATT, parties to the regional trade agreement are required to eliminate duties and other regulations restricting trade. However, Article XXIV allows parties in regional trade agreements to exclude certain GATT articles from the general requirement to eliminate all trade barriers. The article states that "a free-trade area shall be understood to mean a group of two or more customs territories in which the duties and other restrictive regulations of commerce (except, where necessary, those permitted under Articles XI, XII, XIII, XIV, XV, and XX) are eliminated on substantially all the trade between the constituent territories in products originating in such territories" (WTO 1994).

The article covering antidumping measures (Article VI) is not explicitly included among the articles that may be excluded from elimination in the regional trade agreements. If the intention was to permit the exclusion of antidumping measures from elimination in regional trade agreements, a reference to Article VI should have been made in the paragraph (Teh, Prusa and Budetta 2007). The absence of Article VI from the list of excludable articles could be interpreted to mean that the use of antidumping measures in regional trade agreements may be inconsistent with GATT rules. It has not been legally established, however, whether the list of excludable articles is exhaustive or only illustrative as there is no consensus or dispute settlement understanding in the WTO with regard to its interpretation (Teh, Prusa and Budetta 2007). If the list were exhaustive, which is likely to be the case, the antidumping measures—which are not on the list—should be eliminated upon the formation of regional trade agreements.

There are currently about four hundred notified regional trade agreements in force. These agreements can be grouped into three broad categories according to how they treat antidumping measures. There may be differences, however, between the de jure and the de facto application of antidumping provisions in the regional trade agreements.

A vast majority of the regional trade agreements—about 90 percent—have established regional antidumping regimes which keep the WTO provisions essentially unchanged (Rey 2012). These regional trade agreements make reference to the WTO rights and obligations or contain established rules that are in all material respects similar to the WTO rights and obligations. In cases where regional trade agreements make no reference at all to any antidumping provisions, the multilateral regime remains valid. This category of regional trade agreements does not differentiate between partner countries and third countries in antidumping proceedings. Most EU and all U.S. regional trade agreements fall within this category.

A limited number of regional trade agreements contain specific "WTO-plus provisions" for initiating antidumping investigations or imposing antidumping measures that are more restrictive than the WTO rules as compared to the rules for antidumping measures on imports from third countries. The EU has included certain WTO-plus provisions in some of its recent free trade agreements, whereas the United States has not included any WTO-plus provisions in its free trade agreements.

About seventeen regional trade agreements have explicitly eliminated the use of antidumping measures between the partner countries (see table 10.4). In most cases, these regional trade agreements have prohibited the use of antidumping measures from the outset. The progressive deepening or extension of certain regional integration processes has sometimes also resulted in a renunciation of the right to use antidumping measures. The elimination of antidumping measures is explicitly linked to provisions on competition in some regional trade agreements (Teh 2009). This is mainly the case in a number of European Free Trade Association (EFTA) agreements—with Albania, Bosnia and Herzegovina, Chile, Serbia, and Singapore—and in Australia-New Zealand.

The parties to most of the regional trade agreements that have eliminated the antidumping instrument have never used antidumping measures against their partner countries. Only the EU and Australia-New Zealand have abolished antidumping measures that were previously in force (Rey 2012).

In general, the vast majority of the regional trade agreements—about 77 percent—have been concluded between parties that have never reported the use of any antidumping measures against products originating in their partner countries prior to the establishment of the regional trade agreement. Accordingly, a large percentage of regional trade agreements incorporate regional legal frameworks that maintain

Table 10.4
Regional trade agreements currently in force that have eliminated antidumping measures on intra-regional trade (in chronological order)

Regional trade agreement	Type of agreement	Antidumping measures eliminated	Antisubsidy measures eliminated	Safeguard measures eliminated	Contains chapter on competition	Date of the elimination of antidumping measures
European Union	Customs union	X	X	X	X	1-1-1958
Australia-New Zealand	Free trade agreement	X		X	X	1-7-1990
EU-Andorra	Customs union	X	X	X		1-7-1991
EU-San Marino	Customs union	X	X	X		1-4-2002
European Economic Area	Free trade agreement	X	X		X	1-1-1994
Canada-Chile	Free trade agreement	X			X	5-7-1997
European Free Trade Area	Free trade agreement	X	X		X	1-6-2002
EFTA-Singapore	Free trade agreement	X			X	1-1-2003
EFTA-Chile	Free trade agreement	X	X		X	1-12-2004

Table 10.4 (continued)

Regional trade agreement	Type of agreement	Antidumping measures eliminated	Antisubsidy measures eliminated	Safeguard measures eliminated	Contains chapter on competition	Date of the elimination of antidumping measures
China-Hong Kong	Free trade agreement	**X**	X			1-1-2004
China-Macau	Free trade agreement	**X**	X			1-1-2004
EFTA-Serbia	Free trade agreement	**X**		[X]	X	1-10-2011
EFTA-Albania	Free trade agreement	**X**		[X]	X	1-10-2011
EFTA-Ukraine	Free trade agreement	**X**		[X]	X	1-6-2012
EFTA-Montenegro	Free trade agreement	**X**		[X]	X	1-11-2012
EFTA-Hong Kong	Free trade agreement	**X**	X	X	X	1-11-2012
EFTA-Bosnia and Herzegovina	Free trade agreement	**X**		[X]	X	Pending [Signed: 6-24-2013]

Sources: National Board of Trade 2013b and the EFTA free trade agreements.
Note: The "[X]" indicates that the parties have included a best endeavor clause instead of a complete ban on the use of safeguard measures, provided that this is in line with the WTO rules and practice.

the right to use a trade remedy that the parties have never before used in their previous bilateral relationships. This is supported by the fact that in about 81 percent of the regional trade agreements, the parties have not reported the use of any antidumping measure against products originating in their partner countries following the establishment of the regional trade agreement, even though they are entitled to use this provision (Rey 2012).

EU Use of Antidumping Measures in Regional Trade Agreements The EU was the first regional trade agreement to abolish the application of all three trade remedies between its member states; this includes the use of safeguard measures, which are normally allowed between parties that eliminate the use of antidumping measures. The EU is also one of two existing regional trade agreements that have abolished antidumping measures that were previously in place (National Board of Trade 2013b).

The Treaty establishing the European Economic Community (Article 91) prohibited the use of antidumping measures on intra-EU trade once the transition period for the full implementation of the treaty had expired:

> If, during the transitional period, the Commission ... finds that dumping is being practiced within the common market, it shall address recommendations to the person or persons with whom such practices originate for the purpose of putting an end to them. Should the practices continue, the Commission shall authorise the injured Member State to take protective measures. ... As soon as this Treaty enters into force, products which originate in or are in free circulation in one Member State and which have been exported to another Member State shall, on reimportation, be admitted into the territory of the first- mentioned State free of all customs duties, quantitative restrictions or measures having equivalent effect (European Economic Community 1957).

The antidumping measures have, accordingly, been abolished in all successive EU enlargements in 1973, 1981, 1986, 1995, 2004, 2007, and 2013 as the EU gradually expanded from six to twenty-eight member states.

The Treaty on the Functioning of the European Union, which details the current rules for the internal market, also contains a number of prohibitions that make it impossible for the member states to adopt antidumping measures against each other. In particular, member states are prohibited from imposing unjustified quantitative restrictions on the import of goods from other EU member states such as quotas, technical requirements, or minimum prices. The same prohibition applies to fiscal restrictions in the form of customs duties or charges having equivalent effect or discriminatory taxes (National Board of Trade 2013a).

The EU also eliminated the antidumping instrument, with the exception of agricultural and fish products, in 1994 in the European Economic Area (EEA)—its free trade agreements with European Free Trade Association (EFTA) member states Iceland, Liechtenstein and Norway. The EEA states (Article 26) that "anti-dumping measures ... attributable to third countries shall not be applied in relations between the Contracting Parties, unless otherwise specified in this Agreement" (European Communities 1994). Switzerland and the EU have negotiated a number of bilateral agreements, due to the fact that Switzerland could not ratify the agreement because it was rejected by national referendum. The legal framework for antidumping measures between the EU and Switzerland has not been substantially affected by these bilateral agreements (Rey 2012).

The EU has also abolished antidumping measures in its customs unions with Andorra, with the exception of agricultural products, and San Marino. The EU Customs Unions with Andorra and San Marino (Article 7) agreement requires the countries to "apply ... the laws, regulations and administrative provisions applicable to customs matters in the Community and necessary for the proper functioning of the Customs Union [as well as] the common commercial policy of the [Union]" (European Communities 1990, 2002). As a consequence, the EU, Andorra and San Marino have a common antidumping regime against third countries (Rey 2012).

The EU has opted, however, to include antidumping provisions in most of its current twenty-four free trade agreements in force (Albania, Algeria, Bosnia and Herzegovina, EEA, Central America, CARIFORUM, Chile, Colombia/Peru, Eastern and Southern Africa States, Egypt, the Faroe Islands, Israel, Jordan, Lebanon, Macedonia, Mexico, Montenegro, Morocco, the Palestinian Authority, Pacific States, Serbia, South Africa, South Korea, and Tunisia), as well as in its customs union with Turkey. In general, the EU does not differentiate in the use of antidumping measures against its free trade partner countries and other third countries; in practice, the EU has used antidumping measures against half of its free trade partners, but only to a limited extent (National Board of Trade 2013b).

Currently, the EU has antidumping measures in place against ten of its free trade and customs union partners (Algeria, Bosnia and Herzegovina, Egypt, Israel, the former Yugoslav Republic of Macedonia (FYROM),

Mexico, Morocco, South Africa, South Korea, and Turkey, see table 10.5). When Croatia became an EU member state in 2013, its free trade agreement with the EU ceased to exist. While the free trade agreement was in force, the EU imposed antidumping measures on imports of seamless pipes and tubes, iron or steel, from Croatia. These measures were, accordingly abolished overnight upon accession to the EU (National Board of Trade 2013b).

In some free trade agreements, the EU has opted to include WTO-plus provisions. WTO-plus provisions, meaning, the "Union interest test" and the "lesser duty rule," are only included in the recent free trade agreements with Colombia/Peru, South Korea, and the Central American countries (Costa Rica, El Salvador, Guatemala, Honduras, Nicaragua, and Panama) (see box 10.3). The WTO-plus provisions are also considered in a number of ongoing free trade negotiations.

European Partnership Agreements (EPAs) currently in force state that before imposing definitive antidumping measures on products imported from EPA states, the EU "shall consider the possibility of constructive remedies as provided for in the relevant WTO agreements" (European Union 2008). This might be considered as a "best endeavor" provision.

Box 10.3
The WTO-plus provisions in the EU's free trade agreements

The "Union interest test" in the EU's antidumping regulation should be based on an appreciation of all various interests taken as a whole (i.e., including EU importers, EU user industry, and EU consumers). The EU's antidumping regulation states that antidumping measures may not be applied if it can be clearly demonstrated that applying such measures is not in the Union's interest. Antidumping measures would normally be against Union interest if it can be established that the EU's industry would not be able to benefit from such measures.

The "lesser duty rule" in the EU's antidumping regulation obliges the EU to impose an antidumping duty that is not higher than the lesser of the "dumping margin" (i.e., the difference between the domestic price in the exporting country and the export price to the EU) and the "injury margin" (i.e., the difference between the "non-injurious" EU sales price and the export price to the EU). The lesser duty rule ensures, accordingly, that the antidumping measures imposed are not higher than necessary to remove the injury inflicted on EU producers.

Sources: National Board of Trade 2013d, 2013e.

Table 10.5
Antidumping measures currently in force in EU regional trade agreements (in chronological order)

Country	Regional trade agreement	Antidumping measures
Algeria	**Association Agreement** [9-1-1995]	Urea ammonium nitrate solutions [9-22-2000]
Turkey	**Customs Union** [12-31-1995]	Polyester staple fibres [12-17-1988] Polyester yarn [6-14-1996] Steel ropes and cables [8-14-2001] Welded tubes and pipes of iron or noniron steel [9-27-2002] Tube and pipe fittings, of iron or steel 1-29-2013]
Morocco	**Association Agreement** [3-1-2000]	Steel ropes and cables (anticircumvention) [10-30-2004]
Israel	**Association Agreement** [6-1-2000]	PET film (anticircumvention) [11-18-2004]
Mexico	**Economic Partnership and Economic Cooperation Agreement** [7-1-2000]	Magnetic discs [4-13-1996] Lighters [3-6-1997] Steel ropes and cables [8-17-1999]
South Africa	**Trade, Development and Cooperation Agreement** [7-1-2000]	Steel ropes and cables [2-17-1999] Hot rolled coils [2-5-2000] Manganese dioxides [3-13-2008]
FYROM	**Stabilisation and Association Agreement** [5-1-2004]	Ferro-silicon [2-28-2008]
Egypt	**Association Agreement** [6-1-2004]	Ferro-silicon [2-28-2008]
Bosnia and Herzegovina	**Interim Agreement on Trade and Trade Related Matters** [7-1-2008]	Zeolite A powder [5-14-2011]
South Korea	**New Generation Free Trade Agreement** [7-1-2011]	Tube and pipe fittings, of iron or steel [8-24-2002] Silicon metals [1-19-2007] Steel ropes and cables [5-11-2010] PET [11-3-2010]

Source: National Board of Trade 2013b.

U.S. Use of Antidumping Measures in Regional Trade Agreements The United States has maintained the right to use antidumping measures in all its free trade agreements. It currently has fourteen free trade agreements with twenty countries; in seven of them (Australia, Bahrain, Israel, Jordan, Morocco, Oman, and Singapore), the parties are entitled to the WTO provisions on antidumping even though they have not included a specific chapter on the antidumping instrument.

These free trade agreements state that "the Parties understand that the GATT 1994 rights and obligations incorporated by paragraph 1 prohibit, in any circumstances in which any other form of restriction is prohibited, export price requirements and, except as permitted in enforcement of countervailing and antidumping orders and undertakings, import price requirements."

In five free trade agreements—with Chile, Colombia, Panama, Peru, and the Dominican Republic-Central America (CAFTA-DR), including Costa Rica, El Salvador, Guatemala, Honduras, Nicaragua, and the Dominican Republic—the parties have included a section on antidumping measures in the chapter on trade remedies. These provisions are, however, also in line with the general WTO provisions on antidumping measures.

The agreements state that "each Party retains its rights and obligations under the WTO Agreement with regard to the application of antidumping and countervailing duties." In addition, the agreements state that "no provision of this Agreement ... shall be construed as imposing any rights or obligations on the Parties with respect to antidumping or countervailing duty measures." The parties of CAFTA-DR are, however, entitled to special rules on cumulation in the determination of material injury.

In the free trade agreement with South Korea, the chapter on trade remedies is more detailed concerning the proceedings, but the general WTO provisions on antidumping measures remain unchanged. The parties have also decided to establish a Committee on Trade Remedies to serve as a forum for cooperation and increased understanding among the parties.

In the North American Free Trade Agreement (NAFTA) negotiations, Canada and Mexico bargained with the United States in order to replace antidumping rules with competition rules, but the United States argued for maintaining the antidumping instrument as well as other available trade remedies. The agreement states that "each Party reserves the right to apply its antidumping law and countervailing duty law to goods imported from the territory of any other Party" (NAFTA 1994).

However, the negotiations resulted in a compromise that created a binational panel charged with reviewing domestic antidumping determinations. NAFTA has also established a Working Group on Trade and Competition (Farha 2012).

The United States has not included any WTO-plus provisions in any of its free trade agreements. With the exception of NAFTA and South Korea, and to a certain extent CAFTA-DR, where the provisions on antidumping are slightly different compared to the general WTO provisions, the United States does not differentiate between its free trade partners and other third countries. In practice, however, the United States is not a frequent user of the antidumping instrument against its free trade partners—with the exception of NAFTA and South Korea.

Currently, the United States has antidumping measures in place against five of its free trade partners (Australia, Canada, Chile, Mexico, and South Korea, see table 10.6). The most frequently targeted countries are South Korea, Mexico, and Canada.

In line with the EU, the United States does not use antidumping measures or other quantitative restrictions between individual states. The doctrine of the "dormant" Commerce Clause prohibits states to act in ways that impede interstate commerce. The dormant Commerce Clause, also known as the "negative" Commerce Clause, is a legal doctrine that is inferred from the Commerce Clause in Article I of the United States Constitution (Williams 2006). The Commerce Clause explicitly grants Congress the power to regulate commerce among the states. The idea behind the dormant Commerce Clause is that this grant of power implies a restriction prohibiting a state from passing legislation that improperly burdens or discriminates against interstate commerce (ibid.). The U.S. Constitution (Art. I, para. 8) reserves for Congress at least some degree of exclusive power "to regulate Commerce with foreign Nations, and among the several States" (ibid.). Accordingly, individual states are limited in their ability to legislate on such matters. The central rationale for the rule against discrimination is to prohibit state or municipal laws whose object is local economic protectionism (ibid.).

The Initiative to Abolish Antidumping Measures in the TTIP

The analysis of the initiative to abolish antidumping measures in the Transatlantic Trade and Investment Partnership (TTIP) should be viewed in the context of the empirical findings concerning the imposition and abolition of antidumping measures in the EU. The current antidumping measures between the EU and the United States are analyzed in this

Table 10.6
Antidumping measures currently in force in U.S. regional trade agreements (in chronological order)

Country	Regional trade agreement	Antidumping measures
Canada	**North American Free Trade Agreement** [Fmr. US-Canada Free Trade Agreement] [01-01-1989]	Iron construction castings [5-3-1986] Citric acid and certain citrate [5-29-2009]
Mexico	**North American Free Trade Agreement** [01-01-1994]	Circular welded nonalloy steel pipe [11-2-1992] Fresh tomatoes (suspended) [11-1-1996] Carbon steel wire rod [10-29-2002] Prestressed concrete steel wire strand [1-28-2004] Light-walled rectangular pipe and tube [8-5-2008] Certain magnesia carbon bricks [9-20-2010] Seamless refined copper pipe and tube [11-22-2010] Large residential washers [2-15-2013]
Chile	**Free Trade Agreement** [01-01-2004]	Preserved mushrooms [12-2-1998]
Australia	**Free Trade Agreement** [1-1-2005]	Electrolytic manganese dioxide [10-8-2008]
South Korea	**Free Trade Agreement** [3-15-2012]	Circular welded nonalloy steel pipe [11-2-1992] Welded ASTM A-312 stainless steel pipe [12-30-1992] Stainless steel wire rod [9-15-1998] Stainless steel plate in coils [5-21-1999] Stainless steel sheet & strip [7-27-1999] Carbon steel plate [2-10-2000] Polyester staple fiber [5-25-2000] Polyvinyl alcohol [10-1-2003] Prestressed concrete steel wire strand [1-28-2004] Light-walled rectangular pipe and tube [8-5-2008] Large power transformers [8-31-2012] Large residential washers [2-15-2013]

Source: Based on USITC 2014a.

context. The mere fact that the EU and the United States are currently entitled to use antidumping measures on the imports of the other trading party creates uncertainty in their bilateral relations. The experiences of eliminating antidumping measures in the EEA—one of the largest free trade areas in the world—could be used as a source of inspiration for the TTIP negotiations.

The Use of Antidumping Measures between the EU and the United States The EU and the United States are among the main users of the antidumping instrument at the global level. In 2012, the United States was the world's largest user of the antidumping instrument with 230 antidumping measures in force; the EU was the world's fifth largest user with 102 antidumping measures in force (European Commission 2014). However, the EU and the United States use the antidumping instrument against each other in different ways (see annex 3 for a detailed description of the methodology used in the analysis).

The United States has twenty-two antidumping measures on seventeen products against different EU member states, that is, not against the EU as a whole (USITC 2014a). In general, the import values affected are of moderate size but some of the measures have been in force for several decades. The United States is the main user of antidumping measures against the EU, representing about 25 percent of the total number of antidumping measures against the EU in 2012 (European Commission 2014). The EU, in contrast, has only two antidumping measures against the United States, but the import values affected are among the largest of all the EU's antidumping measures currently in force (National Board of Trade 2013c).

An analysis of EU antidumping measures against the United States shows that only renewable energy products, such as biodiesel and bioethanol, are targeted (see table 10.7). The antidumping measure on biodiesel from the United States is the EU's fourth-largest antidumping measure with regard to the import value affected; the antidumping measure on bioethanol from the United States is among the EU's fifth- to tenth-largest antidumping measure with regard to import value. This implies that EU-U.S. relations are affected by the recent trend in imposing antidumping measures on renewable energy (National Board of Trade 2013c; ICTSD 2013).

The market shares of biodiesel in the EU indicate that the EU producers have a dominant market position of about 80 percent, and that EU producers' market share has increased slightly at the expense of the

Table 10.7
EU Antidumping measures in force against the United States and other countries targeted by the measures (in chronological order)

Product	Targeted country	Imposition of antidumping duty	Expiry of antidumping duty	Countrywide duty level	Import value (EUR millions)
Biodiesel	**US**	**2009**	[2014]	**172.2 EUR/tonne**	**700**
	Canada (anticircumvention)	**2011**	[2014]	**172.2 EUR/tonne**	**122**
	Argentina Indonesia	2013	[2018]	104.92 EUR/tonne 83.84 EUR/tonne	2,081
Bioethanol	**US**	**2013**	[2018]	**9.5%**	**430**

Source: National Board of Trade 2013c.
Source: Brackets around certain years indicate when the antidumping measures are scheduled to expire but that the decision has not been formally taken (and that the measures may be prolonged).

market share of third countries and the United States (see figure 10.21). The U.S. market share of biodiesel in the EU fluctuates at around 8 percent. The imposition of antidumping measures does not seem to have had an immediate impact on the market situation for U.S. imports. The market shares of bioethanol show that the EU producers also have a dominant position on the EU market (about 90 percent), and that U.S. market share fluctuates around 4 percent (see figure 10.22).

Based on this analysis, the effectiveness of the antidumping measures on U.S. imports seems limited. The efficiency of the measures, that is, the cost of using the antidumping instrument on renewable energy—is likely to be much higher for EU user industry and consumers than the benefits for the EU producers due to the high import values affected and the limited impact on U.S. market shares (National Board of Trade 2013c; ICTSD 2013). This is in line with the more aggregate analysis of the effects on the EU of imposing antidumping measures.

The seemingly limited effectiveness and efficiency of the EU's antidumping measures in force against the United States might indicate that abolishing the measures would leave the EU's dominant market shares largely unaffected. At the same time, the cost for EU user industry and consumers would likely decrease if the antidumping measures were

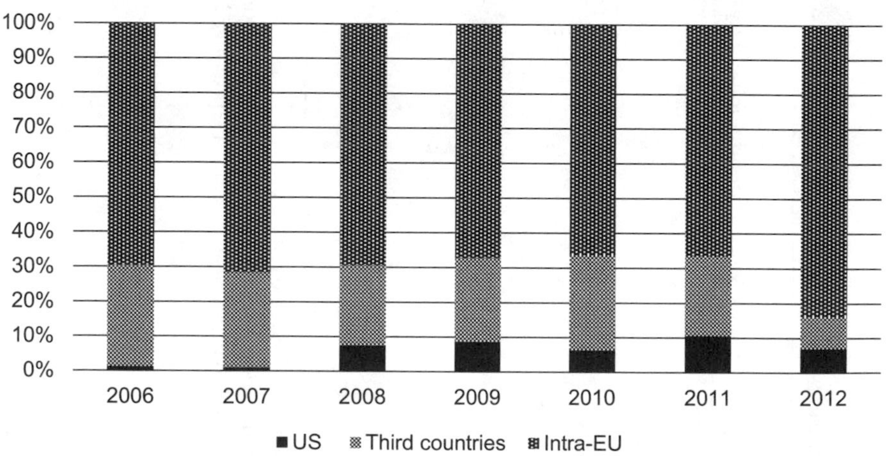

Figure 10.21
Average changes in EU import value market shares of biodiesel (percentage).
Source: Based on U.S. Trade Online database.
Note: Due to the limited number of EU antidumping measures against the United States and the fact that one of the antidumping measures was imposed as recently as 2013, a meaningful aggregate analysis of the effects of import values and prices is not possible at this time.

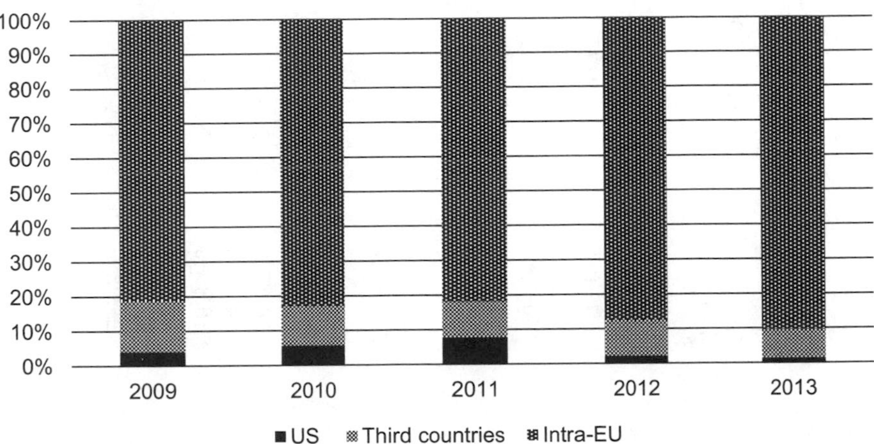

Figure 10.22
Average changes in EU import value market shares of bioethanol (percentage).
Source: Based on U.S. Trade Online database.
Note: Due to the limited number of EU antidumping measures against the United States and the fact that one of the antidumping measures was imposed as recently as 2013, a meaningful aggregate analysis of the effects of import values and prices is not possible at this time.

abolished. This seems also to be in line with the aggregate analysis of abolishing antidumping measures in the EU.

In general, the United States uses antidumping instruments against EU member states on products that are traditionally targeted by antidumping measures, such as iron and steel products (see table 10.8). For many products, the EU member states constitute, either currently or at the time antidumping measures were imposed, only a small fraction of the countries targeted by the product-specific measures, which indicates that EU member states are targeted in spite of small import values. Furthermore, in a great number of cases, antidumping measures against certain EU member states have expired on the products concerned, such as stainless steel bars (France, Germany, Italy, and the UK), ball bearings (France, Germany, and Italy), stainless-steel wire rod (France and Sweden), seamless pipes, small diameter (Czech Republic), stainless steel plate in coils (Italy), and carboxymethylcellulose (Sweden).

The average effects of imposing the antidumping measures on EU imports seem to be immediate and in line with the general effects of imposing antidumping measures (see figure 10.23). Import values decreased 34 percent on average the year before the definitive antidumping measures were imposed (year "0"), and an additional 30 percent over

Table 10.8
U.S. antidumping measures in force against EU member states and other countries targeted by the measures (in chronological order)

Product	Targeted country	Imposition of antidumping duty	Expiry of antidumping duty	Countrywide duty level	Import value (1,000 dollars)
Plastic tape	**Italy**	**1977**	—	**10%**	N/A
Brass sheet and strip	**Italy**	**1987**	—	**5.44%**	**9,463**
	Germany	**1987**	—	**7.30%**	**45,313**
	France	**1987**	—	**42.24%**	**9,147**
	~~Brazil~~	1987	2006	~~40.62%~~	6,204
	~~Canada~~	1987	2006	~~8.10%~~	7,403
	Japan	1998	—	45.72%	22,128
Chlorinated isocyanurate	**Spain**	**2005**	—	**24.83%**	***
	China	2005	—	285.63%	***
Granular resin	**Italy**	**1988**	—	**46.46%**	***
	~~Japan~~	1988	2005	~~91.74%~~	***
Ball bearings	**United Kingdom**	**1989**	—	**54.27%**	N/A
	~~**France**~~	**1989**	**2006**	~~**64.13%**~~	N/A
	~~**Germany**~~	**1989**	**2006**	~~**68.89%**~~	N/A
	~~**Italy**~~	**1989**	**2006**	~~**155.57%**~~	N/A
	Japan	1989	—	45.83%	N/A
	~~Singapore~~	1989	2006	~~25.08%~~	N/A

Table 10.8 (continued)

Product	Targeted country	Imposition of antidumping duty	Expiry of antidumping duty	Countrywide duty level	Import value (1,000 dollars)
Stainless steel bars	**Spain**	**1995**	—	**25.77%**	**13,939**
	Brazil	1995	—	19.43%	9,697
	India	1995	—	12.45%	5,220
	Japan	1995	—	61.47%	37,791
	~~France~~	**2002**	**2007**	**~~35.92%~~**	**11,969**
	~~Germany~~	**2002**	**2007**	**~~15.57%~~**	**24,984**
	~~Italy~~	**2002**	**2007**	**~~6.60%~~**	**45,543**
	~~United Kingdom~~	**2002**	**2007**	**~~83.85%~~**	**15,048**
	~~South Korea~~	2002	2007	~~11.30%~~	18,145
Stainless steel butt-welded fittings	~~Japan~~	1988	2010	~~49.31%~~	10,419
	~~South Korea~~	1993	2010	~~21.20%~~	1,519
	~~Taiwan~~	1993	2010	~~51.01%~~	10,598
	Italy	**2001**	—	**26.59%**	***
	Malaysia	2001	—	7.51%	***
	Philippines	2001	—	7.59%	***
Stainless steel plate in coils	**Belgium**	**1999**	—	**8.54%**	***
	~~Italy~~	**1999**	**2011**	**~~36.69%~~**	***
	~~Canada~~	1999	2005	~~11.10%~~	***
	South Africa	1999	—	41.63%	***
	South Korea	1999	—	16.26%	***
	Taiwan	1999	—	7.39%	***

Table 10.8 (continued)

Product	Targeted country	Imposition of antidumping duty	Expiry of antidumping duty	Countrywide duty level	Import value (1,000 dollars)
Pasta	**Italy**	**1996**	—	**16.51%**	**124,233**
	Turkey	1996	—	60.87%	14,957
Seamless pipes	**Germany**	**1995**	—	**57.72%**	***
	~~Argentina~~	1995	2007	~~108.13%~~	***
	~~Brazil~~	1995	2007	~~124.94%~~	***
Stainless steel wire rod	India	1993	—	48.80%	3,490
	~~France~~	**1993**	**2006**	**~~24.51%~~**	**18,034**
	~~Brazil~~	1993	2006	~~25.88%~~	3,599
	Italy	**1998**	—	**11.25%**	**22,829**
	Spain	**1998**	**2007**	**2.71%**	**6,474**
	~~Sweden~~	**1998**	—	**~~5.71%~~**	**29,931**
	Japan	1998	—	25.26%	25,919
	South Korea	1998	—	5.77%	22,287
	Taiwan	1998		8.29%	28,151

Table 10.8 (continued)

Product	Targeted country	Imposition of antidumping duty	Expiry of antidumping duty	Countrywide duty level	Import value (1,000 dollars)
Steel concrete reinforcement bars	**Poland**	**2001**	—	**47.13%**	**2,049**
	Latvia	**2001**	—	**16.99%**	**60,153**
	Belarus	2001	—	114.53%	14,662
	China	2001	—	133.00%	3,330
	Indonesia	2001	—	60.46%	16,185
	Moldova	2001	—	232.86%	40,228
	Ukraine	2001	—	41.69%	18,412
	~~South Korea~~	2001	2007	~~22.89%~~	59,202
Thermal paper	**Germany**	**2008**	—	**6.49%**	***
	China	2008	—	132.95%	***
Low enriched uranium	Russia	1992	(2012)	115.82%	123,223
	France	**2002**	—	**19.95%**	***
Carboxymethylcellulose	**Finland**	**2005**	—	**6.65%**	***
	Netherlands	**2005**	—	**14.57%**	***
	~~Sweden~~	**2005**	**2010**	~~25.29%~~	***
	~~Mexico~~	2005	2010	~~12.61%~~	***

Table 10.8 (continued)

Product	Targeted country	Imposition of antidumping duty	Expiry of antidumping duty	Countrywide duty level	Import value (1,000 dollars)
Seamless pipe small diameter	**Romania**	**2000**	—	**13.06%**	**18,332**
	~~Czech Republic~~	**2000**	**2006**	**~~32.26%~~**	**2,682**
	Japan	2000	—	70.43%	91,263
	~~South Africa~~	2000	2006	~~40.17%~~	5,680
Sodium nitrate	**Germany**	**2008**	—	**150.82%**	**2,680**
	China	2008	—	190.74%	476

Source: Based on USITC 2014a, b.

Note: The antidumping measures are presented in the order that antidumping investigations were initiated, even though the definitive measures were imposed at a later date. Antidumping measures against EU member states are marked in bold. Expired antidumping measures are crossed out. Antidumping measures against third countries on the same products are presented correspondingly. Antidumping measures on the products concerned during the last decade are considered, even though measures on the products might have been in place earlier.

the first two years of antidumping measures being in force (year "2"). At the same time, the import unit value price increased 47 percent (see figure 10.24). The effects of antidumping measures seem to change, on average, after two years, as the average import value of targeted EU imports increases 23 percent while the average import unit value price remains constant. Third countries not targeted by antidumping measures seem largely unaffected by the use of the antidumping instrument even though there is a slight increase in import value and unit value price. This is in line with the more aggregate analysis of the effects on the EU of imposing antidumping measures.

The share of imports from the targeted EU member states, as a percentage of total U.S. imports of the targeted products, decreased by 8 percentage points in three years from the year the antidumping measures were imposed (see figure 10.25). Other targeted countries, however, increased their import share by 5 percentage points. At the same time, the import share of nontargeted third countries increased by 3 percentage points.

The limited import shares of EU member states in the total import value (in particular, since the intra-U.S. market share is not considered), as well as the increasing unit value price, might indicate that the effects on U.S. producers' market share and price levels would remain largely

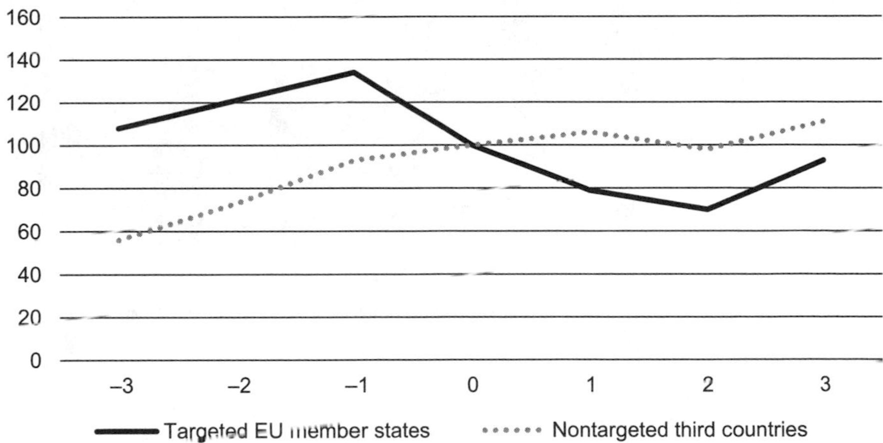

Figure 10.23
Average changes in U.S. import value of targeted products (index 100 = year 0).
Source: Based on U.S. Trade Online database.
Note: Due to the lack of intra-U.S. trade statistics, it is not possible to present the intra-U.S. import value and/or the intra-U.S. import value price in the figure.

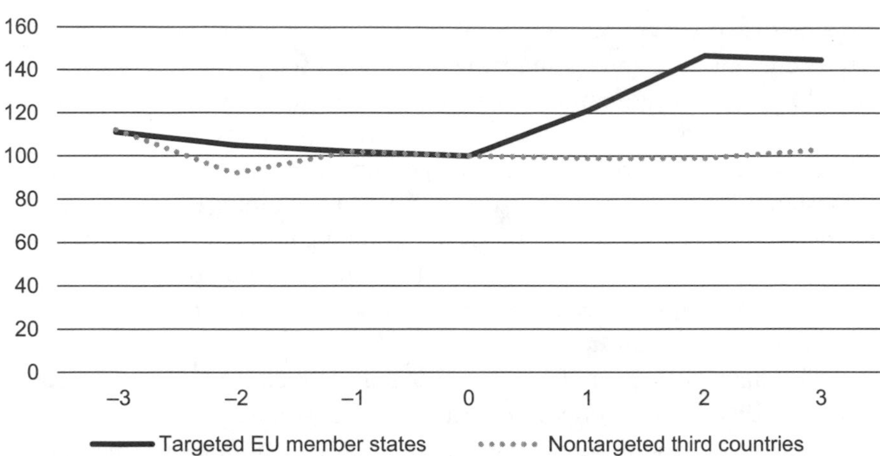

Figure 10.24
Average changes in U.S. import unit value price of targeted products (index 100 = year 0).
Source: Based on U.S. Trade Online database.
Note: Due to the lack of intra-U.S. trade statistics, it is not possible to present the intra-U.S. import value and/or the intra-U.S. import value price in the figure.

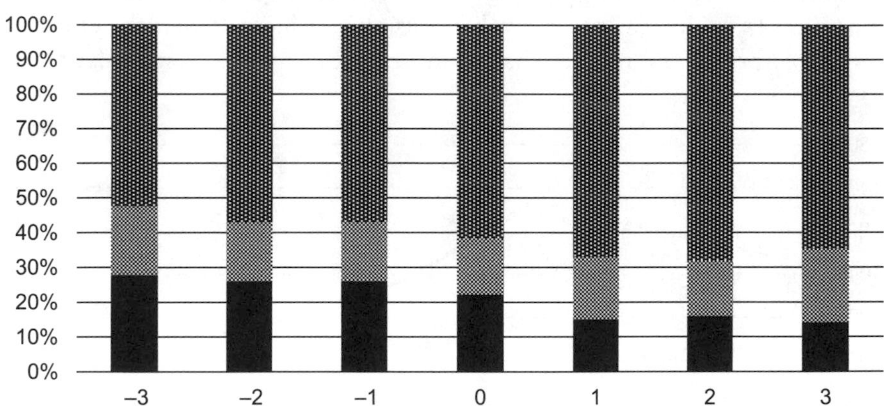

Figure 10.25
Average changes in U.S. import value shares (percentage).
Source: Based on U.S. Trade Online database.

unaffected by an abolition of antidumping measures. This is also supported by the fact that a large number of U.S. antidumping measures against EU members on the products concerned have expired naturally in recent years. Accordingly, there is reason to believe that the trade effects of a possible abolition of the U.S. antidumping measures against EU member states would be in line with the analysis of abolishing antidumping measures in the EU.

EU and EEA Experience as an Inspiration for TTIP Negotiations It is sometimes argued that the elimination of antidumping measures is only possible in regional trade agreements with limited levels of trade and competition between the parties. The thirty-two EEA parties, however, have managed to eliminate antidumping measures among their main trading partners. The EEA parties trade on average about 70 percent of their total value of goods with other EEA parties (see table 10.9). The United States, however, accounts for only about 4 percent on average of the total value of trade in goods of the EEA parties, and antidumping measures are currently used between the parties.

How was it possible for EEA parties to eliminate antidumping measures among themselves, and what aspects should be considered if the EEA were to be used as an inspiration for the TTIP?

The EU abolished antidumping measures among its original member states, something that has also been the case in the subsequent EU enlargements. The EFTA member states have also eliminated antidumping measures among its members. The EU has eliminated the possibility of using any of the three trade remedies (antidumping measures, antisubsidy measures, and safeguard measures) that are available according to the WTO rules against its members. In the EFTA it is possible for the member states to use safeguard measures, but this provision has never been used. This is also the case for the EEA where safeguard measures are allowed according to strict requirements (European Communities 1994).

It is frequently argued that antidumping measures are used to provide a "level playing field" and "fair competition" in trade relations among countries (National Board of Trade 2012b, 2013a). The EU—and by extension the EEA—have proved, however, that it is possible to replace antidumping measures among major trading partners in regional trade agreements and still benefit from "fair competition." It is relevant to note that not a single competition was raised when antidumping measures were abolished in the EU at the enlargement in 2004 (National Board of Trade 2013a).

Table 10.9
Trade levels among EEA member states and between EEA member states and the United States (value in average 2009–2012)

Imports from EEA (percentage)		Exports to EEA (percentage)		Imports from the United States (percentage)		Exports to the United States (percentage)	
Liechtenstein	89	**Luxembourg**	87	**Ireland**	14	**Ireland**	22
Austria	84	**Slovakia**	86	Iceland	9	**United Kingdom**	12
Estonia	80	**Czech Republic**	86	**United Kingdom**	8	Liechtenstein	12
Luxembourg	79	Iceland	83	**Netherlands**	7	Switzerland	9
Latvia	79	Norway	81	**Belgium**	6	**Germany**	7
Denmark	77	**Poland**	81	Norway	6	**Sweden**	7
Malta	77	**Hungary**	79	**Luxembourg**	5	**Finland**	6
Sweden	77	**Netherlands**	79	Switzerland	5	**Denmark**	6
Czech Republic	77	**Slovenia**	78	**France**	5	**Italy**	6
Portugal	76	**Austria**	77	**Germany**	4	**Malta**	6
Romania	74	**Portugal**	75	**Sweden**	3	**France**	6
Slovakia	74	**Belgium**	74	**Spain**	3	**Belgium**	6

Table 10.9 (continued)

Imports from EEA (percentage)		Exports to EEA (percentage)		Imports from the United States (percentage)		Exports to the United States (percentage)	
Slovenia	74	Romania	74	Italy	3	Norway	5
Poland	72	Denmark	73	Denmark	3	Estonia	5
France	72	Estonia	71	Liechtenstein	3	Austria	5
Cyprus	71	Spain	69	Malta	3	Greece	4
Ireland	71	Latvia	69	Croatia	2	Iceland	4
Belgium	71	Sweden	68	Finland	2	Netherlands	4
Switzerland	71	Cyprus	66	Greece	2	Portugal	4
Hungary	70	Germany	65	Austria	2	Spain	4
Germany	70	France	64	Portugal	2	Croatia	3
Finland	67	Lithuania	64	Hungary	2	Lithuania	2
Norway	67	Ireland	64	Cyprus	2	Hungary	2
Iceland	65	Bulgaria	63	Poland	2	Luxembourg	2

Table 10.9 (continued)

Imports from EEA (percentage)		Exports to EEA (percentage)		Imports from the United States (percentage)		Exports to the United States (percentage)	
Croatia	64	**Italy**	62	**Slovenia**	2	**Czech Republic**	2
Bulgaria	60	**Croatia**	62	**Czech Republic**	1	**Cyprus**	2
Spain	60	**Finland**	59	**Romania**	1	**Poland**	2
Italy	58	Liechtenstein	58	**Lithuania**	1	**Romania**	2
Lithuania	58	**United Kingdom**	57	**Estonia**	1	**Slovakia**	2
United Kingdom	56	**Greece**	52	**Bulgaria**	1	**Bulgaria**	2
Greece	54	Switzerland	52	**Latvia**	1	**Slovenia**	1
Netherlands	51	**Malta**	41	**Slovakia**	0	**Latvia**	1

Source: Based on Eurostat/Comext.
Note: For the purpose of this analysis, Switzerland is included among the EEA parties. EU member states are highlighted in bold.

At the EU enlargements, the accession countries are required to adapt their legislation in relevant areas to the EU's *acquis communautaire*, meaning, to harmonize their national regulatory frameworks with EU law. These harmonization requirements involve stringent conditions with regard to production standards, labor rights, health standards, environmental standards, and consumer quality standards, for example, and create the conditions for a "level playing field" (National Board of Trade 2013a). This provides for the free movement of goods, persons, services, and capital, usually referred to as the "four freedoms." The harmonization requirements, in combination with a common mechanism for enforcing the rules, make "unfair" competitive advantages less likely on these grounds and decrease the need to resort to contingency protection measures such as the use of the antidumping instrument (National Board of Trade 2013a). In line with the harmonization requirements, the EU has established common competition rules that aim to guarantee "fair competition." The EU's competition law contains, for example, rules on cartels, market dominance, mergers, and state aid. Even though no formal link has been established between the elimination of antidumping measures and the application of common competition rules, the rules were established to guarantee fair competition in the EU's internal market (National Board of Trade 2013a).

The same is true as regards the EEA where antidumping measures have also been eliminated with the only exception being agricultural and fishery products. The EEA might be seen as an extension of the EU's internal market with the exception of common agricultural policy and the common fisheries policy. During the EEA negotiations, the EFTA states agreed to harmonize their domestic law in relevant fields to the EU's *acquis communautaire*. The elimination of antidumping measures was made conditional on the full enforcement of EU competition rules in the EFTA member states (Rey 2012). In the EEA, two supranational bodies—the European Commission and the EFTA Surveillance Authority—are responsible for enforcing the competition rules.

The situation looks different, however, in the EU's other free trade agreements. In general, the EU favors the inclusion of competition rules in its free trade agreements with third countries (National Board of Trade 2013b). The free trade agreements negotiated by the EU normally contain strong language regarding anticompetitive agreements and the abuse of a dominant position in line with the common competition rules. However, they contain only limited provisions when it comes to coordination and cooperation with regard to the exchange of information (Solano and Sennekamp 2006). In addition, they do not establish a common authority for the enforcement of the competition rules. This implies that the provisions for competition are not as easily enforceable in the free trade agreements as they are within the EU or in the EEA. In addition, a general harmonization of the relevant domestic policies and rules does not take place in the EU's free trade agreements (National Board of Trade 2013a).

It is therefore evident from experience from the EU—and by extension the EEA—that in comparison with the EU's other free trade agreements, it is not only the introduction of competition rules that creates the preconditions for eliminating antidumping measures. It is apparent that the provisions for competition, where included in the free trade agreement, must also be enforceable. The EU and the EEA have also proven that harmonization of relevant policies and rules among the parties is key to prospects for eliminating antidumping measures. In order to make it possible for the EU and the United States to eliminate antidumping measures in TTIP, the negotiations should preferably focus on the harmonization of different policies and rules to a greater extent than is normally the case in free trade agreements.

In the case of TTIP negotiations between the EU and the United States, the normal customs duties between the countries are low. The greatest potential benefits from a future free trade agreement between the EU and the United States would therefore stem from the harmonization, simplification, and mutual recognition of rules and regulations. Tariff liberalizations would also have positive effects, but these would be more marginal due to the low level of the customs duties (even though the removal of administrative procedures would still be needed). The harmonization, simplification, and mutual recognition of rules and regulations between the EU and the United States is thus a core issue in TTIP negotiations, as well as one of the main preconditions for the success of TTIP (National Board of Trade 2012c, 2014).

A consequence of this harmonization exercise would be that antidumping measures might be unnecessary if conditions for a "level playing field" are created. The parties might also advocate harmonizing the competition rules and establishing relevant enforcement authorities in line with the EEA in order to render the provisions for competition meaningful. This would create the necessary preconditions for "fair competition". The experiences of deeper integration in major regional trade agreements—sometimes referred to as "mega-regionals"—such as the TTIP might serve as a model for other free trade agreements or as a stepping stone for multilateral rules or both. The TTIP might also open up to later joiners who will benefit from the negotiated outcome.

10.3 Conclusions

This chapter indicates that the benefits of antidumping measures in regional trade agreements are limited and come at a high cost. In the case of the EU, the antidumping measures might have contributed in helping EU producers increase their market share by 1 percentage point. However, for every euro EU producers gained from the antidumping protection, EU user industry and consumers lost, on average, 4.5 euro. Third countries not subject to the antidumping measures benefited considerably more, as their market share increased by 8 percentage points. The market share of countries subject to antidumping measures decreased by 9 percentage points.

This chapter also indicates that abolishing antidumping measures does not necessarily cause injury to the protected industry. About ten years ago, the EU abolished a large number of antidumping measures from ten accession countries overnight due to the EU enlargement. Some of the antidumping measures had been in force for well over a decade, and some were as high as 50 percent; they met the criteria of dumping, injury, and causality. Abolishing the antidumping measures, however, did not cause injury in terms of price undercutting or lost market shares for EU producers. The producers from the new member states did not increase their market share as was previously feared. Their market share in the EU increased by only 1 percentage point. The decrease in market share of EU producers—by 9 percentage points—was mainly due to the corresponding increase—by 8 percentage points—in the market share of third countries, and not as a result of the abolition of antidumping measures. The abolition of antidumping measures did not imply any antidumping action against third countries on the previously targeted products. In addition, there was not a single antidumping case that was later replaced by a competition case. Thus, what were once considered third country imports that caused injury to domestic industry and triggered the use of antidumping measures in the EU have—following the enlargement—been considered normal business practices in line with the requirements of "fair competition."

The empirical findings from the abolition of antidumping measures in the EU indicate that parties to regional trade agreements, as well as third countries, have little to fear from eliminating the use of antidumping measures in regional trade agreements altogether. The experiences of abolishing antidumping measures in the EU and the EEA might therefore be useful in initiatives to eliminate antidumping measures in the TTIP negotiations. The inclusion of competition rules and other forms of policy harmonization and harmonization of relevant conditions and standards within the EU and the EEA has proved to be a successful substitute for the use of antidumping measures when certain institutional preconditions, such as a successful enforcement mechanism, are fulfilled. This implies that when conditions for a "level playing field" and "fair competition" are created in regional trade agreements, there is no need to resort to antidumping measures.

If major regional trade agreements—sometimes referred to as "mega-regionals"—such as the TTIP follow the examples of the EU and the EEA and eliminate antidumping measures, regional trade agreements might serve as a stepping stone to a new multilateral regime in this field, that is to say, as a way of 'multilateralizing regionalism."

Annexes

Annex 1: Methodology Used for Calculating the Effects of Imposing Antidumping Measures in the EU

The first part of section 10.1 is based on the report *Do EU Producers and the EU Economy Really Benefit from Antidumping Policy?* by the National Board of Trade, Sweden.

The dataset consists of all antidumping investigations initiated by the EU during the periods 2000–2001 and 2006–2008 that resulted in both provisional and definitive antidumping measures where the measure is expressed as an *ad valorem* duty. The average definitive countrywide antidumping duty is around 30 percent. The antidumping duty level varies significantly, however, with the lowest being around 5 percent and the highest being around 70 percent. The countrywide definitive antidumping duty has been used for each country. The time period was selected to avoid the effects of the EU enlargement in 2004.

The selected sample consists of twenty-two antidumping cases counted on a case-by-product basis. The types of products that are targeted are both intermediate products (chemical and iron and steel products, approximately two-thirds) and consumer products (approximately one-third). Counted on a case-by-country basis, the selected sample consists of thirty-nine cases (see National Board of Trade 2012a). A total of sixteen countries are targeted by the antidumping measures; by far the most frequently targeted is China (thirteen antidumping measures), followed by India (four antidumping measures) and Russia and Thailand (three antidumping measures each).

In the calculations of *effectiveness*, data on trade between EU members (intra-EU imports) and trade between the EU and the rest of the world (extra-EU imports) were collected for all products listed in the antidumping cases. For the cases initiated between 2000 and 2001, data for the EU15 are used; for the cases initiated between 2006 and 2008, data for the EU25 are used. The data were retrieved from the Eurostat Comext database.

Due to the fact that data on EU domestic sales for the products concerned are not available, data for sales within the EU (intra-EU trade) have been used as a proxy. The presumption is that the elasticity of substitution between intra-EU imports and extra-EU imports closely resembles the elasticity between EU domestic sales and extra-EU trade.

For each case, trade data for intra-EU imports and extra-EU imports from three years before and three years after the antidumping investigation were initiated are analyzed. The year the antidumping investigation was initiated is indicated by the year "0." For the selected cases, the provisional duty was generally imposed the year after the antidumping investigation was initiated (year "1"); the definitive duty was generally imposed the following year (year "2"). The import statistics dataset contains information on the value (in euro) of the imported products and information on the corresponding volume (in tonnes) of imported products. A unit value price, which is used as a proxy for the import price, is calculated as the total value of imports divided by the total volume of imports. In order to construct a unit value price that reflects the transaction price as much as possible, the division of value by volume was made on the most disaggregated data, that is, the unit value price of each CN product (eight-digit level) from each targeted country has been calculated separately.

Figures 10.1–10.5 provide graphical representations of the effects of imposing EU antidumping measures on intra-EU trade, EU imports from targeted countries, and EU imports from nontargeted countries. Figures 10.1, 10.3, and 10.5 show the unweighted average changes in imports for each case relative to the year in which the investigation was initiated (year "0"). By using an unweighted average, each case has the same impact on the relative average change, regardless of the value of the total trade in the particular product. Figures 10.2 and 10.4 show the average changes in import market shares (in terms of value and volume) of the EU internal market.

In the context of the analysis, it is important to emphasize that the focus is on the average effects of the antidumping policy on import flows of several different antidumping cases. Naturally, there is a lot of variation among the different cases. Underlying trends that affect imports from different geographical sources in different ways are not controlled for in the analysis.

In the calculations of *efficiency*, the estimated average ratio between EU producers' benefit and EU user industry and consumers' loss is based on an analysis of changes of producer surplus and user industry/consumer surplus for each of the antidumping cases in the selected sample.

Aggregate effects during a three-year period after the initiation of the investigation were calculated using a Carli index (the unweighted mean of the price or volume ratios). The effects are calculated for each product from the year before the initiation of the antidumping investigation (year "-1"). This reference year was chosen because it is assumed to show the ex ante levels of volume and price.

Annex 2: Methodology Used for Calculating the Effects of Abolishing Antidumping Measures in the EU

The second part of section 10.1 is based on the report *Effects on Trade and Competition of Abolishing Anti-Dumping Measures: The European Union Experience* by the National Board of Trade, Sweden.

The dataset consists of the antidumping measures that were in force in EU15 and thus were abolished at the EU enlargement with ten accession countries in May 2004. The analysis ends in the year 2008 as the economic crisis, which began that year, may blur the analysis of the economic effects in the years that follow.

The analysis does not include the antidumping measures that expired normally before the enlargement. The effect of abolishing EU25 antidumping measures on imports from Bulgaria and Romania as a consequence of the enlargement in 2007 is not included in this analysis. These countries are therefore counted as third countries for the purpose of this analysis, which only considers the effects of abolishing antidumping measures in EU15, and not antidumping measures that were abolished in the accession countries.

In total, sixteen antidumping measures were abolished as a direct consequence of the EU enlargement in 2004 (see table 10.1); these measures covered eight products originating in six accession countries. The Czech Republic and Poland were the two most targeted accession countries, as EU15 had five antidumping measures in place against each of these countries. The measures had been in force for different lengths of time, the shortest for two years and the longest for eleven years. The targeted products were all intermediate products: five iron and steel products (four different types of pipes and tubes) and three chemical products (all used as fertilizers). The average countrywide *ad valorem* duty applicable to the iron and steel products was around 30 percent, and the average countrywide specific duty applicable to the chemical products was around 15 euros per tonne.

The three chemical products (ammonium nitrate, urea, and urea ammonium nitrate solutions) are excluded from the aggregate and product-specific analyses since the average unit prices are due to factors other than the abolition of antidumping measures that took place at the same time and contributed to a reduction in exports and higher world market prices: (1) the exclusion from subsidized Russian gas prices to producers in EU accession countries following their accession to the EU; (2) an increase in the international price of oil; and (3) an increased demand for urea and ammonium nitrate in China and India. In the calculations of injury to the EU15 producers, data on trade between EU15 members (intra-EU imports) and trade between the EU15 and the rest of the world (extra-EU imports) were collected for all products listed in the antidumping cases. The data were retrieved from the Eurostat Comext database.

Due to the fact that data on EU domestic sales for the products concerned are not available, data for sales within the EU (intra-EU trade) have been used as a proxy. The presumption is that the elasticity of substitution between intra-EU imports and extra-EU imports is very similar to the elasticity between EU domestic sales and extra-EU trade.

The import statistics dataset contains information on the value (in euro) of the imported products and information on the corresponding volume (in tonnes) of imported products. A unit value price, which is used as a proxy for the import price, is calculated as the total value of imports divided by the total volume of imports. In order to construct a unit value price that reflects the transaction price as much as possible, the division of value by volume was made on the most disaggregated data, that is, the unit value price of each CN product (eight-digit level) from each targeted country has been calculated separately.

Figures 10.6–10.10 provide graphical representations of the average effects of abolishing antidumping measures against the accession countries on EU15 imports from the accession countries, intra-EU15 trade, and EU15 imports from all other countries, both those targeted and those not targeted by antidumping measures, between 1998 and 2008. Figures 10.6, 10.8, and 10.10 show the unweighted average changes in imports (in terms of value, volume, and unit prices) for each case, relative to the year in which antidumping measures were abolished. By using an unweighted average, each case has the same impact on the relative average change, regardless of the value of the trade in the corresponding product. Figures 10.7 and 10.9 show the average changes in import market shares (in terms of value and volume) of the EU internal market.

The limitations of the analysis also have to be considered. At the time the accession countries became EU member states, *all* EU15 duties against them ceased. It is not possible to distinguish between the effects of terminating antidumping duties and terminating these other customs duties, where relevant. Furthermore, it is not possible to distinguish between the effects of abolishing antidumping measures and other possible effects on competition and pricing associated with EU membership—for example, the effects of harmonizing with the EU's *acquis communautaire* and the free movement of goods, capital, services, and people. The harmonization process might lead to restructuring of industry and higher production costs, and the "four freedoms" on the EU's internal market might increase competition. These aspects merit further analyses.

The antidumping measures were, in most cases, subject to price undertakings. The exceptions were ammonium nitrate and urea ammonium nitrate solutions from Poland and welded tubes and pipes, iron or nonalloy steel from the Czech Republic and Poland. Price undertakings imply that certain exporters commit themselves to increasing their prices to minimums designed to eliminate the injurious effects of dumping. Minimum prices prevent import prices from falling below a certain price floor. The possible effects of price undertakings have not been analyzed. However, it is reasonable to believe that our findings on the effects of abolishing antidumping measures would have been more pronounced in the absence of price undertakings.

The reasons behind the increase in third country imports when antidumping measures against the accession countries were abolished have not been considered in this analysis. However, it is apparent that EU producers did not request additional antidumping measures against this increase in imports from third countries. These aspects also merit further analyses.

It is important to consider the limited number of antidumping cases that are being analyzed in the chapter. However, these are the only empirical cases available for the analysis of effects of abolishing antidumping measures in any regional trade agreements during the last few decades.

Annex 3: Methodology Used for Analyzing Antidumping Measures between the EU and the United States

Section 10.2 is partly based on the report *Eliminating Anti-Dumping Measures in Regional Trade Agreements: The European Union Example* by the National Board of Trade, Sweden.

The dataset in the analysis consists of all products currently faced with antidumping measures between the EU28 and the United States (as of May 2014). The possible existence of anticircumvention measures on certain products is not considered in the analysis.

In the EU, antidumping measures targeting two products, biodiesel and bioethanol—products that are not traditionally targeted by antidumping measures—are currently in place. The antidumping measures on biodiesel have been in place for about five years, while the antidumping measures on bioethanol have recently been imposed, for about one year.

In the United States, antidumping measures are currently imposed on sixteen products—mainly traditionally targeted iron and steel products—against twenty-two EU member states. The currently most frequently targeted EU member states are Italy (six antidumping measures) and Germany (four antidumping measures). Some of the measures have been in place for almost forty years (plastic tape) and some of the measures for almost thirty years (brass sheet and strip, chlorinated isocyanurate, granular resin, and ball bearings).

Note: In the analysis of U.S. antidumping measures against EU member states, only the EU member states targeted at the imposition of the antidumping measures are covered. In addition, only antidumping measures with data on the unit price level (stainless steel butt-welded fittings, chlorinated isocyanurate, thermal paper, carboxymethylcellulose, seamless pipes, stainless steel plate in coils, and sodium nitrate) were included in the sample. The chapter does not consider previous antidumping measures between the EU and the United States or the effects of their expiration. This is an area that merits further and more detailed analyses.

Data on trade between EU member states (intra-EU imports) and trade between the EU and the rest of the world (extra-EU imports) have been collected for all products listed in the antidumping cases. The data were retrieved from the Eurostat Comext database.

Due to the fact that data on EU domestic sales for the products concerned are not available, data for sales within the EU, intra-EU trade have been used as a proxy. The presumption is that the elasticity of substitution between intra-EU imports and extra-EU imports is very similar to the elasticity between EU domestic sales and extra-EU trade.

Due to the limited number of current EU antidumping measures against the United States and the fact that one of the antidumping measures was imposed as recently as 2013, a meaningful aggregate analysis on the effects of import values and prices is not possible at this moment in time. The market shares of the products are therefore also analyzed separately.

Figure 10.21 provides a graphical representation of the effects on market shares (intra-EU trade, EU imports from the United States, and EU imports from nontargeted third countries) of imposing definitive antidumping measures on biodiesel from the United States. Figure 10.22 provides a graphical representation of the effects on market shares (intra-EU trade, EU imports from the United States, and EU imports from nontargeted third countries) of the initiation of the antidumping investigation on bioethanol from the United States. Due to the recent imposition of antidumping measures on bioethanol, trade statistics are not available in order to analyze the effects on trade of imposing the measures. The analysis of the possible effects of abolishing the EU antidumping measures against the United States is limited in scope and mainly qualitative. This is an area that merits further and more detailed analyses.

Data on U.S. imports from the rest of the world have been collected for all products listed in the antidumping cases. The data were retrieved from the U.S. Trade Online database.

Due to the fact that data on U.S. domestic sales for the products concerned are not available, and intra-U.S. trade cannot be used as a proxy, an analysis of intra-U.S. average changes in import value, intra-U.S. average changes in import value market share, and intra U.S. average changes in import unit value price has been omitted. As a consequence, in analyzing the average changes in import value and in import unit value price, the focus is on the targeted EU member states and third countries not targeted by antidumping measures for the products concerned (figures 10.23–10.24). For the simplicity of the analysis, third countries targeted with antidumping measures for the products concerned are also omitted when presenting the effects of average changes in import value and price.

Due to the limits in data availability, the focus of the analysis is on average changes in the import value shares and not on the average changes in import value market shares (figure 10.25). For the simplicity of the analysis, only the average changes in import values have been considered and not the average changes in import volumes.

For each case, the trade data for U.S. imports three years before and three years after the imposition of definitive antidumping measures are analyzed instead of at the time of the initiation of the antidumping investigation. This is due to the fact that the antidumping investigations in some cases were initiated several years before the antidumping measures were imposed. This fact might, however, have influenced the import levels in the analysis. The year that definitive antidumping measures were imposed is marked by the year "0."

Figures 10.23–10.25 provide graphical representations of the effects of imposing U.S. antidumping measures on imports from targeted EU member states and U.S. imports from nontargeted third countries (as the trade flows from third countries targeted with the measures are excluded in the presentation). The figures show the unweighted average changes in imports for each case relative to the year in which the antidumping measures were imposed (year "0"). By using an unweighted average, each case has the same impact on the relative average change, regardless of the value of the total trade in the particular product.

In the context of the analysis, it is important to emphasize that the focus is on the average effects of the antidumping policy on import flows of several different antidumping cases. Naturally, there is a lot of variation among the different cases. Underlying trends that affect imports from different geographical sources in different ways are not controlled for in the analysis.

The analysis of the efficiency of the antidumping measures between the EU and the United States is limited in scope and mainly qualitative. The conclusions are mainly based on the experience of imposing antidumping measures in the EU (see annex 1). The analysis of the possible effects of abolishing the U.S. antidumping measures against the EU is limited in scope and mainly qualitative. This is an area that merits further and more detailed analyses.

Ideas for future research with regard to the possible abolition of antidumping measures in the TTIP might be (1) modeling the possible effects on trade of abolishing antidumping measures between the EU and the United States; (2) analyzing the effects on trade of the terminated/expired antidumping measures between the EU and the United States; and (3) detailing the requirements for a harmonization of rules and standards in the TTIP that would create the preconditions for creating a "level playing field" and "fair competition."

Note

This chapter is a revised version of a paper prepared for the conference "Challenges Facing the World Trade System" at Johns Hopkins University, October 1–2, 2014. The chapter is mainly based on previous research on the EU's antidumping policy by Jonas Kasteng or Camilla Prawitz, or both, at the National Board of Trade, Sweden. During the preparation of the chapter, various colleagues at the National Board of Trade provided valuable input and ideas. The chapter also benefitted greatly from comments by Thomas J. Prusa, professor of economics at Rutgers University, in his capacity as discussant of the conference paper, as well as from other conference participants.

Disclaimer: The National Board of Trade is a Swedish Governmental Agency. The National Board of Trade provides the Swedish Government with analyses and recommendations on trade policy issues—with focus on the Swedish position within the EU. It also publishes reports to increase awareness of the importance of open and free trade with transparent rules. The ideas presented by the National Board of Trade are not necessarily those of the Swedish Government.

References

Bhagwati, Jagdish, and Arvind Panagariya. 1996. "Preferential Trading Areas and Multilateralism: Strangers, Friends or Foes?" In *Trading Blocs: Alternative Approaches to Analyzing Preferential Trade Agreements*, ed. Jagdish Bhagwati, Pravin Krishna, and Arvind Panagariya, 33–102. Cambridge, MA: MIT Press.

European Commission. 2014. "WTO Member's TDI Activity up to 30 June 2013." Paper based on WTO members' semi-annual report prepared by the European Commission. Brussels: European Commission.

European Communities. 1990. *Agreement between the European Economic Community and the Principality of Andorra*. Official Journal L 374, December 31. Brussels: European Communities.

European Communities. 1994. *Agreement on the European Economic Area*. Official Journal No L1, March 1. Brussels: European Communities.

European Communities. 2002. *Agreement on Cooperation and Customs Union between the European Economic Community and the Republic of San Marino.* Official Journal L 084, March 28. Brussels: European Communities.

European Economic Community. 1957. *Treaty Establishing the European Economic Community (The Treaty of Rome).* Official Journal, March 25. Brussels: European Economic Community.

European Union. 2008. *Economic Partnership Agreement between the CARIFORUM States, of the one part, and the European Community and its Member States, of the other part.* Official Journal L 289, October 30. Brussels: European Union.

Farha, Ryan. 2012. "A Right Unexercised Is a Right Lost? Abolishing Antidumping in Regional Trade Agreements." *Georgetown Journal of International Law* 44 (1) (Fall): 211–248.

ICTSD. 2013. *Trade Remedies on Clean Energy: A New Trend in Need of Multilateral Initiatives.* Think Piece by Jonas Kasteng. E15 Expert Group on Clean Energy Technologies and the Trade System. Geneva: International Centre for Trade and Sustainable Development and World Economic Forum.

NAFTA. 1994. North American Free Trade Agreement. Legal Texts. NAFTA Secretariat. https://www.nafta-sec-alena.org/Home/Legal-Texts/North-American-Free-Trade-Agreement, accessed October 1, 2014.

National Board of Trade. 2012a. *Do EU Producers and the EU Economy Really Benefit from Anti-Dumping Policy?* Authored by Camilla Prawitz. Stockholm: National Board of Trade.

National Board of Trade. 2012b. *Paving the Way for Unfair Competition: The Imposition of EU Anti-Dumping Duties on Ceramic Tiles from China.* Authored by Jonas Kasteng. Stockholm: National Board of Trade.

National Board of Trade. 2012c. *Potential Effects from an EU-US Free Trade Agreement: Sweden in Focus.* Authored by Susanna Kinnman and Tomas Hagberg. Stockholm: National Board of Trade.

National Board of Trade. 2013a. *Effects on Trade and Competition of Abolishing Anti-Dumping Measures: The European Union Experience.* Authored by Camilla Prawitz and Jonas Kasteng. Stockholm: National Board of Trade.

National Board of Trade. 2013b. *Eliminating Anti-Dumping Measures in Regional Trade Agreements: The European Union Example.* Authored by Jonas Kasteng and Camilla Prawitz. Stockholm: National Board of Trade.

National Board of Trade. 2013c. *Targeting the Environment: Exploring a New Trend in the EU's Trade Defence Investigations.* Authored by Jonas Kasteng. Stockholm: National Board of Trade.

National Board of Trade. 2013d. *The Lesser Duty Rule in Trade Defence Investigations. Review of EU Trade Defence Instruments in Brief.* No. 3. Stockholm: National Board of Trade.

National Board of Trade. 2013e. *The Union Interest Test in Trade Defence Investigations. Review of EU Trade Defence Instruments in Brief*. No. 4. Stockholm: National Board of Trade.

National Board of Trade. 2014. *Regulatory Co-operation and Technical Barriers to Trade within Transatlantic Trade and Investment Partnership*. Authored by Heidi Lund. Stockholm: National Board of Trade.

Prusa, Thomas, and Robert Teh. 2010. "Protection Reduction and Diversion: PTAs and Incidence of Antidumping Disputes." NBER Working Paper No. 16276. Cambridge, MA: National Bureau of Economic Research.

Rey, Jean-Daniel. 2012. "Antidumping Regional Regimes and the Multilateral Trading System: Do Regional Antidumping Regimes Make a Difference?" Staff Working Paper ERSD-2012–22, World Trade Organization Economic Research and Statistics Division. Geneva: World Trade Organization.

Solano, Oliver, and Andreas Sennekamp. 2006. *Competition Provisions in Regional Trade Agreements*. OECD Trade Policy Working Papers No. 31. Paris: OECD Publishing.

Teh, Robert. 2009. "Competition Provisions in Regional Trade Agreements." In *Regional Rules in the Global Trading System*, ed. Antoni Estevadeordal, Kati Suominen, and Robert Teh, 418–491. New York: Cambridge University Press.

Teh, Robert, Thomas Prusa, and Michelle Budetta. 2007. "Trade Remedy Provisions in Regional Trade Agreements." Staff Working Paper ERSD-2007–03, World Trade Organization Economic Research and Statistics Division. Geneva: World Trade Organization.

USITC. 2014a. AD/CVD Orders. Excel file on AD/CVD Orders and Revocations January 1, 2006–April 7, 2014. Prepared by the United States International Trade Commission, Washington, DC.

USITC. 2014b. Import Injury Case Statistics. FY 1980–2008. Prepared by the United States International Trade Commission, Washington, DC.

Williams, Norman. 2006. "Why Congress May Not "Overrule" the Dormant Commerce Clause." *UCLA Law Review* 53 (1): 153 – 238 .

WTO. 1994. *The Results of the Uruguay Round of Multilateral Trade Negotiations: The Legal Texts*. Geneva: World Trade Organization.

WTO. 2011. *The WTO and Preferential Trade Agreements: From Co-existence to Coherence. World Trade Report 2011*. Geneva: World Trade Organization.

Contributors

Rahel Aichele, ifo Institute, Munich

Jagdish N. Bhagwati, Columbia University

Steve Charnovitz, George Washington University

Gabriel Felbermayr, University of Munich and ifo Institute, Munich

Dimitar D. Gueorguiev, Maxwell School of Citizenship and Public Affairs, Syracuse University

Bernard Hoekman, European University Institute and Centre for Economic Policy Research

Jonas Kasteng, National Board of Trade, Sweden

Pravin Krishna, Johns Hopkins University and National Bureau of Economic Research (NBER)

Mary E. Lovely, Maxwell School of Citizenship and Public Affairs, Syracuse University

Petros C. Mavroidis, Columbia Law School

Devashish Mitra, Maxwell School of Citizenship and Public Affairs, Syracuse University

Arvind Panagariya, School of International and Public Affairs, Columbia University

Thomas J. Prusa, Rutgers University

André Sapir, Solvay Brussels School of Economics and Management, Université Libre de Bruxelles

Stefan Tangermann, University of Göttingen and Göttingen Academy of Sciences and Humanities

Index

Page numbers followed by *f* indicate figures; page numbers followed by *t* indicate tables.